SAMUEL RICHARDSON

Dramatic Novelist

Mark Kinkead-Weekes

LONDON
METHUEN & CO. LTD.
1973

First published in 1973 by
Methuen & Co Ltd,
11 New Fetter Lane,
London E.C.4

SBN 416 02970 1
Printed in Great Britain by
T. & A. Constable Limited, Edinburgh

Endpapers
Drawing of Samuel Richardson reading by Susanna Highmore reproduced by permission of the Pierpont Morgan Library.

Contents

Preface vii
Introduction 1

PART ONE · PAMELA

1. Pamela and her Persecutor 7
2. In the Wilderness 34
3. The Assault on the World 58
4. Taking Stock 88

PART TWO · CLARISSA

5. Three Worlds (The first instalment) 123
6. A Matter of Delicacy (The second instalment) 171
7. The Inquisition (The final instalment) 219

PART THREE · SIR CHARLES GRANDISON

8. 'Sir Charles' and 'Harriet Byron' 279
9. Crisis, Resolution, and the Family of the Heart 333

PART FOUR · MASTER OF THE HEART,
SHAKESPEARE OF PROSE

10. The Novel as Drama 395
11. Social Realism, Psychology – and Form 462

Index 503

Preface

Richardson has been fortunate in his scholars. Like all Richardsonians, I am much indebted to the work of Alan McKillop and William Sale, lately amalgamated and extended by T. Duncan Eaves and Ben Kimpel in a standard biography. John Carroll has made a very useful and scholarly selection of Richardson's letters, and is about to produce an edition of *Clarissa* based, at last, on the first edition. Eaves and Kimpel have also recently produced in America a first-edition text of *Pamela*; and an edition of *Sir Charles Grandison* by Jocelyn Harris is promised soon. I am sorry not to have been able to make page references to these. Mine refer to the Shakespeare Head edition (numbers in roman type), and also to the Everyman edition (numbers in italics).

He has been less lucky in his critics. Though his affinity with Henry James was noted long ago by E. M. Forster, Percy Lubbock, and Ford Madox Ford; and though Dr Leavis conceded that *Clarissa* was 'impressive', and that he would rather re-read her history than Proust's; Richardson has been treated with extraordinary patronage by academics. When I began, only R. F. Brissenden's 'Writers and their Work' introduction, an early article by Frank Kermode in the Cambridge Journal, a few pages by Arnold Kettle, an essay by David Daiches, and Ian Watt's influential *The Rise of the Novel* encouraged any student to take him seriously. For these I was and remain grateful. There is still too little appreciation of his form and his subtlety, though John Carroll and Rosemary Cowler have now been able to collect some useful criticism in the *Twentieth Century Views* and *Twentieth Century Interpretations* series. Recently, when my book was virtually complete, John Preston published a challenging view of Clarissa in *The Created Self*, extending an earlier approach to Richardson's form by Anthony Kearney.

My study is arranged so that an interpretative reading of the novels precedes a final section on their form, but the two approaches cannot really be separated, and a reader could as easily begin with Chapter 10. The arrangement leads to occasional repetition; and the attempt to read 'to the moment' cannot but lead to length, as writing to the moment did. My defence must be that my work began from an impression that the novels are far more demanding, far more complicated, dense and subtle than has ever been allowed; and that only reading in the way that Richardson wrote could do him an overdue justice. I do not claim that my reading is definitive. Indeed I do not so much contend for my critical conclusions, which might have been argued far more briefly, as for the approach that is necessary before worthwhile criticism can start. In this sense I should like to think that

> In me what spots (for spots I have) appear,
> Will prove at least the medium must be clear.

Having decided I had no space for a bibliography, I have also resisted the temptation to prove my acquaintanceship with the critical literature in the footnotes. It does not necessarily follow, therefore, from the absence of reference to an article or book, that I have either not read it or consider it beneath my notice. I think I have noted my borrowings; but if it seems odd that I do not acknowledge indebtedness to some ideas that have appeared in print, it is because I have been anticipated in production rather than in conception. I blush to admit by how much I have exceeded Pope's and Horace's advice to keep one's piece nine years. There is a character in Angus Wilson's *The Middle Age of Mrs Eliot* who has a pile of manuscript on Richardson yellowing on an upper shelf in his cupboard. I know that man . . .

Preface

That my book should have appeared at all is largely owing to the generous help and encouragement of the late John Butt; and to the friends who have been patient enough to read or listen to bits of it. I am particularly grateful to Frank Kermode, Arnold Kettle, Ian Watt, Graham Midgley, Keith Carabine and Ian Gregor for wise comments, many of which they may no longer remember making. By a happy accident (for me!) Ian Jack is the one person who can say with the endurance of Faulkner's Dilsey, 'I seen de beginnin' en now I sees de endin' '.

I owe a great deal to the Chief Librarians and the Committee of the Johannesburg Public Library, to the University of Cape Town, the Rhodes Trust, and the late Principal and the Fellows of Brasenose College, without whose generosity I should have been neither undergraduate nor research student.

Finally I would like to remind my wife of what Richardson said to his. 'Do you know, that the beatified Clarissa was often very uneasy at the Time her Story cost the Man whom you favour with your Love, and that chiefly on your Account? She was . . . I know so well her Mind, that she would have greatly approved of this Acknowledgement; and of the Compliment I now make you, in her Name, of the Volumes which contain her History.' I cannot speak for Clarissa, and my 'volumes' are duller than his, but the acknowledgement and compliment at least I can make.

Canterbury
September 1972.

Introduction

Only a critical method attuned to the nature of Richardson's art can hope to be true to the experience, and the value, of reading him. If a big book is a great evil he is a notorious offender. Yet *Clarissa* is the finest novel of its century, and one cannot separate the nature of the achievement, the degree of imaginative penetration, the quality of integrity, the courage of self-challenge, from the nature of the art that produced the length. This is no less true of the lesser novels, in their degree. Richardson can be slow, even tedious, but if he is worth reading at all he must be taken in his own terms first. Serious criticism will have to risk offending too, if it is to deal adequately with fictions that demand closer and more exploratory reading than any others of their time.

Richardson's own name for his invention, 'writing to the moment', points both to his attempt to create a dramatic present-tense experience, and to the way his imagination worked. He places his characters in a situation of conflict, and the fiction grows, not through his complicated plotting and design, but by imagining how those characters will react to that moment, and so create the next, and the next. He projects his imagination into different points of view, and the significance of his vision can only be grasped by entering all and earning a comprehension greater than any. The art is also an art of implication, of reading between the lines; and it conceals beneath its naturalness a meaningful structure, a relationship of scenes. If we wish to understand before we criticise, we have to work in the same way from situation to situation, exploring the implications of each in a flexible, changing and complex process. Only in this way, above all, can one establish the quality of imaginative growth in Richardson's art: the power of his dramatic imagination to explore, to challenge, and to transcend the attitudes from which the fiction begins. It is not easy to separate 'the moralist' from 'the artist' in Richardson, yet there is a vital distinction between the kind of exploration that appears whenever his dramatic imagination takes flight, and the didacticism that bores us when that imagination lapses. To read 'to the moment' takes time and trouble, but it is the only way to tap the strength and expose the weakness, without being facile, or distorting. To generalise about Richardson is to be an idiot. (He won Blake's heart.)

The first three sections of this study, then, are concerned to read the novels closely, with due attention to the way they were written and to the nature of the dramatic art. The rewards, I believe, are worth the trouble. A *Pamela* emerges which is far closer to what Richardson thought he had written than the history of its criticism would ever lead one to suspect, and also more subtly probing and critical of its heroine. Once the fallibility of her vision is perceived, a hero also emerges who has been virtually invisible over the years. The novel remains flawed prentice-work, but an understanding of what goes wrong with the form allows one to see how it was possible to write *Clarissa* so soon afterwards, and to explain the formal basis of Richardson's greatest achievement. Reading to the moment will reveal the powerful tragic ironies in the treatment of Clarissa too; and, without detracting from the dramatic strength and social insight of the first instalment, will establish the significance of the different conflict in the second instalment, and place the greatest emphasis where it truly belongs, in the extraordinary challenge to Richardson's deepest beliefs that lies behind the rape. *Grandison* is virtually unknown now, yet one can see why Jane Austen and George Eliot admired the book. Its essence turns out to be a tension between two very different kinds of imagination, whose interaction almost produced a curious masterpiece. Even in its partial failure it contains Richardson's most attractive heroine, his developed sense of moral community, and some of his most subtle writing. There is also a humorous side to him from the beginning, which we have neglected.

The emphasis so far is on interpretation, in the belief that this must come first. The final section, however, starts from the evidence that Richardson knew what he was doing formally – far more so than the many critics who have patronised him as an 'unconscious' writer – and attempts to analyse the implications of his dramatic art of fiction. On this basis it becomes possible to review the major preoccupations of his modern critics, and to suggest (I hope) a sounder and less limited approach.

Justice to Richardson may seem a quaint cry now. Yet we are learning to recognise, in the eighteenth century, not the rise of 'the novel' so much as the invention of several different kinds of fiction, which laid the basis of what has happened since. Together they represent a major effort to come to terms imaginatively with eighteenth-century man and his society; but they could do so only by the discovery and development of forms, distinctive ways of using and articulating the imagination, which remain permanently valuable. The 'new way' of the Master of the Heart, the Shakespeare of prose, was by no means the least remarkable of these. It seems sad that, in the century which has known the greatest development in writing from multiple points of view, the inventor of that mode should be the most neglected and misunderstood of the pioneers of English fiction.

PART ONE

Pamela

CHAPTER ONE

Pamela and her Persecutor

I

If *Pamela* was the making of Richardson the novelist it tends to be his undoing now; for since his greatest art is exceptionally long while our reading life gets shorter, the bulk of *Clarissa* gives just the wrong prominence to the smaller and far inferior work. There must be ten who know Richardson only by his prentice-piece (inevitably shackled to Fielding's *Shamela* and *Joseph Andrews*) for one who has read the major novel through. And Richardson's misfortune is compounded: not only is *Clarissa* more widely respected than read, but *Pamela* gets even less respect than it deserves.

To say this is to swim against the current, for while twentieth-century criticism has shifted in emphasis, it has generally stopped well short of taking *Pamela*'s art or its moral vision seriously. In 1744 a Danish writer already saw European opinion divided between '*Pamelists* and *Anti-Pamelists* . . . Some look upon this young Virgin as an Example for Ladies to follow . . . Others, on the contrary, discover in it, the Behaviour of an hypocritical, crafty Girl, in her Courtship; who understands the Art of bringing a Man to her Lure.'[1] By 1900, the Anti-Pamelists have triumphed.[2]

[1] Taken, without acknowledgement, from the Danish dramatist Holberg's *Moral Thoughts* (1744), by Dr Peter Shaw in *The Reflector* (1750). See A. D. McKillop, *Samuel Richardson, Printer and Novelist* (Chapel Hill, N.C., 1936 reprinted 1960), 101-2.

[2] Clara Thomson, *Samuel Richardson* (London, 1900), 157, 164-6; Austin Dobson, *Samuel Richardson* (London, 1902), 34-5.

Little by little, however, moral attack then begins to modulate into psychological interest. Along with distaste for the heroine we begin to find praise for the psychological realism brought about, we are told, by the completeness of Richardson's identification with her.[1] Conversely, by identifying character with author, the book becomes a case-study, either of bourgeois-puritan attitudes, or of Richardson's psychological urges and fantasies.[2] The effect has been to retain some interest at the cost of devaluing the novel's conscious art and moral imagination.

Nevertheless, flawed though it undoubtedly is, *Pamela* seems to one reader a far more subtle and probing fiction than its reputation suggests. Several linked assumptions, amounting now to received opinion, begin to look distinctly unsound as soon as one tries to read 'to the moment' with the closeness of attention that Richardson's fiction demands, even at its crudest. In the criticism I have summarised the hypocrisy of the heroine is taken as read – for *Shamela* has been disproportionately hypnotic – though the subtler critics may allow that it might be unconscious in the girl, and in her author. Her vitality, on the other hand, is assumed to spring from the completeness of Richardson's identification with his character. It follows, if there be such discrepancy between the overt moral purpose and the subversive imaginative vitality, that Richardson must have been a largely unconscious artist. He hit on a method which produced fictive life by encouraging imaginative identification, but he was incapable of seeing or evaluating the real implications of what he had created.

There is as it happens a 'moment', the first turning point of the novel, where detailed attention will prove that none of these

[1] Brian Downs, *Richardson* (London, 1928 reprinted 1969), 111-12; Ernest Baker, *The History of the English Novel*, Vol. 4 (New York, 1930), 28; J. W. Krutch, *Five Masters: A Study in the Mutations of the Novel* (Bloomington, Indiana, 1930 reprinted 1959), 133; David Daiches, *Literary Essays* (Edinburgh and London, 1956), 38-9. (For a throwback to old-fashioned 'Antipamelist' scorn see Bernard Kreissman, *Pamela-Shamela* (Lincoln, Nebraska, 1960), chapter 1.)

[2] Ian Watt, *The Rise of the Novel* (London, 1957), chapter 5; Morris Golden, *Richardson's Characters* (Ann Arbor, Michigan, 1963).

assumptions can be sustained. Letter 24, where Pamela dresses in her new outfit, will show that Richardson himself has both dramatised and resolved the possibility of hypocrisy in his heroine. To identify him with Pamela is, simply, to mistake. We must learn to read, instead, with some attention to his dramatic art, which requires us to project ourselves into several points of view and gain a greater understanding than any. The scene is 'told' through a single pair of eyes, Pamela's; but must be seen through four pairs, of which the last are our own, having seen through all the others, and their misunderstandings. Also, though Pamela's letter seems artless, there turns out to be a concealed structure which articulates Richardson's 'meaning', though it has received no attention. And the scene reveals what looks remarkably like a sense of humour, at Pamela's expense. Reading 'to the moment', one repeats, takes time and trouble. The reward may be to begin to rediscover the *Pamela* that Richardson thought he had written.

A little background first. After B's first 'attempts' on Pamela – the reason for the inverted commas will appear later, for they are not what she thinks – he has decided to give her notice. His anger and mortified pride intimidate Mrs Jervis, his housekeeper, and his household, but Pamela and her parents appear (we had better say) to welcome her release, though she returns to poverty with her hopes of security gone. Secretly, Pamela procures and makes up a set of clothes more suitable to the future she is going to, than her dress as the favourite of B's dead mother. She then writes Letter 24 to her parents, describing how she dressed herself in her new outfit, and what happened.

Shamela's version of the scene insists of course that it is another example of the minx's politic cunning. Mrs Jervis tells the story. 'Miss Sham being set out in a hurry for my Master's House in Lincolnshire, desired me to acquaint you with the success of her Stratagem, which was to dress herself in the plain Neatness of a Farmer's Daughter, for she before wore the Cloaths of my late Mistress, and to be introduced by me as a Stranger to her Master. To say the Truth, she became the Dress extremely, and if I was to keep a House a thousand Years, I would never desire a prettier

Wench in it.' The pun is deliciously barbed. One thinks immediately of the other kind of House-Keeping, and of the function of dressing (and undressing) there.

We might however notice that Richardson's scene is prefaced by a warning. His epistolary method debarred him from open entrance on his stage, but this need not prevent his contriving to comment, or alert his readers, indirectly. We have what sounds like such a 'signal' when Pamela warns against misinterpretation: 'Don't think me presumptuous and conceited; for it is more my Concern than my Pride, to see such a Gentleman so demean himself . . .' (I, 67; *I, 41*). Richardson has dramatised this, making it lead quite naturally from her realisation that her master may be in love with her; yet the touch of formality in the style may suggest an address from author to reader as much as from Pamela to her parents. We do not of course have to believe what we are told – though we need not hasten to believe the opposite either – but it is clear that neither Richardson nor Pamela is unaware of the possibility that she might have been pluming herself on her conquest. Nevertheless, if the signal tends to head us off in one direction, it also raises a question. Though Pamela may be concerned rather than conceited about having attracted her master's attempts, we are also alerted to the possibility that conceit of some kind may be something she has to struggle against.

We now have her dressing-up, with its realistic and lovingly detailed description of each article of clothing, and its convincing feminine language. 'There I trick'd myself up as well as I could in my new Garb . . . and look'd about me in the Glass, as proud as any thing. – To say Truth, I never lik'd myself so well in my Life.' And then, immediately: 'O the Pleasure of descending with Ease, Innocence and Resignation! – Indeed there is nothing like it! An humble Mind, I plainly see, cannot meet with any very shocking Disappointment, let Fortune's Wheel turn round as it will' (I, 67-8; *I, 41-2*).

It is here that the value of having absorbed the signal becomes apparent. Pamela may well appear to be merely rationalising pleasure in her own seductiveness, with smug morality. The change of style might seem to mark the distinction, so that two opposing traits of her character lie side by side, and show that she is a hypocrite and Richardson naïve. If however the signal is entertained at all, the question surely arises of what other reason Pamela could have for being so pleased and proud? It has only to be asked for an explanation to come into focus that runs clean counter to hypocrisy. For Pamela, her new clothes are primarily a symbolic expression of her attitude toward her changing social condition. In Chaucer's tale of Griselda, by way of analogy, the three changes of clothing mark first the 'Cophetua and the beggar-maid' elevation of the heroine, then her tragic degrading, and lastly her merited restoration. She is shown behaving with uniform sweet humility. In any version of this basic folk-motif one is likely to find the same symbolism. There is also likely to be a vivid concentration on the clothes themselves, to make the story's contrasts more colourful, as in 'Cinderella' for example. Moreover these fables make the same point that Swift and Fielding made: that in a world of social distinctions and materialism, clothes hide us from one another. Griselda is always the same, really; Cinderella always as beautiful as a princess beneath her rags, though nobody will see it until she is gowned at the ball. Richardson is clarifying Pamela's attitude to her persecution in a fiction meant for readers who, in many cases, had their only contact with imaginative writing in moral parable, in sermons, or the puritan domestic literature of the period.

Pamela is pleased and proud, then, because the contrast between the clothes she has taken off, and the clothes she has put on, symbolises a spiritual victory in the terms of material disaster. She has resisted the temptation and falsity of the clothes she has shed. They were given originally as a mark of love, an earnest of her lady's intention to educate and support her above her station. They therefore stood also for Pamela's ambition, and longing for the security her parents cannot offer. After her lady's death her master's gift of more clothing was again symbolic to her – as indeed it was to him, in his very different way. The apparent kindness filled her with gratitude because it promised continuity, and allayed her fear of destitution, as the novel opened. Now her hopes have been dashed all the more cruelly because they had been allowed to rise again. B's lust has turned her clothes into a mockery; a temptation she can and must resist, since she can only go on wearing them at the price of his 'favour', a price she can read correctly now. So the new clothes she puts on instead are the clothes of 'innocence' and 'resignation', precisely. For she has brought herself to accept without bitterness the choice of virtue, against security. She knows that her upbringing has made her quite unsuited to the life her parents lead, and that they can scarcely support her. Thoughts of living 'in rags' and 'upon rye bread and water' are partly comic because so theoretical, but there can also be realistic pathos, as when she practises scouring a pewter plate: 'It only blister'd my Hand in two Places' (I, 99; *I*, *63*). Sentimentality is ultimately avoided because her situation is tethered firmly to social injustice and hardship. Hence Pamela's pride and pleasure in 'descending' fortune's wheel with 'ease', that is, equanimity, are neither evidence of hypocrisy, nor even a moral tag tacked on to a realistic story and imperfectly dramatised, but the essential part of the scene.

Yet, it might be objected, ought she to be so pleased with herself? Perhaps not; yet the pleasures of morality are a central feature of Richardson's ethic. He parts with the puritans decisively on this; he will not have the proof of right-doing placed in self-mortification, or the unpleasantness of the act. Morality gives intense pleasure, harmony, and happiness, and the more one can 'congratulate' oneself, the better. Such ideas are not of course peculiar to Richardson. They go back, as R. S. Crane pointed out[1], to the latitudinarian preachers of the seventeenth century, and are near the heart of the revolt against the 'dominion of the saints'. They are also shared by many of the major writers of the eighteenth century, pre-eminently Fielding.[2]

[1] R. S. Crane, 'Suggestions toward a Genealogy of the "Man of Feeling" ', *English Literary History*, 1 (1934), 205 ff.

[2] Martin Battestin, *The Moral Basis of Fielding's Art, A Study of 'Joseph Andrews'* (Middletown, Conn., 1959).

We arrive then at a reading which places at the centre Pamela's acceptance, with pleasure and pride, of the unpleasant consequences of her moral choice. Since this has as its foundation the rejection of her master, the view of her as 'politician' must be dismissed quite categorically. (*Shamela* makes us laugh by keeping the action but *reversing* the motivation and the symbolism.) Pamela's warning, though open to doubt hitherto, is vindicated now. She is not pluming herself on having attracted her master – let alone plotting to entrap him further.

Yet *Pamela* is no mere moral fable. Richardson's choice of phrase ('I tricked myself up . . .') suggests that he has indeed projected himself imaginatively enough to capture a typical feminine complication: that a girl of fifteen is quite capable of feeling, beyond the pride and pleasure in the moral significance of wearing certain clothes, another kind of pride and pleasure in also looking very pretty in them. This seems innocent enough, and, though certainly amusing, provides no reason to talk of hypocrisy or stratagem. Nor should it, surely, make us dislike her; it prevents her from being too Griselda-like, and makes her both more credible and more human, as we smile.

The fiction is not however 'unconscious' of this, nor, would it appear, is it there by accident. The signal at the start of the scene may have directed us away from seeing one kind of conceit in Pamela, but raised the question of conceit as something to think about. Now Pamela's pleasure in her beauty seems innocent, but it may be dangerous. Pamela's parents have already warned her: 'Besure don't let People's telling you, you are pretty, puff you up: for you did not make yourself, and so can have no Praise due to you for it. It is Virtue and Goodness only, that make the true Beauty. Remember that, *Pamela*' (I, 15; *I*, *9*). But Pamela has forgotten. She has two sources of pleasure in her reflection in the mirror; one, it seems, permissible and earned, the other not so, if a relatively harmless vanity. Yet if Pamela cannot distinguish among her feelings – 'I never liked myself so well' is nicely ambiguous – the structure of the scene proceeds to make her do so. There is again no question of her seeking to flaunt herself in front of B; but in going down to see Mrs Jervis she will be made to confront her master, and see herself through his eyes, in a way which effectively punishes her pleasure in her pretty reflection. The encounter, moreover, has far-reaching effects.

Mrs Jervis's reaction enables us to 'place' her in relation to Pamela. She is basically a good woman, but incapable of seeing past the clothes; Pamela is not 'metamorphosed' (I, 68; *I*, *42*), has undergone no basic change. This short-sightedness is characteristic of Mrs Jervis; even when Pamela explains, she can only grasp the fact that the girl is determined to leave. This concentration on the immediate and practical, and blindness to the more distant moral implications of any situation, mark all her advice to Pamela in the first half of the book. It is a perceptive insight into one kind of bourgeois mentality. This explains also why she proceeds to get Pamela into trouble by making it difficult for her to refuse to see her master without creating another scene. Only someone with the short-sightedness of Mrs Jervis to the meaning of the clothes in relation to B, could have failed to see the blunder of suggesting that Pamela confront him. Pamela sees it clearly enough, and says she was a fool to give in, but she does. Why?

This is the point where she may seem closest to *Shamela*, but all the evidence so far has pointed the other way. She has not sought the meeting and she is clearly unhappy about it. Yet if it is true, since her change of clothes is permanent, that 'she must have been seen by him another time', the reason, like the waistcoat she has stayed on to embroider, isn't quite excuse enough. The most likely explanation of both might be an unconscious feeling for her persecutor. (We shall discover when replacing Letter 24 in its context that the waistcoat has been used to mirror feelings she is unaware of having, and though she has never conceived the possibility of capturing her master, there have been other indications of nascent yet unconscious feeling, clear enough between the lines.) If then, at a moment of hurried indecision, she gives way, it might well be because of a hidden willingness to have her prettiness, as well as her moral decision, recognised by B. Only, if we read this way, the determination to leave that is symbolised by the clothes becomes more, rather than less admirable, because far more difficult. And though there are mixed motives once more, there is no hypocrisy because her moral purpose is always uppermost, as we shall see. Again, the structure of the scene provides a judgement, and punishment, of the secondary motive.

Despite Fielding, and the real deficiencies of B's creation, Richardson's hero is no Booby. He recognises Pamela at once, and though he does not recognise the meaning of her clothes he immediately sees both how pretty she is, and how her 'disguise' can be used to get her into his arms. His is the strategic mind; he shares with Lovelace the intriguer's ability to size up a situation instantaneously and turn it to advantage – cleverly sniping at the same time with his 'you are a lovelier Girl by half than *Pamela*; and sure I may be innocently free with you, tho' I would not do her so much Favour' (I, 70; *I*, *43*). This jibe is full of ironies. It aptly punishes the girl's pleasure in her own reflection. Remove the moral source of pleasure, the symbolic meaning of the clothes which B doesn't understand, and what is left is the purely physical, which is his point of view. The word 'lovely' is also nicely ambiguous; it can mean 'spiritually loveable' or 'worthy of love-making'. To B (it seems), to be lovely, is to be desirable, is to be desired, is to be attempted. Pamela is unexpectedly faced with sexual implications, isolated and underlined. A further irony lies in B's belief that she may be more easily attempted in the clothes which express her determination not to be seduced. (He is already on the way to the idea that she set out to attract him.) His 'freedoms' will be 'innocent' now, because in becoming the ordinary country girl she must have put off the high-flown ideas of chastity that belonged to the over-educated lady's maid. Pamela's further punishment for being puffed up by her beauty in the robes of purity, is to have them construed as their opposite. The irony, and her discomfiture, are complete as she runs from the room. The comedy is at her expense: '"O Sir", said I, I am *Pamela*, indeed I am: indeed I am *Pamela, her own-self*!' (I, 70; *I, 43*). But, it must be repeated, it is vanity that is punished, not hypocrisy, and the agent of the humiliation is more culpable and less discriminating than the offender. Pamela, Mrs Jervis, and B place themselves on a descending scale of moral sensibility.

Given time to think, however, B broadens his view of the situation into an attack which perfectly mirrors his own mental preoccupations – and it is the attack made by most of Richardson's critics. He lives in a mental and emotional world dominated by the war of the sexes, and being incapable of understanding Pamela's values, he can only interpret her clothes in terms of their effect on him, and assume they were put on to achieve that effect. So: 'Come in, said he, you little Villain . . . Who is it you put your Tricks upon; I was resolv'd never to honour your Unworthiness, said he, with so much Notice again; and so you must disguise yourself, to attract me, and yet pretend, like a Hypocrite as you are—' (I, 70; *I, 43-4*).

The charge of hypocrisy actually comes from B, fully dramatised within the scene. One is puzzled then to make out how it can be said either that Richardson was unconscious of the unsympathetic interpretation that could be put on Pamela's conduct, or that he is to be identified with her. At this point he has clearly 'become' B, and has seen with considerable accuracy how Pamela must appear to him. B doesn't suggest that the hypocrisy lies in donning robes of purity to attract him sexually, since he doesn't understand the meaning of the clothes at all. He is angry because he is left, as he so often is, with arms outstretched in a void. The dash implies 'and yet pretend like a hypocrite as you are, that the natural sexual consequence repels you'. The hypocrisy for B consists of behaving like a mare only to shy away from the stallion.

It is only now that Pamela angrily explains at least the social meaning of her clothes, but the effect of even this on B is worth watching closely. 'He then took me in his Arms, and presently push'd me from him. Mrs *Jervis*, said he, take the little Witch from me; I can neither *bear* nor *forbear* her! (Strange Words these!) – But stay; you shan't go! – Yet begone! – No, come back again' (I, 71; *I*, *44*). Richardson certainly has some way to go in creating a style which can carry the to-and-fro of a wavering mind with conviction; but this is nevertheless one of the touches, very crude as yet, but to be developed with far greater accuracy and power in his later fiction, which caused him to be called 'the master of the heart'. B is momentarily in the grip of deep conflict as Lovelace is to be, and for the same reason. He is having to give up, painfully, the view of Pamela on which all his actions are founded. To understand her as she really is – that is, no hypocrite, but a genuinely moral being – is to face not only the need to give up hope of seducing her, but also the need to change his whole view of life if he is not to lose her altogether. His pride cannot bear to change, but he wants her as much as ever; he cannot bring himself either to give her up, or to give up himself.

Nevertheless his first impulse is very like repentance, with an offer to renew the plan of putting her to his sister's service. The irony now is that Pamela's suspicions are so roused, and her temper so frayed, that she becomes the blind one. The gulf between their points of view is too wide for her to appreciate the distance, infinitesimal to her but enormous to him, that he has come to meet her. He is having to humble the pride which is his strongest characteristic. Hence the demand that 'she humble herself, and ask this as a Favour, and is sorry for her Pertness, and the Liberty she has taken with my Character' (I, 71; *I*, *44*). Instead, she is so incensed by the charge of hypocrisy, and so suspicious of his motives, that far from thanking him meekly she begins to throw the past in his face. It is worth noticing how her aside, 'Strange words these!', again serves a double function. It is another warning to the reader to ponder the words' significance, but it also indicates that Pamela herself doesn't understand them. Her failure also to understand the talk of 'robbery' is again tragicomic. She is so far from planning to entrap B that she fails to realise how she has touched his love and admiration again, as well as his lust. But the result of her acid jibes is to drive him into a passion, in which his momentary softening is swept away by wounded pride and rage. This pattern, too, will reappear in *Clarissa.*

When sufficient attention is paid to a Richardsonian 'moment', *Pamela* proves far more complex, subtle, and artful than has been supposed. It is not a work written out of the unconscious by a happy accident of self-identification; it is a novel by the artist who would create *Clarissa*, but at a stage where crudities show that he was still learning to articulate his 'new way of writing'. One does not contend that he need have been completely aware in his everyday consciousness of *all* the implications of this scene. There is bound to be a gap between the work itself – where imagination senses more than the artist has yet grasped, but works nevertheless with a 'logic' of its own towards realisation – and the kind of account his ordinary intelligence might give at the time or later. I shall be arguing reasons why this gap was wider than usual in Richardson's case. There are, moreover, features of Letter 24 that suggest imaginative limits. He seems unworried by the possibilities of smugness in his idea of moral pleasure. Morality for him was always public, but he doesn't seem to question the open angling for approval which, along with her desire to show off her new outfit itself, takes Pamela to Mrs Jervis. (Indeed, he allows Pamela's sensitivity to public opinion to figure more prominently in her own explanations of her clothes than their deeper symbolism of 'innocence' and 'resignation'.) Richardson's ability to modulate style is still uncertain: too abrupt transitions cause unforeseen inferences or smiles. Most of the comedy in the scene is not, however, unconscious – including (I believe) the splendid melodramatic close of Jonathan's warning (I, 73-4; *I, 46*), though we have yet to discover the justification for laughing with Richardson rather than at him. Nevertheless, the fact that so many implications of behaviour are taken up into a structure of exploration, testing, and judgement, convinces me that the 'Richardson' who matters – the dramatic artist visible in the relation between texture and structure in the work itself – was imaginatively aware as very many critics who have patronised him have failed to be.

Letter 24 pits different views of life against one another in a meaningful pattern. The author has projected himself imaginatively into all three points of view; the reader must do the same, and be prepared to read between the lines and consider the implications of speech and action. Pamela herself may be only partly conscious of her mixed motives, and B's; but Richardson has used the ambiguities, and resolved them. To identify him with Pamela is simply to misread, for while she may be nearer to him than the others, he is by no means uncritical. Letter 24 disposes of the charge of hypocrisy, but exposes and judges her vanity, suspicion, and self-righteousness. ('I never found her inclinable to think herself in a Fault' says Mrs Jervis, tellingly (I, 71; *I*, *44*)). On the other hand, B turns out to be no simple villain, but a character in conflict, though we have to infer this from what he says and does, as Pamela herself cannot.

Let us now go back to the beginning.

2

The opening phase, up to the 'Judgement' scene where B declares he will dismiss her, may seem at first remarkable mainly for its crudity. The suspiciousness of Pamela's father seems ludicrously exaggerated – even granted a greater suggestiveness in gifts of underclothes than in our age – and it is annoying when he is so swiftly proved right. B's first fumbling attempts, moreover, seem to show why Fielding called him 'Booby'. Not even Defoe allowed his seducers to behave with such crass materialism. Assuming that his gifts will have softened her enough, B appears to build all on a swift offer to make Pamela a gentlewoman, and when repulsed, attempts to buy her silence. There is no word of compliment or desire, let alone love. He then seems oddly taken aback by her rejection, and simply unable to understand her moral language. For a moment he seems touched, in his mother's dressing-room, by Pamela's outburst about her 'first duty', but moments later he appears to be threatening her with straightforward rape in the manner of Tarquin. Yet he is incapable (it seems) of doing anything much, this clumsy schoolboy impossibly miscast as a rake.

That there is crudity admits of no doubt – yet a re-reading may considerably modify one's first impressions, especially if Richardson is not 'unconscious' nor Pamela's view of B infallible. Ian Watt has argued how deftly 'all the themes of the story are sounded in the opening paragraph'[1]: Pamela's dependence, her awe of superiors and her own feeling of being qualified above her degree, her 'obtrusive piety', and 'the ironic climax that what God should most specifically have done for her is to "put it into my good lady's heart . . . (to) say – My dear son! . . . remember my poor Pamela" '. This is surely right.

If Richardson is not as artless as he looks, however, may there not be as important a theme, not in the first letter itself, but in the sharp contrast between it and those that follow? For the main feature of Pamela's first letter is how happily *unsuspecting* she is. The fear of destitution has been lifted and her master has been wondrous kind. I see no evidence that she suspects anything wrong in his behaviour – and to have read the rest of the book is to throw this into high relief, for it will be a very long time before she sounds like this again. If we look closer, however, there is also a potential fearfulness and suspicion waiting to be activated. She seems too easily frightened when B finds her writing to her parents, and there is a canniness about her dispatch of the guineas wrapped in paper, lest sight or sound provoke envy or theft. Yet it is only potential, in high contrast with the exaggerated suspicion and determination to fear the worst apparent everywhere in her father's reply: 'and, Oh! that frightful Word, that he would be kind to you, if you would do as *you should do*, almost kills us with Fears' (I, 5; *I*, *3*). Can we really

[1] Ian Watt, 'Samuel Richardson' in *The Novelist as Innovator* (London, 1965), 4.

be meant to take that tone and attitude straight? Certainly Pamela herself objects: 'I must needs say, your Letter has fill'd me with Trouble: For it has made my Heart, which was overflowing with Gratitude for my Master's Goodness, suspicious and fearful . . . Sure they can't *all* have Designs against me because they are civil!' (I, 6-7; *I, 4-5*).

Once made suspicious and fearful, however, she grows more and more so; and though her master's conduct might seem to justify her, and her parents, her language begins to exaggerate too. After B's first stolen kisses: 'He has now shewed himself in his true Colours, and, to *me*, nothing appears so black and so frightful' (I, 16; *I, 10*). It hardly seems so to us. In the 'Judgement' scene she records B's complaint of how 'representing herself as an Angel of Light, she makes her kind Master and Benefactor a Devil incarnate – (O how People will sometimes, thought I, call themselves by their right Names!)' (I, 37; *I, 24*). He isn't of course a benefactor, but is he a devil either? The italics and brackets might seem to raise an important question, even at this stage. We are bound to accept Pamela's reportage of dramatic scene, since it is all we have. But may not her exaggerated fears and suspicions make her judgement of character and motive unreliable?

The more closely we listen to and watch B, indeed, the less devilish he seems. A dispassionate legal observer might well conclude, not only from the 'Lucretia' scene, but from the whole of the evidence up to Pamela's abduction, that there must be the strongest doubt that he ever attempted rape at all. Our impression of his boobiness, moreover, comes from what on closer inspection looks like confusion and indecision; the attempts in summer-house and dressing-room are seen to be the effects of anger and wounded pride rather than lust; and he does not fail to register Pamela's outrage, but persists in trying desperately to believe that it is really artful hypocrisy.

On a first reading one may be uncertain what to make of this. When however the pattern – concealed artfulness of texture, a heroine blinded by suspicion, a hero more complex than she thinks – anticipates so clearly the more definite findings of Letter 24, confidence grows.

On re-reading, moreover, we are also possessed of a crucial fact we did not know at first: that John, who carries Pamela's letters, was planted by B after he first found her writing one, so that he could read them all before they leave the house. Given this, much that may have seemed odd or ludicrous looks rather different – indeed a whole new reading of B's conduct begins to proffer itself. The sudden change in his behaviour ('some time after my last letter but one' as Pamela observes with odd precision (I, 17, *I*, *11*)) can be explained if we ask what effect her last letter before the summer-house episode might have had on him. He would discover that he had reawakened her suspicions by refusing to let her go to his sister; but his own jealous pride might also be roused by the first humiliating evidence that she would rather go than stay. He watches her closely, perhaps not with goat's eyes as she thinks, but trying to gauge what she really feels; and his tentativeness when he finally determines to find out in the summer-house, may spring from radical uncertainty. He cannot however bear to find he has made so little impression that she would genuinely rather go, and his first kisses are an irritable reflex, rather than seductive (Letter 11). His subsequent conversation with Mrs Jervis, moreover, becomes ambiguous if he already knows that Pamela has confided in her (Letter 14). His questions seem to be aimed at finding out whether Pamela has 'told' – but he is really trying to discover whether she rejects him because of some rival, and is increasingly irritated by the talk of a serving girl's virtue. It would be intolerable to admit that she could find him simply unattractive, or that her morality could be genuinely more powerful. Hence the accusations of artfulness. Either he must have a rival, though it seems unlikely, or else she must be leading him on by pretending moral distance. He is consequently furious at the blend of disparagement and moralisation in her letters, but they also sap his confidence. Indeed, in the dressing-room, he is momentarily convinced that she means what she says (I, 30; *I*, *19*). Yet it remains unbearable – and his second 'attempt' is again a reaction rather than a seduction. He is less concerned to persuade than to riposte, turning her moral exaggerations on her own head, and taunting her with drawing her morality from her reading of romances (I, 31; *I*, *20*). (For the second and not the last time we find Richardson's hero anticipating Fielding's jibes, this one in *Joseph Andrews*.) Paradoxically, B's conduct is revealed as *defensive*. He is really trying not so much to possess her body as to re-possess his old self-esteem and cynicism, which his reading of her letters continually saps away.

But Pamela really believes she is about to be raped, and faints. In a sense this confirms her integrity, since it suggests that her morality is part of her very being, which finds turpitude literally unbearable. We cannot but share her vision; what is 'real' to her is imaginatively 'there' to us. Yet if we can also see more than she does, the episode need not be taken with the gravest solemnity: if B is only playing a vindictive game, as he says, the episode also fits in with her exaggerated fears and suspicions. One of the advantages of the view I am advocating is that there is truth in B's self-defence, though it is all hateful lies to Pamela; our vision becomes double. Nevertheless on any showing Richardson's control is imperfect. The fainting-device is excessive here, is over-used afterwards, and B peeping through the keyhole is funny in a way Richardson may not have intended.

Indeed, though the overall conception of this first phase may well have been far better than it seems, the presentation is undoubtedly faulty. I believe the interpretation I suggest will be confirmed by the structure of the novel as a whole, but it cannot be argued that Richardson has secured it against misreading – it is far too easy to miss, and so be carried along with Pamela's point of view. Familiar with his own idea of the characters, Richardson clearly failed to see how much more help his readers need than he gives them in this first work. In the case of Mr Andrews, I suspect he was still imagining in the mode of the *Familiar Letters*,[1] where 'character' had to be built up quickly

[1] Samuel Richardson, *Familiar Letters on Important Occasions* (1741), ed. B. Downs (London, 1928).

in a single letter, in 'capitals', and that this tempted him to overplay 'the Poor, and Too-Suspicious Father' without realising that the absurdity might be attributed to himself. He seems not to have noticed that his device to conceal from Pamela that B is reading all her letters, also blinds his readers. (The main evidence that B knows what he shouldn't can be attributed to the letter missing from the dressing-table.) Apart from minute give-aways, then, the only solid pointer to the true situation is B's behaviour itself, and Richardson failed to realise how easily this could be taken as boobiness by readers unwilling to work at inferences. Most of all, the trouble lies with the crudity of the single-focus epistolary form. The fact that Pamela is the only source of narrative makes it too easy to confer the reliability of her reportage on to her interpretation also; and hence to assume that she herself, her parents, and her view of B, are meant to represent Richardson's own vision. A single direct insight into B's mind at this stage would have made a world of difference.

3

From the 'Judgement' scene, however, Richardson shows a surer touch. B's angry verdict of dismissal 'to the Distresses and Poverty she was taken from' (I, 37; *I, 24*) marks one exact revolution of fortune's wheel; but Pamela's attitude to the threat of poverty has changed, and far from being crushed she falls to her knees to bless B for releasing her. He is both nonplussed and moved, and though this seems to produce only further anger and insult, Mrs Jervis convincingly explains that his pride makes him furious at being in love (I, 44; *I, 29*). Moreover, his new accusations of 'witchcraft' are significantly directed at Pamela's power to charm people morally. 'She makes even *you*' he growls at Mrs Jervis, 'who should know better what the World is, think her an Angel of Light' (I, 55-6; *I, 36*). It is becoming steadily harder for him to treat Pamela in terms of knowing the world, and his conflict is no longer merely between his pride and his love, but more explicitly between his cynic's view of human nature and the dawnings of moral sensibility.

Mrs Jervis builds on hopes of change in B, and several times, unable to see the long-term implications, she argues that Pamela could easily stay if she will only mollify B's pride. But while Pamela is certain, as she is, that he wants her only for his 'harlot', the possibility that he is learning to love her makes things worse not better. On the one hand, 'To say my Master likes me' – she will use no stronger word – 'when I know what End he aims at, is Abomination to my Ears', and on the other, 'I shan't think myself safe, till I am at my poor Father's and Mother's' (I, 53; *I*, *35*).

For we should by this time be beginning to suspect that Pamela may be falling in love with B, though the hints are indirect and she clearly has no idea herself. The impression made at the start by generosity and handsomeness was clear, and it may well be, as has been suggested, that her willingness to work out her notice, by finishing the waistcoat, has something to do with unconscious feeling for its wearer. The double-edged remark I have just quoted comes immediately after Mrs Jervis reports B saying that if he could find a lady just like Pamela, he would marry her. In her resentment, Pamela doesn't stop to weigh her words. 'Yet if I was the Lady of Birth, and he would offer to be rude first . . . I don't know whether I would have him.' The waistcoat, we may notice, suddenly becomes 'ugly' just here.

Let us not mistake however; she has procured the clothes which express her determination to go. But before she puts them on, she is confronted with four 'ladies of birth' in an episode which would be pointless but for its bearing on her state of mind. The ladies are full of condescending praises, but Pamela's tone makes clear that she knows they are no better than she is, apart from their 'birth'. She also knows she can expect no good from their teasing B about her. When they have gone, she broods. 'I have finish'd my Task, and my Master is horrid cross! And I am vex'd his Crossness affects me so. If ever he had any Kindness towards me, I believe he now hates me heartily. Is it not strange that Love borders so much on Hate? But . . . how must this Hate have been increas'd, if he had met with a base Compliance, after his wicked Will had been gratify'd . . . Thus we read in Holy Writ, that wicked *Amnon*, when he had ruined poor *Tamar*, hated her more than ever he lov'd her, and would have her turn'd out of Door! How happy am I, to be turn'd out of Door, with that sweet Companion my Innocence! – O may that be always my Companion! And while I presume not upon my own Strength, and am willing to avoid the Tempter, I hope the Divine Grace will assist me' (I, 65-6; *I*, *40*). Almost every line of this, if we think about it, is delicately suggestive of her hidden feeling for B, but Richardson's art is not only realistic, but subtle also in making it so credible that Pamela shouldn't realise the implications of what she says. Mrs Jervis's explanation of B's behaviour is running in her mind – she refers to it again at the start of Letter 24 – and it sets her thinking about his feelings when she had started thinking about her own. She then seems too engaged in cheering herself up about B's 'hatred' to analyse her hidden reasons for caring, or being comforted. Her final prayer is prevented from revealing her to herself because, as she says, it has been a familiar prayer before it received the new significance one can see in it now.

But as Letter 23 closes on her defiant pride in her parents, poverty, and her longing to put on her new clothes, the pathos of Letter 24 should be increased by our glimpses of her heart. She is quite clearly not planning to entrap B, and there is strong support for her statement in Letter 24 that she thinks of her situation with concern rather than conceit. She has no secret hope that B might marry her, and whatever the state of his feelings, or hers, she is determined to go. Only, to don the clothes of 'innocence' and 'resignation' with 'ease' is indeed a test, for she has more to overcome than her fear of poverty.

Moreover, given what we now know of B, one can also see how her suspiciousness in the 'Clothes' scene resolved, in the wrong direction, the first real crisis of the novel. It was a possible turning point, for B is not only strongly moved, and ready to hint openly that she has 'robbed' him of his heart, but he virtually asks her to ease his path to reverse his verdict. His pride still predominates however, and so her 'sauciness' enrages him more than ever. Yet the determination to 'have' her, which Rachel overhears, and Jonathan rouses Pamela's fears by reporting so melodramatically, need not at all mean what they think. In retrospect, we know he had already completed his plans to abduct her when he went to Lincolnshire. He is threatening to revert to an old scheme for getting her firmly into his power, not a new one to rape her that very night . . . as it will appear to Pamela.

4

All the remaining scenes before the abduction are in clear structural relation to scenes we have already discussed. The 'Closet' scene (Letter 25) is counterpart to the 'Summer house' and 'Dressing room' episodes. It has always been taken as an attempted rape, but the closer one looks, the more unlikely it seems again that Pamela's interpretation can be the right one. Of course it is understandable that she should suspect the worst. But should we?

Isn't it intrinsically absurd that B should plan to rape her in the presence of Mrs Jervis? – who is quite unlike Mrs Jewkes, or Mrs Sinclair in *Clarissa* – let alone actually in her bed? What on earth could he have imagined Mrs Jervis would do? He only emerges from the smaller room when on the point of being discovered, and he makes no attempt to pull the girl into it and barricade the door with that convenient chest of drawers, as any self-respecting rapist would have done. When he does threaten her sexually, it seems mainly to frighten her into silence; and though he has a try at getting Mrs Jervis out of the room to quieten the maids, and takes his opportunity to fondle Pamela's breasts again, he does far too much 'expostulation' for any serious attempt on her virginity. He might well have made the best of any weakening on Pamela's part, or Mrs Jervis's, but the verdict on felonious intent would surely be 'not proven'? We cannot of course simply accept his own repeated statements next day that he meant no harm, or his frequent assurances that he abhors force, both before and after this. But one must notice how bewildered and annoyed he is by the fuss – and I shall argue later (p. 90-1) that to see that Pamela's account is fallible, is to see a rich element of comedy when we look at B. He really appears not to feel any guilt about rape, only eavesdropping; and he gives a good reason for that: his growing suspicion that Mrs Jervis has been hardening Pamela's resistance while pretending to persuade her to stay.

It will not have escaped readers of the later continuation of the novel, that this 'more favourable Construction' is the one that B afterwards feels he deserves from readers who haven't Pamela's excuse for suspecting the worst (III, 184; *II, 102*). This of course cannot affect the verdict on the scene itself, since both Richardson and his hero have had time and motivation to construct a different 'intention'. The real case is not only that Pamela's evidence itself wholly allows the more favourable construction, but that it is a great deal more plausible than her own; though once again Richardson cannot be said to have secured it, because we have insufficient access to B.

Now however B's humiliation causes a sharp change of mood. He crushes his growing moral sensibility and reverts to his old cynicism; and Richardson cleverly allows him to guy the very scene in which he had been most deeply touched, by inviting Pamela to express her opinion of his new clothes (Letter 27). Insofar as squires who marry beneath them are not admitted at Court, his Birthday Suit may express the same kind of decision as her outfit, to be free. He is very grand, and in fine caustic vein, as he mocks Pamela's 'hideous Squallings' and 'unfashionable Jargon', her 'pretty romantick Turn for Virtue, and all that', and her preaching (I, 86-8; *I, 55-6*). He equips her imaginatively with gown and cassock, then changes his mind to anticipate, in part, Fielding's cruel jibe about her keeping house with Mrs

Jervis. (Both B and Fielding, of course, had read Letter 12). Here B is mocking the idea of moral friendship as well as the alliance of sex with morality. He deliberately jeers at everything that had touched and shamed him. In his rich waistcoat which 'stood on End with Gold Lace' – as against her humble flowered one – he asserts his power and wealth, his independence of her moral standards, and the conscious superiority of the fashionable buck and man of the world. Once again Richardson can hardly be said to be unaware of possible unsympathetic responses to Pamela, or to be composing texturally or structurally by accident.

Yet there is still the question of whether the clothes 'fit' B. 'You do well, Sir, said I, to even your Wit to such a poor Maiden as me. But, permit me to say, that if you was not rich and great, and I poor and little, you would not insult me thus. – Let me ask you, Sir, if this becomes your fine Cloaths, and a Master's Station?' (I, 88; *I*, *56*). If Richardson were always as clear-cut on social issues!

The next two scenes also have specific reference to Letter 24. In Letter 28, he shows Pamela struggling against the inflexibility and self-righteousness exposed in the 'Clothes' scene, and trying to fulfil the servant's duty that corresponds to the duty of a master. B holds another public court, recalling the first 'Judgement' scene, in front of Longman this time as well as Mrs Jervis. He aims to justify himself before his household, relying on her duty. He insists that he is turning her away for impertinence and indiscretion; conceals his attempts on her; and keeps daring her to forget her station and speak out. Pamela is obviously tortured by the temptation to vindicate herself; but when she is eventually forced to speak, she makes a deliberate effort to humble herself instead.

For the first time since Letter 24, B is touched again – as he should be, for pride should know best how hard it is to subdue. Richardson overdoes Longman's emotion, though it is not wholly inappropriate since he knows so little. The strength of his dramatic imagination, however, is apparent in the way that Pamela's feelings are shown subverting her intentions in the act of utterance. She tries hard to do a servant's duty to respect and safeguard the reputation of her master, but her exaggerations define the limits of her humility. B is not 'the *best* of Masters' (I, 95; *I, 60*), and she clearly does not feel that she deserves nothing but shame and disgrace; the speech has a quality of pretence that leaves her real spiritual pride intact. She is struggling in quite a moving and admirable way, but failing to subdue herself.

Nevertheless, as far as B is concerned, this scene undoes much of the bad effect of Letter 24 and removes the justification for his wounded pride. One might expect a reawakening of the response to her moral qualities which that pride had repressed, and so it proves. Richardson organises his next scene as a kind of rewriting of both the 'Clothes' and the 'Closet' scenes, to give his characters another chance. Mrs Jervis herself hides B in the closet of the Green-room, in the hope of moving him still further in Pamela's favour (Letter 29). He overhears Pamela realising, even more vividly than before, her unsuitability for her new condition, summed up by the attempt to scour the pewter plate. Then, with minute reasoning, she repeats the clothes symbolism, dividing her worldly goods like someone dying to the life they have known, and renouncing the bundles of clothes she has forfeited by her refusal of the only conditions on which they could have been hers.

The effect on B is considerable. The final scene between them in this first part of the novel is remarkable for his kindness, tenderness, and candour. For the first time he confesses his love, and in terms which sound convincing. 'You have too much Wit and good Sense not to discover, that I, in spite of my Heart, and all the Pride of it, cannot but love you. Yes, look up to me, my sweet-fac'd Girl! I *must* say I love you . . .' (I, 107; *I, 68-9*). He begins to enquire after her parents, and counters her suspicion by admitting that her 'worthiness' in the scene before Longman, and the 'Bundle' scene, and the light the servants regard her in, and her letters (which he has seen more of than she imagined), have all made him love her 'to extravagance' – and obviously spiritually as well as sexually now. He wants her to stay another fortnight to give him time to overcome his pride, for he cannot 'descend all at once'.

The open admission about the letters is both a mark of greater honesty, and an invitation to the reader to consider, at this crucial stage, whether the fact might make a difference to one's view of his past behaviour.

For the first time in the novel Pamela is up against real temptation rather than apparent assault. Her heart, consistent with our previous analysis, is on the side of the tempter: 'I trembled to find my poor Heart giving way' (I, 109; *I, 70*). Indeed, the rush of feeling is startling, she hardly knows what she is doing, and begins to say the Lord's Prayer like someone in extremity. B makes no attempt to take advantage of this, but leaves her alone to think the whole thing over – another point in his favour.

What he is asking seems little enough on the surface. Yet he has made no promises about his future conduct and there is no guarantee that things will be any different. That he wants time to subdue his unruly pride shows just how strong it is. She cannot bring herself to trust him. (In a sense, by waiting so long to have his heroine seriously tested, Richardson has weighted the scales.) Yet her first thought is that she cannot trust herself, especially in a situation in which B will feel free to talk to her openly of love. This is in her mind, along with her distrust of him, when she makes her final decision – in keeping with the prayer we met before – 'to go away, and trust all to Providence, and nothing to myself' (I, 111; *I, 71*).

How sincere does B seem to us? There seems no reason to doubt the sincerity of what he actually says in the first part of the scene. We have seen how his feelings have been changing again. His solemn oaths ought, I believe, to be taken on trust if only for the moment of utterance, for the Richardson who courted difficulty by insisting that the Lovelace Clarissa would reject, had to be a believer, would hardly have wanted B, whom Pamela is to accept, to blaspheme. Above all B *sounds* sincere, and there is nothing to suggest calculated hypocrisy in the scene itself.

Yet we know, in retrospect, that the waiting chariot marks a long-laid plan to abduct her to Lincolnshire if she insists on leaving the house. Nevertheless, the difficulty is more apparent than real. It is very like the character of B that Richardson has built up, to back himself to win all three ways. If Pamela is willing to stay, she gives him time to settle his own conflict one way – or the other. If she refuses, the chariot awaits.

He returns apparently confident that she will meet his wishes. Surprisingly, however, when she refuses he doesn't storm, but comes out instead with the proposal about Williams which (Pamela is probably right) he has invented while he was out of the room. It is of course a blunder. Pamela's feelings being as they are, the idea of marrying her to a man she has never seen makes her very angry, and she is not likely to miss the inconsistency with B's earlier declarations. He is playing for time, and an excuse to kiss her, but to the Pamela who had been so affected by his talk of loving her, 'his very Breath was now Poison' (I, 113; *I*, *72*).

Richardson risks having all B's conduct in the scene read as hypocrisy now, instead of as a conflict becoming resolved in the wrong direction once more. Pamela is meant to see him as a 'black-hearted wretch', and hate him with a vehemence that is the direct outcome of her awakening love. But we are not, or the whole complexity vanishes, and leaves us with a cardboard villain false to the impressions Richardson has lately been building up much more carefully. One may be annoyed again also, as at the beginning, by an apparent overeagerness to vindicate suspicion immediately, and prove right what could easily have been wrong. Given the disadvantage of the single focus which bars us from direct access to B's mind when we need it most, the risks were too great. As on so many occasions however, if one stops to ask *why* a man of intrigue should miscalculate so badly, an answer appears that almost makes the risk worth taking, since it explains so much that will follow.

B surely miscalculates because he cannot imagine her feelings for himself – and this proves how much he has changed. At first, rather than imagine she could possibly find him unattractive, he angrily sought evidence of a rival. Now he invents a proposal that is obviously meant to be more attractive than his own, and seems quite blind to the feelings for himself that could make it 'poisonous'. It seems that her letters, and her intransigence, have developed a moral sensibility in B that shows him how his behaviour could have made him hateful – the irony of his miscalculation is all the finer. I think we shall understand B better if we see how love could have destroyed his personal vanity, though it battles still against his social pride.

The scene gives us our last sight of Pamela as a free agent. It is a greater 'might-have-been' than Letter 24, though B's motives are still dangerously mixed, but to read with attention is to dispose once and for all of interpretations which suggest that Pamela is a scheming minx. One will certainly have many reservations about her, but hypocrisy isn't one of these, and there is evidence that Richardson has some too. If we ceased to assume she was offered for unquestioning admiration, we might be able to respond to the fifteen-year-old girl much more sympathetically. It seems certain, too, that B's behaviour is far more complex and his conflicts already deeper than is apparent on the surface, though the major flaw in the novel is that we have to infer this, risking far too much if we fail to do so. Yet Richardson, in spite of flaws and crudities, is managing to create the day-to-day fluctuations in feeling and behaviour that give depth to moral analysis and make his fiction seem 'like' life. For all their apparent naturalness – or artlessness – however, his scenes are carefully interrelated in a pattern of continuous cross-reference and parallel. Only, we have to read and think as much 'to the moment' as he wrote, if his art is to reveal its subtleties.

CHAPTER TWO

In the Wilderness

I

In the first part of the novel there was a good deal of dramatic action, but with the abduction of Pamela comes a marked change of direction. The fluctuating relationships in the first part, the structurally related scenes, defined both inner conflicts and the essential differences between visions of life. The texture was complex but much of its 'meaning' implicit; so that while the first part of the novel is the most lively it is also the most liable to misinterpretation. Now however Pamela is isolated. For a long time we shall have hardly a glimpse of B. Richardson begins a fuller and more explicit analysis of his heroine and her problems, the most important of which, it turns out, go far deeper than her relation with her master.

Only now does Richardson take care to emphasise the passage of time; not merely dating journal entries, but counting the days of her captivity. From the abduction to the morning on which she and B will confess their love is forty days and forty nights. If this is a coincidence it is at least a suggestive one, for this is not only a period of suffering – of 'persecutions, oppressions and distress', as Pamela puts it – it is also a period of spiritual growth through trial and temptation. In this section, moreover, the novel ceases to be ethical, with a pious or even sanctimonious flavour, and becomes overtly religious, in Pamela's victory over a temptation that for Richardson was the greatest of all she had to face, though it has nothing to do with B.

The emphasis now is therefore internal, and concerned more with consciousness than behaviour. Consequently there is much less action but much more discussion and analysis, and if Pamela in one sense is immobile, in another her very immobility is the condition of battle. The critic, too, has to sharpen his focus on certain moral and spiritual questions. These are introduced immediately, at the very beginning of the journal Pamela will keep through her captivity, and the language of the Bible and of prayer itself indicates the new dimension, and the point at which the moral becomes the religious.

Pamela's moral self-vindication is true to our experience, but also less than the whole truth. Her trials are not of her seeking, – but she has a dawning love for her master. They are not caused by presumption, by looking above her station, or breaking her duty to respect and obey her master where his commands do not conflict with a Higher Duty – but she is inclined to be 'pert', and even openly contemptuous, and has achieved only partial success in humbling herself. Her trials are not caused by vanity or pride – though these, with self-righteousness, are among the faults to which she is most liable. So the vindication is both true, and also defines the areas in which she is open to moral question, like the author direction in Letter 24. All of these will be further explored.

The first part of Pamela's prayer, however, takes up previous prayers with a new emphasis on an element common to them all: the distinction between faith and self-reliance. The conditions on which she hopes that her God will deliver her from the wilderness include not only duty and humility, but resignation. Yet she recognises that she prays 'imperfectly, as I am forc'd by my distracting Fears and Apprehensions'. One begins to see that Pamela may be fearful in a much deeper sense than merely being afraid of her master. The greatest danger in her abduction is that fear will drive her towards the deepest of sins, despair. ('But yet what can I hope for, when I seem to be devoted' – that is, doomed – 'as a Victim to the Will of a wicked Violator of all the Laws of God and Man! – But, gracious Heaven, forgive me my Rashness and Despondency! O let me not sin against thee; for thou best knowest what is fit for thine Handmaid!') (I, 129; *I, 82*). Pamela's battle with despair, her struggle to regain faith and trust, not only in God but also in Man, will become the major theme at the centre of the novel, and will incidentally reverse the irony about Providence that Ian Watt spotted in the first paragraph. But it is not only a battle to gain something; it is also a battle to give something up, one of her strongest characteristics: her self-reliance, and indeed pride in her own prudence. For to be 'resigned' is to trust God rather than oneself. We begin to confront a paradox. It is her self-reliance that makes the embattled little girl so vividly real and interesting – yet to rely too much on her own prudence, ingenuity, suspicion, is to rely on the fallible, and fall from pride to despair when the inevitable failure comes.

Pamela glimpses this now, and Richardson brings it squarely to our attention. Yet Pamela's self-reliance is ingrained; her pert calculating intelligence and her vanity are perhaps the qualities above all that provoke the charge of hypocrisy. She can seem so wide-awake, so carefully estimating the effects of her actions, that this impression tends to obliterate others no less important: her little girl's naïveté, her loneliness, her inability to understand the complexity of other people, her fearfulness. Now her isolation is to develop strongly, and disastrously, her tendency to intrigue in the interests of prudence. Although she has glimpsed the need to trust God rather than herself, what B will call her 'little plotting guileful heart' is soon as active as ever if not more so, and delighting in her own cunning. She fails to win anyone over to help her on the journey to Lincolnshire, but as she busies herself hiding pens, paper and ink behind Mrs Jewkes back she thinks how 'something . . . might happen to open a Way for my Deliverance, by these or some other Means'. Of course we would not care for a Pamela who folded her hands. And yet – 'O the Pride, thought I, I shall have, if I can secure my Innocence, and escape the artful Wiles of this wicked Master . . . So I must set all my little Wits at Work' (I, 149; *I, 96*). Presumption, vanity, self-reliant prudence and despair, do all have a connection through a common reference to pride. Pamela's sojourn in the wilderness is an opportunity to investigate these more deeply, and to see her developing as she battles with these tendencies herself.

2

In our more egalitarian times there may not be much appreciation of the problem of 'presumption': the implications of Pamela's status and duty as a servant. Modern readers are likely to sympathise with her rebelliousness, her assertion of human rights, her flings at social injustice and the abuse of power and privilege by the rich. It seems, and is, of central significance that B should finally be made to treat her as a human being, not his property or a mere object of his power. This vein of social protest is certainly wholesome and forward looking – but how is it to be reconciled with Pamela's increasing meekness, leading to dove-like submission when she marries, which is apparently also important to Richardson, though exasperating to us? The seeming contradiction may begin to resolve itself, however, if we realise that what is a social problem to us is a moral problem to him, and moreover (in keeping with the tendency of this whole section) becomes a religious question in the end.

Some sharp criticism of *Pamela* was directed at its social subversiveness, encouraging the lower classes to aspire above their station. Richardson was aware he was skating on thin ice, and took pains to have it argued that Pamela's elevation was only possible because of her exceptional talents and qualities. He gave her a quite exceptional upbringing by favour of her lady, and was careful to make her remember her origins at every point. Yet we cannot regard this as a timid betrayal, for prudential or commercial reasons, of his 'real' views, for his was in many ways a deeply conservative and orthodox temperament. That it should also have issued in some rather revolutionary directions is one of the pleasant puzzles about him. What from our point of view is a conflict, however, ceases to be so, once we see that Richardson is only interested in the social as an aspect of the moral. Social implications may arise from moral positions, but always come second. The 'egalitarian' tendencies of Pamela's story are only a by-product of Richardson's concept of Duty as a moral imperative, not a social contract that can be renounced by one side when broken by the other.

Pamela's first letters are all signed 'Your most dutiful daughter', and this is no accident, for the theme of Duty is important from the start. Her dutifulness to her parents is constant. It is also simple, because it involves no conflict, being always synonymous with the absolute morality which her parents have instilled. In the servant-master relationship with B, however, real conflict occurs; not the opposition of mere social convention, and true morality, but the opposition of two moral duties equally real. They are not however finally equal. Though there is never, throughout the book, any attempt to minimise the duty of servants to obey their masters and know their places, yet there is a definition of the limits within which obedience should operate, which Pamela opposes to B's view that it is her duty to obey him in all things. 'I should be loth to behave to my Master unbecomingly;' she writes, 'but I must needs say, Sir, my Innocence is so dear to me, that all other Considerations are, and, I hope, shall ever be, treated by me as Niceties, that ought, for that, to be dispens'd with' (I, 186; *I, 120* misprinted). Where the commands of a master conflict with the demands of morality (let alone the commandments of God) there can be no question where true duty lies. This point is made several times in the first part of the novel, and in the wilderness Pamela is made to argue it more fully with Robin, and John, and over and over again with Mrs Jewkes, while it also bears on the question of Williams's duty to B, as charged against him by Sir Simon Darnford and by B himself.

Yet it is by no means enough to point to the clarity of this distinction. For it does not in the least absolve Pamela from her absolute duty to give her master humble and complete obedience in all things in which no such moral case can be made out. And duty is not only a matter of actions, but of demeanour, and of state of mind. This is where the real conflict lies, for Pamela finds it very hard. She is proud, pert, 'saucy' by temperament; her quick tongue and intelligence are always liable to run away with her. Her moral clarity on the limits of duty is one thing, her progress to true dutifulness another.

Here then is the significance of her growing meekness, and the apparent paradox that it is just when what we would call 'class distinction' has been broken down on B's part, that it is reasserted by Pamela. She is already aware of the problem in the first part of the novel, hence the almost ritualistic attempt at self-humiliation in the scene before Longman. Yet her language was exaggerated, her actions melodramatic, her real pride left intact. By the end of her sojourn in the wilderness, however, her tone has completely changed. Obedience does not come easily. When she is first asked to forgive Mrs Jewkes she is politic: 'for you know, my dear Parents, I might as well make a Merit of my Compliance, when my Refusal would stand me in no stead' (I, 283; *I, 182*). Yet she does school herself to obey with grace, until finally when she has the freedom to act as she wishes, she seems to have no will but B's. There is a continual effort to subdue her pride and her pertness, to remind herself of her lowly origins, and to act on the realisation with genuine humility. This was obviously important to Richardson. Her reply to B's proposals to make her a kept mistress is firm, but never disrespectful, and it contains the assertion that she had 'not once dared to look so high' as any prospect of marrying him (I, 261; *I, 167*). In the first amazing and disconcerting experience of being consulted, and taken into B's confidence, about the social problem of marrying her, she maintains that he 'ought to regard the World's Opinion, and avoid doing any thing disgraceful to your Birth and Fortune' – though, seconds later, she cannot help exclaiming, 'But were I the first Lady in the Land, instead of the poor abject *Pamela*, I would, I *could* tell you' (I, 293-4; *I, 189*). Significantly,

B rhapsodises rather more over the 'generosity' of the first statement than the confession of the second. The question of presumption is clearly a vital one. Moreover, after Pamela has been finally dismissed in anger, and before B's courier arrives to ask her to go back, she realises that it is even presumptuous to say to herself that she will 'never be able to think of any body in the World but him' (II, 8; *I, 220*) – presumption that only love can excuse. This is significant evidence because she is alone and cannot hope for any effect from her words. Pamela's humility is hard-won, but once won it is absolute. Her tone in the discussion, in B's coach, of what their married life will be like, will strike a modern reader as excessively, even ludicrously meek. Richardson clearly meant her renunciation of consequence, her desire to accept her own lowliness uncomplainingly and without disguise, her effusive gratitude for B's favour in making her his wife, her insistence on continuing to refer to him as her 'master', to represent a triumph over the self, and a reconciliation of the real duty of obedience to moral standards with the equally real duty (now) of her servant status. Clothes symbolism reappears to make the point clear. In her rejection of B's 'articles' Pamela rejected fine clothes for the same reason as before. But when she refuses to change out of her homespun dress for a finer one, to go out in the coach with B, a new reason has come into play, for she must avoid giving herself consequence or being eager to aspire to his level (II, 24-5; *I, 230-1*). The clothes of Letter 24 have become the clothes of humility, but she is wearing them with no less ease, and avoiding any very shocking presumption, let fortune's wheel turn as it will.

Thus Pamela's rejection of obedience where her master's demands are irreconcilable with absolute morality, is only justifiable in terms of her complete acceptance, in her inner thoughts as well as her outer behaviour, of her duty and place as a servant in all other cases. Social status and duty are referred directly to the bar of morality and denounced if they offend; but where there is no offence, morality strongly reinforces the status quo of social relationship. This can look revolutionary from one point of view and extremely conservative from another. The same paradox appears in the discussion of social hierarchy.

Here however we may see how the moral law is itself referred to religion: the high status of the rich and noble is seen in relation to their duty to do good, in furthering the design of Providence. 'O the unparallel'd Wickedness, Stratagems, and Devices of those who call themselves Gentlemen, yet pervert the Design of Providence, in giving them ample Means to do Good, to their own everlasting Perdition, and the Ruin of poor oppressed Innocence!' (I, 129; *I, 83*). Where such perversions occur, the moral condemnation of social oppression and pride is clean and uncomplicated; but where there is no conflict, the existing hierarchy is endorsed and strengthened by morality, and Pamela will welcome her elevation, not as a privilege for its own sake, but as a multiplication of her opportunities to do good.

This involves, too, some distinctions about pride, analogous to those we met in Letter 24. In her reaction to the letter from Lady Davers that B shows her, Pamela plays on words to distinguish a proper pride from a sinful one. She ends a long meditation on the folly of snobbery by calling it 'this proud Letter of the *lowly* Lady Davers, against the *high-minded* Pamela. *Lowly*, I say, because she could *stoop* to such vain *Pride*; and *high-minded* I, because I hope, I am too *proud* ever to do the like! – But, after all, poor Wretches that we be! we scarce know what we *are*, much less what we *shall be*! – But once more pray I to be kept from the sinful Pride of a high Estate' (II, 23; *I, 230*). In keeping with Richardson's admittedly less than ideal views on moral pleasure, there is clearly a proper pride in reconciling status and duty, both upwards and downwards, with morality; but this is to be sharply distinguished from the improper and sinful pride in status for its own sake. So Pamela can take a proper pride in her own high-mindedness and her parents' honest poverty. But when she begins to blossom forth into a new status there are new dangers. It is only on B's direct orders that Pamela-Cinderella changes her clothes at last and begins to flower, dress by dress, into a lady. There is no presumption, but there is an exact and deliberate recall of Letter 24: 'and so put on fine Linen, Silk Shoes, and fine white Cotton Stockens, a fine quilted Coat; a delicate green *Mantua* Silk Gown and Coat, a *French* Necklace, and a laced Cambrick Handkerchief, and clean Gloves; and taking my Fan in my Hand, I, like a little proud Hussy, look'd in the Glass, and thought myself a Gentlewoman once more; but I forgot not to return due Thanks, for being able to put on this Dress with so much Comfort' (II, 85; *I, 270-1*). We can see that, though fortune's wheel has turned another half-circle, Pamela has not yet lost her little girl's vanity in her appearance. But the 'comfort' resides in her reconciliation of morals with finery, of moral and social duty with privilege, and she is sharply aware of the danger of sinful pride in her elevation. Over and over again at the end of her time in the wilderness she prays for humility. 'O my dear Father and Mother, now pray for me on another score! for fear I should grow too proud, and be giddy and foolish with all these promising Things, so soothing to the Vanity of my Years and Sex. But even to this Hour can I pray, that God would remove from me all these delightful Prospects, if they are likely so to corrupt my Mind, as to make me proud, and vain, and not acknowledge, with thankful Humility, the blessed Providence, which has so visibly conducted me thro' the dangerous Paths I have trod to this happy Moment' (II, 45; *I, 244*).

3

If, in the wilderness, the analysis of social duty leads steadily through morality to Providence, this is equally true of the more important investigation of self-reliant prudence, and its relation to despair. Like the other problem too, this can now be seen to have been present from the very beginning.

Prudence is a worldly virtue dependent on the Fall, for essential to it is the capacity to fear and suspect hidden darkness in fair appearance. Pamela's very first letter was almost Eden-like in its happiness and innocence, but we noticed a potential fearfulness and suspicion already present, which the exaggerated fears and suspicions of her father activated, and her master's conduct steadily increased. On the face of things, moreover, she is justified. Yet we also saw that the face of things might be deceptive, and how suspicion produced a blindness to the real complexity of B, particularly at turning points like Letter 24 and their final interview before the abduction. Fear can be even more dangerous; it makes her pray imperfectly, and tempts her towards despair. She prays for resignation, emphasising what previous prayers have suggested, that she must trust in God rather than in herself. Yet almost immediately the characteristic activities of her self-reliant prudence revive again: her suspicious fear of the worst, her ingenuity, calculation, and intrigue, but most of all her pride in these.

The effects are often distinctly unpleasant. When she first realises that the coachman seems to have lost his way, she immediately suspects him of having designs on her himself, in spite of his obvious distress at her unhappiness. Suspecting the worst connects with calculation: in the midst of moral reflections about her clothes, she is strongly influenced by a careful calculation of the most uncharitable things people might say. Calculation connects with contrivance. On two occasions, having renounced her finery, her native canniness cannot resist speculating about how, without actually wearing them and spoiling the moral gesture, she could turn the clothes into money if they should be sent after her. Musing on John Arnold's agonised letter of confession she thinks 'I will, if it lies in my way, encourage his Penitence; for I may possibly make some Discoveries by it' (I, 159; *I, 103*). Intrigue connects with pride; she begins to hug herself over her cunning about the paper, pens, and ink. Finally it is the cunning of the clever evasion, the equivocation, the 'white' lie. We saw in Letter 15, how B's knowledge of her letters enables him to catch her out in three equivocations in as many minutes. Now, in the wilderness, she moves from equivocation to lie, and the question of the innocence of her deceptions is raised, albeit in a comic context. Nan returns a moment too soon, and nearly catches Pamela picking out Mr Williams's first letter from under the broken tile by the sunflower. 'You seem frighted, Madam, said she. Why, said I, with a lucky Thought, (alas! your poor Daughter will make an Intriguer by-and-by; but, I hope, an innocent one!) I stoop'd to smell at the Sun-flower, and a great nasty Worm ran into the Ground, that startled me; for I can't abide Worms. Said she, Sun-flowers don't smell. So I find, reply'd I' (I, 170-1; *I, 110*). And though she never takes delight in equivocation, she does begin to hug herself more and more over her cunning and her plots. The thing that annoys her most about the early part of her captivity is being tricked out of her money by Mrs Jewkes; and the vexation is as much at being outsmarted as at the consequences for her escape.

We cannot be sure yet, from the evidence of the fiction itself, what the Richardson one cares about – the artist visible in the relation of texture and structure – thinks of all this. It is all only too understandable in Pamela's situation; we feel with and for her. One would not care so much for a Griselda who possessed her soul in patience; one admires the battling courage, intelligence, quick-wittedness, the refusal to sit quiet. If we smile sometimes, there is also a sense in which the small contrivances and equivocations are pathetic – there is so very little she *can* do. There is always the possibility that Pamela's suspicious prudence and delight in subterfuge simply reflect her creator, as indeed they must in some way. Might he not feel straightforwardly that prudence is a virtue, and that Pamela is not only natural but entirely innocent? Yet his imagination is essentially a probing one. Whatever his orthodox daily self may have felt about prudence, there is already evidence of uneasiness about the dangers of the fear and suspicion which cause blindness and risk despair. Though he may have enjoyed intrigue imaginatively, the 'alas' about Pamela's deception is as evident as her 'hope' of its ultimate innocence in resisting a wicked conspiracy. The dramatic imagination, from the start, has gradually posed more and more questionmarks about what seems ordinarily an obvious virtue – this is one of the strengths of a kind of art which leaves the artist free to explore what he does not have to take immediate responsibility for expounding.

Now however the questions begin to be resolved in what cannot be an accidental fashion, since it involves the central structure of the novel. Pamela's self-reliant prudence is seen to lead directly to worldly and spiritual disaster. Conversely, it is only when she learns to give up self-reliance and trust herself wholly to Providence, when she learns to replace caution and suspicion with faith in Man as well as God, when indeed she learns – it will be specifically stated – to have the faith to be imprudent, that she escapes from the wilderness into happiness.

It is Pamela's love of intrigue that brings about the first worsening of her position in the wilderness. B's state of mind when we (and she) last saw him was still ambiguous, but distinctly hopeful. He showed real tenderness in their last interview and confessed what sounded like genuine love and admiration. He also confessed, it is true, how great a hold his pride had over him, and could not resist his own love of intrigue in backing himself to win all ways. His quite unnecessary proposal of Williams as a husband, moreover, turned Pamela against him at a crucial moment; made her see him as a 'black-hearted wretch' and insist on leaving, and so ensured her captivity. Yet we remember from Letter 24 how Pamela's suspicion could blind her; and the B who abducts her should not be simply a 'black-hearted wretch' to us. His motivation is complex and the outcome of his conflict still very much in the balance. His insistence on honourable intentions may be no more than a rather adolescent self-pluming on the vast progress he has made by his own way of it; it may be only in the meantime, while he makes up his mind. Yet he does promise to stay away from her, and in his second letter tells her something which has great significance for the future: that she will achieve most by placing confidence in him.

Now it is in reply to this letter that Pamela makes a serious blunder. For no good reason but the promptings of an intriguing mind, she writes a crucial sentence, among her reasons for distrusting him, that he now makes no mention of the Williams proposal (I, 185; *I, 120*). Since it was precisely this that made her really distrustful of him in the first place, she is being extremely disingenuous to say the least. Her intrigue, stalling for time, misfires disastrously – ironically recalling exactly B's own blunder not only in its motive, but also in its cause and effect. The cause is her inability to believe that he loves her. The effect, when Mrs Jewkes confirms that she would prefer Williams after B has laid a trap to test her, is to convert Pamela in his mind from a complex person to a type of perfidy. She not only outrages his social pride – a clergyman, his dependant! – she also subverts his new moral sensibility, that is the fine irony of it. For the more we judge that love and a moral admiration of her resistance may have made him see the unattractiveness of his past conduct and begin to reform; the more we can appreciate how her apparent eagerness to throw herself at a virtually unknown man makes her morality look hypocritical. The advantage of taking the inference in his own proposal of Williams, is that we can understand the unmistakeable note of *betrayal* when Pamela seems keen to act on it. It is natural that he should be furiously jealous; what is more interesting is the bitterness of his reversion to his old cynicism. 'Henceforth, for *Pamela's* sake, whenever I see a lovely Face, will I mistrust a deceitful Heart: and whenever I hear of the greatest Pretences to Innocence, will I suspect some deep-laid Mischief. You were determin'd to place no Confidence in me, tho' I have solemnly, over and over, engag'd my Honour to you . . . Yet how have you requited me? The very first Fellow that your charming Face, and insinuating Address, could influence, you have practis'd upon, corrupted too, I may say, (and even ruin'd, as the ingrateful Wretch shall find) and thrown your *forward* Self upon him. As therefore you would place no Confidence in me, my Honour owes you nothing' (I, 222-3; *I, 143*). All his prospective improvement seems destroyed at a stroke. Williams is thrown into jail, Colbrand is sent down to guard her, and B promises to decide her fate in three weeks.

To look from B's point of view is not of course to find it justified; yet Pamela's inexperience of the complexity of human behaviour, her little girl's inability to see things other than in black and white, coupled with her suspicion and her tendency to intrigue, have landed her in a predicament not wholly undeserved. She may insist that she contrives only in self defence, but this will not excuse all – and it will certainly not excuse her frame of mind when she fails. From having delightedly plumed herself: 'O good Sirs! Of all the Flowers in the Garden, the Sun-flower, sure, is the loveliest! . . . How nobly my Plot succeeds!' (I, 174; *I, 113*) – she is thrown into the depths of despair. Even before the arrival of B's letter, she is so frightened by the beating of Williams, the change in Mrs Jewkes, and by the bull that had been in the pasture, that when she has a chance to escape she flees back into the garden in terror, scared half out of her wits by two harmless cows. She herself begins to be 'persuaded, that Fear brings one into more Dangers, than the Caution that goes along with it, delivers one from' – and proves it by telling a sadder lie than ever as soon as she has safely turned the key (I, 206; *I, 133*). B's letter, however, with the arrest of Williams and the arrival of the 'terrible' Colbrand – her description of him is a fine example of imagination heightened by fear – spur her to contrive a last desperate attempt to get away, and she comes near to committing suicide when it fails.

The scene by the pond is not only the centre of *Pamela*, the turning-point of the whole novel, it is also the first important and sustained self-analysis in English fiction; though it cannot be said to succeed. Richardson has not yet created an adequate dramatic language for the colloquy of a mind with itself, and so tends to fall back on the idiom – the 'theeing' and 'thouing', and the often unintentionally comic 'poetic' imagery – of domestic puritan traditions of devotional introspection. Hence, though he is writing about despair, he never really succeeds in creating it. Yet there are parts of the scene where there is a masterly to-and-fro of thought that looks forward to *Clarissa*, where the ponderousness disappears and the effect is both moving and realistic.

Pamela's self-reliance has led inevitably to despair. Because she has trusted to herself, the miscarriage of her intrigues and contrivances has left her nothing to look to, or hope for. The blow on her head and the effects of terror, pain, and weariness may have helped to break her spirit, but it is the breakdown of her self-reliance that brings her face to face with her darkest temptation – which has nothing to do with B. Despair is deadly sin, and the change of language again emphasises that at this point the novel has ceased to be merely ethical and becomes overtly religious. The decoy clothes floating in the pond, that so nearly anticipated real self-destruction, remind us of something . . . that round-eared cap and coat . . . words from the past: 'innocence', and 'resignation', 'no very shocking disappointment, let fortune's wheel turn round as it will'. The innocence and resignation then were social and moral, and could easily co-exist with a certain pride in herself. They receive a fully religious dimension now.

Pamela is tempted by *herself*: her self-dramatisation and self-pity, her longing to be publicly well thought of and pitied. Her calculating mind is as busy as ever: how after her death B would repent of accusing her of hypocrisy (always the charge that hurts her most), how he may cover things up but men and maids will pity her; and yet, how much she hopes she won't become the subject of a popular ballad (I, 233-4; *I, 150*). This little progression is a deft and characteristic stroke of Richardsonian art, and his psychological subtlety is shown again where both her self-dramatisation and her calculation come into play. She wonders whether she need throw herself into the water after all, whether '*these Bruises* and *Maims* that I have gotten, while I pursued only the laudable Escape I had meditated, may not kindly have furnish'd me with the Opportunity I now am tempted with to precipitate myself, and of surrendering up my Life, spotless and unguilty, to that merciful Being who gave it!' (I, 235; *I, 151*).

Yet through such claptrap her own insight cuts cleanly and firmly. Who is she to set a limit to the power of God who can touch B in an instant, or a limit to what she is prepared to bear, or to lose faith in God's power to bring good out of evil and suffering? Finally the 'theeing' and 'thouing' give way to one sentence that is the core of a new self-knowledge. 'And how do I know, but that God, who sees all the lurking Vileness of my Heart, may have permitted these Sufferings on that very score, and to make me rely solely on his Grace and Assistance, who perhaps have too much prided myself in a vain Dependence on my own foolish Contrivances' (I, 236; *I*, *151*). From this point she begins to find the resignation she had prayed for on her first entry into the wilderness, and when she tells Mrs Jewkes that her contrivances are at an end, she means it. She has learnt the first of two great lessons that come to her beside the pond: to renounce, not perhaps prudence itself, but whatever in prudence may be proud and self-reliant, in favour of faith in God.

This of course is no help with B. When he arrives she has to reap the consequence of her intrigue, first in insult, then in B's 'articles' putting into black and white what she has to look to now, and finally, his last 'attempt'.

We can be sure this time that B did set out to take her, for he tells her so afterwards. Nevertheless, there is evidence in the build-up and within the scene itself that suggests, again, that the attempt is not nearly as serious as Pamela imagines. B is still enraged when he arrives in Lincolnshire, but he has only to see her to begin to relent, as the scene in which he makes her wait on him makes clear. In her reply to the articles, moreover, she says things which are likely to mollify both his re-aroused vanity and his pride: that if she preferred anyone it would be her master, but that nevertheless she has never imagined he might marry her. Yet – anticipating a situation in *Clarissa* – it is also clear that Mrs Jewkes is inciting him to have the girl and have done; and since his desire for vengeance is still uppermost, he lays a careful plan to fulfil the threat he made at the close of the 'articles'. When he is disguised as the drunken Nan, however, he hears Pamela running through her whole story to Mrs Jewkes; and knowing him as we do, and as Pamela does not, we should expect him to be softened both by the reminder of her consistency, and also by her earnest declaration that she never thought of marrying Williams. When Pamela describes 'Nan' coming to bed, then, though it is open to us to believe that the quick breathing and the trembling are signs of sexual excitement, the reader who has learnt to understand Richardson's hero is more likely to think the opposite. (Rightly, for B will confess that his 'resolution' was 'half disarmed' before he approached the bed.) Pamela's 'Simplicity' has removed any justification for wounded pride and revenge; instead, as has happened several times before, moral sensibility is re-awakened. If then B goes on with his plan, it is through another kind of pride, a stubbornness, that will not let him give up what he has already carried so far. Yet if this be so, the trembling suggests not excitement but fear; a mind divided against itself and already nervous at its own wrongdoing. We ought once again to see the scene from two very different points of view: from one it looks like a sexual scene, whose only puzzle is why the booby rapist stands 'dilly dallying', as Mrs Jewkes says; from the other it is not really about sex at all, but about pride.

'Now, Pamela, said he, is the dreadful Time of Reckoning come, that I have threatened!' – we can now appreciate the note of hollow melodrama, for B cannot sustain his role, and within seconds is trying to use the situation for salvage rather than rape. He tries to threaten Pamela into accepting his articles, and the hand in the bosom this time has little to do with sexual excitement, it is a strategic threat. 'Swear then to me, said he, that you will accept my Proposals! – and then (for this was all detestable Grimace) he put his Hand into my Bosom' (I, 279; *I*, *179*). It is grimace, though in almost the opposite sense to Pamela's. B is playing a game he knows to be a losing one long before it is lost, and he is trying to extract whatever advantage he can salvage from the wreck. It is an extraordinary scene for an eighteenth century novelist to write, but what is chiefly extraordinary about it is that it should have so little to do with sex, given the initial situation. It is the last kick of a doomed pride, struggling to assert itself when the will to do so is almost gone, and brought remorselessly to see the only possible end of such assertion in the 'deathlike' state of the girl he cannot make his by force. The scene ends with tenderness, and B's 'change of heart' the next morning should not seem surprising.

One is of course justified in feeling that Pamela's fainting fit has been over-used by this time. Yet we have also noticed that Richardson's technique has time and again involved making one scene recall another, but with a new point or a different emphasis; and on closer inspection this fainting fit *is* different. As B observes, it is far more frighteningly deathlike, but more important, it has a different significance. If her fainting before was a sign of moral integrity, a proof that Pamela's morality is ingrained in her being, this time her 'fit' reinforces the religious significance of the scene by the pond. She says afterwards that she has 'Reason to bless God, who, by disabling me in my Faculties, impower'd me to preserve my Innocence; and when all my Strength would have signified nothing, magnified himself in my Weakness' (I, 280-1; *I, 180*). She herself, it is clear, takes her fit as an act of Providence in direct reply to her agonised cry 'O God! my God! this *Time*, this *one Time*! deliver me from this Distress! or strike me dead this Moment!' (I, 278; *I, 178-9*) – and sees herself as saved, not by self-reliant strength, but by the faith of acknowledged weakness.

The sight of her suffering, and the knowledge of her sincerity, affect B more and more strongly. Her intense prickliness at any tendency to 'indecency' causes temporary setback; but her self-justification shows him the consistency of her actions and explains why she will obey him in all directions but one, and disobey and resist him to the end in that, on the same moral basis. He finally understands now that he cannot hope to have her on his terms; that neither force nor intrigue will do it; and the knowledge that the only way open is the road into Pamela's moral world, brings him to the first scene in the novel in which he treats her as an independent human being, and in full sincerity himself. Moreover the dawn of happiness for Pamela, the end both of her forty days and nights in the wilderness, and of the first volume in the first edition, takes place by the pond again – and Pamela herself is made to emphasise the connection between this second pond scene and the first.

For the first time, B is completely open with Pamela. He confesses that he cannot live without her, and that his passion is increased by his growing understanding of her virtue; but that he cannot overcome his pride and his aversion to marriage enough to make her his wife. What does she think he should do? Pamela is powerfully affected by this appeal. She is careful not to presume, insisting that the world's opinion is not to be despised, but this 'generosity' (as we noticed) only makes B admire her more – and his ardour makes her give away her feeling for him, beyond mistaking. In fact, as he cross-examines her about Williams, she is as honest with him as he has been with her. It is, indeed, the first time they can be said to have communicated. Yet this is not only a change in B, but an equally important change in Pamela. For to communicate in sincerity with another human being is to put oneself in his power, and when the other person is B this is true *a fortiori*. The context is still his inability to defy society and his pride. Whatever else Pamela may be at this moment, she is not prudent; and she recognises this. 'I will tell you, perhaps, the unnecessary and imprudent, but yet the whole Truth' (I, 297; *I*, *192*). But if it is not prudent, her act may be something better, and deeper. It is indeed an act of *faith* – and that, once again, is what *Pamela* turns out to be 'about'. The heroine had to learn faith in God in the first scene by the pond. In the second she, and B too, learn faith in human beings, at the expense of suspicion, intrigue, and disguise. The result, in B's words, is to 'have known, in this agreeable Hour, more sincere Pleasure than I have experienced in all the guilty Tumults that my desiring Soul compell'd me into' (I, 299; *I*, *193*). The lesson for Pamela is that faith in the inherent goodness of other people is the necessary groundwork of human relationship; that this faith encourages that inherent goodness to grow; and that on the other hand, as B puts it, 'your Doubts will only beget *Cause* of Doubts' (I, 300; *I, 194*). It seems quite clear now that Richardson's exploring vision has established that the suspicious element in prudence can entail a kind of blindness, and become a block both to understanding and relationship.

Pamela's suspicion and timidity are not, however, to be overcome in a day. B often calls her 'fearful and doubting Pamela', and this is as good a shorthand characterisation as any. Immediately after this scene she is in agonies, having to remind herself that her father is a man in order to silence her fears of the desperate wickedness of the masculine heart. Yet her future happiness will hinge on her ability to act on the meaning of the second scene by the pond. Very soon afterwards, this is tested. While B is away, a gypsy succeeds in slipping her a note from 'Somebody' – in fact, Longman – warning her that B is planning a mock-marriage. Immediately after this, Mrs Jewkes finds her with part of her journal, and on B's return he demands the rest. Both events bear directly on the implications of the second pond scene. B's desire to read her journal is not mere curiosity, but the logical outcome of his experience of sincerity and true knowledge. The journal is important in two ways: it will help him to know and understand Pamela as a person, and it is also a moral education – as Richardson hoped the novel would be for its readers, of whom B has been the first, from the second letter onwards. Yet giving up her journal does involve the last ripping away of Pamela's secrecy and caution, and she bears it very hard. Only a combination of bullying and cunning on B's part, and her duty as a servant, bring the surrender about; although her experience, and still more our own, show that complete knowledge can do her nothing but good with B. In fact, the effect of the journal on him will be a crucial element in his moral regeneration.

Her belief or disbelief in the mock-marriage will however turn out to be even more important. On the one hand there is the evidence of the past: a record, from her point of view, of lust, cruelty, and double-dealing. There is the even more recent evidence of his bullying over the journal, which takes a typically sexual form. There is his stubborn pride, still just as evident as ever in the second pond scene. And there is Pamela's innate fearfulness and suspicion. *But* – there is also the crucial evidence of the pond scene itself: B's new sincerity and openness, his confession of a love that is struggling to become moral, the newly-perceived complexity of his motivation, and above all the new insight, that faith begets human growth even if it be imprudent, while suspicion, the 'despair' of relationship, destroys, even if it be prudent. Pamela with her new knowledge is being asked to choose between the pasteboard villain who has been an old inhabitant of her mind, and her new experience of a complex human being. She is being asked to keep growing in perception and understanding, to remain willing to replace prudent suspicion with imprudent faith.

At a crucial moment, she fails disastrously. The reading of her Journal, and most particularly the account of her near-suicide which he now hears about for the first time, has an enormous effect on B. As they walk beside the pond once again, he is moved enough to make what is the nearest he can get to a proposal of marriage. 'Come, kiss me, said he, and tell me you forgive me, for pushing you into so much Danger and Distress. If my Mind hold, and I can see those former Papers of yours, and that these in my Pocket give me no cause to alter my Opinion, I will endeavour to defy the World, and the World's Censures, and make my *Pamela* Amends, if it be in the Power of my whole Life, for all the Hardships I have made her undergo. All this look'd well; but you shall see how strangely it was all turn'd. For this Sham-marriage then came into my Mind again; and I said, Your poor Servant is far unworthy of this great Honour; for what will it be, but to create Envy to herself, and Discredit to you? Therefore, Sir, permit me to return to my poor Parents, and that is all I have to ask' (I, 330-1; *I, 214*).

Cynicism, suspicion, fearfulness, disingenuousness triumph in the third pond scene . . . and the effect is disastrous. B flies into a rage, and she is finally dismissed to what she has claimed to be her heart's wish, the life of poverty with her parents. Once again the wheel has come full circle – but this time the cause is not in Fortune, but in Pamela herself.

Moreover, she soon finds out, in some of the finest passages in the book, that she doesn't really want to go to her father's at all. She brings to full consciousness for the first time the strength of the love of which she has had no conscious suspicion before, though the signs have been there for a careful reader from a very early stage, and have been growing more and more explicit. In keeping with Richardson's conscious technique in *Pamela*, however, he proceeds to give his characters yet another chance. B has lacked faith too. His inability to believe in the quality of Pamela's feeling is revealed to him, with the full strength of his own passion, by reading her journal when she is gone. He sends a message after her, begging her to come back, which represents a real triumph over his pride. The B that writes, 'But spare me, my dearest girl! the confusion of following you to your father's; which I must do, if you persist to go on; for I find I cannot live a day without you', is a completely different B. He has won a notable victory over *his* suspiciousness and pride. Can Pamela do the same? There is no guarantee at all that the change in B will be permanent. There is every chance of incurring the censure of the world, with which the calculating element of her prudence has always been vitally concerned. What she is being asked to do is the antithesis of prudent caution and suspicion. She is also asked to send for the rest of her journal voluntarily, and hence to lay the whole of her mind and heart bare before him, the antithesis of secrecy and reserve. The two together are an exact duplication of the tests she failed. But faith, and love, triumph this time, and both Pamela's happiness, and the regeneration of B, become possible.

4

The central concern in this section of the novel then, has been with Pamela's spiritual growth, and her victory over some of her greatest weaknesses. In her forty days in the wilderness she learns a truer perception of duty and schools herself to follow it completely, and with good grace. She learns much more about the danger of pride and struggles for a truer humility. Most important of all, she learns two crucial lessons of faith, in God and in Man, both of which involve self-abnegation and certain discriminations about prudence. In learning faith in God and Man she has to abjure the elements, in prudence, of suspicion, pride, intrigue, disguise, and fear. It is equally clear, moreover, that the development of B repeats and reinforces this pattern: he too has to replace plotting and disguise with open sincerity, to learn faith in the integrity of another at the expense of equally innate suspicion, jealousy, and pride. Human relationship and happiness can only be established when faith and trust, however dangerous and difficult, replace sexual war and intrigue. Only on such a basis can the regeneration of B become confirmed.

We can also see, however, that the disadvantages of the single focus become even more serious in this part, for it encouraged Richardson to concentrate even more on his heroine, at his hero's expense, and blinded him to the dangers of doing so. In the first place, the danger of misinterpreting B becomes still more serious when we see so little of him, and inhabit so continuously a mind in which he appears as a 'black hearted wretch'. It is even more essential that a reader should pick up inferences and ponder implications in watching and listening to B when he does appear. Even if one does so, however, an ineradicable difficulty about his 'conversion' remains. Even if a reader is sensitive to implications, and reads with discrimination, and proper allowance for the over-simplifications and distortions of Pamela's view of her persecutor, the change in B cannot possibly be as convincing as the change in Pamela. We can see that B does change, and when he changes, and even why he changes, but we cannot experience how he changes, because we cannot get inside him and know him directly for ourselves as we know Pamela. Thirdly, Richardson seems so concerned with his analysis of Pamela that he seems to forget the gap between her knowledge of B and ours. He carefully creates the opportunity for B to understand all Pamela's behaviour, and remove his misapprehensions, by reading her Journal. He seems to see no need to do something similar on B's behalf, though Pamela's misunderstanding of him has been far more radical, and his behaviour a great deal more in need of explanation and mitigation. It is not that a defence could not have been effectively mounted; reading 'to the moment' confirms the existence of the 'more favourable construction', even of the blackest of B's attempts. Yet no retrospective defence, covering his behaviour before the abduction as well, is ever made, within *Pamela* itself.

Nevertheless, if there be something seriously amiss with the treatment of the hero at the crisis of the novel, the treatment of the heroine is a subtle, penetrating and revolutionary criticism of a central middle-class virtue. (It is ironic that both Richardson and Fielding have been taken to be great upholders of prudence.) The sadness is that the defect has totally obscured the achievement. Accounts of the novel which recognise the central concern with faith are remarkable by their absence.

CHAPTER THREE

The Assault on the World

I

With Pamela's marriage her 'story' ends – but the telling of it does not. The characters are established, there is no longer conflict between or within them, and only when Pamela confronts B's arrogant and passionate sister, or discovers that he has an illegitimate child, is there any tension. The last quarter of the novel seems to consist mainly of endless social visitings (starting in fact before the wedding), in which the happy pair discuss their story with extraordinary complacency while Pamela is deluged with praise and blessing – and of long discussions of the duties of man and wife, or rather, largely of wife.

This spinning out confirms that Richardson's main interest was not in pursuit and capture, and we shall discover in *Clarissa* and again in *Grandison* that he never knew when to have done, but the result is tedious enough. He was however obviously determined to convert his story from a private relationship to a public manifestation of value, and to hammer home in the novel itself the response he hoped for from his readers. It was important for him, not only to demonstrate the consistency and integrity of his heroine's behaviour before and after her marriage, but also to enforce the validity of her standards over a wider field than her struggles with B. The novel becomes a kind of 'Whole duty of Woman' (a fictional counterpart of the *Whole duty of Man* which Pamela sends to Farmer Jones), throwing out the challenge of an old-fashioned morality to a frivolous and lax society. The scenes of choric praise enact Richardson's hopes for the educative power of his story. Pamela's first reader, of course, already exists within the fiction as its hero, and he already bears witness of regeneration; but now the response of his entire circle both confirms his own, and prefigures the idea of moral community which was to be central to *Sir Charles Grandison*.

Pamela has had to struggle more and more consciously against her own vanity and pride, and towards a deeper understanding of social and moral duty. Before the wedding her increasing meekness suggested that she was achieving humility, but the elevation of her marriage is a more difficult and complicated challenge. Here is the first reason for the social visitings: they seem intended to show her behaving with uniform meekness, subjecting herself entirely to the will of her husband-master, and showing amid the flood of praises no sign, either with her sometime superiors, or with her sometime equals who are now her inferiors, of arrogance or presumption. Mrs Jewkes is made to tell her that she is more humble and sweet natured than ever, and this theme is often uppermost in the choric praise of her new society friends. It was obviously important enough to Richardson to require scene after scene to ram it home. Pamela also sums up directly on many occasions, in meditation or prayer, of which one example will suffice to illustrate the tone. 'For my part,' she writes, 'I was dressed out only to be admired, as it seems. And truly, if I had not known, that I did not make *myself*, as you, my dear Father, once hinted to me; and if I had had the Vanity to think as well of myself, as the good Company was pleased to do, I might possibly have been proud. But I know, as my Lady *Davers* said, tho' in Anger, yet in Truth, that I am but *a poor Bit of painted Dirt*. All that I value myself upon, is, that God has raised me to a Condition to be useful in my Generation to better Persons than myself. This is my Pride: And I hope this will be *all* my Pride. For, What was I of myself! – All the Good I can do, is but a poor third-hand Good; for my dearest Master himself is but the Second-hand. God, the All-gracious, the All-good, the

All-bountiful, the All-mighty, the All-merciful GOD, is the First: To HIM, therefore, be all the Glory! (II, 359; *I, 449*). The vanity in her personal appearance which we saw both in the original 'clothes scene', and in its later Cinderella counterpart, is here finally recognised and abjured, with a specific reminiscence of her father's original warning. So is any personal pride in her elevation. The counter-productive effect of making her constantly retail the praises she receives is, of course, another matter, but this is largely a formal blunder and I discuss it later.

Yet her new situation is more complicated than her old, and humility itself is no longer enough. This is where the dramatic scene with Lady Davers, as well as being the best episode in the last section, makes a further distinction. On the one hand the behaviour of Lady Davers is used, as her letter had been earlier, to point the full force of the contrast between the arrogance of the high-born in their status for its own sake, and the unassuming meekness of Pamela. Lady Davers realises for us dramatically the full impact of pride. It is seen, as it was by Pope in *The Rape of the Lock*, as a product of disordered passions, amounting to hysteria if uncontrolled, and eventually to disease. (Lady Davers has a violent bout of colic before she can be brought to her senses!) B's sister also marks the pole towards which the rather adolescent pride of B himself tended, the pride he had to quell in order to marry Pamela. But we are meant to watch Pamela as much as Lady Davers, and if we do, we realise that the scene's major function is to define the proper limits of her humility. To be meek and unassuming is not enough.

Though Richardson conceived her duty to her husband-master as one of almost complete submission, so that there is continuity between her status as servant and as wife, he also obviously felt that her duty to others was affected by her new position. She owes Lady Davers respect and humility as her husband's sister; but this is firmly limited by the equally strong, and new duty, to do nothing unbecoming the position of B's wife, and it does not extend to Lady Davers' nephew or her servant when they attempt to follow her lead. So the scene has a curious double direction. Pamela must not cringe, must not wait on Lady Davers as she is ordered, must not sit down to dine with milady's woman, must not deny her new status. Yet she must not cease to be humble and meek in herself – for the firmness is not for herself, but for her husband's dignity. Interestingly, the pert miss of the early part of the novel has developed far enough to make us realise how much harder she finds it to be firm than to be humble now. This is partly owing to her excessive timidity not to say cowardice, of which there are several examples in the book, and a particularly extreme one here when the puppy Jackey draws his sword. This is not, however, the whole explanation. Pamela insists that, for her own part, she would gladly wait on Lady Davers or kneel at her feet, but that the honour she has received makes it necessary 'to act another Part, not to be utterly unworthy of them' (II, 206; *I, 349*). On the other hand, in her discomfiture of Beck and Lord Jackey we have flashes of the old Pamela. Indeed the dramatic structure of the scene seeks to compensate for the apparent lack of spirit towards Lady Davers by the spirited onslaughts on the presumption of the others – but this is not to be interpreted merely psychologically, or even in terms of what we usually mean by snobbery. It is a tricky course for Richardson to steer, and its full impact may well be lost on a modern reader; once again the point lies not in social hierarchy for its own sake, but in its moral basis. Lady Davers' arrogance does not exempt Pamela from her double-edged duty; but Richardson demands that those on the higher rungs of the social ladder should realise that the responsibilities of their position are more important than the privileges. So Pamela prays that '(I), tho' nothing worth in myself, shall give Signification by my *Place*, and multiply the Blessings I owe to thy Goodness... This, as I conceive, is the indispensable Duty of a high Condition...' (II, 170; *I, 326*). So, in the last part of the novel she distributes largesse, happily undertakes on B's orders the settling of her parents on his Kentish estate, and prepares to keep a ledger of her charities with the thematic, if unintentionally comic title of 'Humble returns for Divine Mercies'. There is humility because the status is separated from the person, defined in terms of responsibility, and referred not only to moral duty but to Providence. On this basis status is important and respectable to Richardson. The scene with Lady Davers provides a contrast not only between humility and arrogance as personal characteristics, but between one concept of status that refers it to morality, and another that refers it only to snobbery and pride.

Richardson's concept of the family is equally hierarchic – reinforced of course by Pamela's special position of servant-turned-wife-but-always-remembering-her-past. Here is the bearing of the several conversations about the proper behaviour and duties of wives. The last section attempts to cover a wider field than the morality of Pamela's trials: B gives her lengthy instructions on her dress, regulation of mealtimes and domestic economy, behaviour to his friends, conduct to himself, the bringing up of children, and so on. Many of these precepts are obviously a challenge to a frivolous society to return to old-fashioned regularity and order. At one point Pamela reduces a curtain-lecture to forty-eight articles to be pondered (II, 290-4; *I, 406-9*): we may perhaps concern ourselves only with those which bear on the Whole Duty of Wifely Submission. The wife should bear with her husband even when he is in the wrong, should be flexible, should overcome by sweetness and complaisance though not slavishly, should show no reluctance to oblige and obey him, and, if he be set on a wrong thing, should not dispute with him unless it is a really important point, but do it first and expostulate afterwards. Now Richardson obviously did not expect the first and last points to be taken wholly seriously, for Pamela finds them debatable and they obviously relate to B's imperious temper. Yet the overall picture resembles what Richardson feels about the whole structure of society closely enough to make his general intentions clear. Once again the view is deeply hierarchic: morality endorses the husband as Head, and the duty of the wife to submit unless some important principle is at stake. But, once again this is considerably modified, and its most unpleasant features softened, by referring the hierarchy directly to an absolute morality. The husband must desire nothing of his wife but what is just, must take care to make her compliance reasonable, and consistent with her free agency in points that ought to be allowed her. In fact the words 'command' and 'obey' are even for B, to be blotted out of the vocabulary insofar as they imply orders and obedience for their own sake; they stand only insofar as they can be referred to morality, but once this is so, morality endorses them.

It is clear that Richardson's mind was hierarchic in the most orthodox and conservative manner, and that provided he could refer the hierarchies of society and the family to moral standards, he upheld them with old-fashioned strictness. Although there is a good deal of social criticism in *Pamela*, it is founded on a conservative and not a radical temperament; and on old-fashioned morality, rather than any new desire to question the reality of social distinctions, or the existing status of women. The greatest feminist of the eighteenth century is no apostle of Women's Liberation. Yet simply within his uncompromising reference of hierarchy to morality lie the seeds of latent radicalism, and a challenge to his society. Because Pamela is uniformly virtuous and does not presume, she is wholly worthy of translation from servant to Lady, and can fulfil her new duty and status as well, if not better than, the proudest duchess.

Yet Richardson is very cautious, obviously aware that he is crossing a firmly established social boundary and laying himself open to angry criticism. He inserts into this last section what will seem to modern readers an unpleasant little bit of casuistry designed to forestall his critics (II, 253-4; *I, 381-2*). In answer to the angry Lady Davers, B argues that for her to marry her groom would be sordid and degrading in a way quite different from his own marriage. This is because a man takes his wife to his rank and remains her head, while a woman takes her rank from her husband and makes him her head. Given Richardson's views on the family this is perfectly logical, and it accords with orthodox eighteenth century thinking on social precedence; yet it allows us to see the limits of his radicalism too.

Nevertheless the social visitings show him illustrating, in the fiction itself, his awareness that his 'Whole Duty of Woman' represents a twofold assault on the world. In a society of rigid social distinction the story of Pamela would seem subversive. To a pleasure-loving and lax milieu it would be something of a puritan and old-fashioned bore. So the scenes in which Pamela is deluged with choric praises attempt to condition the reader to acceptance. Pamela and her husband win over rakes and cynics, servants and proud ladies, all in fact who hear their story. The imagined triumph within the fiction prefigures Richardson's hopes for the coming assault, on the real world, of his novel's intransigent morality.

Most modern readers however will find these choric praises tedious and counter-productive (to put it mildly); and since they are not confined to the last section, though they are most concentrated there, this may help to explain the eagerness of critics to pick holes in characters so endlessly and effusively held up for admiration. Moreover, although it is clear that one point of the scenes is to show Pamela behaving with undiminished humility, Richardson apparently failed to see what damaging implications could arise from her hearing and relating these praises with such apparent complacence.

This is primarily a technical blunder, a consequence of the novel's single narrative focus. Pamela has to record the chorus because she is our only source of information; and Richardson seems to have thought that numerous disclaimers could make it clear that she is quite unaffected by the praises she retails. Unfortunately in literature the effect of comment cannot outweigh the effect of action; for comment applies only to the intelligence while action lays hold of the imagination too. Not only do we see her listen, apparently without embarrassment, in scene after scene, but we can never be unaware that she herself is describing what she hears. The experience thus gradually built up is bound to outweigh any disclaimer, and leave us with the impression that she is really far from humble. The less we are aware of the formal difficulties of a wholly new technique, the stronger these feelings will be.

Richardson's technique and his intention are therefore at odds. Yet when this was later brought home to him by many of his readers, he was less than penitent. In *Clarissa* he learnt a far greater tact, but as late as *Grandison*, when he had nearly finished the manuscript, he wrote to Lady Bradshaigh: 'I am not a little embarrassed in my new piece, (so I was in my two former) with the affectation that custom almost compels one to be guilty of:– to make my characters disclaim the merits of the good they do, or the knowledge they pretend to; and to be afraid of reporting the praises due, and given to them by others . . . although the praises given are as much to the honour of the giver's sensibility, as of the receivers. Does any body believe these disclaimers? Does not every body think them affected, and often pharisaical? and even their pretences to modesty, are what Lovelace calls, traps laid for praise? Yet custom exacts them; and who is great enough to be above custom? I think I would wish that my good man, and even my good girl, should be thought to be above regarding this custom. To receive praise with a grace, is a grace.'[1]

We can perhaps understand Richardson's view more easily when we remember that, like Addison and Steele before him, he was much concerned to remove any shamefacedness with regard to morality that might linger in the wake of the reaction against puritanism. Morality and its recognition ought not to be hidden, require no self-deprecation, and where custom seems to demand this, custom must be resisted. Richardson moreover goes beyond all others in demanding that a man should not only be ready but eager to discuss his own virtue and vice, and those of others, with as much freedom and candour as any other subject. Morality is a matter of public concern. So Pamela and B must discuss their story with friends or semi-strangers, without either affectation or pride as Richardson sees it; and the scenes of choric praise, though their relation to complacency remains awkward, must also be seen as a product of an exceptionally public concern for morality.

[1] Richardson to Lady Bradshaigh, 22 April 1752; John Carroll (ed.), *Selected Letters of Samuel Richardson* (Oxford, 1964), 212-13.

Moreover these public discussions, forming part of a living exemplum in the relationship of Pamela and B, are a logical extension of the educative power of Pamela's journal. As Pamela's behaviour, backed up by the deeper revelation and analysis of the journal, was responsible for the regeneration of B; so the behaviour of the married pair, backed up by the discussion of their story, has a morally educative effect on all who see and hear them. Richardson had a profound and enthusiastic belief in the power of example. It is this, of course, and not hypocrisy, that is the basis of Fielding's satire on Richardson in *Joseph Andrews*, the idea (shared by Richardson and Parson Adams) that virtue can be learnt by example and hence from books. It is not only that Richardson believed that morality should be essentially public; but also that by making it public it could be made to grow and spread throughout society. The force of example awakens moral sensibility, and the example of that awakening creates another, and another.

This is connected at a deeper level still with Richardson's longing for secure personal relationships, which is reflected in his heroine. Pamela writes to her parents: '(I) hope to make myself as much beloved about you as I am here' (I, 50; *I, 33*) – and the agency of awakening love, as Richardson sees it, is virtue. 'Now this pleases one', she writes again, 'to be so belov'd. – How much better, by good Fame and Integrity, is it, to get every one's good Word but *one*, than by pleasing *that one*, to make *every one else* one's Enemy, and be an execrable Creature besides!' (I, 57-8; *I, 38*). Morality is the great binding force of society. Lonely individuals reap true and secure friendship and affection through their pursuit of good, creating a fellowship from which only the wilfully selfish and wicked exclude themselves. With this, as *Grandison* will show, we reach one of Richardson's most deep-seated concerns.

So in *Pamela* we have the awakening of B through his growing understanding of Pamela's virtues, from pride and sensuality to love and tenderness. 'Your person made me your lover, but your mind made me your husband.' Hence the importance of the journal, not only for the conversion of B, but for the later conversion of Lady Davers. Hence, finally, the real importance of the concord of praise. The public discussion and the living example awaken the sensibility and the inherent good nature of all who experience them. The chorus of praise and blessing that results is not only the reward of the happy pair, but is also the sign of a community of spirit binding them to their household and their neighbours with true and stable bonds. Everyone is 'improved' – even the dirty old man Sir Simon, the cynical Mr Martin, the imperfectly pious Jane, the penitent John, the brutal Mrs Jewkes. All, in joining the concord of praise, find their truest selves and the true sense of fellowship. The experience of these scenes is meant to be the same for the reader. It is an enactment of a felt sense of moral community, a stilling of criticism, an impulse to regeneration. The onslaught on the world is complete and the world is won over – in the novel.

The trouble is that Richardson the didactic moralist has taken over from Richardson the imaginative dramatist in this last section. Insofar as the imagination is at work it is, apart from the Lady Davers scene, in a much more naïve and self-indulgent way than in the rest of the novel. When one thinks about the moral implications, one may realise that quite serious ideas lie behind the tedious lengthening, but it remains true that there is little really exploratory, reaching through the dramatic imagination to new insight. The impetus behind the writing is too simply didactic, the result more exposition than exploration.

There is however one new contribution to the whole complex of the novel's meaning: Pamela's reaction to the discovery of B's past affair with Sally Godfrey, and the existence of 'Miss Goodwin', his illegitimate child. This is a last example, in contrast, of the way that Richardson's dramatic imagination could take fire in an exploratory way, and lead him to assert deeper values than he seems to have had in mind to start with. We have seen in the treatment of prudence how he explored his way to more sensitive attitudes; here, in the apparently still less amenable area of sexual misdemeanour, there is an even more decisive break with orthodox morality. Sally Godfrey not only failed to resist seduction but to a great extent took the initiative in her own disaster. Only, she was so affected by the warning of her 'child-bed terrors' that she rushed into exile to avoid falling again, though she was still in love with her seducer. We might expect Pamela to rail against her for her fall; instead she voices a judgement that excludes the fall altogether. 'Indeed, indeed, Sir, said I, I bleed for what her Distresses must be in this Case: I am griev'd for her poor Mind's Remorse, through her Child-bed Terrors, which could have so great and so worthy an Effect upon her afterwards; and I honour her Resolution, *and should rank such a returning dear Lady in the Class of those who are most virtuous*, [my italics] and doubt not God Almighty's Mercies to her; and that her present Happiness is the Result of his gracious Providence, blessing her Penitence and Reformation' (II, 339; *I, 437-8*).

The implication is clear. There is in Pamela – as Richardson tries in a concrete dramatic scene to imagine what ideal conduct would be like – a quality of forgiveness which erases the past and begins moral judgement afresh, provided there is a genuine turning-point of reformation. Richardson has moved well away from the simple puritan horror of sexual excess and its outcome which one might have expected from the vehemence of Pamela's revulsion earlier in the book. We may further notice that there is no stigma of the slightest kind attached to the illegitimate child.

This can have thematic importance for the novel as a whole, for we can now detect another kind of progress in the heroine. She decided to encourage John's remorse originally because 'I may possibly make some Discoveries by it'. She forgave Mrs Jewkes as a mark of her duty to B where her innocence was not at stake, but she did it grudgingly at first, 'for you know, my dear Parents, I might as well make a Merit of my Compliance, when my Refusal would stand me in no stead.' On the other hand, though the point is never explicitly handled, her forgiveness of B is complete and unqualified, along with the faith and love which mark her final development in the wilderness, and after this her attitude to Mrs Jewkes and John becomes warmer and untainted by prudential calculations. It would seem then that the logic of the novel's structure marks as strong and humane a development of the theme of forgiveness as of the theme of faith. Interestingly, in both cases, it is Pamela's parents who are left behind; the residue, perhaps, of attitudes Richardson grew out of in the act of writing the novel. The contrast in forgiveness is with Goodman Andrews, insisting that he will refuse to own his daughter if she has fallen (II, 70; *I, 261*).

If Richardson had managed to make this more explicit there might have been less criticism of the ease with which, as soon as B begins to behave moderately decently, he is greeted by Pamela with such effusive, even excessive praise. By the most extreme of Richardson's critics this has been taken as the final evidence of her hypocrisy; it was not the man she objected to all along, but his terms.[1] By others it is put down less to moral insensibility or impurity than to snobbery; printers don't become angels by merely ceasing to threaten girls with sexual violence, but evidently squires do.[2] But the implication of the Godfrey episode is that Richardson imagined a kind of forgiveness that would permit B as well as Sally Godfrey to be ranked 'in the Class of those who are most virtuous' simply because of the sincere wish to break with the past. The novel in Richardson's hands is always liable to move over sharply from the human and psychological, and even the moral, to the overtly religious; Pamela's forgiveness of B may be extraordinary, but the Godfrey episode warns us not to be too sure of its motivation. There is after all a certain parable which insists that moral blame must be completely wiped out, and the returning sinner treated with excessive joy and welcome, simply because he has returned. Perhaps not only squires, but seduced women, and wicked servants can deserve the same treatment when they decide to take the road home. It is all doubtless most unethical and unjust, as the Prodigal's elder brother thought. And lest we be too certain that Richardson had no idea what he was doing, it is worth reminding ourselves

[1] Krutch, *Five Masters*, 129-30. [2] Daiches, *Essays*, 37.

of the text B proposes for Williams's first sermon in the rededicated chapel: 'There is more Joy in Heaven over one Sinner that repenteth, than over Ninety-nine just Persons that need no Repentance' (II, 96; *I, 278*). I am not making Lovelace's mistake of confusing the parable of the Good Shepherd with that of the Prodigal Son, but the message is the same.

While it remains true, then, that the last section of *Pamela* is its dullest and least successful part, we can at least see that some of its implications are important for the meaning of the whole. Richardson converts his dramatic story of private relationship into a public exemplum, embodying theories of behaviour over a wider area of life. The novel becomes a challenge to the world, on behalf of an unfashionably strict morality. There is a final clarification of Richardson's view of social and family duty. The Godfrey episode suggests a deeper way of looking at the novel's attitude towards its sinners. Finally, the success in the fiction of Pamela's assault on the world is meant to enact in its readers' imaginations a felt sense of moral community, a stilling of criticism, an impulse to moral regeneration.

2

What actually happened was partly triumph—and partly not. The dream did come true: the anonymous little volumes hit the Town's fancy and became all the rage; and they also won the wide middle-class and moral readership he had hoped for. The novel became one of the century's best-sellers, going through five editions in its first year, and being rapidly translated into most European languages. Fashionable ladies showed off copies in public and held fans decorated with pictures of its best-loved scenes. *Pamela* became a play, an opera, even a waxwork. It also had the very unusual distinction, at a time when fiction tended to be morally suspect, of being recommended from a London pulpit; and the letters that poured into the booksellers left no doubt that the blend of fiction with morality had secured the attention of the kind of readership the *Spectator* had created – though the comments rarely showed critical intelligence. Even Mr Pope was reported as saying that he had lost a night's sleep over the book, and that it would do 'more good than many volumes of sermons'.[1]

At the height of triumph, however, came the dissident voices. *Pamela* came out on 6 November 1740. *Shamela* appeared the following April; *Pamela Censured* in May; *Anti-Pamela: or Feign'd Innocence Detected; In a Series of Syrena's Adventures* in June, almost certainly by Eliza Haywood; and Povey's *Virgin in Eden* before the end of 1741. There followed a spate of ephemera connected with *Pamela* in one way or another.[2]

The attacks have in common the charges of social subversion and lasciviousness, but they come from very different angles. Eliza Haywood played the market on both sides, trying to imitate Richardson in another work. Fielding was wittier, and was also hitting at more than *Pamela*. He clearly associated the anonymous author with Cibber and Conyers Middleton, and hence with a worldly, an armoured, and a successful vanity and hypocrisy that were long-standing and favourite targets from his point of view. (He may well have been disconcerted to find out who the real author was: a man admired by the original of Mr Allworthy. There is certainly a very sharp distinction between the nature of the satire in *Shamela* and in *Joseph Andrews*, by which time the authorship of *Pamela* was widely known.) But Fielding and Eliza Haywood are both authors of the sophisticated 'Town', whose scheming minxes travesty their original. In *Pamela Censured* and the *Virgin*, however, the attacks come from a zealous puritanism, and in the case of the former a prurience, well in excess of Richardson's own; the charge is immodesty, and the 'artful and alluring amorous Ideas' which inflame the imagination.

1 Cheyne to Richardson, 12 February 1741, quoted McKillop, *Richardson*, 50; Leake to Richardson,? February 1741, A. L. Barbauld (ed.), *The Correspondence of Samuel Richardson*, I, lix.

2 These are discussed by McKillop, *Richardson*, 73 ff.; Kreissman, *Pamela-Shamela*; T. C. D. Eaves and B. Kimpel, *Samuel Richardson, A Biography* (Oxford, 1971), 127 ff.

The year 1741 also saw a kind of attack that was even more embittering. By April a spurious continuation of *Pamela* was well advanced, commissioned by an unscrupulous bookseller from a hack called Kelly. Richardson tried to warn Chandler off, and advertised against him, but the spurious *Pamela's Conduct in High Life* duly came out in May. His only redress was to announce that he would continue the work himself, and he set about it in mid-April. *Pamela* itself had come from a spurt of creative imagination in only two months; the continuation took three times as long and proved hard labour. As he told James Leake in August: 'it is no easy Task to one that has so much Business upon his Hands, and so many Avocations of different Sorts, and whose old Complaints in the Nervous way require that he should sometimes run away from Business and from himself, if he could.'[1] It cannot be emphasised too much that *Pamela* was complete in its original form, with no thought of going on. *Pamela in her Exalted Condition* was begun unwillingly, and finished laboriously. It is hardly surprising that it is the least effective of his novels. There was no longer a dramatic situation to begin from and the original inspiration was exhausted – as it had begun to be, indeed, in the last part of the book itself. He had, moreover, to compete with his own triumph, and he could hardly have hoped to succeed.

Nevertheless the continuation is not wholly without interest to us. We can see it as an opportunity for Richardson to review and to some extent to defend himself: to meet whatever charges he thought worth meeting in the light of the attacks of 1741, and the criticisms within the praises he had received. He did manage also to create one new situation which implicitly suggests some awareness of the limits of his hero's reformation, and allows him to test his heroine again. On the other hand, the continuation allows us to pin down even more clearly the difference between the moral dramatist and the moral instructor, and hence the dangers of generalising about 'Richardson's views'. And in some formal ways the continuation was a five-finger exercise which

[1] Carroll, *Letters*, 45.

extended his technical repertory, in preparation, as it turned out, for *Clarissa*.

The points he thought worth answering in set terms are the social criticisms; the objections to the forgiveness of Mrs Jewkes; and the objections to the sexual scenes.

In several particulars, Richardson obeyed the 'good natured letter' which pleased him most of all the anonymous comments sent to his booksellers.[1] Pamela's style is further raised to suit her 'exalted condition' – though this had already begun in the original where the style at the beginning was even homelier than it is in the edition we now read. She is given much more dignity, and will write to Lady Davers on increasingly equal terms – though the gentleman is denied his wish to have B accept a title and make her a Lady indeed, since B argues his preference for the status of a plain country gentleman of ancient family.

On the other hand, from the very beginning of the new work there is great sensitivity to the charges of social subversion. If the meek servant-wife was irritating, the minutely-discriminating consciousness of rank with which Pamela now writes to her parents will win even fewer friends – but it springs from a desire to show the whole Andrews family alive to the danger of encroaching, or seeming to trade on the new situation. So the accommodation in the Kent farmhouse must be nicely adjusted to suit both the old people coming up in the world again, and B on his occasional visits; not too little, not too much, but just right, a little grand for them, a little plain for him. B must not be saddled with employing more members of the family, though they can be helped in other ways. Goodman Andrews insists on making himself useful and earning his new good fortune, and becomes a steward beloved by B's tenants.

Pamela and her husband also explicitly answer the charge of setting a bad example 'to young Gentlemen of Family and Fortune to marry beneath them' (III, 323-30; *II*, *168-72*) – but more

[1] Forster MS. Collection, XVI, 1, fols. 34-6; partly reprinted by McKillop, *Richardson*, 48. The criticisms are summarised in the prefatory letters, Shakespeare Head edition, I, xvi-xvii.

effective than argument are the dramatic episodes Richardson invents to enforce it. He offers his own parody of the original situation in the foiled affair of Jackey and Pamela's maid, the compliant Polly Barlow. Polly gets a salutary fright and is good thereafter, and though Pamela isn't convinced that she has the true virtue appropriate to a clergyman's wife, she does not stand in the way of her marriage to the young chaplain. Jackey however goes on to marry the well-born cast mistress of an earl, with predictably disastrous results. The arguments of B and Pamela are enforced: the 'example' holds precisely in the degree to which the girl is as moral and as worthy of exaltation as Pamela, and the gentleman capable of discrimination, not 'such a Booby, that he cannot *reflect* and *compare*, and take the Case with *all its Circumstances* together' (III, 328; *II*, *171*). This is as close as Richardson ever gets to an explicit comment on *Shamela*, and a reply to its naming of his hero.

His anonymous correspondent also felt that Pamela had been too timid with Lady Davers. The point is not argued explicitly this time (though Aaron Hill had answered it in the prefatory material to the second edition), but one of the best episodes of the continuation is something of an alternative. This is the winning over of the ill-mannered and arrogant Sir Jacob Swynford, where Richardson's comic talent gets its first sustained opportunity (III 304 ff.; *II*, *156 ff.*). Because B's overbearing uncle has never seen Pamela, Richardson is able to invent a way of exposing his insolence and snobbery without forfeiting Pamela's dignity. The Countess and Lady Davers persuade her to play up as the former's daughter, and the surly bear is allowed to think that his presence has banished Mrs B from her drawing-room and dinner-table. But the more he is taken with the captivating 'Lady Jenny', despite her odd hoop (for she is beginning to show her pregnancy) and the wedding ring he never notices, the more it must finally come home to him how superficial the fixed ideas of his snobbery have been, and how insolent. Pamela is allowed to be respectful, especially at the end when she asks his blessing and his pardon, without making a doormat of herself; and she reveals the same power of absolute forgiveness as before. But much more important: the scene is imaginatively alive, the dialogue well sustained, and there are some good comic moments. The episode is far more effective than a straight argument in making its point, that the arrogant are best overcome not by open opposition, but by the kind of submission that reveals them to themselves.

In defence of the sexual scenes, however, nothing but the most explicit argument will do. In reply to Pamela's worries about the propriety of Lord Davers and his nephew being allowed to read her accounts of her two 'grand trials', Lady Davers is adamant. Only by knowing exactly what happened is it possible to judge the merit of Pamela's resistance, and to be convinced that she really deserves her elevation. Defence then moves to attack, 'for it must be a very unvirtuous Mind, that can form any other Ideas from what you relate, than those of Terror and Pity for you. Your Expressions are too delicate to give the nicest Ear Offence, except at him. – You paint no Scenes but such as make his Wickedness odious; and that Gentleman, much more Lady, must have a very corrupt Heart, who could, from such Circumstances of Distress, make any Reflections but what should be to your Honour, and in Abhorrence of such Actions. Indeed, Child, I am so convinc'd of this, that by this Rule I would judge of any Man's Heart in the World, better than by a Thousand Declarations and Protestations' (III, 44-5; *II, 27*). She goes on to argue that, far from inflaming the imagination, the narrative sets bounds to it and to the guilt of B, by preventing a reader from imagining that more might have happened than actually did.

Much more significant and effective, however, is the creation for the first time of B's point of view of one of those scenes. Lady Davers puts her brother to public trial, on the charge that to have attempted Pamela's virtue in the presence of Mrs Jervis 'was the very Stretch of shameless Wickedness' (III, 182; *II, 100*). B reads Pamela's account again, and comments: 'This is a dark Affair, as it is here stated; and I can't say, but *Pamela*, and Mrs *Jervis* too, had a great deal of Reason to apprehend the worst: But surely Readers of it, who were less Parties in the supposed Attempt, and who were not determined at all Events to condemn me, might have made a more favourable Construction...' (III, 183-4; *II*, *102*). He then gives quite a long narrative account of how his passion for his mother's maid (and his plan to abduct her) began before Mrs B's death and grew after; with explicit reminiscence of Letter 24 and of his conflict between pride and love; admiration of her virtue and anger at her resistance; determination to have her, and jealousy lest she throw herself into the arms of some inferior to escape his advances. He concludes with his own account of the 'Closet' scene, which would have made the fallibility of Pamela's quite unmistakeable, if we had had it at the time. He meant only to eavesdrop and there was no attempt at rape at all, though he might have taken advantage of the situation if Mrs Jervis had been prevailed upon to leave.

As I suggested earlier, those who wish to believe the worst of Richardson could conceivably argue that this is all afterthought, and that he had had many months in which to concoct a plausible defence of what had originally been just what Pamela thought. But though the account of events before the death of Mrs B may well be a new idea, I do not think that such an argument can dispose of B's self-defence where the original material is at issue. His version of himself in the 'Closet' scene is a great deal more plausible than Pamela's; it fits his repeated protestations at the time, and the whole pattern of the character in conflict, which can be detected by close enough attention to what he says and does throughout the original *Pamela*. The defence comes too late of course to alter anything. Yet we may place beside the reproach to superficial readers – the first of many to come – a dawning realisation of the need for sustained access to more than one point of view, which was to be a vitally important factor in the difference between the botched prentice work of *Pamela*, and the major achievement, at the cost of length, in *Clarissa*. Moreover there are moments when B now anticipates both Lovelace's style and his rake's ideology. And when Pamela observes that the 'saucy Air' of these moments isn't 'very like the Style of a true Penitent' (III, 212; *II, 119*), Richardson seems to become aware that his hero's reformation had been somewhat facile. Once again the dramatic imagination moves beyond defence, and straightforward moral argument, to growth.

The treatment of the problem of forgiveness will show up still further the difference between the ordinary Mr Richardson and the dramatic artist when he allows his imagination scope. There had been objections to the forgiveness of Mrs Jewkes both in Fielding's attack and in Ralph Allen's good-will.[1] Pamela now argues that she was in no position to require the woman's dismissal; that if she had provoked B he might have resumed his wicked purposes; and that when she was bid to hope 'beyond her highest Ambition' and asked to forgive Mrs Jewkes as a sign that she could forgive B himself, who was she 'to take upon me Lady Airs, and to resent'? (III, 66; *II, 39*). She lays claim to rather more inclination to forgive than was actually the case at first, and goes on to argue that the change in the power-situation was a triumph which allowed her to pity 'the poor abject Creature' at her feet, rather than be guilty of the mean pride of trampling on her. Wouldn't a refusal of B's request have shown her incapable of generosity, but just 'as capable of Insolence, and Vengeance too, in her Turn, as the better born'? (III, 71; *II, 42*) – and wouldn't this have suggested to B that she had a pride, through which he could hope to overcome her after all? What is most noticeable here is how Richardson descends again into the kind of prudential reasoning which his dramatic imagination had enabled him to transcend in *Pamela* itself. There is no sign, either, of the enthusiasm, the real generosity and wholeheartedness, he had captured when he imagined her reaction to Sally Godfrey. There clearly are two Richardsons, both 'moral', but in perceptibly different senses.

We may refine a little. As Richardson goes on now to imagine a letter from the penitent Mrs Jewkes, and Pamela's reply, the

[1] See Parson Oliver's fourth objection in *Shamela*; and Richardson to Allen, 8 October 1741; Carroll, *Letters*, 51.

treatment becomes more humane, and the justification by human results more persuasive than the arguments of prudence. Mrs Jewkes isn't 'abject', and Pamela's tone improves. But there is still too much *de haut en bas*. The arguments of Mr Richardson, asserting her moral superiority, seem to have hobbled the imagination by which the dramatic artist had made the original Pamela leap beyond her orthodoxy, and his own, to a higher morality of forgiveness. There is no prodigal's welcome from the 'exalted' Pamela. Even with the Godfrey affair, in this book, Richardson cannot rise to former heights, because he lacks the right dramatic setting to heat his imagination. There is one promising flash of psychological insight: Pamela's confession of a 'strange Passion' for the baby of her alter-ego (III, 119; *II*, *67*); but it isn't developed. The need to reply to 'Mrs Wrightson's' letter in terms that will not give away Sally Godfrey's past, effectively prevents Pamela from expressing herself, as she might otherwise have done, to the mother who had lost that baby; while the tone of her commentary to Lady Davers is not likely to encourage the old enthusiasm. We can measure the difference between 'I should rank such a returning dear Lady in the Class of those who are most virtuous', and, 'Must not such a Lady as this, dear Madam, have as much Merit, as many even of those, who, having not had her Temptations, have not fallen?' (IV, 278; *II*, *359*). The sentence hesitates, the tone is perceptibly cooler and more cautious. Mr Richardson is at work, not the Master of the Heart.

The crux of the problem of forgiveness however, as several of the censurers and many later critics point out, is not Mrs Jewkes, nor Sally Godfrey, but B himself . . . and this is the bearing of the central episode of the new book. In the masquerade, and the affair with the dashing young widow that develops out of it, Richardson the dramatist comes into his own again.

We see through Pamela's eyes. At the masquerade (IV, 94 ff.; *II*, *258 ff.*) the Quaker (a nice touch), is more than a little jealous of her Spaniard's flirtation with the dashingly inappropriate Nun, but the episode passes entirely from mind as Pamela is brought to bed with her first child. Later however, when all is safely over, we get the first hint of trouble in the B household from Polly Darnford. Lady Davers, too, hears rumours from Town, and enquires anxiously. Eventually Pamela opens her heart to her sister-in-law. It is clear that she fears the worst, though she is trying hard to be patient, and to see that her 'Apprehensions were ever afore-hand with Events' (IV, 145; *II, 284*). Yet there seem very good reasons to fear. B is 'cold and a little cross', impatient with what he regards as signs that the baby is spoiling her cheerful temper. He spends a good deal of time away from home, on the excuse that she is wholly taken up with the nursery. Worse still, the lawyer Turner has carried tales that B has been corresponding with the young Countess Dowager, and has been jaunting to Oxford with her. Then a letter from her is brought to the house and B is rather aggressively touchy, hawk-eyed for signs that she dares to question his honour. Pamela takes herself to task: she must 'not exasperate him by Upbraidings, when I should try to move him by Patience and Forbearance. For the Breach of *his* Duty cannot warrant the Neglect of *mine*' (IV, 152; *II, 288*). This is consistent with the idea of overcoming by duty and submission throughout the original book, and the Swynford episode in this one, but one is also reminded of the 'Judgement' scene with Longman in the first section of *Pamela*. For, as she imagines giving up B to her rival, and agonises lest he take her baby with him, there is the unmistakeable and betraying note of exaggeration again. She may know the role she wants, but she finds it exceedingly difficult and cannot play it truly yet. She is very jealous as she had pointed out to Lady Davers some time back, and the affair has also struck at her Achilles heel, the belief that B had reformed. Lady Davers rubs in salt by passing on the gossip about the Countess's quarrel with her uncle, when she reputedly argued for polygamy, and said 'She had rather be a certain Gentleman's second Wife, than the first to the greatest Man in *England*' (IV, 156; *II, 289*).

Now the affair moves to crisis. B insists on bringing his Countess and her sister on a formal visit. He is none too pleased with the plainness of Pamela's dress, her melancholy air, and the loss of sparkle in her eyes. She forgets her role for a moment with the quick retort that the change may be in his eyes rather than hers, but in the tensely-polite scene that follows she acquits herself quite well – sustained by her child, and the fact that her rival has to keep calling her Mrs B. But the moment it is over, a compliment from B suddenly releases her overcharged feelings in helpless tears – and B stalks angrily out of the house.

He comes back late and locks himself in his study. She writes him a note, but he will not see her yet, lest things get worse. She goes down to tap at his door, with a 'tragedy speech' about Hester risking her life to break in on her royal husband, which suggests to him that she is a little unhinged – as indeed she is. He is quite kind however, and promises to have it all out with her after a journey he has to make to Tonbridge the next day. 'Only', he says, 'think as well of me, as I do of you. Would to Heaven, thought I, there was the same Reason for the one, as for the other!' (IV, 173; *II*,*300*). B falls asleep, or pretends to, as soon as his head touches the pillow, which effectively prevents any further talk; but Pamela 'had all my own entertaining Reflections to myself; which gave me not one Wink of Sleep; but made me of so much Service' as to wake him, 'when the Clock struck Four' – so as not to keep her rival waiting. The tart tone is nicely caught.

She has complained of cruel suspense, but on the Friday a misspelt letter from an unknown Thomasine Fuller seems to put the matter out of doubt. (The reminiscence now is of 'Somebody's' letter in *Pamela*, about the mock marriage.) Thomasine warns that B and his Countess plan to set up together at Tonbridge. Pamela has a passing thought that the letter may be an intrigue of Turner's, but on the whole she believes it. With eddying feelings, she has to wait until Monday, for B sends word he will be delayed.

When he returns, however, he is both touched and troubled by the 'moving Sedateness' of her manner (IV, 180; *II*, *304*). She insists on dining first, and then on making the 'éclaircissement' a formal trial in her closet, putting herself in the dock behind three chairs, and making B promise not to look at her, and to hear her out before he judges. He fears for her head, as he may well do when she compares herself to St Paul before Felix, but her 'romantic airs' are a bid for 'magnanimity'. She aspires 'to be an humble Means of saving the Man I love and honour, from Errors that might be fatal to his Soul' (IV, 183; *II, 306*) and she must rise above herself. She will not allow B's quick temper to create an argument when she begins to produce her evidence, and she does her best not to upbraid him. For, what might in another novelist have become a scene of bitter repartee, in Richardson's hands must forgo secular conflict for religious self-sacrifice. She tells B she loves him as much as ever, but for his mind as well as his body as the Countess cannot do. Nevertheless she will give him up to her beautiful rival, she will go to her parents with her son, for she must have the boy to have 'something worth living for' (IV, 192; *II, 311*). She will never recriminate. But it will be her constant prayer that he will be touched by divine grace, and 'I will receive your returning ever-valu'd Heart, *as if nothing had happen'd* [my italics], the Moment I can be sure it will be wholly mine' (IV, 192; *II, 312*). We hear again the note of absolute forgiveness; this time at a crisis which reverses the Sally Godfrey situation, for Pamela now believes she has lost B, whereas then she could perhaps afford to be magnanimous. Richardson the dramatic novelist recaptures his former position, as Mr Richardson failed to do. (That the difference is a matter of whether the dramatic imagination is operating or not, and not a development from one part of the novel to another, is shown by the fact that the 'Sally Godfrey' letters and comments come *after* this whole episode.) His implicit sense that this required an extraordinary flight of imagination is embodied in the peculiarity of the scene, and the 'romantic' and 'uncommon' heightening of his heroine's manner. He can have been in no doubt of the reaction of 'Town' sophisticates, or of puritans like Povey, or of the morally orthodox – but this time at least the absolute forgiveness cannot be 'explained' in terms of social ambition and self-seeking hypocrisy.

Nevertheless, though Pamela's magnanimity reinforces the theme of forgiveness, insofar as she believes B guilty, there is also a reinforcement of the original pattern of her fallibility. Once again, if we look closely enough at what B actually says and does, it is clear that his conscience is relatively untroubled, that he feels *he* has a grievance, that he has not ceased to love her, and that his whole behaviour is consistent with a far 'more favourable construction' than Pamela's. The reminiscence of 'Somebody's' letter would itself be enough to alert sensitive readers of *Pamela*, and she remembers enough to have a fleeting suspicion that Turner might have written it. We were reminded at the beginning of the episode how characteristic of her it is to allow her imagination to leap ahead of the facts. And this time we do not have to work by inference alone, for Richardson has learnt the lesson of the need for direct access to B's point of view.

He tells her immediately that, though he 'has been inconsiderately led on by blind Passion for an Object too charming, but which I never thought equal to my *Pamela*, I will (for it is yet, I bless God, in my Power) restore to your Virtue a Husband all your own' (IV, 196; *II, 314*). Both overwrought, they part, and B promises to clear up the whole affair. He spends all night writing, and sets off the next morning with assurances of his, and the lady's honour, but he will postpone the explanation until he can satisfy her completely. He asks Pamela to get her letters back from Lady Davers, and forward them to him.

His detailed account of the affair, when it comes (IV, 207 ff.; *II, 320* ff.), shows that he has been guilty of no more than love of intrigue, inordinate vanity, and thoughtlessness, both about the reputations of himself and the Countess, and about the suffering he might be causing to Pamela. He makes the best of the affair of course, and we need no more accept his version uncritically than Pamela's. He spoke in his new awareness at the 'trial' of 'blind passion', and he admits at the end that he could have tumbled into bed if the lady had been less virtuous (or, we may see, if Pamela had turned shrewish, though for once Richardson avoids the prudential point). Nevertheless, though his equivocation at the masquerade gave the Countess the impression he was unmarried, which he failed to set right himself, his continued friendship with her after she found out the true state of affairs was reckless rather than guilty. He is an ancestor of Henry Crawford, drawn into a relationship by the vain gallant's inability to resist making up to a pretty girl who makes up to him, but he was saved in time. All the circumstances in Pamela's narrative fall into a different perspective, revealing folly and self-centredness rather than vice. He felt the new father's sense of neglect, and, pluming himself on his honour, failed to imagine what Pamela might be feeling, so that he could only see her changed temper as unjustified doubt of that honour, jealousy, and vapours. The uncle's distorted gossip, Turner's malicious intrigue, and Pamela's own tendency to fear the worst did all the rest.

The crucial points seem to be the unwarranted confidence in his honour which is at the root of B's lack of imagination, and Pamela's lack of faith once more, despite the lessons of the pond. She soon draws her inference, that the episode was necessary to ensure that she would never be jealous again (IV, 247; *II*, *340*). But B still has some way to go. Richardson has now clearly realised the limits of the hero's reformation in *Pamela* and how shaky its foundations of love and honour might prove; he goes on to develop the point. While B is at Tonbridge, breaking with the Countess, little Billy gets smallpox. At first B tries to keep Pamela from nursing him, but then with a deeper understanding of her feelings he gives way, and she contracts the disease. The threat to her looks makes him in his turn see how his 'affair' had been necessary, to bring home to him how much more valuable her mind is than her beauty. When he takes Pamela to Tonbridge, after the Countess has gone, he has realised that honour, and even morality, are insufficient guides and guardians – nothing but 'RELIGIOUS CONSIDERATIONS, and a Resolution to watch over the very *first* Appearances of Evil' will do (IV, 378; *II*, *423*). An enraptured Pamela blesses the mysterious workings of Providence, and from that time B becomes a religious man.

This central episode, then, has three bearings. Richardson's dramatic imagination recaptures a vision of absolute forgiveness, even if this be extraordinary and 'romantic'. There is a wholly proper realisation of the limits of B's original reformation. And the episode develops the technical advance that had been implicit in B's account of the 'Closet' scene. For now we have both the fallible narrative and its immediate modification by a second point of view, later supplemented by a third, for the Countess is also allowed to speak for herself (IV, 289 ff.; *II*, *366* ff.). This is by far the most important advance on the road to *Clarissa*.

Unfortunately, along with Sir Jacob Swynford and B's earlier narrative, this virtually closes the profit balance on the new book, for the bulk of it has the tedium of the last part of *Pamela*, and worse. We may however briefly notice some five-finger exercises which do contribute further moments of liveliness, and also extend the scope of Richardson's epistolary form. He begins to develop what Spence was to call his orchestra of styles. We have already noticed the first anticipations of Lovelace in B's narratives, but they remain narratives; the idea of a masculine correspondence as such has not yet arrived. Yet the joking exchange of letters between B and Sir Simon Darnford provides, in its small way, the first hints of what he might be able to do. The straight-faced role-playing, the comic imagery, the mock high-style of B's letter are all to bear fruit later. With Sir Simon's and Jackey's letters we have experiments in 'characteristic' styles, the rueful *roué* and the booby lord – and Sir Simon becomes a more genuinely comic creation than he had been in *Pamela*. The idea of a lively female correspondent is also taking shape. Lady Davers has moments of raillery which can hold both tartness and affection, and Polly Darnford anticipates Anna Howe more closely in her accounts of her tussles with her father and sister. One notices the modulation between the saucy and the serious, the greater ease of syntax and colloquialism, the speech rhythms, which will play against the greater formality associated with the purer virtue speaking seriously. In the verbal battles between Polly and her ill-natured sister we have a preliminary sketch of Clarissa and Bella: the dramatically rendered bitchiness and petulance in the authentic cadences of the human voice, and the combination of conscious virtue with a sharp tongue.

Unfortunately, however, the rest of the book is by Mr Richardson, who told Dr Cheyne: 'I labour'd hard to rein in my Invention . . . and indeed had so much Matter upon my Hands to give probable Instances of what a good Wife, a tender Mother, a faithful Friend, a Kind Mistress, and a worthy Neighbour shou'd do (including the first parts of Education, which might fall under the Mother's Eye) that . . . (I) had not Field for Excursions of Fancy & Imagination . . . For I always had it in View, I have the Vanity to repeat, to make the Story rather *useful* than *diverting*'.[1] We are back with the Whole Duty of Woman, the Exemplary, and the central impulse to instruct; as entertainingly as possible perhaps, but mainly to sugar the wholesome pill lest it be rejected.

So B and Pamela must show what ideal conjugal manners should be: the husband tender and considerate, too affectionate to stand too much on ceremony, but respectful of her privacy; the wife acknowledging him as her head whenever there is a serious disagreement (as over the argument about whether she should suckle her child herself), but otherwise benefiting from his compliance with all her reasonable requests. They are fond of each other's company, unlike fashionable pairs, and he teaches her French and encourages her to develop her mind, as Mr Richardson believes all husbands should do, instead of regarding women as an inferior species. We are shown Pamela as the ideal manager of a household, turning the servants into a harmonious, efficient and religious family. We watch her instituting family worship with all the household, careful of the dignity and the prospects of chaplain Williams and his successor Mr Adams, and regular in churchgoing. We see how she organises her funds for charitable purposes, go with her on her rounds of the sick, and hear of her arrangements with apothecary and surgeon to care for her people when she is away. We see her through her first pregnancy and childbirth, Billy's smallpox, and the prudent precautions which make the disease relatively manageable when she

[1] Richardson to Cheyne, 1742; Carroll, *Letters*, 54.

gets it. She goes on to bear B five sons and two daughters eventually (though only five in the book); she accompanies him on tours of Britain and Europe, and we leave her (not without great relief), the cynosure of all who know her, and still in her prime. Mr Richardson is assaulting the world again.

The relationship with the *Spectator*'s ideal of correcting taste and manners becomes even more explicit as Pamela gives us her essays too, with the encouragement of Lady Davers and B. She criticises a tragedy, *The Distressed Mother*, and a comedy, *The Tender Husband*, and encloses with her remarks on the Opera a short essay by B, observing that the Italians themselves do not divorce sound and sense like the cobbled-together versions that had become so popular in London. She describes the masquerade, and attacks the vogue for such dubious freedoms. B even persuades her to prepare a little book on the education and management of children, in a series of letters commenting on Locke. So she writes on the treatment of babies, on the use of rewards (where she differs from the sage), on discipline, on toys, on the proper relations of children and servants (differing again in several of these subjects), and on the first steps of education supervised by the mother. She argues at some length the respective advantages and disadvantages of educating boys at home with a tutor, or sending them to school, and comes up with a compromise. She has things to say about the education of girls to fit them as intelligent companions for their husbands, and a new idea about sending boys on miniature Grand Tours of the British Isles to prepare them for the real thing. There are signs that Mr Richardson the printer would not have been averse to unloading his commonplace book on the World if these foretastes had created a demand.

A little more sugaring appears in some sketches which might also have made *Spectator*-like papers. There are 'characters': a rather 'pi' vignette of the Good Family in Adversity, and a more amusing one on an Old Maid pretending to be younger than she is. There are 'conversation pieces': on titles, and a gentleman's duty in politics, on whether there should be laws to cover seduction, and a picture of four rakes on a visit. There is a full-scale Ladies'-piece, when the Dean and Mrs Towers bring three young women to hear Pamela's instructions, not very artfully disguised as conversation, though she plumes herself on her management of the talk to give the romantic one, the soft one and the over-lively one the necessary moral nudge. There is a fable for little children, and one for little women too on the histories of Coquetilla, Prudiana, Profusiana and Prudentia. Miss Goodwin is in no difficulties about identification: 'PRUDENTIA is YOU – is YOU indeed!,' she cries; 'It *can* be nobody else! O teach me, Good GOD! to follow *Your* example and I shall be a SECOND PRUDENTIA'. On this the continuation ends.

Once again the assault on the world accentuates the difference between Mr Richardson and the novelist. We have seen how the 'exalted' Pamela fell back into prudential calculation, as Mr Richardson tried to argue her justification for forgiving Mrs Jewkes. Similarly, after the episode with the Countess, it can seem wholly 'proper' to the heroine in didactic mood 'that I should be so very uneasy, as to assume a conduct not natural to my Temper, and to raise his generous Concern for me!' (IV, 376; *II*, *422*). Finally Prudentia is simply exalted too, with no hint now of the dangers of suspicion, calculation and fear which were the discoveries of the original novel. Complexities are flattened; distinctions blurred. To Mr Richardson his heroine can do no wrong; whereas the strength of the novelist lies precisely in the power of his imagination to criticise and transcend his ordinary self.

CHAPTER FOUR

Taking Stock

I

The attempt to recover the *Pamela* that Richardson wrote has involved making the best of it. This needs no apology, I hope, since the opposite has been the case for so long; yet the time has come now to right the balance, and try to establish how it was that so much went wrong, when so much had gone right.

As we have seen, there has been serious misreading: far too little close attention to texture and structure, too little willingness to puzzle over implications and difficulties, too little awareness of form, method, and technique. Yet one does not dispose of the misreadings by showing their myopia. For they could not have arisen to such an extent if Richardson's control over his medium, and his understanding of some of its implications, had not been so imperfect at this stage. He made *Pamela* far too easy to mistake. Conversely however, it is surprising how many of the moral charges levelled against the book are traceable to technical imperfections. This is why it was technical improvement and not a moral revolution which enabled the same man to write a major novel so soon afterwards.

If, then, readers have been too ready to treat the heroine 'as a real person' without remembering that what we know of a fictional character depends entirely on the fictional form, and not ready enough to work at subtle inferences; Richardson seems not to have realised how much a reader's response could be damaged by a formal defect, and how simply and easily unwanted inferences could arise from flaws of technique and style.

The first plank in the 'hypocrisy' platform, for example, is supplied by inadequacies of plotting. Richardson often overlooked the need for invention, as his habit of repeating himself shows, but he seems never to have noticed how failures to contrive could have unwanted psychological effects. It ought to be obvious, for example, that the reason for Pamela staying on after B's first attempts is neither a moral nor a psychological matter, but an absolute necessity of the novelist. In the *Familiar Letters* a girl in the same situation leaves at once, but that of course is the end of that, in one page.[1] If Pamela is not to pay the price of her author's necessity, however, it is rather important that he contrive some convincing excuse for her to stay. Her parents have told her to be guided by Mrs Jervis, but that is hardly enough. Richardson should have made much more of the timidity he develops later; particularly if he had contrived some recent episode in the neighbourhood which, in that age of violence, might convincingly have given Pamela and her readers pause about the advisability of trying to get all the way home by herself. Yet all he manages to produce is the waistcoat which she must finish before she leaves. Moreover, the subtlety with which he then uses the waistcoat to show her unconscious feeling for B and its fluctuation, actually compounds the inadequacy. He does not notice how, having put his character on the spot to serve his needs, he has not only failed to protect her, but has actually exposed her to doubts about the sincerity of her moral decision, which need never have arisen. A similar case occurs in Letter 24, when Richardson obviously needs Pamela in her new dress to meet her master, but contrives the meeting so clumsily that it is possible for a careless reader to assume that she intended it all the time. In neither case would one wish to lose the psychological complexity: the waistcoat does reveal Pamela's feeling for her persecutor, her giving in to Mrs Jervis does hint that she isn't

[1] *Familiar Letters*, ed. Downs, letters 138 and 139, 164-5.

entirely unwilling to be seen by B when she looks so pretty; and a sensitive reading will put these points into perspective with all the other evidence. The trouble is that the crudity of contrivance, with readers insensitive to all the other evidence, makes it too easy to simplify her behaviour into hypocrisy.

Problems also arise from crudities of style. The most obvious is the problem of unwanted comedy, but there can be unwanted psychological inferences too. I have argued that there is far more conscious humour in *Pamela* than has been supposed. Our close look at Letter 24 showed that the humour at Pamela's expense there was not only intended, but part of the structure of the episode, and that the melodrama at the close is a comedy of misunderstanding. Eaves and Kimpel are 'tempted to hope' that there could be intended humour in the 'Closet' scene.[1] They point to the splendid bathos of B's rage with Mrs Jervis, 'He was desperate angry, and threaten'd to throw her out of the Window; and to turn her out of the House the next Morning', to Pamela's equally splendid 'expostulate To-morrow if you must expostulate!', and to what they call 'Mr B's ridiculous request to Mrs Jervis to step upstairs'. But they are still very unsure, because they clearly think of the scene as an attempted rape, and hence can only ask whether we are 'forced to take all of this as deadly serious if we are to adopt Richardson's official view of Pamela's situation'. Whereas, in fact, there is no 'official' view in 'multiple point of view' writing – and to see through all the points of view is to discover that Pamela has wholly mistaken B's purpose, while B in turn, knowing his own motives, is deliciously unaware at first of what all the fuss is about. The scene in its entire conception, once we can see it from all its points of view, really does have its funny side and is not an attempted rape at all. Moreover the comic point in all three instances is that they are quite natural from one point of view and deliciously absurd from another. This is what convinces me that all three are intended, because the full joke depends on commanding a double point of view, which is characteristically

[1] Eaves and Kimpel, *Richardson*, 107-8.

Richardsonian. The one place in the book where Pamela is actually called a comical girl, by Mrs Jervis in the 'Bundle' scene, is a case in point. For the comedy is not just that Pamela makes a joke: 'Now I come to the Presents of my dear virtuous Master: Hay, you know, *Closet* for that, Mrs *Jervis*!' – but also the joke at Pamela's expense, for we know that B is in the closet *again*! (I, 100; *I*, *64*). So here, the jokes are only rich when we see why B is so flustered, why he is so angry at Mrs Jervis's biblical denunciation, and why he wants to 'expostulate' – and see on the other hand that (to him) the bathos is flustered rhetoric followed by a serious threat, and the suggestion about quietening the maids not ridiculous, though he might well have taken advantage of it.

Yet the same episode furnishes an example of what I take to be unconscious humour, produced by a momentary inattention to language. This is a favourite of mine: I always cherish the note of absentminded surprise in 'I found his Hand in my Bosom' (I, 79; *I*, *50*). One can see that Richardson intended to make clear that it happened before Pamela was aware of it, but both the tone and the turn of phrase are wrong. (One has only to substitute the word 'felt' to see the difference, for the odd tone is produced by the word that seems to make the bosom no part of the girl.) And here I think one can be sure that the humour is unintentional, both because there is no 'point of view' comedy, but still more because it is very difficult to believe that Richardson could have meant us to laugh at the beginning of his heroine's terror, where the scene is obviously meant to darken.

A rather different example is the comedy produced by Pamela's rhetorical excesses. I suspect that many of these may be intentional too, since both B and Mrs Jewkes get in some good digs about her exaggerations; but I think I can produce an example of one that is clearly unintentionally funny, because it comes immediately after the most serious moment in the novel, and is a continuation of it. ' "What then, presumptuous *Pamela*, dost thou *here*?" thought I: Quit with Speed these perilous Banks, and fly from these curling Waters, that seem, in their meaning Murmurs, this still Night, to reproach thy Rashness!"' (I, 236; *I, 152*). The trouble with this sort of thing is that it connects with the problem of unwanted psychological inference: the style may seem to disqualify the sincerity. In the continuation the now genteel Pamela disapproves of 'allegorical or metaphorical style' and says that 'no style can be proper, which is not plain, simple, easy, natural, and unaffected' (IV, 415-17; *II, 447-8*). Yet Richardson lapses again in another wholly serious context in *Grandison*, which I discuss later on.

This is particularly likely to happen when there is too sharp a juxtaposition of, or transition between, an elevated moralisation and a colloquialism. There are two examples of this in Letter 24. Pamela's plea not to be thought presumptuous and conceited about B is immediately followed, with only a dash for transition, by 'But I am to tell you of my new Dress today'; and later, her look in the mirror, 'To say Truth, I never liked myself so well in my Life', is sharply juxtaposed with the key moral bit about descending with ease, innocence, and resignation. To a modern reader, disposed in any case to resent overt moralising, the colloquial speech will seem natural, hence sincere, and the moralising an insincere rationalisation. Two Pamelas lie tellingly side by side, and too many readers feel sure they know which is the 'real' one . . . hence, again, the charges of hypocrisy. Yet Richardson has only to learn to manage the transitions more tactfully (like the similar over-sharp transitions in the attempt to show a mind in conflict, which cause smiles rather than sympathy) and the problem will disappear.

The major source of unwanted psychological inference, however, is a flaw not merely local but in the basic epistolary form itself, as Richardson first conceived it. In focussing the novel through Pamela alone, he failed to count the cost of her letters having to carry all three major formal functions: the narrative, the analytic, and the revelation of character. And this cost proved remarkably high.

The problem of recording praise of the heroine is made insoluble. As I suggested earlier, Richardson's desire to shower his heroine with constant praise is the main cause of the eagerness of many readers to pick holes wherever possible. But when Pamela's overcoming of her vanity becomes a theme, the position is hopeless. Every time someone praises her, as we saw, she is the one who has to tell us, since there is no other way for us to know in the novel as Richardson has organised it. Yet when a reader is encouraged to make psychological and moral inferences by the subtlety of the 'revelatory' techniques, he has to have a sharp sense of fictional form to prevent himself doing likewise from what is, properly, mere narrative. And no amount of disclaiming on Pamela's part can erase the effect of *apparently* watching her receive praise with complacency and retail it with relish – indeed, the apparent discrepancy between the disclaimers and the relish feeds the 'hypocrisy' misreadings once more. If there must be praise, it is far less damaging (though it may still irritate) if it is done through somebody else's letters – as it is in *Clarissa*.

Interestingly, psychological inferences can be drawn almost as easily from the narration of insults. A critic who sees Pamela as lovingly hoarding up the epithets B hurls at her, secretly determined to invite another insult, because she would rather be raped than ignored,[1] is again failing to distinguish where inference is appropriate, and where properly speaking there is merely narrative. We are often quite unaware of the devious ways in which impressions can form in our minds; and where a technique is unfamiliar, and especially where, as in this case, it is still in a formative stage, the danger of making false inferences is acute. Only, if Richardson is at fault for failing to distinguish the problem, he is perhaps more forgivable than critics who show no more awareness, with over two centuries of development in fiction behind them.

One of Richardson's maligned female circle made an interesting point about Clarissa when she told him that however much she admired his heroine, she could not help liking Anna Howe much

[1] F. C. Green, *Minuet* (London, 1935 reprinted 1939), 381.

more because she was less self-conscious.[1] This kind of feeling often underlies a preference for Fielding, and an enthusiastic use of Coleridge's 'sick-room' analogy[2] in undergraduate essays to express the difference. Yet Richardson's main characters seem self-conscious largely because they are made the focus, not just the pawns, of their author's analysis of the human mind. It is through their constant self-examination that the analysis goes on, whereas in Fielding the analysis is the direct responsibility of the author. We confront here the basic formal distinction between epic and drama. Again, however, where there is only one epistolary focus, there is especial danger of half-conscious psychological inference from the form itself. When a critic contends that Pamela's 'dreams are filled with ideas of rape' while 'her waking moments resound to prate about her "honour",'[3] the sheer inaccuracy (for she dreams of rape precisely once, with every excuse) betrays the pressure of the belief that her consciousness is basically unhealthy. A criticism derived from this may show why. 'Innocence is surely not the word best suited to describe the quality of a mind which spent most of its waking hours in a feverish contemplation of the possibility that the body which contained it might conceivably be seduced or violated. Though the ways of the world were not known to her by experience, the defect was made good by the activity of an imagination very ready to conceive and perhaps exaggerate all the dangers which an innocent spirit would discover with surprise.'[4] The view of innocence as a *tabula rasa* is extraordinary – one much prefers Milton's very different concept in *Areopagitica* – but it is useful to have the preconception bared because something like it may well lie behind much more sophisticated

[1] Sarah Chapone to Richardson, Forster XII, 2, fol. 55. See the footnote to Richardson's reply of 18 April 1752; Carroll, *Letters*, 210. A similar point was made by Hazlitt, 'On the English Novelists', *Complete Works*, ed. P. P. Howe (London, 1931), VI, 119.

[2] Coleridge, *Table Talk*, 5 July 1834. See also p. 420 below.

[3] Downs, *Richardson*, 111.

[4] Krutch, *Five Masters*, 128.

criticism. When Ian Watt suggests[1] that we remove the discussion from Pamela's mind to Richardson's reflection of his age, because in the eighteenth century, as Steele pointed out, prude and coquette alike had 'the distinction of sex in all their thoughts, words and actions', the subtlety of the point should not blind us to the fact that there is a vital category missing. Unless we believe that sex has nothing to do with morals, it is not only the prude and coquette who are interested in it in all their thoughts, words and actions, but the analytic moralist also.

Yet may there not be too vibrant a suspiciousness in Pamela, an unhealthy fear? We have already dealt with this question: there is, it is revealed at certain specific points, it is thematic, and whatever Richardson's original ideas may have been, the crux of his novel critically places that fear against the deeper values of love and faith. Unfortunately, this specific and thematic point is constantly being blurred by the more diffuse and half-conscious feeling in critics that the prolonged analysis of a sexual situation, carried through in the mind of a character, *itself* suggests a psychological deduction about the unhealthiness of that mind. Pamela does not spend most of her waking hours in feverish contemplation of seduction; she does spend them in constant analysis of a sexual situation, the moral implications of B's behaviour and her own, and the conclusions that are to be drawn about the future – and she does this as the formal surrogate of her author, the moralist.

Let us imagine another *Pamela*, in which the behaviour would be exactly the same, the analysis would be exactly the same, but both the carrying on of the story and the dissection of its moral implications would be done by the author, except for letters from Pamela at points of crisis to show the state of her mind. We should lose heavily: lose all the advantages of living in a mind and coming to know it intimately in its day-to-day fluctuations. We would gain only one thing: the ease with which we could differentiate between narrative and analysis on one hand, and the revelation of character on the other. We would be prevented

[1] Watt, *Rise of the Novel*, 170.

from making inferences from the mere existence of exhaustive narration and analysis of sexual behaviour – or, for that matter, from the passing on of *double entendre*, of which there are several examples. The novel would be immeasurably the poorer, only accurate criticism would be easier. Yet one can acquire a tact in judging what is a legitimate 'character' inference and what is a consequence of form. There must not of course be any tampering with the impression the fiction makes on our imaginations, but we can attempt to discipline the critical conclusions we draw from our experience. And once again the development of a multi-focus form in Clarissa eased the problem, for it then became not the fact, but the differing tone and quality of narrative and analysis in different correspondents, that was important.

The greatest of all the formal flaws in *Pamela* however, which is also the result of the single focus but is far more damaging, and causes fissures in all sorts of directions, is the failure to give us access to the hero's mind. As we have seen, one of the central ways of misreading *Pamela* is to adopt her view of her master. To pay close attention to what B actually does and says, and to puzzle over what is puzzling about Pamela's account of him, is to discover a character by no means so black and so boobyish, and a great deal more complex and interesting than one had supposed. Yet the true B has apparently remained almost invisible since 1740.[1]

The first reason for this is that Richardson's art of implication is so demanding. It depends absolutely on a reader's willingness to read closely and to ponder for himself the significance of what characters do and say. The real B is 'there' in Pamela's reportage of every dramatic scene, but not obviously, because there is no author to explain and the reader must do the work of understanding. A second reason is the tendency to identify Richardson with Pamela. If this were indeed so, then of course we would expect her account of B to be reliable. In fact, however,

[1] After writing this, I came upon Gwendolyn B. Needham, 'Richardson's Characterization of Mr B and Double Purpose in *Pamela*', *Eighteenth-Century Studies*, 3 (1970), 433-74; a notable exception.

though we cannot but accept her reportage of dramatic scene, since it is all we have, her judgement of her master's character and motives is demonstrably unreliable. Most important of all, however, is the sheer cumulative effect of the single focus itself. Although both B and Pamela are 'on stage', and we are required to understand and judge them both in their opposition, we live almost entirely in her mind, and almost never in his. It is an inevitable danger in point of view writing that readers are tempted to identify with only one point of view, but this is rendered not only possible but probable when the novel is written from a single focus. So to discover the real B through the distorting medium of Pamela's suspicion and fear in the first part of the novel is much more difficult than it need or should have been. His presence is far too sketchy.

It is only too easy to see B's first 'attempts' as merely boobyish and to miss their real meaning altogether, especially on a first reading when one has not yet discovered that all her letters are going straight to him. A single direct insight into his mind before Letter 24 could have made a world of difference in a reader's response to the whole book. Again, if B's defence of his presence in the closet had been available at the time, the critical fortunes of *Pamela* would have been utterly different. In the final scene before the abduction, too, we noticed what a risk Richardson took by giving us no access to B's thoughts and motives – though it may be that one or two earlier glimpses would have been enough to alert readers to the fallibility of Pamela's judgements of him. Just three letters from Lovelace in the first two volumes of *Clarissa*, while not enough to prevent misreading by the careless, were enough to remove all excuse for it.

In 'the wilderness' the difficulty is increased by the long absence of B from the stage. Pamela has left Bedfordshire feeling that he is a 'black-hearted wretch', but even if we suspect how much of a simplification this is, the effect of living in her mind uninterruptedly for so long puts pressure on our memories of his complexity, and if we have not grasped that complexity in the first place, we simplify all the more. So the significance of

B's plea for confidence will be missed, and there will be no imaginative response to the enormity that his suspicion of Pamela and Williams must seem to him.

Our first glimpses of him again, seem to show him in his most brutal and vengeful mood, apparently confirming Pamela's view, and this culminates in the last and most serious of his attempts – though even that is not what Pamela thinks. Then however all is suddenly sweetness and light. A reformed B makes love to her in the garden, and though there is a temporary setback, soon everything in that garden is lovely. Obviously, nearly all critics who have missed the real man have felt that the conversion of Pamela's B is too easy by half, and their irritation works itself out in several directions. Some cast doubts on her apparent abhorrence of his actions throughout, and see the resolution as the final proof that she is only a little politician, whose real objection was merely to B's terms. Others blame Richardson's snobbery: as soon as B ceases for a moment to think of rape he obviously becomes an angel because he is a squire. Whatever the particular line, however, there is disbelief in the reality of B's conversion. If the reformation were truly there, there would be no need to criticise Pamela's acceptance of it.

Yet Richardson obviously intended it to be there and thought that it was; and once the real complexity of B's character and behaviour in the first part of the novel is grasped, this is no longer at all difficult to understand. For the real B, as opposed to the black-hearted wretch and rapist, the reformation is only one rather longer stride on a road we have watched him advancing along steadily, albeit with some backslidings. The 'turn' is easily identified. The firmness of Pamela's rejection of his Articles, and the violence of her reaction to his last 'attempt', finally convince him that she can never be won from any position outside her moral world. Her denial to Mrs Jewkes (when she has no idea of B's presence) of any feeling for Williams; the humility of her behaviour and her disavowal of presumption in advising him not to despise the world's censure; and finally her confession of deep feeling for him, in an atmosphere of sincerity on both sides, remove all the irritants to his pride which caused his lapses and destroyed his previous moral progress. All this makes possible the break with his former self towards which he has been moving throughout. The journal completes the work of re-education which Pamela's example had begun. Moral sensibility is reawakened and confirmed – Richardson always believed, unlike Fielding, in the inherent goodness of all human beings – and after many setbacks B is established in what he now recognises as true happiness.

There is surely nothing incredible or unamiable in this, and it is wholly consistent with the pattern revealed by close attention to both the structure and the texture from the beginning. Yet even after misreadings have been removed, Richardson's perfectly good intentions are not sufficiently achieved in our imaginative experience. We may see when and why B conquers himself, if we read with the sensitive attention the book deserves, but we can never feel how he changes. We do not have a full enough imaginative experience of the battle with himself and its resolution, which is vitally necessary at this point. The build-up of pride, cynicism and callousness throughout the book has been too strong, and the experience of moral progress too far back, for us not to need a powerful experience of his conversion now, if we are to be convinced. This could only be achieved by direct insight into his mind, of comparable strength to the experience we have of Pamela – and the single-focus epistolary form prevents this. To see so crucial a change only by glimpses is not nearly enough; it is not proved on our pulses. And if the conversion is not real enough, doubts are liable to be cast on Pamela's enthusiastic welcome of it, her return to B, her gratitude and meekness, which ought never to have arisen. Critics who thunder at these ought to be discussing B not Pamela, and his character as realised not as intended; but the fault is Richardson's and it is a very bad one. Nevertheless it is basically a failure in technique, not in morals, and it comes about because he was so enthusiastically exploiting the resources of his new discovery on Pamela's behalf, that he failed completely to notice its disastrous limitation for his hero. Richardson's haste to draw over-simple moral lessons is also visible in the editorial link between Pamela's letters and her journals, where he speaks of 'the base Arts of designing Men to gain their wicked Ends' (I, 120; *I, 76*).

2

The first set of distorting factors in *Pamela*, then, which help to explain its ultimate failure, are technical. We can account for the great achievement of *Clarissa* so soon afterwards by showing how Richardson's growing understanding of his medium helped him to solve or at least temper each of these problems in his new novel. At a stroke many apparently moral failings are removed, not through moral change, but technical development.

Yet these technical factors, though they go a surprisingly long way towards explaining what went wrong with *Pamela*, do not themselves go quite far enough. As soon as we ask why such a subtle and analytic mind failed to see the effects of his technical failures early enough to remedy them, we are led to deeper considerations. Though it is disastrous to treat a novel as a psychiatric case-book or as autobiography, it is of course true that novelists do reveal themselves in their books, and it may be that the final comment on puzzling features will be found in the author's character . . . in the last resort.

I suspect that behind Richardson's failure to see early enough how these technical blemishes were distorting his book, lie ambivalences in his own attitude to vanity, to the elements of calculation and intrigue in prudence, and to social distinctions.

The discussion of vanity is prominent in *Pamela*, but in dealing with it Richardson was dealing with one of his own greatest weaknesses. This is well illustrated in a gleaning of Boswell's. 'One day at his country-house at Northend, where a large company was assembled at dinner, a gentleman who was just returned from Paris, willing to please Mr Richardson, mentioned to him a very flattering circumstance – that he had seen his

Clarissa lying on the King's brother's table. Richardson, observing that part of the company were engaged in talking to each other, affected then not to attend to it. But by and by, when there was a general silence, and he thought that the flattery might be fully heard, he addressed himself to the gentleman, "I think, Sir, you were saying something about", . . . pausing in a high flutter of expectation. The gentleman, provoked at his inordinate vanity, resolved not to indulge it, and with an exquisitely sly air of indifference answered, "A mere trifle, Sir, not worth repeating." The mortification of Richardson was visible, and he did not speak ten words more the whole day.'[1]

There is much evidence to support this. Richardson was extremely diffident, and there can be no doubt that he had deep need of praise, naturally accompanied by marked sensitivity to criticism and hostile challenge. He could not have written as he did without his coterie of admirers, a circle of more intelligence and charm than is often allowed, who recognised both his merits and his needs, and indulged the latter, as Boswell's gentleman refused to do, because of their genuine admiration for the former. Yet this need for praise remains a weakness which could have unpleasant consequences. One of the most revealing sections of Richardson's correspondence has remained largely unnoticed.[2] He was hoodwinked by an oily projector and lawyer called Eusebius Silvester, to whom he gave great encouragement in various plans to better himself and also, with characteristic generosity, lent sums of money which he never recovered. Silvester won Richardson over by excessive flattery, not of his mind or personality but of the moral worth of his writings; flattery which any reader of the correspondence should see through, but which Richardson, the master of judging character by style, was unable to recognise. Because of his own nature and psychological needs it would seem that flattery did not immediately repel him, for the very reason that it was directed towards moral characteristics. He

[1] Boswell, *Life of Dr Johnson*, ed. G. Birkbeck Hill, rev. L. F. Powell (Oxford, 1934), IV, 28-9.

[2] Forster, XIV, 4; XV, 1. But see Eaves and Kimpel, *Richardson*, 465-70.

seems to have confused apparent moral direction with real moral quality. Yet his pain and anger on discovering how he had been duped are surprisingly moving, and his reaction was characteristic – he kept the correspondence intact for the rest of his life as an exemplum for his family.

Now this trait may help to explain some features of his novel. The 'puffing' letters he prefixed to the first edition were parodied by Fielding, and Dr Johnson and many others found them objectionable. We need to remember that Richardson was printer and publisher as well as author, that he felt shielded by his anonymity, and that the letters were meant to serve exactly the same function as a modern publisher's blurb.[1] Yet this can only be a partial defence, and Richardson himself realised subsequently that he had gone too far. Once again he had failed to be repelled by fulsomeness in praise of morality. Similarly, behind the deeper and more worthy reasons for the choric praise in the last section, may lurk the half-conscious need to surround his character with the same supply of admiration that he found necessary to his own wellbeing and happiness.

This may at least help to explain why he failed to see any danger in Pamela's retailing of these praises. The problem remains primarily technical and in *Clarissa* he learned a good deal about how to solve it; but behind the technical crudity there may lie this personal weakness. If he had seen the danger he could easily have provided another source of letters – say, Pamela's father staying on and writing to his wife – in order to carry the narrative of the choric scenes. His inability to see any danger argues some personal insensitivity.

I have however already argued that the matter is more complicated still, for when the problem was brought home to him he would not alter his basic position, and developed it into some by no means despicable ideas about the essentially public nature of morality, and the sense of moral community. I have also

[1] See McKillop, *Richardson*, 42-3. The prefatory material has been edited, and Richardson's revisions studied, by Sheridan W. Baker, Augustan reprint no. 48 (Los Angeles, 1954).

argued that he was not alone in feeling that the pleasure of moral self-approval is a good thing that needs no apology. It could be argued that he came to these ideas in an attempt to rationalise his own weakness, but even so one would have to admit that he develops them in worthy directions.

Yet the awkwardness of reconciling self-congratulation with true modesty remains. It is all too easy on the basis of such ideas for author or character to slip into complacency, priggishness, self-righteousness, pride. There is still greater danger when it is not only self-approval or the graceful acceptance of praise that is in question, but the engineering of it. Not only does Richardson seem to have believed too easily that self-congratulation could co-exist with true humility, but he also failed to see that there could be unamiable calculation behind the impulse to secure the moral approval of others. This is a marked feature of Pamela as Richardson presents her, and it often occurs in a context of unmistakeable authorial approval, as in the 'Bundle' scene. We can see how it relates to her loneliness and youth, and to Richardson's idea of community, but there remains an awkwardness of which he seems insufficiently aware. One feels that he knows too little at this stage of how good impulses can contain less good ones, and that he takes the desire and pursuit of virtue too much at face value, as he did with Eusebius Silvester. At some points there can be a failure of analysis which is at least partly owing to his inability completely to analyse himself. Yet at the centre his imagination transcends his defects. By the pond, pride, calculation and contrivance are firmly rejected for faith in God and Man; and at the crisis of her return to B, Pamela rises above her hypersensitivity to public opinion, learning the faith to be imprudent in going against the wise world's censure.

I have indeed argued that the greatest moral achievement in *Pamela* is the way in which Richardson's understanding of some of the limitations of prudence grows in his act of creation. Yet one way of appreciating this is by detecting how strong the pressure against this growth could be in Richardson's mind, and consequently how he was always liable to slip back into more native and congenial but less wholesome and humanly attractive attitudes, as soon as his imagination flagged and he became Mr Richardson again. Perhaps the reason why his achievement has not been sufficiently recognised is the presence of inconsistencies which distort it.

The critical placing of the elements, in prudence, of suspicion and fear remains firm, and is indeed repeated, if less explicitly, in the continuation. But the placing of the ways in which prudential calculation can issue in intrigue, equivocation and deceit is far less secure. At the height of her new self-knowledge Pamela realises there had been something wrong with her contrivances; and in the new emphasis on faith and trust, openness and sincerity, there is implicit judgement of her equivocation and intrigue. It does not matter that B, when he reads her journal, condones and even praises her artfulness with some amusement, for this is quite in keeping with his character. But Mr Richardson, in the moral summary which he appended to the novel, has sunk back into his ordinary self. Where the dramatic artist is constantly driven to test, question and criticise, Mr Richardson will see or allow no flaw in his heroine. He contends for her 'signal *veracity*' and 'the innocence she preserved in all her stratagems and contrivances' (I, 452), and it would seem that only her pride in them was wrong. Of course she was forced to scheme to get away, in her own defence, and we would think less of her if she had not; but there is more than that involved, all the same, more even than pride and self-reliance. It is not these which make her decide to encourage John's repentance in the hope of strategic advantage, or which explain the facility with which she equivocates and finally lies. At the full stretch of the artist's imagination the pond scenes imply a criticism of these traits and an endorsement of sincerity, truth and trust; but Mr Richardson seems either to have forgotten, or not to have fully grasped what the dramatic imagination had done. And, once again, the myopia may connect with his own personality. He unquestionably loved intrigue: the story of his own first meeting with Lady Bradshaigh is the best known of many illustrations from his correspondence.

He also enjoyed equivocation in bantering argument. In his life these things were always harmless and playful, the result more of a rather naïve and amusing delight in his own ingenuity, than any real tendency to dishonesty. In his art, the same tendencies were also of course active in the creation of B, and still more so in the far greater creation of Lovelace. Yet we can see once again how his own traits may help to explain his apparent inability to see a problem clearly.

Lastly, while the failure to create B's reformation remains a technical one, and wholly avoidable by technical improvement, the failure to see at once that something had gone badly wrong may have been partly owing to a latent snobbery. His imagination seems to get caught up in the fairy-tale elevation of his heroine, and its appeal is dependent on the glamour and kindness of the prince, seen quite uncritically. Richardson obviously had his own idea of B firmly in mind, but he allowed himself, in giving the rein to his interest in status, to forget that Pamela's idea of B had been very different. So though he had been careful to satisfy B of Pamela's integrity through the reading of the journal, it seems never to occur to him that it is far more necessary to satisfy Pamela that her view of his past actions had been distorted. Moreover Richardson allows B to behave with palpable condescension towards her and this, together with the extraordinary meekness and humility on her part which must show her avoidance of presumption, is quite enough to justify the irritation many readers feel. The central social vision of the novel, of course, is not snobbish. Though Richardson's mind was deeply conservative and hierarchic, we have seen how uncompromisingly social distinctions are referred to morality and to religion, and how on that basis there can be a questioning of social injustice and arrogance, a latent radicalism, an insistence that Pamela should be treated as a human being, who is indeed as worthy of her new station as any duchess. Nevertheless, if B is allowed to show far too much condescension and too little contrition, if he is not obliged to satisfy Pamela that he never was the villain she thought him, the failure to spot the flaw may well be the effect of a snobbery latent in the sense of hierarchy.

I do not believe that these traits of character explain the technical failures. They merely help us to see why Richardson did not immediately diagnose and remedy what had gone wrong, and why in some directions he could seem curiously blind to the nature of his own imaginative achievement. Moreover we must not be glib: character flaws can spring from impulses not at all bad in themselves, and can have odd relations to artistic strength. The way that good is liable to become bad if not held in proportion, and bad lead to good, is one of the paradoxes of life and the challenges of art. Richardson's humility and diffidence are by no means unamiable, but they have the closest connection with his vanity and snobbery. His devious ingenuity and his delight in intrigue, his sharp calculation of effect and inference, may be responsible for one or two moral wobbles in his work, but they are no less responsible for a great deal of its strength and subtlety. Finally, as Lawrence's famous dictum insists, it is the tale that is important, especially since one of the things it shows us is how a 'teller's' imagination may raise him above himself.

3

What however of another contention of Lawrence, that Richardson had an unhealthy attitude to sex? As we saw, *Pamela* ran into trouble in this respect from the beginning. Povey and his kind objected to the 'warm scenes' as inflammatory, while Fielding insinuated that the real appeal was the offer, behind a cloak of prudery, of vicarious sexual experience, which squares well enough with Lawrence's 'calico purity and underclothes excitement'.[1] From this it is only a short step to make Richardson an exemplar of puritan sexual maladjustment. At the end of this line a critic writes: 'What is it that the Puritan cannot get out

[1] *Phoenix – The Posthumous Papers of D. H. Lawrence*, ed. Edward D. McDonald (London, 1936), 552.

of his mind, so that it is a mania and an obsession? It is sex. Richardson is mad about sex. His is the madness of Paul Pry and Peeping Tom . . . Prurient and obsessed by sex, the prim Richardson creeps on tiptoe nearer and nearer, inch by inch . . . he beckons us on, pausing to make every kind of pious protestation, and then nearer and nearer he creeps again . . . working us up until we catch the obsession too.'[1] This would obviously be a totally disabling charge if it were true. But is it?

There is no inference to be drawn from the choice of a sexual subject. It is easy to see how in any century when the position of women was subordinate and confined, the world of sexual relationship and love would seem the one in which the feminine character could be most subtly analysed. Richardson is indeed part of a puritan development in this direction so marked that it brought about a change in the meaning of the word 'virtue'. One can see this happening in *Comus*, where Milton starts by talking of virtue, then defines it as chastity, and ends by talking of virginity. In writings strongly influenced by puritanism 'virtue' may indeed *mean* chastity, or even virginity, as it often does in *Pamela*. But however one may sense dangers in this of denying the value of sexual love on the one hand, or unhealthy interest in sex on the other, the answer will lie in the treatment, not the choice of subject, or the definition of virtue within a single area of experience.

Now it is hard to see how any normal reader could possibly find the treatment of sex in *Pamela* inflammatory, or even mildly exciting. The sexual scenes are constructed with mechanical repetition. They all follow the same pattern: the verbal sparring, the offer of indecency which is always the same ('I found his hand in my bosom'), and the ending in shrieks, tears, and fainting fits. The dramatic high point tends to be near the beginning, after which any narrative excitement there had been steadily declines. The scenes are markedly theatrical, and to most modern readers would seem to cry out for parody rather than underclothes excitement. Indeed if they were meant to be pornographic, the inference would surely be that Richardson knew too little

[1] V. S. Pritchett, 'Clarissa' in *The Living Novel* (London, 1946), 10.

about sex to excite any but the hotly prurient, for whom the mere existence of a sexual situation with an uncertain outcome would suffice.

In fact, as we have seen, the really important and surprising thing about the sexual scenes is that they are not essentially about sex at all – they are about pride. Hence the potentially comic verbalising, the absence of action (what Mrs Jewkes understandably calls 'dilly dallying'), the eagerness to 'expostulate', the techniques of blackmail. And this, strangely enough, is why the scenes do have an obsessive quality, though it has little to do with sexuality and nothing with Peeping Tom. The motivation is cooler, in some ways deadlier than lust, which may make the whole business unpleasant, but in no way that runs counter to Richardson's intention. Moreover, once it is clear that the scenes are not about lust, the narrative repetitiveness leaves one free to concentrate on the key question of why things happen as they do, and then it appears that the scenes do differ, and differ thematically. The 'events' remain the same, but what is going on behind them is quite different, as the implicitly invited comparisons bring out. The episodes in the summer-house and the dressing-room are both attempts by wounded pride to reassert itself, but they differ sharply in tone – the eagerness of the first, the taunting cynicism of the second which betrays B's characteristic reaction to humiliation – and they differ also in the mounting degree of Pamela's misunderstanding of his behaviour. The Closet scene, on the other hand, is founded on so great a misunderstanding that B is, amusingly, as much a victim as Pamela. The episode has a splendidly comic side, which depends on two of the actors believing it is an attempt at rape, while the supposed rapist is increasingly embarrassed and infuriated by the volume of fuss which he doesn't understand – and isn't allowed to discuss or defend himself against. Whereas the final attempt does begin with the intention of rape, though for revenge and subjugation, not desire – but it continues in mere stubborn pride, unwilling to give in to fear of wrongdoing, and trying hopelessly to salvage something. The melodrama and the sexual action (and inaction) are 'all detestable grimace' because B is playing a game he knows to be a losing one and for which he has already lost heart. It is an extraordinary scene but what is most extraordinary about it is that it has really as little as possible to do with sexuality, given the initial situation. It is the last kick of B's pride, brought remorselessly to face its consequences in the 'death' of the girl he loves. The result is tenderness, and there is no need for B's subsequent change to seem surprising.

The 'sexual' scenes then are not about sex; they are extensions and intensifications of a treatment of pride. Richardson, one suspects, knew little about sexuality but he did know a great deal about the monomania of pride, and hence these scenes do have a certain compulsion once they are understood. In the discrepancy between the theatricality and the baffled, obsessive twistings and turnings of the ego, lies the meaning. The scenes are scenes of humiliation, of B.

Yet if the charge of prurience will not hold water, there may nevertheless be some substance in the feeling that Richardson's general attitude to sex in Pamela is unsatisfactory. Daiches objects to 'Richardson's narrow and mechanical view of sex and indeed of love. . . . Sex, wherever it is treated in Richardson, is presented as something violent and violating. The notion of mutual sexual satisfaction does not occur to him.'[1] This seems to me a much more searching and accurate criticism, though the last assertion is open to challenge. The charge is not that Richardson goes on too much about sex, but too little; or rather that he sees too little of its full human potential and significance, that he degrades it in treating it too narrowly and mechanically. Sex can be violent and violating and there is nothing wrong with showing this, but an author ought not to suggest that sex is always and only so.

Richardson's idea of purity does seem to involve a hypersensitive delicacy. It is not only that Pamela's abhorrence of sexual violation makes her faint at the suggestion of it; she is confused and embarrassed by B's gift of stockings at the beginning

[1] Daiches, *Essays*, 41.

of the book, and hardly less so at her future husband's delicate insinuation that part of her time after marriage may be occupied with children. This exaggerated delicacy has led to questionings of the 'purity' it tries to suggest. Yet surely Shaw's remark that 'Delicacy is indelicacy's conspiracy of silence' is too pat.[1] Does a horror of corporal punishment reveal a secret sadism? It may, but it surely need not. Pamela's delicacy is both unnecessary and ridiculous by our standards, but it is misleading to isolate its sexual manifestations, for it is the product of a would-be refinement that points in many other directions too. Ladies must not discuss politics as well as sex; it is indecorous for them to hunt as well as wear breeches; true ladies are physically as well as morally delicate. We watch a definition of femininity which is silly in many different ways, but it is hardly necessary to call the sexual ones indecent. It is not so very long ago that a young girl could be embarrassed by a gift of underwear from someone she 'hardly knew' and could feel that it was 'too personal'; or that a bride-to-be might colour up if the discussion turned to her future motherhood. Do we have to brand such things as morally questionable; and, conversely, are we quite so sure now that outspokenness is a sign of moral health?

I argue so, not to dispose of the charge, but to suggest that the discussion has been altogether too glib, has proceeded on questionable evidence, and has come to quite unnecessarily harsh conclusions. In the process, the one crucial piece of evidence has never been mentioned: Pamela's reaction to her wedding night. Her journal up to eleven o'clock is marked by the excessive apprehension that has been obvious all day, though she knows it is wrong and has tried to control it. The entries conclude with the sort of prayer a gladiator might make before entering the arena. So far, so bad. Yet the following morning she writes exultantly: 'O How this dear excellent Man indulges me in every thing! Every Hour he makes me happier, by his sweet Condescension, than the former. He pities my Weakness of Mind, allows for all my little Foibles, indeavours to dissipate my Fears;

[1] Quoted by Ian Watt, *Rise of the Novel*, 169.

his Words are so pure, his Ideas so chaste, and his whole Behaviour so sweetly decent, that never, surely, was so happy a Creature as your *Pamela*! I never could have hoped such a Husband could have fallen to my Lot...' (II, 156; *I, 316*). The emphasis still falls far too heavily on delicacy, on Pamela's delighted surprise that B should be so 'sweetly decent'. One smiles – yet the passage hardly shows that the idea of mutual sexual satisfaction never occurs to Richardson, for behind the primness Pamela's happiness and satisfaction seem to me to come through clearly enough. (We would hardly expect her to be explicit.) Moreover the point she so appreciates in B's delicacy is not merely prudish, but is the manifestation of tenderness, consideration, and generosity.

Richardson's treatment of sexual love in *Pamela* still leaves a great deal to be desired. It is indeed too narrow, too prim, too apologetic, too frightened. There is too vibrant an awareness of what is potentially violating, frightening, degrading or embarrassing about sex; and too little idea of what is potentially exciting, liberating and enriching. But I do not think that there is any more prurience in his delicacy than there was in the apparent 'sexual attempts'. Richardson has not escaped the narrow conditioning of his environment and upbringing; yet, as with the problem of prudence, we can watch his imagination beginning to transcend the limitations of his ordinary self.

Indeed, the whole growth of Pamela's feeling for B represents an imaginative break with puritan strictness. In her very first impression of B – 'he gave these good Things to us both with such a Graciousness, as I thought he look'd like an Angel' – gratitude, moral approval, and physical attraction happily coincide in the girl's fervour (I, 12; *I, 7*). But her feelings go on developing below the surface of her consciousness when gratitude and approval are impossible; as we see from significant slips of language (I, 53; *I, 34*), from her revealing distress at B's hatred (I, 65; *I, 40*), and her frightened self-mistrust when he treats her tenderly (I, 109; *I, 70*). There is no hypocrisy and no design, but there is a nascent love of which she is never aware, precisely because she is a puritan to whom it cannot occur that she could love where she heartily disapproves. She may wonder why she feels only relief when B escapes drowning; but when she cries 'O what an Angel would he be in my Eyes yet, if he would cease his Attempts, and reform', she cannot see how the echoing of that never-effaced first impression suggests a feeling that has already escaped the moral conditions she sets (I, 243; *I*, *156*). This shadowing-in of a dimension of unconscious conflict is something that Richardson does particularly well. His imaginative realisation of the eddying and often amoral feelings behind the moral choices we make is one of the great leaps forward in the history of the novel, and one of the reasons why he was called 'the Master of the Heart'. Long before Pamela finally realises the state of her heart on her way home, we ought to have been aware of her eddying feelings adding meaning to half a dozen thoughts and remarks I have not touched on. (Richardson's only tactlessness is to be too explicit in her reply to B's first Article.) Pamela may assure her parents that B's 'Vices all *ugly him over*', but it isn't true (I, 269; *I*, *172*). When all is past, she finally realises and tells Lady Davers that she had always 'thought all his good Actions doubly good; and for his naughty ones, tho' I abhorred his Attempts upon me, yet I could not hate him; and always wish'd him well; but I did not know that it was Love' (II, 296; *I*, *410*).

Nevertheless, on every occasion when she is required to make a decision she decides on the moral course against the secret feelings. There is no hypocrisy, unless the unsuspected presence of mixed emotions is hypocritical, in which case scarcely one of us is not so. Yet Richardson's imagination does imply a more humane and realistic attitude towards sexuality than Mr Richardson would be prepared to admit – as we shall see when we come to *Clarissa*. The dramatic artist knows very well, and apparently sees no reason to condemn, the fact that Pamela is sexually in love with a man whose behaviour she believes to be corrupt. The repression involved in this helps to explain why her feelings flower so abundantly whenever she can sanction them or give them some moral expression. Her outburst on her knees, when B defends her from Mrs Jervis as she is leaving, has been called 'ludicrous',[1] but the fact that it is referred to several times shows that it must be significant, and its significance is that B's 'goodness' is not the cause, but the *excuse* for her real feelings to escape.

So though Richardson's treatment of sex is far too narrow, there are signs of imaginative progress beyond the rigidity of puritan positions. There remains however a last difficulty about the apparent equation of the loss of virtue with the loss of virginity. There seems to be a muddle when Pamela, rejecting the Articles, begs him to consider 'what Remorse will attend your dying Hour, when you come to reflect, that you have ruin'd, perhaps, Soul and Body, a wretched Creature, whose only Pride was her Virtue!' (I, 263; *I*, *168*). Yet the 'perhaps' is a warning, and we may notice that twice during her detailed reply to the Articles she is perfectly clear that her innocence will be unchanged because her will would play no part in her violation. Moreover the Godfrey episode both adds a final comment on Richardson's attitude to sin even when the will is guilty; and, in a passage subsequently cut from the moral which deals with her, provides the probable explanation of the 'perhaps' in the suggestion that one fault makes another and another easier to commit, so that a first fall through moral ignorance can land up in prostitution. We may perhaps accuse Richardson of so much imprecision in using 'virtue' to mean both innocence and virginity, that 'rather my life than my vartue' becomes an obvious parody hit; but if his own attitude was ambiguous when he began the book, the ambiguity is resolved by the end.

Related to this, however, is the failure to differentiate between kinds of 'trial', and hence between kinds of virtue called into play. Pamela tends to treat her resistances as morally equivalent, or rather, she is allowed to speak of two of her 'trials' – the ones she takes to be attempted rape – as the worst of all. This they may be in a simple physical sense, but in any moral sense they are the occasions on which she is least tried. One does not praise

[1] Eaves and Kimpel, *Richardson*, 107.

someone for morality in not allowing themselves to be raped if they can help it. Had she been tried in a scene where B's gentleness and tenderness brought out her own secret feelings, that would have been 'worst of all' because her purity would be tested as it clearly is not, for example, in the Closet episode. Of course Richardson does write such a scene, and Pamela triumphs, though by postponing it to the end of the first section the scales are a bit weighted, since she has by that time very solid reasons for distrusting B. The same point needs to be made about the Articles, and the final 'attempt'. If we talk of Pamela's resistance, we are for much of the time talking about resistance in physical and economic terms rather than terms of purity. There are values involved, of courage, determination and disinterestedness, but they amount to less than Pamela seems to think.

On the other hand, this is not a criticism of Richardson's creation itself, but of the apparent attitude towards it, or evaluation of it, that one may infer from Pamela's language, the choric praises, and Mr Richardson's own moral summary. The undifferentiated praise of Pamela's 'resistance', and her own view of the 'rape' scenes as her worst trials, leave the assumption too open that there is as much emphasis on resistance to force and finance as on the far deeper values which send Pamela into the wilderness, and then in the two pond scenes and the return, send her back in love and faith.

4

A similar distinction between creation and creator ought to lie behind the discussion of another fundamental criticism of *Pamela*: the implications of the sub-title 'Virtue Rewarded'.

The fairy-tale element in the novel reaches its apotheosis here. Behind *Pamela* stretches a long history of domestic sub-literature where everything always comes right in the end, the good little girl gets her quite specific reward, and the children are encouraged to believe that this is the way of God's world. One can also see how Mr Richardson's uncompromisingly didactic view of the novel encourages the impulse to sort out the sheep from the goats with a very explicit and material bill of lading, so that moral evaluation is confirmed by results. Yet in a novel as serious, indeed, as our analysis has shown, ultimately as religious as this one, such insistence of rewards and punishments will not do. It is true neither to life, nor to morals, nor to Christianity.

Yet one must be aware once more of what precisely one is objecting to. The root of the common criticism is the contention that Pamela is good not for goodness sake, but because it pays. 'Virginity is the best policy.' Mrs Barbauld began this, with her assertion that 'She has an end in view, an interested end, and we can only consider her as the conscious possessor of a treasure, which she wisely resolved not to part with, but for its just price.'[1] Yet on every single occasion bar one, Pamela acts against her own secret wishes, with materially nothing to gain and everything to lose. There is not a shred of evidence that she ever imagines, in Mrs Peachum's words, that 'by keeping men off, you keep them on' – though this is indeed the case with B. On the exceptional occasion, when she does turn back to B, it is to a man she at last knows she loves, whose reformation though by no means fully enough explored is 'there' by the implications of his behaviour over a long and subtle development; and most of all, the decision is in specific disobedience to the dictates of calculating prudence. It is made to depend on a new, very imprudent faith in God and Man, and is structurally related to the excessively imprudent and unjust dictates of full Christian forgiveness.

It is open to the critic to say that it is immoral to love a man who has behaved like B, even if he seems to have made a break with his past; and that it is immoral to be able to blot out that past in a forgiveness excessive enough to enrol repentant sinners 'in the rank of the most virtuous', simply because they have made a fresh start. Only, if this is what we want to say let us

[1] Barbauld, *Correspondence*, I, lxiii.

say it clearly, in awareness of what saying it implies. Let us not, on the other hand, talk too much about the jewel market.

Pamela herself makes a very relevant remark about the way 'the World' will probably judge her decision to go back to B. 'For, to be sure, the World, the *wise* World, that never is wrong itself, judges always by Events. And if he should use me ill, then I shall be blamed for trusting him: If well, O then I did right to be sure! – But, How would my Censurers act in my Case, before the Event justifies or condemns the Action, is the Question?' (II, 14; *I*, *224*). And so it is, indeed. Only Pamela does not foresee that the world may come to censure her because things turn out *well*, feeling in an unformulated way that the happy ending mars the disinterestedness; that her virtue would have been greater if things had fallen out badly; or even that the event shows what the motivation was really like. Yet if she had foreseen this, she might presumably have made the same reply: that the moral value of the decision is not to be sought in the rewards or punishments, be they what they may.

On the other hand she could also not have foreseen that her creator would argue by results – not in the book itself, but in his way of referring to it and recommending it by moral summary. 'And the Editor of these Sheets will have his End, if it [sic] inspires a laudable emulation in the Minds of any worthy Persons, who may thereby intitle themselves to the Rewards, the Praises, and the Blessings, by which she was so deservedly distinguished' (*I*, *453*, cut from 1st edition in S.H. ed.). One can see the difference between author/creator and author/commentator by watching the slipping from one little word to another in parallel accounts. It is one thing to praise God as Pamela does because He *can* change distress to happiness, or even frequently *does* reward sufferers with good. It is quite another for her creator to recommend the novel to clergymen, those of desponding heart, those of poor estate, and so on, as evidence that God always *will*. This is precisely liable to imply a kind of insurance or market value for virtue, and one does find commercial imagery creeping into the discussion.

The sub-title, and the state of mind that appended it, are naïve, crude, and inconsistent with the faith Mr Richardson professes; but once again the trouble lies with the ordinary self of the author, commenting on the work of his imagination when the imagination has lapsed. In recommending his novels he always goes for their simplest and most immediately didactic message. He believed, rather crudely, that books had specific and immediate moral effects on their readers, and his recommendations usually go bald-headed at capitalising these effects. This partly explains, though it by no means excuses, the discrepancy between the naïve sub-title and 'morals', and the complexity of the moral experience in the fiction itself. It takes close reading and some thought to appreciate that complexity, and the placing of prudential calculation in it, but the implication that virtue is the best policy can be hammered home without delay. Furthermore Mr Richardson was recommending his book to a very unsubtle middle and lower class audience; though quite how unsubtle he was not to discover until the mangled readings of *Clarissa.* We must look to the fiction, not the packaging.

What the fiction shows is that there is a strong element of prudential calculation in the heroine, but directed rather to the reward of moral approval than material interest. The structure of the novel, and its central concern with faith as a criticism of prudence, implies a critical placing of her strategic calculations. Nevertheless the element of prudential calculation is a native characteristic of Richardson himself, and he is always hypersensitive to public opinion. So though at the centre of the novel he becomes aware of the unamiable elements of prudence, he is always liable to slip back; and because the securing of public approval connects so closely with his ideas of community, while rewards of moral pleasure are also crucially part of his break with puritanism, one is never confident that the element of calculation is firmly placed throughout. There is no point at which Pamela's decisions are materially 'interested', but one is not at all sure that Richardson sees anything wrong in Pamela's angling for the rewards of moral approval, and fairly certain that he believed in the reward of moral pleasure. This is a far cry from parting with her jewel when the price is right. It is also very different from the crudity visible in Mr Richardson's sub-title and moral summary – though it is worth pointing out that in the summary the 'rewards' are glossed by 'praises' and 'blessings', not income and status. Nevertheless we see again very clearly the power of Richardson's dramatic imagination, in seeing the ordinary mentality it develops from and is in tension with, what it leaves behind in its reaching out beyond prudence to faith, love, forgiveness, and their power of regeneration.

5

In just two months, Richardson achieved a whole new dimension in English fiction. For the first time the inner life of a character was conveyed in an intimate, complex, and convincing way. Nobody has ever doubted Pamela's vitality; the way she lives to the imagination. Again for the first time, a character was created who convincingly developed, through day to day fluctuations, during the whole course of the novel. There is also far more to the hero and more development of him, than has ever been realised, though Richardson's failure to give us full enough access to his mind is the most serious flaw in the book. For all its apparent artlessness, moreover, the novel patterns and structures its scenes, both in themselves and in relation to one another, with a serious and interesting purpose that goes far deeper than mere characterisation. Two opposing mental worlds are set in conflict, and out of that conflict emerges not only an attempt to show the nature of regeneration, but also to analyse the nature of virtue and the foundation of happiness more searchingly than had ever been attempted before in English fiction. The exploration is not only ethical but overtly religious, and the final issues at stake go far beyond the sexual situation from which they begin.

Nevertheless *Pamela* clearly fails to achieve its full potential. Had Richardson been able to articulate and explore his medium and his meanings successfully, such widespread misreading could not have occurred. I have tried to get at those meanings at some length, but I may well have made them clearer than the book. Although Richardson is by no means an unconscious artist, and was far more aware of what he was doing than the numerous critics who have patronised him, he was still feeling his way; exploring and testing his own attitudes in projecting his dramatic imagination into the minds of his characters. He brings up more problems than he fully realises or resolves, and he is unaware of some difficulties and hazards, but since he is in the act of evolving a complex new literary form this is hardly surprising.

I have tried to show how most of the distortions are caused by technical flaws, though some of Richardson's personal traits may explain why he failed to spot the trouble, and there are crudities in several of his attitudes. Indeed, there are sufficient reasons to conclude that the work is ultimately a failure – though on a far higher level than has been supposed. One's reservations about Richardson's attitudes to sexual love, to social distinction, and to vanity, and above all the very serious effects of the restriction to a single epistolary focus, are enough to reduce the novel's full potential.

Yet the exciting thing about *Pamela* is that it develops so far in the direction of success. So much was against Richardson: the cramping narrowness of his environment and his experience, the limitations of his education and his reading, the lower middle class and rather puritanical outlook in which his mind was moulded. What is astonishing – and moving – is the way that the dramatic imagination of this rather ordinary man explores and transcends the kind of attitudes from which it starts – to quite extraordinary effect. He may never quite succeed, in *Pamela*, in getting some things clear, in suffusing the whole texture with the understanding he reached at the centre, so that the meaning is articulated beyond all power of mistaking. He sometimes seems unaware of the implications of his own achievement, is liable to slip back, resimplify, coarsen. Yet it no longer seems extraordinary that he should have written *Clarissa* so soon. The development of technical understanding removed at a stroke most of the major flaws, and the development beyond uncertainty and hesitation of some of *Pamela*'s hard-won insights, led to a work of whose sombre and compelling power there has seldom been any doubt. If Pamela fails it is not ignobly, for it is clearly the foundation of success.

PART TWO

Clarissa

CHAPTER FIVE

Three Worlds

(*The First Instalment*)

I

Clarissa is actually three novels in one, each with a different focus. Unfortunately, later editions have obscured the divisions that were clear in the original publication by instalment; and the deepening exploration from one dimension to another tends to be obscured by the sheer length of the whole. This may prompt even admirers who read to the end to base their judgements too narrowly on the more social focus from which the book begins.

The best known discussions have indeed come from those who are interested in fiction as a reflection of society[1]; while the work of social historians, especially Professor Habbakuk,[2] has cast new light on certain social changes in the eighteenth century, which lie behind the persecution of the heroine in the first instalment. We have, consequently, a new sense of the novel's relevance to its time and of the quality of its social criticism. Where Clara Thomson at the turn of the century found the behaviour of the Harlowes, and hence the whole basic situation,

[1] Arnold Kettle, *An Introduction to the English Novel* (London, 1951), I, 65-71; Ian Watt, *Rise of the Novel*, chapter 7; Christopher Hill, 'Clarissa Harlowe and her Times', *Essays in Criticism*, 5 (1955), 315-40.

[2] 'Marriage Settlements in the 18th Century', *Trans. of Royal Hist. Soc.* (1950), 24-5; 'English Land-ownership, 1680-1740', *Econ. Hist. Review* (1940), 6-10. See Christopher Hill, 'Clarissa Harlowe and her Times', 315-19.

incredible,[1] we have now been given a lively sense of the forces which did in fact go to create such situations, and can see how accurately Richardson diagnoses contemporary problems. We have also been taught to read Clarissa as a paradigm of the finest kind of protestant or puritan rebellion: the refusal to bend before the forces in contemporary life which threatened individual freedom and integrity. Clarissa's tragedy is an exposure of a materialist and acquisitive society; of the moral decay of both the aristocracy and the 'middle class'; of a view of human relationship grounded on money and property. It is a revelation of the tensions, within the bourgeois world to which Richardson himself belonged, between its twin inheritances from the seventeenth century: capitalism, and individualism. We have been given a *Clarissa* in which all that makes the individual life valuable is in danger from the pressures of a morally corrupt materialism.

This is all gain. Yet *Clarissa* is no more an essentially social novel than *Pamela*, though its social criticism is far sharper and more profound. The exploration of social problems serves the same function in both: it brings into focus the moral and religious problems that lie behind. To overemphasise the social dimension of *Clarissa* is to simplify more and more dangerously as the book proceeds; to say valuable things about the original first instalment (volumes 1 and 2), but to be unable to account for the shifting focus which accompanies – is indeed the reason for – the increasing isolation of the heroine in *Clarissa* as much as in *Pamela*. Richardson probes through the social, to the ethical, to the religious, and his final volumes are concerned with dying to the world. Even in the first instalment the social cannot be separated from the moral and religious without distortion.

Furthermore, as in *Pamela*, the central exploration and achievement are to be found in the probing of the heroine. It may seem at first that Clarissa is simply being used as a touchstone to

[1] Clara Thomson, *Richardson*, 187. Richardson himself was worried about the family's 'inveteracy', however, and wrote the intrigue with Leman into the manuscript to explain how it was kept up. See Richardson to Hill, 29 October 1746; Carroll, *Letters*, 74.

expose the false values of the corrupt bourgeoisie and aristocracy. The Harlowes and Lovelace, linked, for all their mutual hatred, by a common belief in the only divinity of self and the only reality of power, are opposed to Clarissa's world of moral value; and the clash of the three worlds seems motivated by a simple desire to show the superiority of Clarissa's, even in defeat. There is truth in this, but it is not nearly so simple. For from the very beginning, as the conflict develops, Richardson is forced once again to probe the implications of his heroine's values; and to confront their helplessness in the kind of society he depicts so well. More and more painfully he is driven to test his convictions about her; to use her persecutors as inquisitors to discover what she really is; to try to find, in face of the worst her world can do, what grounds there may be for her justification. This results inevitably in the need to isolate her, and finally in the need to break her soul open in asking the harshest questions of all: What *is* man? And *is* God mindful of him? From the very beginning we need to be aware of this questioning of Clarissa herself, and hence of the values Richardson holds dearest, or the full complexity and value of the fiction will remain hidden.

It is especially important, with Richardson's kind of art at its height, to follow as faithfully and simultaneously as one can *all* the resonances of the conflict, for only then will the range and depth of the art become apparent, and only in that complexity can one be certain of the 'meanings' and of their relative importance. As opposed to the epic fiction, the dramatic is exploratory and tentative. A Fielding novel produces a clear analysis because it is an instrument to articulate a structural and analytic scheme, which the author conceives before he writes. But Richardson works by projecting himself into characters and developing their conflicts, from which 'meanings' emerge far more gradually, to him as well as to us. He starts with only one certainty – what the creatures of his imagination are like – and at his greatest he imposes no pattern on them. *Clarissa* shows its huge advance over *Pamela* as much by its quality of inevitability as in any other way. Given the characters as Richardson conceives them and the situation from which the book begins, one feels that things could not have turned out otherwise. Yet the implications of each situation within that development emerge only as the conflict is explored, and only then can the nature of the next situation be foreseen. The 'meanings' which emerge from this way of writing are bound to be more tentative and more complicated than in other kinds of fiction, since many more tensions and problems arise than the author anticipated, or can immediately clarify. It is of course impossible to criticise a work as long as *Clarissa* really 'to the moment', following all the twistings and turnings of the exploration as it occurs. Nevertheless one may be sure that criticism which is selective in any direction, and does not retain some sense of what the experience of reading the fiction is like, will be even more inadequate than might be the case with other authors.

2

The Harlowe family has become a byword for cruelty, gloomy hypocrisy, and greed. Nowhere in the eighteenth century is there such a penetrating analysis of the worst tendencies of bourgeois ambition. It is important to emphasise, however, that both our understanding and their own development are gradual processes. Their full motivation does not appear for some time; several facts do not lock into place until their persecution of their daughter is well under way; and the whole truth only reveals itself to Clarissa long afterwards. They are by no means equally to blame, and the complexity of Richardson's creation can be seen in the way that the better and more loving ones, Mrs Harlowe, Uncle John, and Aunt Hervey, are gradually assimilated to the others and drawn into an 'embattled phalanx' which inhibits their better feelings and their power to act. Ultimately, however, and with far greater intensity and penetration than Defoe, Richardson shows what it means to reduce human relationships to terms of money and power.

Clarissa's father, in marrying her mother, has annexed to an already prosperous bourgeois family a considerable fortune, and also a connection with the nobility which feeds his pride and fires his family ambition. His wealth is further increased by bequests from his wife's family. His elder brother John makes a fortune by the discovery of minerals on his land, while the younger brother Anthony gets equally rich as an East India merchant. His son James is left estates in both England and Scotland under his godmother's will. As Grandfather Harlowe puts it in his last testament: 'never was there a family more prosperous in all its branches, blessed be God therefore' (I, 30; *I*, *21*).

These riches, however, merely fire greed and social ambition, and they become obsessed with the desire to 'raise a family' by breaking into the peerage. As Professor Habbakuk has argued, political power was becoming more dependent on the possession of landed wealth; and titles were increasingly given as reward for the political interest that went with great estates, rather than by the personal favour of the monarch. Owing, moreover, to certain legal changes in the seventeenth century whereby the father of a family became in effect life-tenant of the estate, the estate itself became more important than the individual 'owner', and the eldest son, who was to carry on both it and the family name, came to occupy a unique position of authority. The darling plan of the Harlowes could have been very meaningful to many rich families at the time. If *all* the family estates can be concentrated on young James Harlowe they might well 'make such a noble fortune, and give him such an interest, as might entitle him to hope for a Peerage' (I, 79; *I*, *54*). Also, as Habbakuk explains, the concentration of estates was necessary in any case if the landed families were to maintain their power in an increasingly money-based economy.

This ambition obsesses the entire family, and both bachelor uncles vow to remain unmarried in order to further the plan, by preventing the dispersal of their fortunes among children. The family acts as a unit, therefore, from strong economic motivation;

but their thinking also shows the influence of a highly conservative view of the nature of family organisation. They still see 'the family', not as the modern conjugal unit of father, mother and children, but as the extended feudal complex which includes a number of other relations married and unmarried, dependants, and even servants, all ruled as one monolithic whole by patriarchal authority. So the Harlowes blend social climbing and economic acquisitiveness, the marks of the 'new man' of the late sixteenth and seventeenth centuries, with a deeply conservative view of the nature of the family and of authority. The patriarch's control of the economic activity of the whole family unit must be upheld, but the centralised direction can be justified by appealing to old-fashioned morality – the doctrine of absolute filial obedience.

Marriage is very much an economic activity in the Harlowe view and, as Habbakuk again shows, in the view of upper class eighteenth-century families in general, but there is a radical difference in the position of sons and daughters. Young James Harlowe is in a uniquely privileged position which swells his natural arrogance. He is largely independent through his acquired estates; deferred to by an all-powerful father who is savagely jealous of prerogative as far as his wife and daughters are concerned; uncontrolled by a crushed and passive mother; and both pampered and feared by his other relations. On the strength of his great expectations he comes to regard his uncles as merely his stewards, and is capable of treating even his father with condescension. His power to prevent foreclosure on a mortgage held by his Uncle Hervey allows him to behave to his mother's sister with unconcealed contempt. Because he is the spearhead of his family's ambition and pride he gains the power to make himself virtually its head, and his arrogance and selfishness, thus supported and encouraged by his economic position, know no bounds.

Where property is paramount, however, the mere existence of daughters is a potential encumbrance. James asserts with characteristic brutality 'That a man who has Sons brings up chickens for his own table . . . whereas Daughters are chickens brought up for the tables of other men . . . (and) to induce people to take them off their hands, the family-stock must be impaired into the bargain' (I, 79; *I, 54*). Habbakuk reminds us that the most common way of raising a dowry was by mortgage on the family land. Yet a daughter's marriage may, with proper direction, be made to serve the family advantage. There may be no direct acquisition of property, as in a son's marriage, but there should be desirable connections, social or economic, and there may be at least a chance of property by entail, if there are no children. Thus the father's right to direct the marriage of his daughters to the maximum economic advantage must remain unquestioned.

These, then, are the motives which govern the Harlowes; but before the novel opens their ambitions have taken one jolt which proves to be of crucial importance. Clarissa's grandfather, considering the others well provided for, ignores primogeniture and leaves his personal estate, for private and moral rather than economic reasons, to his youngest grandchild who has been the delight of his old age. It is true that Clarissa gives over its management to her father, moved by ideas of filial duty that have nothing to do with economics; true also that the estate is only one part of her grandfather's wealth. Yet her action does not, as she hoped, restore equanimity to her family; it only forces resentment underground where it continues to fester, particularly in the breasts of her brother and sister. The grandfather has 'lopped off one branch' of James's expectations (I, 80; *I, 54*); he has broken the united front; and he has planted a rancour that is personal as well as economic.

It is into this situation that Lovelace enters, introduced by Uncle Anthony on the look-out for an advantageous match, but by a misunderstanding he is introduced as a suitor to Arabella. Clarissa and James are away from home, but the rest of the family see the match as highly suitable, for Lovelace has a large fortune himself, is heir to a Lord, and has further expectations from the rest of an aristocratic family whose last male descendant he is. Lovelace cleverly extricates himself from his error while remaining on good terms with the family; and after meeting Clarissa on her return, he duly asks for the hand of the younger daughter. Mrs Harlowe's 'only dislike of his alliance . . . was on account of his reputed faulty morals' (I, 13; *I, 9*), but this counts for nothing with the uncles, and the sister in a mood of bravado makes no objection. Clarissa's father indeed hesitates, as he had not before, because of a letter from James about Lovelace's character; but the key point is not so much his morals as his extravagance, which may mean that he is not, after all, a good enough economic bet to risk alienating his son. Clarissa alone makes a judgement which shows at least the conception of marriage as a human relationship. 'I immediately answered, That I did not like him at all: He seemed to have too good an opinion both of his person and parts, to have any regard for his Wife, let him marry whom he would' (I, 15; *I, 10*).

On the return of James, however, there is a marked change, and the suppressed rancour of brother and sister bursts out. They insult Lovelace, and James finally forces a duel in which Lovelace wounds him slightly, in disarming him. Harlowe Place is thrown into tumult, gouty father and irate uncles flame out at this threat to their darling hopes. Arabella blames it all on her sister, and on his recovery James contrives a plan to revenge himself on both Clarissa and Lovelace. To prevent her falling into the hands of a vile libertine for whom she is alleged to cherish a secret liking, he proposes several suitors he knows she will refuse, and finally proposes to give her to the sordid miser Solmes. His personal motives are clear. He has been humiliated, both earlier at college and now in the duel, by a man whom he consequently loathes with the obsessive hatred of wounded arrogance, but knows himself too weak to attack directly. The marriage of Clarissa to Solmes is the only revenge he can take. It would also be a satisfactory revenge on Clarissa for his disappointment over the grandfather's will, and for a lifetime of jealousy at her power to inspire affection and admiration. Bella too has cause to hate her sister, not only through rooted jealousy, but more immediately because of the conquest of Lovelace whom Bella plumed herself on attracting, and for whom she still cares more than she will admit.

So hatred and jealousy poison the atmosphere as the persecution of Clarissa begins, but behind these lie hidden economic motives, which explain the marked change I have mentioned, as also the inveteracy with which the persecution is pursued, and how far it goes. His grandfather's will has shown James that his position is not as secure as he thought; and a chance conversation with the uncles he has regarded so complacently suddenly opens up the appalling possibility that they might follow their father's lead. Anthony has been in treaty with Lord M about Lovelace's proposal. Lovelace is already heir to his uncle's title, but Lord M holds out the dazzling prospect of an even higher one, that of the father of Lady Sarah and Lady Betty which has been vacant since his death. There is a strong possibility that Clarissa could become a high ranking peeress herself and pull her family into eminence behind her, and the Harlowe brothers are seriously considering putting their financial weight into the scale. Their attitude to James depends purely on his role in their plans for family advancement and their fear of his passionate arrogance, but they have cause to love Clarissa for herself. Since she already has her grandfather's estate the family property can no longer all be concentrated on James, and Anthony feels that 'there was wealth enough in their own family to build up three considerable ones' (I, 84; *I*, *57*). James would still have enough from his father and his godmother to set up for a smaller title, and two are better than one. The threat to the ambitions which mean everything to James is an appalling one. ' "See, Sister Bella," said he in an indecent passion before my Uncles . . . "See how it is! — You and I ought to look about us! — This little Syren is in a fair way to *out-uncle*, as she has already *out-grandfather'd*, us both!" ' (I, 85; *I*, *58*). Consequently Clarissa must at all costs be prevented from marrying Lovelace. The strategy which ends in the duel succeeds in inflaming the whole family, but a continual pressure has to be kept up because the family greed, which is all James has to count on, may swing them back to the alliance at any moment – especially since James was the aggressor, and Lovelace behaves at first with great self-control and apparent desire for reconciliation. Clarissa must be married off in a hurry.

The proposal of Solmes gives rein to the Harlowes' *parvenu* resentment of the real thing in Lovelace, and offers them more direct prospects of aggrandisement, because he is a nobody. He has inherited from a miser who preferred a fellow spirit to closer relatives; and because Solmes himself is aware that he has not a single non-economic quality that can recommend him to Clarissa, and lets it be known that he will feel no responsibility to his own relatives in bargaining, he may be prepared to bid high for an alliance with the Harlowes. They hope to dictate to him as they could not to Lovelace. He may be induced to exchange his local estate for James' northern one, so concentrating the Harlowe property in one area and increasing their hopes of an English title. Or he may buy the northern estate on advantageous terms, enabling the Harlowes to buy in their own area with the proceeds. Solmes' own motives are clear to them – he is a man they can understand. Clarissa's estate borders on two of his own and thus has immense value to him; but he holds out the dazzling prospect that he will entail all three away from his own family back to theirs. So the certainty of losing Clarissa's estate on her marriage to someone else (even if that were not Lovelace), becomes the enchanting hope of one day getting it back with rich additions. Clarissa sees how craftily Solmes dangles the bait of remote contingencies – but the Harlowes are sure they can tie him down. For this, since parental authority must be absolute in directing economic policy, and since that is what matters most in marriage, Clarissa is to be given to a man she utterly despises and who is indeed despicable. (One might say that the real function of Solmes in the novel is to illustrate what purely economic man looks like, uncomplicated by any of the non-economic qualities which make men attractive or even bearable.)

Yet the Solmes proposal is only part of James Harlowe's scheme, and not the most important part. His full revenge on Clarissa, and his full security, cannot be accomplished without ruining her with her family *whatever happens with Solmes*. He is not by any means the fool his sister supposes. If the Solmes proposal is what he wanted he chooses an odd way to bring it about, contriving that she be presented with a *fait accompli* delivered in the most unpleasantly formal, self-righteous, and authoritarian Harlowe manner, inflamed by scorn and passion from himself. He makes it impossible ever to discuss it, and stokes his father's authoritarianism until he succeeds in making the issue a straight question of absolute obedience. Behind the scenes he may constantly be detected trying to prevent Clarissa from meeting the family to plead her cause. He makes every effort to exacerbate the clash of wills, to infuriate both sides, to keep the atmosphere overcharged. He knows his sister better than she thinks: what spirit underlies her normal meekness. The more he can put her back up by persuading his family to indulge the harshness so natural to them, the more he can prevent her meeting them and appealing to their pity, the more he and Bella can provoke her to speak out sharply and enrage the authoritarians, the better his whole plan will be served. To a reader who grasps the full scope of his purposes as Clarissa, in spite of a momentary suspicion (II, 27; *I, 257*), never manages to do until it is too late, the strategy of James and Bella stands out point by point and situation by situation, with sinister clarity. It has the advantage of giving full rein to their native rancour, and every time either enters the scene, in person or by letter, the emotional temperature rises as they fully intend it should.

James succeeds in every direction. He contrives that Clarissa should first be confined to the house and forbidden to correspond outside; then that she should be 'sent to Coventry' with her own servant dismissed and Bella's set over her, with instructions, obviously, to annoy her; then that her room should be searched several times; and lastly that she should be threatened with a forced marriage outside the protection of her parents. Under this kind of provocation he succeeds in tempting her to several strategic errors. Since her family will have it that she cherishes a secret attraction to Lovelace, and uses her denial against her, she is provoked to see what will come from allowing it to seem that she does. Still better, from James's point of view, she is provoked into a reminder of the existence of her estate, which he can easily convert into a threat to resume it. This seals her doom. The family is forced to 'Jehu-drive' since they have every reason to fear the arrival of Colonel Morden, her cousin and trustee. The more persecution James contrives with the open admission that it is to break her spirit, the more she is driven to obduracy, and the better his real purposes are served.

Where persecution achieves such results, any attempt by the rest of the family to treat her more gently must be sabotaged, and in every case he or Bella manage to do so. This applies still more to Clarissa's alternative proposals. It is part of her tragedy that when she has come to see her family's greed, she should fail to see her brother's interest in demolishing the efforts she makes to satisfy it, and should continue to hope for results. She proposes to live single and renounce Lovelace unconditionally; then to guarantee this by putting up her estate as surety, to her father, or even to her brother. Then, seeing that the estate itself, and the family greed, are the real points with most of the Harlowes, she proposes to make it over entirely to Bella if *she* will marry Solmes, thus effectively answering the family's economic ends. Yet her hopes are pitiful because she cannot see, until it is far too late, that however her proposals might satisfy the rest of the Harlowes, they will not serve her brother. He uses the opportunities of inflaming the others that are cunningly provided by Lovelace, or the unfailing resource of direct appeal to prerogative, to ensure that each counter-proposal is rejected. Nothing but the maximum disgrace will do; and if the Solmes proposal comes off as well, so much the better.

James Harlowe succeeds because of the Harlowe greed and pride, but these could not have closed the trap on Clarissa so remorselessly had not his vindictive jealousy and hatred driven him to adopt the strategy he does, which in its later stages works against his short-term interest, and Bella's. This is the first of many points where a purely economic and social analysis will fail to account for the complexity of Richardson's creation. The point about economic motivation for Richardson, as we shall see, is that it opens the door of the soul to the deadly sins, releasing the evil in the hearts of men. *Radix malorum est cupiditas* – as Clarissa tells her Uncle Anthony (I, 228; *I, 156*).

Bourgeois capitalist though he was himself, Richardson was in no doubt about the corrupting power of money, and the alienation of economic man from all that is most worth while in life. 'You are all too rich to be happy, child' (I, 60; *I, 41*), writes Anna Howe, and again, 'I think you might have known, that AVARICE and ENVY are two passions that are not to be satisfied the one by *giving*, the other by the envied person's continuing to *deserve* and *excel*. – Fuel, fuel both, all the world over, to flames insatiate and devouring' (I, 59; *I, 40*). There is nothing original here, indeed the language shows the influence of a sermon tradition stretching back to the Middle Ages. What is original and revealing, though, is the dramatic novelist's power to show in the grain of dialogue – to prove on our pulses as we read – how cupidity corrupts the moral language the Harlowes purport to use; how it involves them in hypocrisy and dishonesty; how it alienates them not only from reason and truth but from feeling; how it distorts human relationship; and how, at the deepest levels of personality, it liberates ugly passion, cruelty, and sadism. It is hard to illustrate this adequately, when every speech in a long development adds its particular and emotional involvement, with a vitality no schematic analysis can match – but at least the outlines can be made clear.

What happens to moral categories is visible in the language of the best of the Harlowes, as Clarissa's mother contrasts the motivation of her husband and his daughter. 'What therefore can be *his* motives, Clary Harlowe . . . but the welfare and aggrandizement of his family; which already having fortunes to become the highest condition, cannot but aspire to greater distinctions? However slight such views as these may appear to you, Clary . . . your Father will be his own judge of what is and what is not likely to promote the good of his children. Your abstractedness, child, (*Affectation* of abstractedness some call it) savours, let me tell you, of greater particularity, than what we aim to carry. Modesty and Humility therefore will oblige you rather to mistrust yourself of *peculiarity*, than censure views which all the world pursues, as opportunity offers' (I, 144-5; *I*, *99*). To Bella, whose view of human motivation knows no other categories but egotism and its power to achieve desired results, there is no need of such verbal pieties. Clarissa's values are a confidence trick, and the girl herself a 'creeper-on' and an 'insinuator'. 'How often, said she, have I and my Brother been talking upon a subject, and had every-body's attention, till *you* came in, with your bewitching *meek* pride, and *humble* significance? . . . Did you not bewitch my Grandfather? . . . How did he use to hang, till he slabbered again, poor doting old man! on your silver tongue! . . . And what was all this for? Why, truly, his Last Will shewed what effect your *smooth* obligingness had upon him!' (I, 316-7; *I*, *216*). To anaesthetise moral distinction, or brutally to travesty behaviour; to purse the lips or to spit venom – Richardson's control of tone, diction and speech rhythm is equally masterly.

Where moral language is sterilised, authority – which Clarissa accepts on moral grounds – becomes an instrument of naked power. While the Harlowes rely on her concept of duty, founded in reason and conscience, they will not allow reason and conscience to operate. From the first announcement of the Solmes plan, which is signed and sealed before being mentioned to Clarissa, they are determined to allow no discussion. 'Clarissa Harlowe,' her father thunders, 'know, that I will be obeyed . . . No protestations, girl! No words! I will not be prated to! I will be obeyed! I have no child, I *will* have no child, but an obedient one' (I, 52-3, *I*, *36*).

The Harlowes also deny truth. An early example of their urge to shape the world to the image of their desire is their refusal to accept the facts of the duel. Yet at every step in their battle with their daughter they turn her honesty into a weapon against her. Time and again they force her into intransigence by such calculatedly dishonest inferences from what she says and does that she can make no move to meet them without having it construed into capitulation. She hesitates to maintain that her heart is free because she knows this will be turned into a confession that only wilful obstinacy makes her refuse Solmes, though her mother knows perfectly well that is a lie. Since she can only meet her family downstairs on the assumption that she is prepared to give in, she has to allow her isolation to seem her own choice. Her mother even tries to trick her into being excused because of 'modesty on the occasion' (I, 111; *I, 76*) – that is, that she *is* prepared to think of Solmes as a husband – so that she is forced to seem unprepared to be excused at all. Her readiness to have one interview with Solmes as a mark of duty, is immediately construed into agreement to consider him as a suitor; and the whole family adopts a hypocritical behaviour to support this construction which they know is completely untrue. Where false inferences are drawn from every move, intransigence is the only integrity.

The denial of truth of feeling, moreover, strikes at one of Richardson's deepest convictions. In his world, a man who permits himself to feel for others can open the fountain of goodness in himself, no matter how immoral he has been; and only the man who will not or cannot feel is irredeemable. The Harlowes, however, set their faces against the world of the heart. Though Mrs Harlowe appeals for pity for herself and even the 'gouty paroxysms' of her husband, the better Harlowes crush their natural feelings, and refuse to see Clarissa lest their pity be touched. Mrs Harlowe locks herself in her room at one point, to avoid seeing her daughter; and she and Uncle John and Aunt Hervey often simulate or even induce an anger which will harden their hearts. Arabella admits in an off-guard moment that only her brother and herself can be trusted to see Clarissa (I, 316; *I, 215*); and we glimpse them preventing even the enraged patriarch from going upstairs where he might be touched by pity, or, in the language of James and Bella, by 'pug's tricks' and 'whining vocatives'. (When Eaves and Kimpel perceive how shadowy Mr Harlowe is, this is of course the reason.[1] We cannot

[1] Eaves and Kimpel, *Richardson*, 250-1.

know him because he is kept from his daughter, and hence from us.)

By subjecting feeling to the demands of economics and power, the Harlowes end in denying relationships. Look where one will in the family, one finds this denial; and also in the attitude of Solmes to his relations, which the Harlowes so obviously approve. They have no time for the concept of family feeling that underlies the eighteenth-century synonym of 'friends' for 'relations'. Anna makes the point by refusing to use the former word, though she cannot deny the fact of the latter. Yet Harlowe language seeks to make even the fact depend entirely on Clarissa's willingness to bend her will to theirs: 'I *will* have no child but an obedient one'. Relationship is defined in a context of money and power, and if this concept is refused there is no room for any other; or for forgiveness since '*Too ready forgiveness does but encourage offences*: That's your good Father's maxim' (I, 238; *I, 163*). Or, in the good gentleman's words on announcing the forced marriage: 'when Mr Solmes can introduce you to us, in the temper we wish to behold you in, we may perhaps forgive *his* Wife, altho' we never can, in any *other* character, our perverse Daughter . . . Nor shall you hear from me any more till you have changed your name to my liking' (I, 309; *I, 210-11*). True enough, she never does, unless we except the passing on of his parental curse.

In such a world we should expect a low view of marriage, and indeed the uncles have renounced it altogether, without regret. Uncle Anthony tells Clarissa not to let 'matrimonial differences' – a typical Harlow euphemism for what she may expect in marrying a man she loathes physically, intellectually and morally – 'frighten you: Honey-moon lasts not now-a-days above a fortnight . . .' (I, 239; *I, 164*) Clarissa lives day by day with an example of what the marriage bond, conceived in terms of money and power, means, even when the woman was allowed her choice. She maintains that her father originally loved her mother, but all traces of this have been obliterated by his obsession with prerogative. The money she brought has merely fired his ambition without producing any gratitude or consideration. Her readiness to give in to him, which Clarissa ascribes partly to worry about his illness at first, has merely fostered his imperiousness, and the woman has become a crushed nonentity. She lives in such fear that she now flies in the face of her own knowledge of right and wrong, rationalising as the 'preservation of family unity' the sacrifice of the only admirable Harlowe to the greed and hatred of the others. Yet her compliance brings her nothing but ill-treatment from those who have learnt to tyrannise over her. Her son treats her with contempt and her husband treats her as he treats his daughter. Examples of unhappy marriage in the bourgeois world abound. The Herveys are not happy, neither were the Howes. Anna sees the reason clearly in terms of materialism and masculine power (I, 191; *I, 131*): behind the fiction of courtship is the reality of commerce in female property. Even the better inhabitants deny importance to love, and the fact that this can come clearly from Mrs Howe reminds us that we are dealing with a widely held eighteenth-century view (II, 80-1; *I, 294*). It remains only for Solmes to put into words the facts of the Harlow marriage and draw a final and logical inference. 'Fear and Terror . . . looked pretty in a Bride as well as in a Wife: And, laughing . . . It should be his care to perpetuate the occasion for that *Fear*, if he could not think he had the *Love*. And, truly, he was of opinion, that if LOVE and FEAR must be separated in Matrimony, the man who made himself *feared*, fared best' (II, 66; *I, 284*).

The love of money, power, title, drives the Harlowes then to deny all that is most valuable in human life: moral discrimination, reason, conscience, truth, feeling, relationship. *Radix malorum est cupiditas*, proved on our pulses as we hear them speak and watch them behave. The deepest truth of the old saw, however, is the demonstration not only of what *cupiditas* denies, but also of what it liberates. It opens the floodgates to ugly passion, issuing ultimately in sadism. The vividness with which the Harlowes are created (with the partial exception of the father) makes them live in the memory like an old family portrait gallery, each quite distinct through all the family likeness. What one remembers longest is not the individual features, however, but the similar expressions of swelling passion. Bella speaks 'with a face even bursting with restraint of passion. The poor Bella has, you know, a plump high-fed face' (I, 44; *I, 36*). The father sits with 'his fingers, poor dear gentleman! in motion, as if angry to the very ends of them. My Sister sat swelling. My Brother looked at me with scorn, having measured me, as I may say, with his eyes as I entered, from head to foot' (I, 51; *I, 35*). Uncle Anthony comes up 'as if he would have beat me; his face violently working, his hands clenched, and his teeth set – Yes, yes, yes, hissed the poor gentleman, you shall, you shall, you shall, Cousin Clary, be Mr Solmes's wife' (II, 207-8; *I, 380*). We have a wide choice for James, looking at his arm in a sling when things are not going well enough, or 'his eyes flaming with anger' (II, 230; *I, 396*), or 'with a settled and haughty gloom,' (II, 222; *I, 390*) or tossing Clarissa's hand 'from him with a whirl, that pained my very shoulder' (II, 209; *I, 381*). Or, an audio-visual: 'Sister, Sister, Sister, said he, with his teeth set, act on the termagant part you have so newly assumed . . . leave her, leave her, Mr Solmes: Her time is short. You'll find her humble and mortified enough very quickly – Then, how like a little tame fool will she look, with her conscience upbraiding her, and begging of you (with a whining voice, the barbarous Brother spoke) to forgive and forget!—More he said, as he flew out, with a glowing face' (II, 235-6; *I, 400*). One or two are more complicated. 'Never was there a countenance that expressed so significantly, as my Mother's did, an anguish, which she struggled to hide, under an anger she was compelled to assume – Till the latter overcoming the former, she turned from me with an uplifted eye; and stamping . . .' (I, 148; *I, 101*). But the issue is the same, and there is the same note of childishness that accompanies the loss of perspective and control. The weaker natures are just as capable of cruelty and blackmail, just as prepared to vent their inner discomfort on a helpless prey. Her 'truly maternal indulgence' is often in Mrs Harlowe's mouth, but her crushed nature can taunt her daughter with her supposed prepossession, or torment her with coldly calculated suspense.

John Harlowe is the only one of the three brothers with something of a heart – it is an interesting sign of how clearly Richardson attributes the corruption of the Harlowes to the pursuit of the economic life, when we contrast John, whose riches are accidental, with Anthony the working capitalist and self-made man – but John also uses his affection as a blackmailing weapon, and plays the family game of false inferences in face of Clarissa's mounting distress.

What is finally liberated in the Harlowes is sadism. The most powerful pictures we are left with are pictures of humiliation and torture. The end of the interview with Solmes, which James whips up with intrusion after intrusion, sees Clarissa made to sprawl from her knees flat on her face on the floor of an empty room, with her brother standing over her. With greater refinement, one of the finest scenes in the novel has a malevolently whispering Arabella touch an open nerve with every sentence, as she forces Clarissa to imagine dressing up as Solmes's wife on the wedding night, and the first public appearance afterwards. The purpose again is to heat up a situation that is going the wrong way; and thematically the scene is a perfect illustration of the Harlowe substitution of clothes, jewels and money for kindness and love; but the real achievement is the way that Richardson creates, in the sibilant inflections of Bella's voice, a caressing enjoyment of inflicting pain. She 'took up the patterns which my mother had sent me up . . . and, offering one, and then another, upon her sleeve and shoulder, thus she ran on, with great seeming tranquillity, but whisperingly, that my Aunt might not hear her. *This*, Clary, is a pretty pattern enough: but *This* is quite *charming*! I would advise you to make your appearance in it. And *This*, were I you, should be my wedding night-gown – And *This* my second dressed suit! Won't you give orders, Love, to have your Grandmother's jewels new-set? – Or will you think to shew away in the new ones Mr Solmes intends to present to you? He talks of laying out two or three thousand pounds in presents, child! Dear heart! How gorgeously will you be arrayed! What! silent, my dear! Mama Norton's *sweet dear*! What! silent still? . . .' (I, 345, *I*, *235-6*). The last result of Harlowe pride, placing the self at the centre of existence and denying all human reality but power, is a world of torture. Clarissa sums up the crucial difference between herself and her family by referring to the second of the two 'great' commandments and its dependence on the first. In so doing she touches briefly, but tellingly, what will be the novel's deepest chord. 'Is it not a sad thing, beloved as I thought myself so lately by every one, that now I have not one person in the world to plead for me, to stand by me, or who would afford me refuge, were I to be under the necessity of seeking for it? – I who had the vanity to think I had as many friends as I saw faces, and flattered myself too, that it was not altogether unmerited, because I saw not my Maker's Image, either in man, woman, or child, high or low, rich or poor, whom, comparatively, I loved not as myself . . . I don't know what to do, not I! – God forgive me, but I am very impatient! I wish – but I don't know what to wish, without a sin! – Yet I wish it would please God to take me to his mercy! – I can meet with none here – What a world is this! What is there in it desirable? The good we hope for, so strangely mixed, that one knows not what to wish for! And one half of mankind tormenting the other, and being tormented themselves in tormenting!' (II, 38; *I, 264-5*). This is not merely a Hobbist vision of the war of all against all. It is a Christian vision, of a kind of hell.

3

The darker our vision of the Harlowes, the more attractive Lovelace must seem - at first. His gaiety, his apparent candour, his wit and charm, even his rakehell insouciance and energy, are like suddenly coming across a portrait of Charles II among a gallery of Breughels. Yet there is a trap for the unwary and superficial here, into which not a few of the book's first readers proceeded to fall. For in these opening volumes we see him mostly through the eyes of Clarissa (and sometimes Anna) and these are innocent, ignorant, and subject to emotional clouding. There is talk of Lovelace's 'immorality', but it is nearly all vague hearsay, enough to raise a question-mark but not enough to convince, or produce any real hardening of attitude. The more Clarissa is embittered by her persecution the more attractive Lovelace seems to her, and hence to us. There are stages of anger, of jealousy and disgust over the 'Rosebud' affair, of deep misgiving. Yet Lovelace manages to make her forgive his presumptions; when the truth about his behaviour to the country girl is revealed, disgust turns into tenderness and admiration as he had hoped; and though the misgiving remains, he comes out far better than his reputation, through Clarissa's eyes.

Furthermore, in isolating him so much from our direct vision, Richardson insulates him from the imaginative certainty and emotional response that are characteristic of his new way of writing. Most of the time Lovelace is given merely narrative treatment. Where our knowledge of the Harlowes is carried alive and certain into our minds by narrative bursting into drama, scene after scene, giving us not only the words of the speakers but also their inflections, expressions and gestures, we never get much more of the few encounters with Lovelace than the gist of what he said. Similarly only one of his letters to Clarissa actually appears, the rest are merely summarised. Richardson himself knew how little the content of behaviour and speech convey without their style - it is that which the dramatic form concentrates on conveying, and that which enables us to know with the most imaginative certainty. We hear Clarissa agree with Anna in her very first letter that 'air and manner often express more than the accompanying words' (I, 8; *I*, *5*), and as far as letters go we have Richardson's own word for it that 'styles differ, too, as much as faces, and are indicative, generally beyond the power of disguise, of the mind of the writer'.[1] We have only to compare Clarissa's account of her encounter with Lovelace in the garden with any of the big scenes with her family; or her summary of one of his letters with any of the actual letters of James or Bella or Uncle Anthony, to realise how much is being kept from us.

[1] Richardson to Miss Westcomb, ? 1746; Carroll, *Letters*, 64.

Yet, as was disastrously not the case in *Pamela*, there are four precious exceptions, where we get direct access to Lovelace for ourselves. In three of these - Lovelace's three letters to Belford - we are given knowledge of him that is denied to Clarissa; and with this behind us the fourth, the only one of his letters to her that we get intact, ought to carry a wealth of meaning that she cannot see, provided we have not merely let our eyes slide over the others. Most of the time we share the deficiency of her knowledge and the fluctuations of her feelings; and even the Belford letters are cunningly placed in contexts likely to react in Lovelace's favour if they are not read with a sensitivity to implications. Yet we have been given, beneath the gay and candid surface, a kind of insight no character in the book possesses.

The first letter to Belford reveals that Lovelace is pursuing a strategy very similar to James Harlowe's. He is well aware that his only hold on Clarissa is her fear of violent reprisals for the Harlowe insults. It is by threats that he puts her unwillingly under an obligation, and forces her to continue a correspondence whose secrecy makes it 'lover-like', allowing him to presume a kind of intimacy he could not otherwise have gained. Moreover, as she sees, the persecution so avowedly aimed against joining her with Lovelace produces just the effect it is meant to avoid. Indeed, the more hopeless her position and the more bitter she feels, the less she can help turning to Lovelace in spite of her original objections. The Belford letters show him so aware that the persecution is doing his work for him, that he is exerting every effort to make it *worse*. He is enflaming the Harlowes through the very servant James has paid to spy on him. 'I am playing (James) off as I please; cooling or inflaming his violent passions as may best suit my purposes; permitting so much to be revealed of my life and actions, and intentions, as may give him such a confidence in his double-faced agent, as shall enable me to dance his employer upon my own wires . . . By this engine, whose springs I am continually oiling, I play them all off. The busy old tarpaulin Uncle I make but my embassador to Queen Annabella Howe, to engage her . . . to join in their cause . . .'

(I, 215; *I, 147*). Lovelace is closing the trap as ruthlessly as James Harlowe, indeed using James to do so, in order to make sure that there is no escape from Solmes but himself.

So we see him as another cause of the Jehu-driving. It is his 'continued menaces and insults' that convince Mr Harlowe, with her obstinacy, 'that a short day is necessary to put an end to all that man's hopes' (I, 145; *I, 99-100*), and so bring on the 'frightful precipitance' of the preparations for an early wedding, and the turning down of Clarissa's first counter-proposal. Lovelace's threats are given as a reason for her confinement, and his reported boast that he is sure of her is a powerful argument in the rejection of her last offer which, as we shall see, he hypocritically encouraged. He deliberately throws Harlowe Place into tumults by threatening armed rescue if the family try to remove her to her uncle's; thus keeping her where he has means and opportunity to carry her off. This also provokes a definite date for the forced marriage, which in turn is directly responsible for Clarissa agreeing to use his help to escape. She of course never sees what a deliberate strategy this is, though she does get as far as noticing that the persecution has worked out well for him.

Yet the strategy is less important than its implications; for it can only be accomplished at the cost of increasing misery to Clarissa. What she says of Solmes sheds light on Lovelace too, with powerful irony for the future: 'he that can see a person whom he pretends to value, thus treated, and approve of it' – let alone helping it on – 'must be capable of treating her thus himself' (II, 212; *I, 383*). The charm of Lovelace's gaiety never sobers into any sense of what she must be suffering, or any idea of what is involved for her in the breaking of family ties which to him are 'Mere cradle prejudices'. He is no more willing than the Harlowes to abide by her choice: the real object of his schemes is to substitute his power over her for theirs, with a strong hint that he will marry her only if he has to.

Behind the gaiety and candour then, refreshing as they may be after the anger and gloom of the Harlowes, lies the revelation that Clarissa is in far greater danger than she ever supposes.

Lovelace sees much deeper than the Harlowes, is dancing them on his wires, is deliberately provoking them to block any escape to the Howes (his advocacy of which is wholly hypocritical), and all to one end: to have her in his power to seduce or marry as he pleases.

We can of course explain much of this in terms of revenge on the Harlowes which is continually in conflict with his love. He thinks of himself as Dryden's lion, quietly dissembling in order to rend his enemies more effectively (I, 257; *I*, *175*). Yet his eagerness to use the woman he purports to love as the chief weapon remains in question. 'But now am I *indeed* in Love. I can think of nothing, of nobody, but the divine Clarissa Harlowe – *Harlowe* – How that hated word sticks in my throat – But I shall give her for it the name of Love', that is, Lovelace (I, 214; *I*, *146-7*). It may yet be asked how the name of Love differs from that use of other people for one's own selfish ends that is a mark of the name of Harlowe?

Lovelace's preoccupation with love seems to distinguish his world from the obsessive Harlowe pursuit of economic and social power. He is a good if rather feudal landlord, but wholly uninterested in money and property. (He can of course afford to be, but so can the Harlowes.) He despises them for being 'sprung up from a dunghil, within every elderly person's remembrance' (I, 249; *I*, *170*), but he shows no social ambition himself, and no interest in his family's plan to regain the earldom. Of that other preoccupation of the landed aristocracy, politics and the pursuit of power at court, we gather he knows something but cares not at all. With all the advantages he could want, and the freedom conferred on him by birth, fortune and connections, he devotes all his powers to the pursuit of love.

Yet the difference is less important than it looks, for Lovelace shares the basic ideology of the Harlowes: the one divinity of self and the one reality of power – only the field is different. We gather from the Belford letters that his rake's career springs from a jilting by his first love, in a romantic and poetic affair that he now mocks effectively enough. Yet it reveals a lasting pattern. His 'love' had little interest in the real woman; it was largely a projection of his ego; and the chief pleasure it gave was the exercise of power. The real hurt when he was jilted for a coronet was not to his feelings but his pride; and we gather later that this was enough to send him into a Byronic kind of exile. For this he has vowed revenge on the whole sex – we note again the touch of childishness. He has now swung full circle from romance to cynicism, he is pledged to faithlessness and unlimited seduction, but the pattern remains the same. Having felt the power of women to humiliate, he is out to use the power of masculinity to revenge, or simply assert, his own ego. His world substitutes the war of the sexes for the economic war, but the foundations in pride and power are the same.

In the idea-world of Restoration drama,[1] Lovelace finds an echo of his needs and a convenient notation of his feelings. He echoes its view of the sex war; and both the cynicism of its Comedy, and the indulgence in the stormier passions of its Tragedy. Indeed, as our knowledge of him extends, we shall find that he builds a coherent structure of values on its basic assumptions about men and women. One could clearly hold that he represents a Cavalier throwback, a continuing aristocratic reaction against the derivatives from puritanism which Clarissa and her family represent in their different ways. Yet we should not put too much emphasis on this. Richardson goes out of his way in the Belford letters to give Lovelace a moment of self-knowledge that puts the stress on his basic nature – 'I believe I had been a rogue, had I been a plough-boy' (I, 253; *I, 172*) – and sees his class and fortune only as catalysts. Both Lovelace and the Harlowes shed light outwards on eighteenth-century society; but Richardson's real interest is the inward one, in which the superficial differences between their codes and preoccupations are less significant than the basic similarities.

Lovelace distinguishes between the two kinds of love the Restoration poets express, and coming immediately after his

[1] For a discussion of Lovelace and libertines in the theatre see Ira Konigsberg, *Samuel Richardson and the Dramatic Novel* (Lexington, Kentucky, 1968), 36-48.

citation of 'the name of Love', the distinction is significant. He adapts Otway to express his feeling for Clarissa, but immediately reacts against him as 'over-tender'; for to admit the softening power of love on the heart is an admission of female power. He rebels at the idea of being 'favoured', is amazed that he should think for a moment of being 'shackled' in marriage... and in revulsion, the humanising power of love is decisively rejected as sentimental, belonging to 'the family of the whiners' (I, 215; *I, 147*). The concept of love he seizes on instead (from Dryden) is stormily masculine; a proud assertion of the male ego and a threat to wreak revenge on all who question or thwart it. At the moment this means the Harlowes, but it may come to mean Clarissa too.

For there is already a love-hate quality in his fascination with her. She is already a standing challenge to his pride because he has not been able to make any impression, or force any acknowledgement of his sexual attraction. All he can get is 'a few cold lines... only to let me know, that she values the most worthless person of her very worthless family, more than she values me; and that she would not write at all, but to induce me to bear insults, which *un-man* me to bear' (I, 218; *I, 149*). His strategy of unfulfilled threats, though it works well enough, is obviously partly a torture because it involves reining-in his manhood. Only the fact that there is no rival makes it bearable, but the letters are already full of threats to Clarissa if she should seem inclined to give in to her family; or should he fail to make her admit his male power once she is in it. His attitude to his Rosebud is a significant pointer. The country girl is humble and anxious to please, and her grandmother has implored him not to take advantage of her. 'This is the right way with me. Many and many a pretty rogue had I spared, whom I did *not* spare, had my power been acknowleged, and my mercy in time implored. But the *Debellare superbos* should be my motto, were I to have a new one' (I, 250; *I, 170*).

Now Clarissa is clearly a 'superba' in Lovelace's sense, who is most unlikely to make any such acknowledgement or plea.

And Lovelace believes (with a certain justification, as we shall see) that this is a class-phenomenon, the product of a class-code which makes women unnatural. The first of his assumptions about the nature of women to become clear, is that it is 'natural' for them to submit to the male, and acknowledge his power. In Rosebud's mind is to be found 'all that her superiors have been taught to conceal, in order to render themselves less natural, and of consequence less pleasing . . . No defiances will my Rose-bud breathe; no *self*-dependent, *thee*-doubting watchfulness (indirectly challenging thy inventive machinations to do their worst) will she assume' (I, 250-1; *I, 171*). Lovelace is right to believe that Clarissa's code is hostile to the confession of love before marriage (let alone the admission of sexual attraction), but he has no conception of any moral reasons which could be involved, and might make this more complicated than mere class-education. Consequently he tends to read Clarissa's 'reserve' as a direct female challenge to a war of pride against pride; the opportunity for a triumph over the whole sex; an invitation to his 'inventive machinations to do their worst'. It might be natural for an angel to resist male attraction where it is unnatural for a woman, but there is only one way to find out which Clarissa is, and until he knows the answer his ego will not let him rest. 'Until by MATRIMONIAL, or EQUAL intimacies, I have found her *less than angel*, it is impossible to think of any other' (I, 220; *I, 150*).[1]

It is remarkable how intellectual Lovelace's world turns out to be. He is obsessed with sex-war, but its delight is the challenge to his intellectual powers, intrigue, ingenuity, quickness of thought. It is in the stalking and trapping, not the kill, that he finds the fullest expression of his ego; and in the manoeuvring which gets women into his power, against their will and wit, that he experiences the real sense of his superiority. As a rake, the strangest thing about him (which however he shares with B) is the relative absence of lust. '*Preparation* and *Expectation* are in

1 This passage represents a darkening of Lovelace even in the manuscript. See Eaves and Kimpel, 'The Composition of *Clarissa* and its Revision before Publication', *P.M.L.A.*, 83 (1968), 420-1.

a manner every-thing: *Reflection* indeed may be something, if the mind be hardened above feeling the guilt of a past *trespass*: But the *Fruition*, what is there in that? And yet That being the end, nature will not be satisfied without it' (I, 253; *I, 172-3*).

The 'name of love' turns out to be remarkably Loveless, as it was pronounced in the eighteenth century. It is as loveless, because it is as self-centred, as the world of the Harlowes; indeed, it is remarkable how similar they basically are. There is a strong parallel with James (as Aunt Hervey notices): the spoilt childhood, the arrogance and ruthless ego, the pride in intrigue, the similar tactics. As with the Harlowes in general, there is a sterilisation and inversion of morality, a tendency to ascribe others' actions to one's own motives, a denial of honesty oneself, yet a use of it in strategy, a basic rejection of conscience. Lovelace is gayer and cleverer of course, as one sees in his neat inversion of Richardson's customary distinction between legitimate and illegitimate pride. Lovelace's egotism rejects any pride in inward qualities which one is born with; he prides himself on the outward ones, dress, manner, 'debonnaire', that are one's own manufacture. But more significant than this *jeu-d'esprit* is what happens to 'honour'. All 'the life of honour' means is sexual union outside marriage; there is no sense of an honour that could prevent the most deliberate dishonesty and hypocrisy. 'Honesty' becomes merely strategic. To confess 'ingenuously' what one cannot hide turns disadvantage into advantage and keeps eyes away from what one can keep hidden. We have noticed his tendency to ascribe Clarissa's scrupulousness to pride; being without conscience himself he is incapable of allowing for its operation in her. 'What a *worse* than Moloch deity', Clarissa later remarks of his concept of love, 'is That, which expects an offering of Reason, Duty, and Discretion, to be made to its shrine!' (II, 74; *I, 289*). Lovelace is also as scornful of his own family relationships as he wishes her to be; and being a man without deep human ties, he has no sympathy for hers. He too rejects the softer feelings; and his idea of marriage is as low as the Harlowes', sharing with them the idea that it should involve the subjection of women, if for different reasons. Finally there are already hints in him of what we see clearly in them: a callousness and latent cruelty.

Yet Lovelace is much more complex than the Harlowes, and it is important that we should not see him too simply, as Richardson himself did in his later comments on the novel. He was infuriated by the misreadings which stemmed from the failure of his first readers to grasp the darker implications of the Belford letters; and his later recensions of the novel set out, both by notes and by changes in the text, to blacken his villain. The anger was justifiable, the recension less so. It was one thing to write to Lady Bradshaigh: 'And did you not perceive, that in the very first Letter of Lovelace, all those Seeds of Wickedness were thick sown, which sprouted up into Action afterwards in his Character?'[1]; but quite another to assert (in a note whose tartness is typical of many inserted at the same time), that Lovelace had only two motives in his behaviour to Rosebud: the gratification of his pride, and a politic scheme to advance Clarissa's opinion of him (II, 168; *I, 353*). There is quite obviously more than that; and to ignore what there is so blandly was to play false to his own creation, in his haste to rectify a faulty response.[2]

For we can see in the Belford letters a potentially deep conflict in Lovelace. He half realises that his Restoration rake's code will not really do to explain this woman. He shuffles through his stock explanations for feminine coldness: pride, scorn, insolence – but finds them unsatisfactory. He is capable of recognising virtue, if not of understanding it, and he cannot help knowing

[1] Richardson to 'Mrs Belfour', 26 October 1748, Carroll, *Letters*, 92.

[2] In my 'Clarissa Restored?', *R.E.S.* 10 (1959), I argued that much of the material supposedly 'restored' by the second and third editions from the original manuscript, was actually added by Richardson to counter misreadings of the first edition. In many respects 'the revision simplifies, and in doing so, distorts, so that the third edition, on which all modern texts are based, 'is a novel perceptibly different from, and in many ways cruder than, the first'. I am glad to hear that John Carroll is about to produce a new text, based on the first edition, for the Oxford English Novels series. Meanwhile it is worth remembering that the irritable and heavy didactic emphasis of the new notes, italics and index, are the result of Richardson's anger at the carelessness and superficiality of many of his earliest readers. (See also p. 195 below.)

that it increases his love. His instinct is to resort to the easy Cavalier scorn of puritanism, the belief that the conscious pursuit of virtue is always hypocrisy; but though he knows this would be true of him, he cannot help knowing that Clarissa is 'truly admirable' – 'For what a mind must that be, which tho' not virtuous itself, admires not virtue in another?' (I, 212; *I, 145*). There is a clash between his rake's code and the genuine admiration and tenderness that reveal themselves in his adaptation of Ferdinand's view of Miranda in *The Tempest* (I, 219; *I, 150*). There are already the seeds of suspicion that there may be no way to win her but her own way, by reforming. Yet he is obviously unprepared for that; unprepared even to pretend, and spend years of siege and 'merit-doubting hypocrisy' which, even then, might not come off. He will try to prove her 'less than angel' to restore his freedom and his code. He heartily hates the love that responds to virtue, but hates it most 'because 'tis my master'.

The Rosebud affair bears directly on this. It is true that the girl's humility does gratify his pride, and that he has a clear eye for the strategic advantages of good behaviour, which indeed he later reaps as he intended. Yet the real significance is the evidence that once his pride is mollified, a better self and a better vision can operate. He again shows a genuine admiration for innocence, which he himself associates with his feeling for Clarissa. 'What would I give (by my Soul, my angel will indeed reform me, if her friends' implacable folly ruin us not both! – What would I give) to have so innocent and so good a heart, as either my Rose-bud's, or Johnny's!' (I, 252; *I, 172*). He becomes quite grave for a moment or two. On the basis of this admiration his generosity to the young couple, though it smacks a little of conscience money, is not to be ascribed to that. It is on a par with his generosity to his tenants (I, 83; *I, 56*): both show how a capacity for goodness comes out in him when his pride is laid to rest, or indeed pushes him in the right direction.

This does not really affect the danger he represents to Clarissa because the admiration for goodness, the pity, and the generosity can only operate when his power is acknowledged and his pride mollified, and she is unlikely to meet either condition. Yet there clearly is a side to Lovelace which is not only not expressed in his rake's code, but is in conflict with it.

Indeed, now is the time to notice that there is something artificial about Lovelace's *style*. The 'Roman' thee-ing and thou-ing, the posturings, the rhetorical bursts of 'passion', the quotations from plays, all have the effect of artifice; and promote suspicion that Lovelace is putting on a mask which represents what he thinks he is, or wants to be, rather than his true or full nature. I think we begin to see signs of a real human being trying to peer out from behind the rake's mask; and we ignore this at the cost of missing the truth that the tragedy is Lovelace's as well as Clarissa's, and its beginnings are here.

When we have grasped what we can of the implications of these letters, then, the rest of the first instalment gains greatly in complexity, and we begin to see a good deal more than Clarissa can. We see, for instance, how much deliberate art lies behind that encounter in the garden which impresses her so much in his favour. The last letter to Belford actually shows Lovelace planning how to behave, rehearsing his humility, his lack of presumption, down to the last trembling of the lip. Where the first two letters direct us to his character and ideas, and his strategy towards the Harlowes, the third draws our attention to his strategy towards Clarissa which is no less deliberate. From this moment the action fills with dramatic irony.

It wells up now when Clarissa perceives 'such moderate notions of that very high Prerogative in Husbands, of which we in our family have been accustomed to hear so much' (I, 263; *I, 180*); when she assures herself that his candour in admitting his faults, and what a struggle it is to reform, cannot be hypocrisy; or when Lovelace insists that his offer of protection is a last resort, and applauds her attempt to heal the family rift by resigning her estate (I, 270; *I, 184*). Behind each of his moves we can now detect the workings of an alert and subtle intelligence, watchful of implication, as when he deftly sidesteps the trap of seeming to think himself entitled to resent on her behalf (I, 267;

I, *182*). Only once does he apparently let himself flame out, and then on the issue that most touches his pride: the suspicion that her desire to give up their correspondence means she is weakening about Solmes. Yet so strong is the impression of policy, so quickly does he catch himself up, and then convert what might have been sincere impulse into a theatricality, designed to intimidate, that the 'passion' seems as contrived as the 'humility' – to *us*. One notices the stagey quotation from *Othello* (I, 268; *I*, *183*). It is a very clever performance, which succeeds in its object of keeping the correspondence going, and yet is controlled enough to leave Clarissa prepared to forgive. Coming as it does, immediately after we see Lovelace planning it, the scene should put us finally on our guard.

The alternation between passion and humility is moreover the pattern of much of Lovelace's subsequent behaviour when we no longer see him directly. The impression left by the garden scene is a good one, but Clarissa must be in no doubt of the danger to her relatives of any weakening in her resistance, so Lovelace gives Anna a glimpse of the desperado which is duly conveyed to her friend. Clarissa is angry, fails to answer three letters, and is angered still more when Lovelace complains 'in high terms' of her silence. Now it is time for humility – and humble excuses, garnished with apparent willingness to be reconciled to her family if she can guarantee no new insults, soon bring her round again. A further letter filled with concern for her, and accounts of his own suffering, even brings her to agree to another meeting.

However, in the new situation brought about by an apparent change in the family policy, when she agrees to one interview with Solmes, she decides to cancel the arrangement. The 'passionate' letter from Lovelace that follows is the only one she gives us verbatim, and so provides our last direct glimpse of him in the first instalment. It is at this point that the difference between Clarissa's point of view, and our greater knowledge, is both most acute and most revealing. The significance *she* sees is the letter's presumption of a closer relationship than Lovelace has ever been entitled to, its reflection on her sex, and its revelation of a fierceness only too similar to that of the Harlowes. She angrily breaks off the correspondence again. Yet she is obviously uneasy through all her anger; she is worried when he does not reply; her jealousy over the false report about Rosebud shows how much she still cares; and when the truth is revealed, and a humble letter arrives to explain that Lovelace has been ill because of his soaking in the coppice, she forgives him with only a show of sternness.

Yet, as I believe, the significance conveyed by the letter to *us* is a revelation of quite a different kind. The letter is strongly reminiscent of the theatrical passion in the garden, and we may suspect a similar strategy. It is difficult not to agree with Anna, a little later, when she perceives how regular the pattern of alternate humility and passion has been, and guesses its strategic purpose. (Anna, of course, shares something of Lovelace's sex-war language and ideology.) She sees how the strategy must accustom Clarissa to take account of his feelings, cement the lover-like relationship he must intrigue for, and gradually break down her reserve. Moreover, as Lovelace confesses, it suits his book as well to make her angry as to soften her, since both are admissions of his power to move. Finally we may notice that, like the outburst in the garden, the letter is vehement enough to serve its purpose, but it carefully avoids going too far. The tone is deftly controlled; the caressing note that underlies the rhetorical outbursts is enough to prevent the 'Sweet and ever adorable – What? – Promise breaker – must I call you?' from taking too deep and indelible offence (II, 130; *I*, *328*).

There is however another inference which our private knowledge of Lovelace should enable us to draw, and which is even more important. For neither the spontaneity ('I know not what I write') nor the 'anguish of mind' rings wholly true. The graphic detail, the word play, the dashes, the bursts of despairing passion, have a strong flavour of artifice. Yet the point is not hypocrisy, but rather that the falsity comes from his whole concept of love. It is this that drives him to a rhetoric that falsifies whatever sincere feelings there may have been to begin with. There may well be real unhappiness, wounded pride, genuine anxiety – but Lovelace inflates the situation with stormy passion, theatrical, much larger than life, because he thinks that this is what love should be like. The lover writing his heart out on his knee in the cold and gloomy dawn comes straight from Restoration tragedy and its debased indulgence in whipped-up passion; and the stagey attitudinising blots out whatever real man there may be underneath – to himself as well as to us. Lovelace is an incurable playactor, and is also his own primary audience, satisfying his own inner needs by his performance before it has anything to do with anyone else. Even at his most passionate moments, he cannot help making what he feels into a role, watching himself playing it, and often improving the performance as he goes along. The Belford letters have shown us this process in private, and shown us also, in their picture of his first affair, a pattern of love as pure self-projection. We see the same thing in his letter to Clarissa now, and see (as she cannot) that to think of love as he does is to be cut off from sincerity and self-knowledge. The Lovelace she will be involved with for the rest of the novel is a man playing a stage-part he thinks is real, in a performance for which she does not possess a script, on a stage of whose conventions she is completely ignorant.

The real nature of the trap Clarissa is in, is now apparent. On one side are the Harlowes, obsessed by greed and selfishness, degenerating as she refuses to bend to their will into creatures of blind passion and cruelty. Yet the attractive alternative (at first sight) that Lovelace seems to present, is revealed as even more dangerous. His world of 'love' is no less self-centred and callous, no less obsessively intent on bending her to his will. But he is more dangerous both because he is more radically hypocritical, more intelligent, and more capable of concealing what he is really up to; and also, in an equally radical way, because he is self-blinded, made incapable of understanding Clarissa or himself by the Restoration-coloured spectacles he insists on wearing. The way of looking which he has made his own through the compulsions of his ego, is a rhetorical fiction which hides from him his own better impulses and falsifies his true feelings, while committing him to an equally false view of Clarissa. After the rift over the passionate letter is healed there are no more. As the persecution mounts in hysteria, Clarissa turns more and more to Lovelace, trying to assure herself that he is simply offering her freedom of choice; that he will leave her as soon as she is safe; that he will not press marriage until she has tried to be reconciled with the Harlowes – all of which he promises with alacrity because he sees how well such preconditions will suit his deeper plans. But Clarissa has no idea how they will be used against her, no idea what Lovelace is really like, because she has no idea of the compulsions which are casting her in the role of Proud Restoration Beauty, who *must* be made humble and suppliant, so that Lovelace's vision shall retain its power to flatter and satisfy his ego.

4

Against these worlds of selfishness, radical deceit and power, we may measure the values by which Clarissa tries to live.

The bourgeois materialism of her family has no meaning for her. Money and property are valuable only when they are humanised by benevolence and the acceptance of responsibility. All estates are essentially stewardships (I, 134; *I, 92*), not in the Harlowe sense of property to be increased and passed on to the heir, but implying the responsibility to foster happiness and prosperity for as many people as possible. Money, as she retorts to Bella's taunts of improvidence, is not to be hoarded but spent gladly in works of charity (I, 318-9; *I, 217-8*). Behind this lies the concept of a universal human relationship expressed in the second of the 'great' commandments. Against the narrowly private and acquisitive sense of property she asserts the idea of the Family of Man: 'the World is but one great Family. Originally it was so. What then is this narrow selfishness that reigns in us, but relationship remembered against relationship forgot?' (I, 49, *I, 34*). Money and property then become valuable only insofar as they can be used to remember what has been forgotten.

Throughout her persecution moreover, she struggles to preserve the narrower sense of family too, and to keep alive in her heart not only the sense of duty towards her persecutors, but also a loyalty and love. She keeps trying to find reasons for their behaviour, to temper Anna's angry criticism, to assert family feeling long after the Harlowes have denied it. This goes so far that many readers may feel irritated. If so, Anna serves as she does in so many ways, to express a more normal reaction and act as a safety valve for our own less than ideal feelings. There is no doubting the genuineness of Clarissa's struggle, however: at the first sign of gentleness, even from Bella, her heart is ready to open, even if only to be humiliated again. 'Have you not a Thomas à Kempis, Sister? with a stiff air. I have, Madam. *Madam*! How long are we to be at this distance, Clary? *No longer*, my dear Bella, if you allow me to call you Sister. And I took her hand. No fawning neither, girl! I withdrew my hand as hastily, as you may believe I should have done, had I . . . been bitten by a Viper' (II, 187-8; *I, 367*). Clarissa's appeals for pity, too, are anchored in a system of value. She is trying to open the hearts of her family because she believes that anyone who 'wants a *heart* . . . wants everything' (I, 296; *I, 202*). Sure enough, she fails; not in 'whining vocatives', but in the attempt to assert a world of unselfish feeling, for 'Love that deserves the name, seeks the satisfaction of the beloved object more than its own' (II, 126; *I, 325*). In this light, the Harlowe view of family and the 'love' in the mouths of Solmes and Lovelace are, as she calls the last of these, 'a profanation'.

As against the way the selfish egotisms of her persecutors distort the truth, she aims at absolute sincerity. She tries to act so that no inference, however unscrupulous, can cloud the truth; she 'cannot give a hope of what (she) cannot intend' (I, 157; *I, 108*). If truth must be absolute, so must the moral law. There can be no relativity or social contract: 'whether the Parent do his duty by the Child or not, the Child cannot be excused from doing hers to him' (II, 60; *I*, *280*). So she flatly refuses to take the advice of Anna to resume her estate, which would be playing the family game of power against the call of duty. She does get so far as to remind them of it and ask to live there, but only after extreme provocation, and she is still to be under her father's control. Her next move, indeed, is to offer to give it up altogether and be more in his power than ever. She has no desire for independence – again one notes the limits of Richardson's 'radicalism' – and will obey her father whenever reason and conscience do not unmistakeably give their voice contrary to his. Even then, as with the Solmes proposal, she contends only for the right to refuse, and it is clear that her father has, in her view, a right to veto any positive proposal of her own.

Conscience forbids obedience in the Solmes affair because her view of marriage is so serious. It is precisely because she will feel bound to give her husband the same power over her that her father has, that she places love, and moral and intellectual respect, at the heart of marriage as the Harlowes and Mrs Howe do not. Marriage is not an economic contract, it is 'a very solemn engagement, enough to make a young creature's heart ake, with the *best* prospects, when she thinks seriously of it!' (I, 223; *I*, *152-3*). She takes the marriage-vows given at the altar absolutely seriously and literally. (The contrast here is with Anna, who shares Lovelace's view of the relation of man and woman as ceaseless war, and pours scorn on Clarissa's 'meek regard to that little piddling part of the marriage-vow which some Prerogative-monger foisted into the office, to make That a *duty*, which he knew was not a *right*' (II, 150; *I*, *341*), in other words 'the little reptile word OBEY') (II, 152; *I*, *342*). Intellectual and moral respect are almost as essential as love, not merely on personal grounds, but because any failure in respect or difficulty about obedience, which become very likely when the husband is inferior, is 'a breach in an altar-vowed duty' (II, 71; *I*, *287*). 'Convenience' and 'interest' cannot be allowed any weight, and conscience must reign over all, where vows cover a state of mind as well as behaviour, and are taken for a lifetime.

Clarissa's values, then, make the sharpest of contrasts with her family and Lovelace. Hers reject the selfish and grasping ego, and the seeking of power to gratify it. Richardson obviously tried to embody his own ideals in his heroine; not only universal values, but feminine ones too. (I take it that 'Clarissa' is related to 'clarissima' as 'Grandison' is to 'grandest-son' – i.e. 'what is best and most beautiful in woman'.) So she must be utterly gentle and meek, though with a deep moral strength, a 'steadiness' at the core, and a spirit, both in word and action, when she is driven too far. She must be intelligent, sensitive, and imaginative too, for she tells Betty Barnes that women have great advantages over men 'in all the powers that related to imagination' (II, 117; *I, 319*). She must have the most punctilious purity – hence her sense of deep insult over her brother's taunt of '*Amor omnibus idem*' (II, 26; *I, 256*). She must be capable of seeing deeply into the moral implications of events and behaviour. Finally she must, as created by the Richardson who was nicknamed 'Serious' and 'Gravity' at school, have a high seriousness behind her sweet disposition, though she ought to have enough self-deprecation to contrast her 'grave airs' with the liveliness and humour of Anna.

Yet this contrast of ideas and specifications does not account for Clarissa, or for the value of her world. What is most important about the worlds that oppose hers, is our *experience* of them. The Harlowes live insofar as dialogue and gesture bring home to our imaginations the slow but steady growth of their ugly passion, deceit, and self-righteous cruelty, making us experience what it feels like and means to be a Harlowe. Similarly what is important about the Love-less world is our experience through his style of the interplay of egotism and tenderness; the way that rhetorical attitudinising and playacting are broken into by flashes of a deeper self; above all, the experience, beneath the gaiety and charm, of hectic eddying energy, confused and dangerous – what it feels and means to be a Lovelace. We need to abstract and schematise values in order to understand what is involved, but the question we really need to ask is what the experience of sharing Clarissa's mental world is like.

It is of course obvious that our first experience is one of moral evaluation, of continuous analysis, of living in a mind that submits every detail of action and thought to intensive and scrupulous examination. Only in this process of sifting, probing, and argument are her values brought home to herself and to us. Moreover this implies a process of self-discovery too. In no other eighteenth century novel does one so register the painful effort of self-knowledge.

Apart from *The Pilgrim's Progress*, Richardson's novels are in this respect the first really imaginative use of the habits of mind which produced the Puritan diaries of the seventeenth and eighteenth centuries. Of course Richardson is not a puritan in any strict sense. He was no Dissenter in religion; he criticised the economic individualism which went hand in hand with some kinds of puritan thinking, and he did not see independent-mindedness as a virtue. He urges implicit obedience to absolute moral law in a recognised social code. Yet there is a final appeal to the individual reason and conscience, as there was in puritan thinking, and this brings with it the need to make self-scrutiny, in the light of reason and conscience, a feature of daily life. Yet there is an important difference from the puritan diary. For Clarissa's self-examination is not individual and private; it is a deliberate attempt to lay bare her heart and her behaviour for the judgement of her friend. This is not merely a consequence of Richardson's epistolary method, or his didactic intentions. As in *Pamela*, it is a search for moral community to counteract the loneliness of the individual. It is also part of Richardson's growing awareness of the heart's self-deception. The effort, often painful, to search feelings, probe motives, and lay the whole truth open to someone else, is an attempt to guard against the heart's disguises and find objective reassurance. So the friendship of Clarissa and Anna is founded on ruthless honesty. If things lurk in Clarissa's heart and mind that are not being brought into full consciousness, both friends realise it is Anna's duty to search them out, however painful it may be. In keeping with Richardson's ideas about community, also, Clarissa does not only feel answerable to Anna but to Mrs Norton, all who know her, the eyes of the moral world. Morality, we remember, is essentially public.

So the first experience of Clarissa is not only of a continuous process of sustained moral analysis, but of soul-searching and self-discovery that come from a willingness to try to be objective about herself, and to submit her mind and conduct not only to standards, but to human judgement, outside herself. In a situation where nearly all the other characters behave like blind engines roaring along the mono-rails of self-interest, we experience an awareness of the heart's disguises and self-partiality, and the need for a felt sense of moral community, the importance of relationship in Richardson's world.

Yet the multi-focus epistolary form, as it now develops, creates an even more interesting and significant experience: for we not only live within Clarissa, but within Anna and Lovelace as they experience her – a much more sustained and complex knowledge than was possible in *Pamela*. If she enables us to realise her creator's deepest values, as he then saw them, Anna and Lovelace enable Richardson, and us, to test those values in a crucible of conflict. Here is the real vitality and growth of the book, for as it proceeds in its exploration it makes even more significant and disturbing discoveries about its heroine than *Pamela* had done. Richardson may have started out simply to use Clarissa as a mouthpiece or touchstone, but as he makes her examine herself, and also separates himself from her, to examine her through the very different eyes of his other characters, he comes upon more and more that is disturbing about her absolutism.

'People who act like angels', says Lovelace, 'ought to have angels to deal with', but Clarissa has not. The effect of her aspiration to absolute probity is to put her more and more in the power of people less scrupulous than herself, to play forever into their hands, and to prevent herself from acting to save herself. In the world as it is rather than as it should be, the result of absolute probity looks like absolute passivity, not to say helplessness. Clarissa refuses to resume her estate, because duty must be absolute as long as it is reconcilable with conscience. Because sincerity must be absolute she can be forced with her eyes open, by the family game of inferences, to seem to imprison herself. She cannot take Anna's worldly-wise advice to 'part with a few of your admirable punctilio's' (II, 258; *I, 146*) or try to escape in Anna's company. She can only act negatively and refuse to give in – the first passive resister in fiction.

Anna embodies another side of Richardson's mind, and he develops through her an acute challenge to his own idealism. She is more likeable than Clarissa, not only because she is given vivacity and wit, spirit, sturdy independence; but mostly because she is less absolute, far more willing (like ourselves) to compromise absolute standards if she must. If she is less sensitive and scrupulous than her friend, she could not be so victimised. If with her similarity to Lovelace in ideology, and also in style, she enters the world of power and ego – her vivacity of style represents, as his does, an assertion of her sovereignty over language and her right to play tricks with sober truth in words – she also keeps us in touch with a sublunary landscape, a human norm, from which the refinement of Clarissa's absolutisms can seem both admirable, and senseless or unreal. She helps Richardson pose a very awkward question for him: *can* it be right to be absolute, if the results are as we see they are?

There is indeed a further query: can one hope to *be* absolute in such a world, or is one bound to be sullied? For Clarissa is not wholly untouched. She does remind her family of her estate, under extreme provocation admittedly, which is almost to play the power game, though she does not mean it so, and soon renounces it altogether. She does show us, in her response to Bella and James, that she is right in thinking she has as much of her father's as of her mother's side in her. She has a tongue as sharp as Pamela's, once stung out of her normal gentleness. She also gets involved in artifice. One can see how much Richardson has learnt since *Pamela*, for there is no pleasure or pride in it now, indeed Clarissa sees very clearly that it is wrong. Yet the question remains; another sign of how the dramatic imagination is probing and exploring.

Many of the feminine characteristics that Richardson obviously admires also increase her helplessness. To be meek and gentle may be attractive in the abstract, but both Clarissa and Anna realise that she could do with a great deal more of her friend's spirit; for meekness merely encourages tyranny, as may be seen in Mrs Harlowe's responsibility for what her husband has become. This means that Clarissa, too, is partly responsible for the degeneration of her family, in that her meekness and absolutism tempt them to go further, and further. It is not that Clarissa is wishy-washy – there is a core of great strength as the novel will witness, and her own word 'steadiness' will do very well to describe her behaviour when she knows she is right – but she does find it difficult to be assertive. She can be provoked into showing defiance or temper, but it is almost impossible for her to sustain this for more than a moment or two. Though there is also an unpleasant side to Anna's spirit, much of which derives from pride and wilfulness as we shall see, one cannot but become more and more aware of the disadvantages of being a Clarissa, however much, like Cordelia, her low voice may be an excellent thing in women. Her sensitivity and imagination are also little help to her. She is easily frightened, like Pamela again. The thought of fleeing to London holds all sorts of terrors for a mind which always thinks too precisely on the event, and she is more terrified, by her imagination, about the forced marriage than she ought to be. Like Pamela again, she has bad dreams which mirror an inherent fearfulness, and perhaps something more (see p. 231). Lovelace will manage to 'abduct' her through pure fright, when she had determined not to go. Feminine characteristics that may be beautiful and lovable in the serene mistress of a secure household, or the beloved daughter of a happy home, look very different when she is forced to rely on herself.

There are, indeed, dangers in certain eighteenth century attitudes to women that are increased in Clarissa's case by her values. The sheltered background of an eighteenth century girl made her knowledge of evil necessarily theoretic. So, for all the talk of Lovelace's immorality, Clarissa has little idea of what might be in his nature, and her own values can make her even more naïve than Anna – as in her 'innocent observation' (the words are Anna's (II, 84; *I, 296-7*)) that the man who resents the imputation of lying wouldn't be guilty of it. The attempt of her family and Solmes to produce evidence that Lovelace had sworn to seduce her might at least have opened her eyes; but she angrily refuses to listen to the traducing of a man behind his back. Several motives coincide here: her hatred of Solmes, her feeling for Lovelace, perhaps even an instinctive fear of his sexuality, yet it is above all her sense of justice that aggravates the innocence and ignorance that are in any case the lot of an eighteenth-century girl. We see something similar in her failure to understand the real wickedness of her family, especially James and Bella. Her own loyalty seems to make her incapable of seeing what they are really up to, renders it unimaginable. Even when she has been made to recognise their greed and jealousy as we do, she cannot grasp how far it will go until it is much too late.

Some features of the feminine code also encourage a kind of blindness. Clarissa does not share Anna's militant feminism, but she does share the code that believes unmarried girls should keep men at a distance, and is angry with Lovelace for trying to make himself familiar. She does not call men 'wretches' or 'fellows' (let alone 'monkeys' and 'baboons'), but she does share Anna's deep suspicion, and regards the male sex as 'encroaching', 'mischievous' and 'hard-hearted'. Of course the Harlowe men and Lovelace give her cause to think so, but the generalising suspicion, coupled with the code obligation of distance, hardly encourage the knowledge of masculine nature she will need later on. She will turn out to be dangerously blind to Lovelace's complexity, and will indeed try to fit him to formula as he does her.

Equally disturbing are code attitudes to love. Mrs Howe declares that no 'nice creature' would be thought to have 'very violent inclinations' (II, 79; *I, 293*). Clarissa wishes to give love a central importance in marriage as Mrs Howe, and the widely held view she expresses, do not. Yet she shares the suspicion of sex, and implies at one point a discrimination between *eros* and truer forms of love. She has been accused by her family of 'prepossession', that is, of a physical and sexual attraction that possess her before duty and morals have a chance to sway her mind. In reply she distinguishes love that is '*relative*', '*social*', and '*divine*' from love 'in the narrow, circumscribed, selfish, peculiar sense' (I, 197; *I, 135*). The first kinds, it is implied, negate the ego in terms of moral and communal value, and unselfish feeling; the latter seeks only its own satisfaction. The view is of course far too circumscribed. While the distinction is basically the same as Fielding's in Book 6 of *Tom Jones*, one misses his sense of how *eros* can heighten *agape*. Nevertheless, although one cannot be certain that the narrowness is not Mr Richardson's, the dramatic novelist becomes aware, through Anna, of a serious defect in Clarissa. She believes much too simply that love not only ought to be, but *is* governed by morality. The only feeling for Lovelace she will admit to is 'something that might be called – I don't know what to call it – A *conditional kind of liking*, or so' (I, 197; *I, 135*) – that is, something conditional on Lovelace's morality, when it shall become clear. Anna makes short work of this, realising clearly enough that a state of feeling is not necessarily governed by moral discrimination. Of course feelings are affected by moral judgement, and of course one can control what one shall do about them, but Clarissa seems to believe that morals can determine their very existence – and there is thus a dangerous tendency to close her eyes to what is really in her heart.

Much the most moving experience of Clarissa's world, apart from her suffering the Harlowe persecution, is indeed her struggle to see into her heart. She will not admit her feelings to begin with, but once again Richardson has her subtly give herself away by slips of the tongue and unconscious movements of the mind, long before she herself has any idea that Lovelace attracts her more strongly than he should. The phrasing of several comments is curiously defensive for the indifference she says she feels, and before ten letters have passed, ambiguity gives the game away. 'For my regards are not so much engaged (upon my word they are not; I know not myself if they be) to another person as some of my friends suppose . . . What preferable favour I may have for him to any other person, is owing more to the usage he has received, and for my sake borne, than to any personal consideration' (I 57; *I 39*). From this moment the eagle eye of Anna is continually on the lookout, and so should ours be. Her claim that Clarissa gives herself away in fifty instances may be exaggerated, but there are certainly enough to show the progress of a strong attraction, difficult though it may be to distinguish from the way the persecution turns her towards Lovelace, and little though she realises it herself. Anna has to taunt and prod her into examining her heart, and it is unquestionably painful. Yet she vindicates her integrity by the serious effort she makes, in the 'solemn stillness' at midnight, after the storm of Mrs Norton's visit.

After saying all she can in Lovelace's favour she admits that 'all that command of my passions which has been attributed to me as my greatest praise . . . has hardly been sufficient for me' (I, 293; *I, 200*). After a deliberately harsh review of his failings she admits again 'with all his preponderating faults, I like him better than I ever thought I should like him; and, those faults considered, better perhaps than I *ought* to like him. And I believe, it is possible for the persecution I labour under, to induce me to like him still more . . .' (I, 298; *I, 203*). Even now, however, though she can imagine Anna's response to what has been an exclusively moral analysis, she still cannot accept it. She still concludes 'were he *now* but a moral man, I would prefer him to all the men I ever saw', whereas it is obvious that she already does, as it is. She still thinks of the feeling itself as 'conditional' because she 'could yet, without a *throb*, most willingly give up the *one* man to get rid of the *other*' (I, 299; *I, 204*). She still confuses moral analysis with emotional analysis, and the state of her heart with the action she could take. There is of course nothing dishonest about this. Dr Johnson's remark that 'there is always something she prefers to truth',[1] which Ian Watt echoes, is deeply

[1] *Johnsonian Miscellanies*, ed. G. Birkbeck Hill (Oxford, 1897), I, 297.

misleading because the verb is too active. No character in fiction tries harder to be true, and what is interesting of course is what the something she 'prefers' is. It is because she thinks so instinctively and exclusively in moral terms that even now, when she is trying hardest, she cannot quite plumb her heart – and this spells danger, for she thinks herself thoroughly in control of her feelings as well as her actions after this, and she is not.

The feeling for Lovelace continues, in fact, to grow. Before long we know that giving him up would cause a '*temporary* concern' (II, 100; *I, 307*) – the wording is suspiciously defensive again – and would be a 'sacrifice', though she is still quite prepared to make it. Though she is angry at the 'freedoms' of his passionate letter, she is obviously uneasy at the moment of sending her tart reply, and gets more so at the silence which follows. There is much jealousy as well as morality in her contempt at the false reports about Rosebud; and a rush of feeling, however guarded, at the truth. As the persecution intensifies she turns to him more and more; admittedly as her only refuge from the tightening net, but nevertheless with an ironic sense of his 'generosity' and 'politeness'. While insisting that her duty must still be paramount, she actually promises that if she is forced to renounce him she will never marry unless he does – the first indication that she now feels she owes a duty to *him* (II, 299; *I, 444*). Finally, in an unguarded moment, the strength of the physical attraction slips out: 'It is a wonder, nevertheless, that he has not been seen by some of our tenants: For it is impossible that any disguise can hide the gracefulness of his figure' (II, 302; *I, 446*). These are small signs, but in Clarissa's world they are tremendously significant. When Anna raises the pertinent question: is Clarissa's refusal to go off with her the result of a 'latent, unowned inclination' (II, 309-10; *I, 451*), which makes her prefer the alternative of Lovelace without knowing why? – Clarissa denies it, but in words whose familiar ambiguity, 'I know not my own heart, if I have', reminds us that she knows it a great deal less than she thinks (II, 315; *I, 455*). Anna's hint is enough to alarm her, however, and joins with the prompting of her own conscience to make her revoke her agreement with Lovelace after all. Yet, as she is tricked away, we need to remember the true state of her feelings, and her own ignorance of their depth, to appreciate the tragedy that follows.

Finally, her self-scrutiny leads her to glimpse one of the most dangerous implications of her kind of moral being; and there is something very moving about the gravity of her self-criticism here. How much, behind the moral absolutism, the desire for exemplary perfection, the prudence, the best motives, may there not lurk a spiritual pride? Was it not pride perhaps that led her to continue the correspondence, trying to keep 'such uncontrollable spirits' from each others' throats? Has she not perhaps been punished for her pride in being the pride of all her friends? She hopes Anna will acquit her 'of *capital* and *intentional* faults: – But oh, my dear! my calamities have humbled me enough . . . to make me look into myself. – And what have I discovered there? – Why, my dear friend, more *secret* pride and vanity than I could have thought' (II, 264; *I, 419-20*). We are reminded of the deepest chord in *Pamela*, yet the difference is shown again in the way that the exploration presses beyond the point which seems to sum it up. For after having castigated herself earlier for thinking herself 'of too much consequence' (II, 255; *I, 413*), she repeats the fault now, in another dimension. In her gloom she imagines that she may have been 'singled out . . . to be a very unhappy creature! – *signally* unhappy!' (II, 263; *I, 419*), and 'singled out to be the *punisher* of myself and family' (II, 264; *I, 420*). Is not this, too, making oneself of consequence; is not this, too, a peculiarly puritan pride? We do not know yet, any more than we know what to make of the morbidity of her thoughts of death which close the meditation. Yet more exploration clearly lies ahead; more questions have been raised than can yet be solved. There is, nevertheless, a leading line, struck earlier on, which Clarissa (and perhaps her creator) seem sure about. 'So, my dear, were we perfect (which no one *can* be) we could not be happy in this life, unless those with whom we have to deal . . . were governed by the same principles. But then does not the . . .

conclusion recur, – That we have nothing to do, but to chuse what is right; to be steady in the pursuit of it; and to leave the issue to Providence?' (I, 137; *I, 94*).

This is not only the final comment on the difference between Clarissa's world and those of the Harlowes and Lovelace, it is a clear prefiguring of the religious novel which is to follow. Richardson has been embodying his ideals in his heroine, and using her to clarify the inhuman and life-denying implications of those who tighten the trap on her. The vision is sharply social, and deeply moral but it is already becoming religious too. In the process of exploration, Richardson has begun to see deep into the complexities and dangers of his own ideals, and to challenge them at a depth and with a courage Defoe and Fielding never managed. The first instalment is already a major achievement, asking major questions about itself.

CHAPTER SIX

A Matter of Delicacy

(*The Second Instalment*)

I

The original first instalment ended dramatically with the short letter from St Albans, and readers then had five months' suspense before volumes 3 and 4 came out in April 1748. Unfortunately another misreading began here, compounding the tendency to miss the sinister side of Lovelace in the first volumes. Someone as close to Richardson as Aaron Hill could speak of the abduction as a 'rash elopement', much to Richardson's hurt and annoyance,[1] and far too many readers could see no more in Clarissa's behaviour afterwards than prudery. We have to understand exactly how she came to 'go off with a man' if we are to grasp the nature of the new trap Lovelace sets so cunningly; and unless we understand the trap, the irony and the real tragedy for both lovers will remain obscure.

Richardson went to great pains to create a situation which would clear his heroine of wilful guilt, and yet not seem improbable given her nature. It is only in desperation, when she discovers her family apparently determined to confront her on the fatal Wednesday with Solmes and a parson; and anger, when she hears James and Bella exulting over their success; that she decides

[1] Richardson to Hill, 26 January 1746/7; Carroll, *Letters*, 82; in reply to Hill's letter of 23 January; Forster, XIII, 3, fols. 82-3.

to accept Lovelace's help to escape. It is to avoid coercion, and on the most unambiguous conditions. Her willingness to accept his help in order (she thinks) to avoid a forced marriage implies no consent to be his. She indeed warns him not to imagine that 'my withdrawing is to give him any advantages which he would not otherwise have had'.

Almost immediately however her conscience begins to worry her. Anna points out that it must inevitably seem that she has chosen Lovelace; that he will be the judge of when it is safe to leave her; that 'Punctilio is out of doors' the moment she leaves her father's house; and that her best course must be to marry Lovelace as soon as she can. Yet her own injunctions will make this difficult, even should she wish it. So she revokes her decision and writes to tell him so. He sees the letter but guesses its message and leaves it uncollected, relying on her promise to give him her reasons in person should she change her mind. He makes a detailed plan to scare her away with him, with the help of his double-agent Joseph Leman. From the first moments of their meeting he puts her in an emotional flurry by bustling her away from the gate, and goes on alternately imploring and bullying, particularly by the well-tried device of threatening her family. Leman is agonisingly slow and misses the first cue altogether – there is rich irony in re-reading – but at last he raises the alarm, apparently, for the Harlowes at his heels, Lovelace draws his sword, and Clarissa is in such a state of terror that she hardly knows what is happening as he rushes her away.

Richardson risks improbability to achieve an action both decisive, and unwilled. What saves him is that the story is so consistent with Clarissa's psychology as we have now come to know it. She is highly strung, hypersensitive and emotional, very imaginative. Though she has great moral courage she can be a coward physically and emotionally, in the special sense in which one might apply the word to a man with no head for heights: in the situation he most fears his limbs become paralysed and his brain will not work, he becomes hysterical, he *cannot* obey his will. Clarissa knows this hysterical propensity in herself. This is why the (otherwise ridiculous) threat of a forced marriage seems wholly possible to her, and to be feared, not because of any lack of will, but because she may not be able to control herself. Her family also know it; hence the full assembly and the parson, though there is no evidence that they would actually have gone beyond the threat, and some evidence that the threat was to have been their final effort.[1] Lovelace knows it: that is why he too fears the Wednesday, since tactics he expects to succeed by, might do no less for the Harlowes. Yet we must notice that Clarissa's terror affects only her limbs and the clarity of her understanding. Her will is unaffected, and she screams 'No' all the way between the gate and the carriage.

It might however appear that, however one defends it as 'natural', the tragedy has become a matter of circumstance. Yet this is only partly true, for Richardson, because of his view of evil. It will soon become clear that he sees Clarissa's tragedy as proceeding inevitably from her first fault: continuing to correspond with Lovelace after her father's prohibition. She did so at first, with her mother's connivance, in order 'to prevent mischief'; but she will learn to see it as pride and presumption, and as the 'one pace awry at first' that 'has led me hundreds and hundreds of miles out of my path' into 'a wilderness of doubt and error' (IV, 38; *II, 263*). Her motives now in promising to meet him and explain herself if she changes her mind, and in holding to that promise, are the same – and equally mistaken. We recognise the phrase 'to prevent mischief' in the mouth of 'honest Joseph' as moral stupidity; what we may not recognise is the directness of the comment on Clarissa. She too, in her much more admirable nature and her much more complex situation, is indulging a wrong and dangerous pragmatism. Even if the desired end is good, the wrong means can only produce greater and greater evil.

Clarissa does not, then, 'elope'. Had she gone willingly with Lovelace, she would have done so only to avoid coercion and to

[1] II, 335; I, *468*. See also III, 39; *II, 4* (though Anna is sceptical); and III, 271-3, 296-7; *II, 162-3, 179-80*.

be free to refuse Solmes, using Lovelace's help without committing herself to him. In fact she goes entirely against her will, and is guiltless of choosing to leave her father's house. Yet this is not a tragedy of fate or circumstance. The evil is a remote, but also an inevitable result of small but significant errors, without which the situation could never have arisen and Lovelace would never have had his chance.

2

The tragic irony is that the situation she thought would allow her freedom of choice, turns out to be an imprisonment more absolute and far more dangerous than the one she has escaped. Almost immediately we begin to get the direct insight into Lovelace's mind that we were so largely denied in the first instalment, and can therefore gauge, as Clarissa cannot the nature of the new trap.

The whole of the strategy with Leman shows how well Lovelace realises her unwillingness to leave Harlowe Place; but not the least important part of the plan is the care he takes to have the family think that her departure was wholly deliberate. The reason is, of course, to make reconciliation impossible. He is quite determined not to leave her, to find fault with wherever they may be on grounds of safety, and to keep up her fear of pursuit by her brother as long as possible, so that she will remain in his power. He can cheerfully suggest that she seek refuge with his family, knowing she will refuse any course that seems to commit her to him and could wreck the family reconciliation that is her dearest hope. He recommends several companions: Mrs Norton, Hannah, one of the Sorlings girls, knowing that there is something in each case to make the idea impracticable. In this way he can both make himself agreeable, and keep her with him. To the people at the inn of St Albans he pretends they are brother and sister in order to have an excuse for innocent 'freedoms'; and though he quickly realises from her anger at his easy deceptions that this sort of thing is to be avoided, he goes on trying to break down the distance at which she keeps him.

All this is directly against the 'injunctions' he had accepted so readily; but the cleverest part of his strategy is to *use* the injunctions as an excuse for not urging her to marry him. Time after time he distantly approaches the subject and then breaks off, pleading respect for her known wishes; knowing full well that her sensitivity and her punctilious regard for social decorum will prevent her from pursuing the subject, and from converting his distant hinting into anything more specific. This tactic gives him the position and the credit of an ardent and yet so considerate lover, while it frees him from all danger of marriage, and keeps Clarissa in his power to treat as he pleases. Meanwhile the whole situation is made to seem Clarissa's own doing – as was also the case with the Harlowe strategy. Lovelace is a master tactician. It is not merely that, as he tells Belford, he realised at once what use could be made of the injunctions – they were actually his own suggestion. He now proceeds to refer himself to them in the very first conversation at St Albans, and the trap they enable him to complete, is a masterly construction. On the one hand his abuse of the injunctions ensures that she shall not escape him by reconciling herself with the Harlowes. On the other, his use of them prevents her escaping her difficulties by marriage. She is left with the worst situation: wholly compromised by remaining with him unmarried. The longer this goes on the worse it must become, and the less chance of reconciliation. She is humiliatingly without clothes and money. She has no power to make him leave her, and no means to get away from him without (she thinks) compromising herself even further. She had warned him not to imagine she was giving him any advantage he had not enjoyed before – the irony is a grim one. Her moral theory confronts a power situation cunningly engineered by him, which puts her increasingly at his mercy.

Lovelace's motives are, as Richardson claimed in the only footnote he thought necessary in the first edition (IV, 338;

II, *466*), wholly consistent with what we should already know of him. His instinctive aversion to the 'shackles' of marriage – as instinctive as Clarissa's 'delicacy' – had been obvious in his first letter to Belford. The Rosebud affair showed how acknowledgement of his power and mollifying his pride could humanise him, whereas his rake's motto was 'debellare superbos'. Now Clarissa not only makes no move to soothe his pride, she outrages it at every turn. He is infuriated by her coldness and the distance she keeps him at, by his inability to impress her or make her admit his attractiveness. He is determined not only that she must love him, but that she must show openly that she prefers him to everyone and everything else, before she can hope for marriage.

This hurt pride, and his inability to see anything but childishness in her feeling for her family, make him interpret her anger and distress as a direct preference of the Harlowes to himself. Her continual pointing to his lack of true politeness infuriates as well as impresses him. Failing to understand the basis of her attitudes, he translates them as he converts everything, into pride. Her behaviour becomes conscious superiority, another mark of the proud beauty, another insult offered by the female to her proper master, and by the bourgeois girl to the last of the Lovelaces. Her superiority and coldness begin now to turn on her, as he had only distantly threatened before, the vengeful feelings hitherto reserved for her family. He begins to draw up an account of indignities which grows longer every day. He simply cannot see that she could hardly be expected to hold herself responsible for the hardships of a lover she never encouraged; or to be all loving gratitude for being run away with against her will. We become more and more aware of the peculiar egotistic blindness of the man who has always seen more of the game than any other player.

Clarissa also inevitably falls victim to his greatest loves: intrigue, and power. Resistance and watchfulness are, as he confessed at the beginning, an irresistible stimulus to try to overcome them, a direct challenge to his cunning and his power. One of the things that fascinates us most about Lovelace is his ebullient energy. 'I am taller by half a yard in my imagination than I was . . . I took off my hat, as I walked, to see if the Lace were not scorched, supposing it had brushed down a star; and, before I put it on again, in mere wantonness, and heart's-ease, I was for buffeting the moon' (III, 33; *I, 515*). He is a born playactor, a perfect Proteus as Clarissa complains; and it is both his nature and his greatest pleasure to give his volatility free play. It would be hard for him at the best of times to behave with any steadiness or consistency; but what he sees as Clarissa's challenge, and later even as her artfulness since she can be trapped into showing that she cares for him, is an open invitation to unleash on her all the arts and inventiveness of his mercurial temperament. It is also an ironic and psychologically lifelike fact that his worlds of appearance become so real to him – and to us, another source of mistake – that they tend increasingly to obscure the realities. Above all, the fact of his power begins to fascinate him. In only his second letter in volume 3 we find him imagining a Belford shocked at the idea that he could intend ' "to break thro' oaths and protestations so solemn". That I did *not* intend it, is certain. That I *do* intend it, I cannot (my heart, my reverence for her, will not let me) say. But knowest thou not my aversion to the State of Shackles? – And is she not IN MY POWER?' (III, 31; *I, 514*). We shall see more and more clearly how corrupting the sense of his own power can be. What he rationalises as a testing of Clarissa's virtue, is the irresistible urge to try the extent of power, to see what the victim can be made to bear. It has hardly come to this yet, but the beginnings are here, and we begin to detect hints of the sadist's delight in playing with his victim. Necessarily accompanying this is a touch of brutality; always implicit in him, but now starting to open out. It must be emphasised, however, that the strength of the first edition lies in the *gradualness* of its development. The later Lovelace is implicit in the earlier, but grows out of him because of pressures not wholly in his own control. He may become a monster eventually but he certainly doesn't start as one. The mark of the relative crudity and intransigence of the third edition is its desire to blot out the development and get a fully hostile response from the start. In the first edition, at this stage, it is not so much cruelty we see as a kind of insensibility: a defect in imaginative realisation. 'But seest thou not now (as I think I do) the wind-out-stripping-Fair-one flying *from* her Love *to* her Love? . . . Nay, flying from friends she was resolved not to abandon, to the man she was determined not to go off with? - *The Sex! the Sex, all over!* – Charming contradiction! – Hah, hah, hah, hah! – I must here – I must here, lay down my pen, to hold my sides . . .' (III, 30; *I, 513*). If we realise the full implications of this, it isn't funny at all; but if we don't think, it is not only Lovelace's servant who might find the laughter infectious. As a 'situation' it *is* amusing; but that 'wind-out-stripping Fair-one', like so much of Lovelace's language, is imaginatively unrealising, blinding one to the real girl and the real terror. (The same is true of Lovelace's 'imperial' language; the metaphors of mining and fortification, the digging of pits with 'Oho, Charmer, how came you there?', the animal imagery.) At the same time Lovelace's humour and rascality is delightful in a way, precisely because it is a holiday from the burden of awareness and responsibility that the rest of the novel imposes on us. That is its fascination; yet we also have to learn its cost.

Even more significantly, Lovelace, like B, inhabits an idea-world that he *must* vindicate against the challenge of Clarissa. He must either prove that she fits it, or give it up, and with it his whole view of human nature, and in a way *himself*, the personality he has built on that view. Unlike B however, Lovelace has a fully worked out theory about women, logically coherent once its assumptions are grasped – and it is a theory he has successfully proved in practice. He has a kind of intelligence and a zest in argument wholly lacking in B; and nobody has ever been tempted to call him 'Booby'. Yet it is important to realise that his arguments are not *jeux d'esprit*, but rationalisations of deep-seated psychological needs. His determination to 'test' Clarissa is also the need to prove that she is no different from any other woman, and hence that his belief in the stature and irresistibility of his own maleness is real. For this is the only thing he really does believe in.

The 'rake's creed' can be reduced to three basic maxims. First, Pope was right, 'Every woman is at heart a rake' (III, 115; *II, 55* – but implied several times before). This implies a refusal to believe in the reality of moral feeling, or desire for chastity. To Lovelace, such ideas are merely the product of custom and education on one hand and female pride on the other. The reality so overlaid is that woman's nature is primarily sexual, and so she finds her true and natural role in submitting to the male. If so, it is hypocrisy for anyone who has seen into the truth of things to pretend to morality, and it is also unnecessary, since the rakes-at-heart naturally, and in spite of their education, can't help being attracted by rakes. We have seen how the submissiveness of Rosebud seemed to Lovelace to bear out this theory: the low-bred girl behaved 'naturally' because she had never been taught otherwise. If Clarissa is different it is because of her education, and the bourgeois morality it foisted on her. Consequently Lovelace will admit no pleas on behalf of her values or her social status; the values are the unnatural products of the status, and both make her a rebel to love and to true womanhood. She has simply been taught from childhood that it is man's part to ask, but woman's to deny (III, 305; *II, 185*); and what custom and education have started, is completed by female pride, 'the principal bulwark of female virtue' (III, 86; *II, 36*), as he tells Belford. A proud woman is the unnatural but most exciting opponent of the dominating male in the sex war. To overcome her is the greatest triumph and satisfaction for the masculine ego.

The second maxim is '*Importunity* and *Opportunity* no woman is proof against, especially from a persevering Lover who knows how to suit Temptations to Inclinations' (III, 85; *II, 35*). If woman's nature is primarily sexual, this follows logically. All the lover has to do is find the right approach, and for Clarissa the best stalking horse is the promise of reformation. With great acuteness, Lovelace detects that fallibility, her belief that love not only ought to be but actually is determined by reason and morality. She has to rationalise and moralise sexual feeling before she will acknowledge it; and conversely, the growth of the attraction can be disguised from herself by imagining that her pleasure is that of reforming a sinner. On the other hand, if feminine pride is the bulwark of virtue, it also follows that importunity and opportunity must seek to humble that pride 'effectually' (III, 86; *II, 36*). Lovelace does some coldly practical thinking about this. He recognises from his own experience that one of the quickest ways of humbling pride is financial obligation (III, 132; *II, 67*). This, rather than generosity, is the main reason for his attempts to get her to accept money from him, as he privately admits. He keeps inflaming the Harlowes through Leman so that they will not send her her own money and clothes, and is also responsible for the hint that sends Uncle Anthony to Mrs Howe, to persuade her to borrow enough from Anna to prevent financial help from that quarter. The whole of Lovelace's marriage-dangling is also intended to humiliate her and make her reveal that she wants him as a husband. These two opposed tactics effectively explain the way he behaves. On the one hand he can be all kindness, all promise of reformation, softening her up until he can find the right time and place to reveal her true nature to herself. On the other hand the kindness is interspersed with bullying, violent behaviour, deliberate marriage-dangling, designed to frighten and humble her out of the attitude of serene and conscious superiority which is the product of her education and the feminine code. If she is a woman and not an angel, she is bound to lose against love within and Lovelace without.

The last maxim, and the most important one for the eventual tragedy, is the belief that '*Once subdued . . . always subdued*' (III, 94; *II, 41*). This, too, follows logically from the first cardinal assumption. If the 'real' nature of woman is wholly sexual, if the only barriers to free sexuality are custom and pride, then the seduction which overthrows pride, puts a woman at one stroke outside the pale of custom, and reveals her 'true' nature to her, must be a decisive and irreversible change. We will not understand Lovelace's eventually almost pathological obsession unless we detect its roots here, in the belief that sexual penetration itself must alter Clarissa permanently. He simply assumes that marriage will always be in his power because she is. He can see no reason why she should 'hate the man who loves her upon proof'. He has no idea what she is really like, because his ideas give him an 'expert' inside-story that is more real to him than the living woman in the next room.

Indeed, by another tragic irony, the history of her behaviour seems to bear out his diagnosis. How, despite all her coldness, has so dutiful a daughter twice broken through her duty, unless it be love? She will not acknowledge that love; therefore she is guilty of affectation or pride or both. If she can want a man against her morality, and found her behaviour on affectation and pride, she exactly fits his definition of woman and the expectation of being able to fulfil the other rakes' maxims follows as of course. The fact that she has already failed her own morality warrants the belief that she could do so in the greatest point. Most unfortunately of all, Belford, in pleading for her, allows that she may be overcome (III, 265-6; *II, 158-9*) and it is to this over and over again that Lovelace returns. He cannot forget it, even in his best moments. It underlies all his rationalisations about testing her virtue: that virtue untested is worthless; that the honour of the whole sex is involved; that it is for Clarissa's own sake since it will redound to her credit if she wins and enable her to atone for her errors; that it is for his sake too, since rakes with their expert knowledge of women are 'nicer' (i.e. more discriminating) than other men (III, 85; *II, 35*). All this is a verbal cover to the central prospect that she is as female as the more naturally seducible, and that what appears most real about her, her intense moral sensibility, is superficial or even sham. It is Richardson's dramatic triumph once again that he should be able to see so clearly from Lovelace's point of view, and see to some extent truly too, since Lovelace does have 'something to say for himself to himself, though it could not have weight to acquit him with the rest of the World'.[1] Clarissa's feelings for him are real, and they and her willingness to marry him in the teeth of her objections, if he will only ask her properly, *are* inconsistent with her moral sensibility. Yet it is Lovelace's tragedy that his ideology drives him to so simple and cynical an explanation: the sexual attraction alone is real, the moral sensibility not, she can be overcome. This mesmerises him, and he cannot help trying to prove it. It continually opens the door to all that is most compulsive about him.

His dearest dream, to persuade her to live with him unmarried, completely fascinates him because it would fulfil all his urges. It would satisfy his pride since it would demonstrate that she cared more for him than for anyone or anything else. It would satisfy his power-longings because he could treat her as he liked, since she would be wholly at his mercy with no social or legal rights. It would satisfy his revenge on Women, and on the Harlowes, a mighty victory over the feminine code and the bourgeoisie. It would suit his volatile nature, keeping love interesting and 'new' because he would be free to roam, and when he does come home it would not be to a stale familiarity. Last, but perhaps most important, it would guarantee his view of life, his confidence in and his valuation of himself. It is his tragedy that he should believe, as we never do because we do not share his assumptions, that all this is a real possibility.

3

Clarissa of course has no idea of the kind of mind she is dealing with, or the kind of trap he has set for her. Yet it is as true here as it was in the first instalment that the trap could not work without Clarissa herself. Her behaviour is often the most unwise possible in her special situation, without her realising it, and she continually

[1] Richardson to Hill, 10 May 1748; Carroll, *Letters*, 88. This letter, only a fortnight after the publication of the second instalment, shows Richardson's attitude before the extent of the misreadings hardened him into intransigence. A comparison of this tone with that of the notes added in the second and third editions is the most obvious measure of the difference. See also p. 195 below.

makes things worse for herself. Only, given the integrity of her character, could she or should she have behaved otherwise?

As soon as one recognises the true nature of her abduction, her anger, distress and suspicion are as natural as her attitude to the Harlowe persecution, and for the same reason. On the pretence of giving her freedom Lovelace has robbed her of her will and plunged her into social disgrace without any faulty intention on her part. There is no doubting the sincerity and force of her resentment. At a cooler distance and with a more strategic mind, Anna can see how much Lovelace hates to be reminded of her unwillingness to leave Harlowe Place, and suggests that Clarissa 'throw off a little more of the veil' (III, 98; *II*, *44*); but Clarissa equally resents the implication that her anger and reserve are put on. If she were not angry at what has happened, her previous behaviour might be open to a suspicion of insincerity; and though she will try to control her anger she will not disguise it or apologise for it.

Her 'reserve' is also to be explained by her desire to be reconciled with the Harlowes. She still cares very much about her parents – Lovelace is surprised by her unexpected sorrow – and she realises how she will have upset them. She is inclined to believe, as Anna is not, that the fatal Wednesday was to be the last of her trials, and while this makes the abduction all the worse, it also holds some hope of a softer attitude once the first passions have cooled. If she can stay independent of Lovelace and not seek the protection of his family, nor inflame her own by demanding her estate, she thinks there is a possibility still of being taken back. She has of course no means of knowing how Leman has been instructed to make her escape seem deliberate. Once again Anna is quick to see that her hopes will keep her balancing and prevent her from taking action, and urges her to give them up (III, 261; *II*, *155*), but she cannot. Even after Bella's hateful letter and the news of her father's curse, she sees a ray of hope in her mother's hesitant move before she left, and from Mrs Harlowe's opinion that Uncle John might have helped her. It is too precious for her ever to give up.

Yet we know from the first instalment that she has begun to be in love, though she misleads herself about it. Lovelace, and we, soon discover now that she could be persuaded to marry him in spite of her objections (III, 75 and 82; *II, 28 and 33*). How is it that she plays into his hands, and allows her 'delicacy', 'punctilio', and 'decorum' to make her incapable of bringing him to the question? And what do these odd words mean? Do they not simply amount to prudery, as so many of the book's first readers thought?

Once we remember the context, however, 'prudery' would be a gross distortion. By his agency she has been deprived of the protection of her parents through whom proposals would normally pass. She has only her own judgement to rely on, and she has no experience of men. She is with a man of suspect reputation, and she has reason herself to doubt the quality of his love and his honesty. She can see some evidence of plotting, though nothing like its full extent or she would not stay with him or consider marriage, but even the artifice he confesses calls his love in question, since true love is unselfish, generous, and respects the beloved's integrity and freewill. Marriage, as we have seen, is an extremely serious matter to Clarissa because she will promise at the altar to give her husband the same obedience as she gave her father; and this would be intolerable if vowed to a truly selfish, heartless or immoral man. If she is 'punctilious' (believing that every detail of behaviour is an important index to the state of heart and mind), or 'delicate' (sensitive to the implications of what is said and done), it is partly because she has a highly developed moral sensibility, but it is even more because in her present situation she can *only* tell from her lover's behaviour what he is really like and how he really feels about her. Every detail is significant, and the more right she has to feel suspicious, the more responsibility she has to be meticulous. All she demands is that he should approach her with 'decorum', that is, in the mode accepted as fitting by the society to which they both belong, and which would have been axiomatic if she were still at home. Anna tells us what that is. 'I should expect that the man should urge me with respectful warmth; that he should supplicate with constancy, and that all his words and actions should tend to the one principal point' (III, 261; *II, 155-6*). If he expects her to leap at his first hint, or take the initiative herself in making him stick to the point and speak out, this is intolerable not because of prudery, which is essentially an affectation or pretence, but because it proves a lack of respect, a selfish pride, a lack of reverence for standards which require a man at this point to subject his will and self-consequence to the happiness and dignity of the girl who will promise him absolute obedience.

Social *mores* change, and Clarissa's attitudes may well seem overdone or too much in need of historical reconstruction. Yet we ourselves continue to believe on the whole (no more rationally), that it is the man's part to propose, and the effort of imagination required to understand Clarissa ought not to be beyond us. The second instalment is concerned with a conflict no less searching and revealing than the first, but more obviously focussing through the social to the moral within a single relationship. Beneath their time-bound formulation Clarissa's ideas are basically a demand for moral integrity and responsibility, and a real correspondence between value and behaviour. Lovelace sees human relationships as essentially a power struggle between warring egotisms, in which all 'forms' or 'values' are a superficiality or a sham, and the only 'integrity' or indeed reality is the will to sexual domination.

The really fascinating and moving feature of the experience however, is that the fiction is far more complex than the conflict of ideologies suggests. For Lovelace's world of deception does not wholly deceive, and he is not, particularly in the first edition, a villain. We already know that he loves Clarissa in ways he has never experienced before, and whenever his pride is allayed there is fresh evidence of his love in the third volume too. He is always liable to be surprised by the depths of his own emotion into actions that belie his strategy. We are reminded of a situation we have seen before in *Pamela*, when Anna begs Clarissa again and again to show some confidence in Lovelace. There are good reasons for her not to, and to believe that it is up to Lovelace to show that he deserves any; and yet we saw in the Rosebud affair how surely the best was brought out in him by mollifying his pride and trusting to his generosity. We also see how Clarissa's suspicions, reproaches, and constant irritation of his pride produce the same hardening effect on Lovelace as Pamela's did on B.

When we consider Lovelace's Protean personality, moreover, we can see that his deceptions are to some extent the expression of a side to him that is otherwise thwarted and unrealisable. He poses as the loving brother in St Albans and will pose as the loving husband in London. Behind his false offers of Hannah, Mrs Norton, and the services of his relations, there builds up the persona of an assiduous, generous and affectionate lover-guardian; a man with a murky past, but one capable of reformation and a more serious view of himself and his life. These are all pretence, part of a radically dishonest and dishonourable strategy. Yet his success in these roles comes from the ability to feel at home in them for the time. They are what part of his mind would like him to be. They may be lies but they are not incapable of being actualised. Again, while we see in his first long letter to Belford in volume 3 the hardening effects of Clarissa's refusal to trust and show feeling for him, we also see clear evidence of a latent pity and love, in whose light the cynical arguments, postures, and threats can seem to him merely 'all this vapouring' (III, 34; *I*, *515*). Which side of him is 'real'? Which will end uppermost? 'I resolve not *any way*. I will see how *her* will works; and how *my* will leads me on. I will give the combatants fair play. And yet, every time I attend her, I find that she is less in *my* power; I more in *hers*. Yet, a foolish little rogue! to forbid me to think of marriage till I am a reformed man!' (III, *32*; *I*, *515*). Two attitudes, two languages, two Lovelaces appear side by side or tangle with each other.

We also remember again how letters may be a kind of mask which can slip aside to reveal another face half hidden beneath.

It is noticeable that many of Lovelace's most gaily cynical and brutal moments are reactions against moments of real feeling. In the most apparently repulsive of his letters in the third volume, where the rake's creed is most in evidence, he postures :'Avaunt then' – the language is significant – 'all consideration that may arise from a weakness which some would miscall *gratitude*; and is oftentimes the corrupter of a heart not ignoble!' (III, 86; *II, 36*). It is not difficult to connect this with the 'politeness', 'generosity' and 'compassion' he pushed aside in the previous letter, with its evidence of Clarissa's real feeling for him, and her tears of vexation and humiliation over the first of his mock-proposals. There is visible behind the rake's mask a face that can but *will* not express humane feeling. When Clarissa collapses after hearing of her father's curse he does express unmistakeable compassion and love; but his reaction afterwards is one of his nastiest moments: 'I am terribly afraid I shall have a vapourish wife, if I do marry . . . Not that I shall be much at home with her, perhaps, after the first fortnight, or so' (III, 307; *II, 187*. Italics omitted). Within seconds he is at his gayest and most brutal, his language at its most unrealising. This pattern is repeated many times, and its implication is clear. Much of his writing is an attempt to clamp back the rake's mask, with its fixed heartless grin, to hide the human expression from its owner's eye. The tragedy is Lovelace's too, and there is a sense in which Clarissa's intransigence allows him to be caught in his own trap. For there is a part of him that is not loveless, which might have become actualised.

Clarissa is betrayed by herself, too as well as by Lovelace, for she not only cannot act to bring out the best in him, but cannot refrain from acting so as to bring out the worst. In the first volumes Richardson had already discovered how her absolutism made her helpless. He now begins to discover her fatal rigidity. She is incapable of adapting herself to her new situation, though Anna continually insists that she must; she insists on behaving as though she were still in her own parlour at home. Even when she notionally recognises that punctilio ended when she left her father's house, she cannot make this real to herself and act accordingly. She will not rebate anything from the absolute standards she demands from herself and her lover. Prudery is indeed the last charge that should have been made against her, for while prudery is affectation, her moral strictness is as deeply ingrained in her nature as Lovelace's pride, and appears as much by reflex. Time and again at the most inopportune moments she cannot avoid telling Lovelace what she thinks of his levity, his lack of politeness, his moral shortcomings. She cannot stop preaching, reproaching, upbraiding. One may admire the courage and integrity which care so little for expediency; but I suspect many of us have been known to share Lovelace's irritation, and certainly we cannot fail to see the dangers of such inflexibility.

While appreciating the values that explain her delicacy, too, it is clear that her behaviour is also a matter of temperament. Richardson begins again to focus on that pride which can co-exist with moral absolutism. There is clear evidence of this in a matter which has little to do with Lovelace: her unwillingness to admit to her family, when she writes to Aunt Hervey, that she was tricked away, by which of course she adds another little nail to her coffin. In the third edition, where an intransigent Mr Richardson set out to make Clarissa as pure white as Lovelace pure black, he inserted prudential reasons for this, but none is convincing. She cannot bear the humbling truth to be known. Beside her moral anger then, a personal anger at having been 'tricked out of myself' puts a rasp in her voice from the first conversation at St Albans, and ensures a touchy inflammability on her side as well as his. She is humiliated by her lack of clothes and money, and this also helps to make her 'peevish', 'fretful', 'incensed' and eager to lash out at the man who is responsible. She also has a very feminine captiousness. It is amusing to watch Lovelace tricking her to London in the knowledge that she will do the opposite of what she thinks he wants. More subtly, her vanity and her feminine code are interwoven in one very significant way. She believes that the head and the will should direct the heart, and she acknowledges a code which forbids a woman to reveal her feelings to her lover before he has decorously asked for her hand; but temperament as well as moral value plays a key role here. She is prevented from showing the feeling she really has, which more than anything else would actualise his most loving self, by a kind of pride that is fostered by the feminine code. She will not admit her love to Anna or herself unless it is disguised in some formulation: like her instantaneous memory of his goodness to Rosebud and his tenants and her delight in being able to talk to him about religion, after his proposal to go to Windsor (III, 121; *II, 59*). Her feelings obviously flower at the first encouragement, but we have to detect them beneath the surface. It is not merely, however, that she is incapable of any readiness to confess her feelings to Lovelace, but that every time it happens she is humiliated. She reacts in anger to her blushes and confusion over the first tentative proposal (III, 75-6; *II, 28-9*). On the next such occasion she provokes him in the worst possible way, by suddenly reviving out of nowhere the old idea that she must be prepared to give Lovelace up if her family will free her from Solmes (III, 145 ff.; *II, 76 ff.*). The result is a really stormy scene in which she has a narrow escape, though she never knows it. What on earth was she thinking of? The answer has to be read between the lines, but it is clear enough. Once again it is shame and anger at her blushes, and at her own affectation in pretending not to know what Lovelace is talking about. She has ample reason for anger at *him*, what is significant is how angry she is at herself. 'I have long been sick of myself: And now I am more and more so' (III, 153; *II, 81*). To betray her feelings makes her look, to herself, 'silly' and 'like a fool' – phrases she repeats again and again. There is no excuse for Lovelace's heartless strategy, but though he cannot see the values behind her 'reserve' he is quite right about the personal pride. Furthermore the anger when that pride is wounded makes her over-ready to pick quarrels and re-assert herself. Once again Lovelace does have something to say for himself when he accuses her of 'conscious superiority' and even 'artfulness'. Part of her tragedy is her own making.

No more than in the first instalment is Richardson simply using Clarissa as an uncriticised positive; he is still being driven by his imagination to test her and discover where her shortcomings lie. Consequently the really key scenes in the second instalment contain a deep tragic irony. These are the three scenes in which Lovelace is surprised into genuine proposals of marriage by the unexpected power of his own feelings, and to the potential ruin of his whole strategy.

4

Readers must have their wits about them here, for the whole truth only appears when the separate accounts of these scenes are pieced together.

The first begins (III, 231; *II, 135*) with Lovelace bringing her the news of her brother's plot to recapture her with Captain Singleton's help (for which the first hint, as usual, came from himself through Leman). Instead of anger at her brother, she falls to lamenting the results of the 'fatal step' she has been 'betrayed into', and Lovelace takes her up smartly on her severity to him. As she grows warm, he chooses a beautifully and deliberately doomed way to propose. 'I hope I may, on this *new* occasion, speak without offence, *notwithstanding your former Injunctions* – You see that there can be no hope of Reconciliation with your Relations. Can you, Madam, consent to honour with your hand, a wretch whom you have never yet obliged with one *voluntary* favour?' (III, 234; *II, 137*). The calm offensiveness could hardly be bettered; and he stands enjoying her confusion, anger and shame 'to be thus teazed by one who seemed to have all *his* passions at command, at a time when I had very little over *mine*!'

As she bursts into tears he seizes the chance to take her in his arms; but now their accounts significantly diverge. Clarissa's suggests annoyance at the teasing 'half-sentences' about not taking advantage of her brother's plot, and there is no reason to doubt this; but Lovelace's reveals something else, both more specific and more personal. He is delighted because she seems so preoccupied with her misery that she hardly notices she is crying on his shoulder. He begins an empty little speech about making up for her unhappiness by his 'gratitude' – and breaks off just there, with the rake's reflection that after all he owes her none (III, 240; *II*, *141*). But the word hangs in the air; and *that* is when 'recollecting how like a tame fool I stood with his arms about me, I flung from him with indignation' (III, 235; *II*, *137*). She imagines he is thanking her for tamely responding to his taunt with her first 'voluntary favour' – and her pride cannot bear it.

As she breaks from him, however, it is Lovelace's turn to lose control. Though he 'no more intended all this ecstatic nonsense, than I thought the same moment of flying in the air' (III, 241; *II*, *142*), he is so carried away by his own feelings that he makes an involuntarily sincere, and warm, and explicit proposal — quite how much so one would hardly gather from Clarissa's account, which does not tell us what he said. But she is too angry and ashamed to respond: 'what could I say to this? — Extorted from him, as it seemed to me, rather as the effect of his Compassion, than of his Love? What *could* I say? I paused, I looked silly – I am *sure* I looked very silly. He suffered me to pause, and look silly; *waiting for* me *to say something*: And at last (ashamed of my confusion, and aiming to make an *excuse for it*)' she ascribes it not to his offer and her feelings, but to her fears of her brother's project and the irreconcilability of her family (III, 235; *II*, *138*). Nothing could be worse advised, as well as disingenuous. The moment is gone, and Lovelace bridles. The accounts now diverge factually: Lovelace says that he asked her again, Clarissa that he didn't, but it hardly matters. For Clarissa, still trying 'for a palliation of my confusion', now compounds her mistake by arguing that she wants her cousin Morden to see, when he arrives, that she has made use of Lovelace's help only to free herself from Solmes. The calamitous misunderstanding of Lovelace can be seen in its full extent as she goes on: 'This, altho' teazed by him as I was, was not, you see, my dear, a *denial*. But he must throw himself into a heat, rather than try to persuade; which any other man, in his situation, I should think, would have done: And this warmth obliged me to adhere to my seeming negative.' Finally it is with what she herself calls 'salving Art' that she seizes the opportunity to be angry too (III, 236; *II, 138*).

Without defending Lovelace, or minimising the real values behind Clarissa's 'delicacy', or charging her with prudery, one may nevertheless assert that the subtlety of the dramatic art in this scene is its probing of the complex female nature, behind the moral values. Clarissa's behaviour is understandable enough in the broad context of her situation and the treatment she has suffered. Yet there remain pride and disingenuousness, which at this moment have been more dangerous enemies to her than Lovelace himself.

His second genuine proposal (III, 290 ff.; *II, 175 ff.*) is the direct result of Clarissa's collapse, when a vicious letter from Arabella passes on to her her father's solemn curse. Lovelace is affected enough by her sorrow to offer, quite sincerely, to send for Lord M's chaplain and marry her before they leave for London; and this time she accepts his hand, though she refuses to set a day for the ceremony. Her motives are 'not *merely ceremonious*' (III, 298; *II, 181*). It is partly that there will be no time for decorous arrangements, but mostly it is a religious objection to entering 'so solemn an Engagement' when grief and illness make her singularly ill-prepared (III, 291; *II, 176*). What is significant this time, however, is not the proposal itself but what follows it. 'He presses me every hour (Indeed as *needlessly*, as *unkindly*) for fresh tokens of my esteem *for* him, and confidence *in* him. And, as I have been brought to *some verbal concessions*, if he should prove unworthy, I am sure I shall have great reason to blame this violent Letter: For I have no resolution at all' (III, 290; *II, 175*). One feels sorry for her, and it is clearly no time for Lovelace to be pestering her for attentions. Yet one cannot help being disturbed by the tone and phrasing of that 'some verbal concessions'. Even now she cannot reveal her feelings or accept commitment. The result is sadly predictable. Almost as soon as he has told Belford about it, Lovelace draws conclusions mortifying to his pride. He is half ashamed of his own feelings anyway, and of how they have betrayed him. He soon begins to shape his style back to the ironic and revive his darker plans. In his next letter his plotting heart rises 'to my throat, in such half-choaking flutters, when I think of what this removal' (to London) 'may do for me' (III, 306; *II, 186*). He still feels for Clarissa, still hopes to stay 'honest'. 'But why, Belford, why, once more, puttest thou me in mind, that she *may be* overcome? And why is her own reliance on my honour so late and so reluctantly shewn?' (III, 307; *II, 187*). The rake's mask is soon clamped back on the face. 'Something *more* than woman, an *angel*, in some things; but a *baby* in others: So father-sick! so family-fond! . . . It is infinitely better for her and for me, that we should not marry. What a delightful manner of life . . . would the life of Honour be with such a woman! The fears, the inquietudes, the uneasy days, the restless nights; all arising from doubts of having disobliged me!' (III, 308; *II, 187*). There is no need to re-emphasize the heartlessness and incomprehension, and we must not forget the strategic side of his complaints against the coldness that never allows him to soften her up. Yet at another crisis that could have resolved the potential tragedy, the responsibility for what follows is partly Clarissa's too, and the tragedy is for both.

The third scene (III, 340, ff.; *II, 209 ff.*) takes place just two days after they get to London. She is annoyed when Lovelace returns to the house so quickly, having promised to leave; and even more annoyed (as we learn only from him) by a splendid linguistic blunder. She has at last taken him up on one of his offers to get his cousin to visit her, and struggling to get himself off the hook he makes the mistake of saying Charlotte is 'delicate, which she took strangely wrong' (III, 345; *II, 213*). This is amusing because all he meant was to refer to Charlotte's stomach disorder, which elsewhere he so cynically attributes to her spinsterhood; but Clarissa is clearly wondering in her own mind whether there may be anything in Anna's charges of over-delicacy, though she will not stand for the imputation from Lovelace — who for once doesn't know what he has done wrong.

He begins, then, a strategic plea, but convinces himself as he goes along, and ends by pressing 'without reserve for Matrimony . . . which state I little thought of urging upon her with so much strength and explicitness' (III, 346; *II*, *213*).

But Clarissa yet again allows the moment to pass, and this time for a reason that has nothing to do with morality, punctilio or decorum. 'He was silent. My voice failed to second the inclination I had to say something not wholly discouraging to a point so warmly pressed' (III, 341; *II*, *210* misprinted). Lovelace recovers, and the moment is gone. It is only in retrospect that the full significance becomes clear, for this turns out to have been her last chance. Behind the prissy language, the reason is no more than a complete failure of nerve. Her behaviour to Lovelace and the whole complex problem of her 'delicacy' cannot be treated in moral terms alone. It is not a question of blame, or of might have beens which are no business of literary criticism. It is a question of responding to the truth and penetration of the dramatic imagination. There is working in these three scenes, in purely literary terms, a subtle dramatic irony without which the novel would be infinitely the poorer. Richardson is again discovering something disturbing. Values properly exist only as they are embodied in behaviour, and as soon as they are, they become inseparably connected with much more dubious facets of temperament than would appear when they are debated theoretically. (This is one of the great ethical demonstrations of fiction.) As soon as we read closely, there is no doubting Clarissa's integrity and responsibility. Yet we are no less valuably made aware of the subtle ways in which these values are connected with her pride, and with a kind of emotional cowardice and dishonesty. The peculiar trap of her puritanism is its vulnerability to pride, and it is Richardson's developing awareness of this, far beyond the stage of *Pamela*, which finally determines both the meaning and the stature of Clarissa's tragedy. This is one of the book's big growing points. Again, while the feminine code insists on the seriousness of marriage, and that suitors must show a responsibility and unselfishness commensurate with that seriousness, it clearly encourages a kind of emotional dishonesty.

Clarissa is allowed to repress perfectly honest sexual feeling, and to escape confronting an emotional problem: a kind of horror of sex and of committing herself to a sexual relationship. Richardson in his ordinary self might have skirted this, but his dramatic imagination willy nilly shows that it is there, and this will prove another growing point no less significant. It will have a bearing on one of his greatest achievements: the opening up of Clarissa's subconscious mind in her derangement.

Unfortunately for all modern readers, as I have argued elsewhere,[1] the didactic moralist has interfered heavily with the dramatic artist in the edition of the novel we all read. A fortnight after the first publication of the second instalment, he had a reasonable view of what he had done. 'My Girl is thought over nice by many, I find: But I think I could defend her in all her Delicacies – And yet, I would that she should have some little things to be blamed for, tho' for nothing in her Will; and that Lovelace should have something to say for himself to himself, tho' it could not have weight to acquit him with the rest of the world.'[2] This does less than full justice to the ironies, but as the evidence of misreading mounted he grew angrier and angrier, and in the second and third editions he tinkered with the book to drive its morality home in terms which the crudest of readers – whom he blamed at the same time for carelessness and superficiality – could understand. In irritable footnotes, in the proliferation of italics directed at the reader and breaking the subtle indirection of the epistolary form, in the further directing of response through the index, and in many insertions in the text, he hardened the outlines of his achievement into a cruder black and white. He would have no criticism of his heroine now, but insisted dogmatically on her exemplary perfection; and in order to enforce this he was driven on several occasions to blur or even subvert his original achievement. Yet if we cannot trust the teller of the third edition we can trust the tale of the first. It has the integrity to confront and the courage to explore what proved

1 'Clarissa Restored', *Review of English Studies*, 10 (1959), 156-71.

2 Richardson to Hill, 10 May 1748; Carroll, *Letters*, 87-8.

rd in its author's most deeply felt values. We shall under[illegible] neither the nature nor the magnitude of the tragedy that [illegible] follow unless we see why it is these three scenes, and not the more sensational ending of the fourth volume, which prove the most significant for the novel as a whole.

5

From this point Clarissa and Lovelace are doomed, though one only realises it afterwards. They may struggle against one another and themselves, and at the end of the instalment Clarissa succeeds for a while in a desperate attempt to escape, but after the move to London and Clarissa's last chance in the scene I have discussed, there remains only the long slippery slope to tragedy.

The power situation, from Lovelace's point of view, is complete as soon as he has her safe in 'Mrs Sinclair's' genteel brothel, with Deb Butler planted as her servant 'Dorcas', and with neither Clarissa nor Anna having any idea of the real address. There is another new factor of which Clarissa is completely unaware: the continual urgings, recriminations and contempt of the young prostitutes Sally and Polly, who cannot bear the implicit reproach of Clarissa's virginity or her power over Lovelace, which their succumbing to him has lost them for ever. They keep badgering him to reduce her to their level, using the tactics most calculated to lacerate his sexual pride, and also assuring him of what he most wants to hear, that she really is like them at heart beneath the veneer of custom and education, and the 'superiority' his craven behaviour allows her to assume.

The structure of the fourth volume is a deterioration of the relationship in four phases, each concluding with a physical attempt more personal and serious than the last.

Lovelace is at first mainly concerned to make his trap absolutely secure. Getting Clarissa to accept Dorcas insinuates an agent into her rooms whose supposed illiteracy will be useful for spying into her correspondence. The false scheme about Mrs

Fretchville's house lets Clarissa regard her stay at Mrs Sinclair's as a temporary expedient, so that she is less likely to object to it. Lovelace goes with her to church, partly to foster her hopes of his reformation, and partly to make sure she cannot find out about the fictitious address. He achieves two great points through her fear of the Singleton plot (which James has in fact given over): that she should accept the need for him to stay under the same roof; and that she should, however tacitly, seem to have owned that they are married, before witnesses who could swear in a court of law that she had consented to her situation. The dinner with his companions and 'Miss Partington' increases the number of witnesses who could swear that she went under his name. The plot to get Clarissa to accept Miss Partington as a bedfellow in the crowded house is also an attempt to open the door to a *Pamela*-style sexual foray. This however fails, and awakens her suspicions again.

Yet Lovelace is mistaken in his belief that the dinner has lost him ground badly, and in the nettled pique which follows. Throughout all this, one must remember, Clarissa is under the impression that all he has to do is press her to name the wedding-day she had postponed because of her grief and illness on one occasion, and her loss of nerve on another. She is irritated by his duplicity in pretending they are married already, and upset by his failure to urge a day once more. Yet after the visit to church she tells Anna she 'could prefer him to all the men I ever knew, were he but to be always what he has been this day' (III, 364; *II*, *225*) – and considering what she means by 'prefer', this is quite an admission. She doesn't care for the levity and impropriety of his friends, but embedded in her letter is even stronger evidence of his growing attractiveness. 'He has indeed so many advantages in his person and manner, that what would be inexcusable in another, would, if one watched not over one's self, and did not endeavour to distinguish what is the essence of right and wrong, look becoming in him' (III, 370; II, *229*). The formulation could hardly be more significant. She also infers an original and natural innocence from the 'deceiving sweetness' of his face, his voice, his smile. We have moreover a new pair of eyes to see her with now. Richardson introduced his fourth main correspondent, Belford, in a single letter in the third volume, and he is present at the dinner. He has no doubt, as he watches her eyes, that she loves her tormentor as well as fearing him (IV, 9; *II*, *243*). For all her lively suspicion, she is obviously worried by her curt refusal of Miss Partington's request, and its implications, and Anna's reaction will confirm the worry. She may end her letter 'I am now out of humour with him', but she goes on 'with myself, with all the world, but you' (III, 375; *II*, *232*). Lovelace may have overplotted himself a little, but not seriously.

Yet there is a sudden change in her now; if not for the reasons Lovelace thinks. She is deeply upset by Mrs Howe's letter, demanding that she give up the correspondence, and by Anna's threat to come to London if she does – the tactic reminds one again of Lovelace – but these would have had only a temporary effect. The real reason for the marked change in her mood and temper is the letter from her cousin Morden, sealed by her family with black wax, without any covering word, that she finds in the trunk of clothes she has at last been sent from Harlowe Place. Morden's kind but firm arguments urging her to obey her parents (based of course on James Harlowe's version of Solmes, and Morden's ignorance of how the Harlowes treated their daughter) throw her back immediately into the state of mind she was in just after she was tricked away, bringing back in full measure her regrets and self-accusations. This is bad enough, but a more bitter blow must be detected by inference. Morden quietly but devastatingly urges her to think of the consequences of loving a libertine: the humiliations she must bring on herself by having to divide 'her interest in his affections with half the town, and that perhaps the dregs of it'; the humiliation of his sensuality; the humiliation of having him boast to 'lewd companions, and not improbably, with lewder women' of her 'patient sufferings and broken spirit, and bringing them home to witness to both'. These, and things far worse – there is a very distant reference to venereal disease – will be the consequence of giving in to 'the fading pleasure of the Eye' (IV, 34-5; *II, 260*). Now at this particular moment this comes as a shattering blow precisely because Clarissa has, quite unmistakeably, been succumbing to Lovelace's sexual attractiveness – and she knows it. At once everything looks horribly different. She is 'in my own opinion, a poor lost creature' (IV, 38; *II, 262*), realising how many hundreds of miles she has been led out of the right path by one false step in setting out, blaming herself bitterly for her presumption, and brooding on death and on her father's curse. When she writes again her 'vapourishness' has increased. In her loneliness and self-disgust the very things which most attract her about Lovelace seem only to emphasise her isolation, 'when his bountiful temper and gay heart attach every one to him; and I am but a *cypher*, to give *him* significance, and *myself* pain' (IV, 40; *II, 264*). Everyone and everything is on Lovelace's side: how different a view of that gay party now. She doesn't say so, but one can see how what Morden had said about having to divide his attention with lewd companions, and having to bear him showing off the humbling of her spirit, would bear on that dinner too. And once again he has humiliated her by failing to urge a speedy day. 'Now, my dear . . . I cannot bear the life I live. I would be glad at my heart to be out of his reach. If I were, he should soon *find the difference*. If I must be humbled, it had better be by those to whom I owe duty, than by him' (IV, 41; *II, 264-5*). She begins to think again of making overtures to Uncle John, through Hickman.

The Harlowes' black wax, and the books they send her, show a vindictive playing on her tendency to melancholy and even morbidity, which we have noticed before. Another suspect psychological trait begins to open out; for though her reaction to the letter is tenable in terms of our knowledge of Lovelace, it is arguably excessive in terms of hers. Nevertheless, when it would be difficult for her to communicate and him to understand her feelings, even if he were a truly loving and reforming fiancé, his tactics have made it impossible. In any case he thinks he knows the explanation of the change in her: over-niceness about his companions, and a suspiciousness that is a challenge to give her cause to distrust. He begins to suspect that something must be brewing between Clarissa and Anna; as indeed it is, though for more complex reasons than he can guess. The result is the attempt to steal Anna's latest letter when it slips unnoticed to the floor, and then to wrest it forcibly from Clarissa (IV, 52; *II*, *272*). For the first time he has gone beyond plotting to force, though directed at the letter and not her person, and hardly serious as yet. Nevertheless the incident marks the end of the hopeful phase that had begun with her acceptance of him after her father's curse.

In the second phase, the pattern of the first is reversed, and Clarissa becomes the contriver. This balanced structure, as we saw in *Pamela*, is very characteristic of Richardson.

She deliberately keeps the tiff going for a week, though she is by no means mortally offended. The idea is to keep him at a distance while Hickman approaches Uncle John and while indeed, unknown to Clarissa, Anna asks Mrs Norton to approach Mrs Harlowe as well. This involves art and deception, and the effect is of course to harden Lovelace still further, as the prostitutes taunt him. Clarissa has not made up her mind to leave him, but the effect of Morden's letter continues to grow. She has now come to believe that it was her 'eye', that is, her sexual attraction to Lovelace, that was responsible for her 'officious' entry into correspondence with him in the first place, but she thinks that the 'deluded eye now clearly sees its fault, and the misled heart despises it for it'. Anna, on reading about Morden's letter, also catches the same tone of gloomy moralising. And after a brush with Lovelace, in which Clarissa openly admits her reason for keeping away from him, with a directness in marked contrast to his methods, she suddenly adopts Anna's language for the first time. 'A wretch! when I can say, to my infinite regret, on a *double* account, that all he complains of is owing to himself!' (IV, 71; *II*, *285*). The double account is not only that they might have been married by now but for his hesitation, but also that this could only be true because of a physical attraction on her part that she feels she should be ashamed of, after her cousin's letter.

The overtures to the Harlowes meet with a complete repulse however – a failure as complete from Clarissa's viewpoint as that of the Partington scheme had been from Lovelace's. How is she to behave now? Anna believes she must be his, for 'to leave him now . . . would have a very ill appearance for your reputation' (IV, 82; *II*, *292*). In her most arrogant feminist terms she advises: 'Let us save the wretch then, if we can, tho' we soil our fingers in lifting him up from his dirt' (IV, 84; *II*, *294*). She sees that Lovelace's pride may make him vengeful, but there can be no room for delicacy now, and having put herself in this position, Clarissa must take and keep the initiative and bring the matter to an issue. Clarissa thinks more justly and less arrogantly, but she feels utterly unequal, as indeed she is, to act up to Anna's advice. 'What, *I* to challenge a man for a husband! – *I* to exert myself to quicken the delayer in his resolutions! And having, as you think, lost an opportunity, to begin to try to recal it, as *from myself*, and *for myself*! To *threaten* him, as I may say, into the Marriage State! – O my dear! if this be right to be done, how difficult is it, where Modesty and Self (or where Pride, if you please) is concerned, to do that right?' (IV, 89; *II*, *297*). But the dawning insight into her pride is not continued, for as her active imagination pictures their next meeting, with a Lovelace 'mighty stately, mighty *mannish*, mighty *coy*, if you please!', and herself 'very humble, very submissive . . . With downcast eye' begging his forgiveness for her perversity, her female gorge rises and she cannot see him (IV, 91; *II*, *298*). She weeps fretfully, and when he promises to wait till morning to see her if she will promise to eat her supper, it is '*Very kind in his anger! – Is he not*? . . . How happy, I'll warrant, if I may meet him in a *kind* and *forgiving* humour! I hate myself! – But I won't be insulted – Indeed I won't, for all this' (IV, 92; *II*, *299*). 'All this' is pride, its true accents beautifully caught by Richardson's dramatic art.

When the next morning, with only the addition of a dig at her family, Lovelace urges what she has already admitted to herself: his need for 'some instances of previous and preferable favour from the Lady I am ambitious to call mine' (IV, 93; *II*, *300*), she is only too happy to seize the chance to quarrel with him. She grows warmer and warmer, refusing to talk of love and insisting only on discussing his merit, until she works herself up to the pitch of demanding that they 'resolve to quit every regard for each other that is more than civil' (IV, 96; *II*, *301-2*). Lovelace inevitably flies into a passion which so terrifies her that she is glad to escape, and burst into tears again. They meet again more coolly, and Lovelace begs leave to write to her about settlements – an expedient he has obviously been keeping up his sleeve. But Clarissa again fails to follow Anna's advice, and turns the subject with a little sermon on generosity. True generosity is a greatness of soul which insists on doing more than is strictly required, or hoped for. It will permit no worthy mind to doubt its worthy intentions, and could never shock anyone, least of all someone thrown into its protection. This is a noble enough conception – yet if we remember that Clarissa has no more evidence of perfidy than the attempt to steal the letter; that she is now herself responsible for the distance between them; and that her conduct must be judged on what she knows, not what we know; it is arguable that she is herself less than truly generous by her first canon, however badly Lovelace fails by the second.

Clarissa however is pleased on the whole because 'I am not *meanly* off . . . If it were only, that I can see this man without losing any of that dignity (What other word can I use, speaking of *myself*, that betokens *decency*, and not *arrogance*?) which is so necessary to enable me to look *up*, or rather with the *mind's* eye, I may say, to look *down* upon a man of this man's cast' (IV, 101; *II*, *305*). This surely begs many questions. It is one thing to argue, as she does elsewhere, that every woman has a right to self-respect; but this goes well beyond, to an inner need for the 'conscious superiority' of which both Anna and Lovelace have spoken, which is far less defensible. That Richardson is aware of the question-mark we can tell from Clarissa's own fear, at the end of this letter, that her behaviour is not wholly the outcome of conscience, divinely implanted, but may spring from 'habits and peculiarities' of her 'deceitful' heart (IV, 103; *II*, *306*).

Lovelace's proposals for the marriage settlement are generous, but end coolly: 'You will now, dearest Madam, judge, how far all the rest depends upon yourself' (IV, 106; *II, 308*). He is resolved after her haughtiness that she shall speak out. Clarissa is so sure that the proposals must end by urging a day that she is quite taken aback when she gets there. She simply cannot realise that her own contrivances have given Lovelace some excuse for his coldness. His behaviour is not excused by hers, yet in the next scene she again plays into his hands when he leaves it to her whether or not to delay the wedding by sending for Lord M; and when after hinting thus at delay he becomes effusive about marrying 'to-morrow'. Finally she wholly fails to sense her danger as Lovelace, having played at obedient resignation, tries to kiss her, and is disdainfully repulsed (IV, 110-11; *II, 311-12*). 'This', he vows afterwards, 'I will for ever remember against her, in order to steel my heart, that I may *cut thro' a rock of ice* to hers; and repay her for the disdain, the scorn ... The women below say, She hates me; she despises me! – And 'tis true: She does; she must. – And why cannot I take their advice? I will not long, my Fair one, be despised by *thee*, and laughed at by *them*!' (IV, 117-18; *II, 316*).

This is a letter to which Richardson paid particular attention in his second edition. He made three insertions in the text, of which the first two merely make explicit what had been implied, but the third contains a plea: 'Why, why, will he take pains to make a heart wrap itself up in Reserve, that wishes only, and that for his sake as well as my own, to observe due decorum?' (IV, 111; *II, 312*). This is just, if taken as a defence of her behaviour in the second instalment as a whole, but in this particular context it is disingenuous. It denies the significance of both the structural patterning and the probing by the dramatic imagination, which make it clear that Clarissa is to some extent meeting contrivance with contrivance and pride with pride. In the first edition the answer to her significantly hesitant question: 'Modesty, I think, required of me that it should pass as he had put it: Did it not? I think it did ...' is by no means simple, because of the irony that cannot but hang over the word 'modesty', as a description of the feeling that has filled her mind over the past two days. The long note Richardson added at the end of the letter goes from bad to worse. He begins with a reasonable reminder of her character and circumstances, and the need to keep Lovelace at a distance – though the argument hardly covers the contrived distance lately. Then he tries to justify her in terms of the reader's new knowledge of Lovelace, which is quite beside the point. Most unfortunate of all, he insists heavily that she 'is proposed as an *Example*', and so cannot be dispensed from 'Rules' as others might be, 'altho' if she had *not* observed them, a *Lovelace* would have carried all his points' (IV, 113; *II, 313*). In its dogmatic and prudential emphasis this is Mr Richardson at his worst, but even that is more forgivable than the falsification of his art. It is precisely her intransigence that has played into Lovelace's hands; and her absolutism that has made her as helpless with him as with her family. Though 'might have beens' should play no part in criticism, if one is to be forced into such terms the three ironic scenes suggest that some compromise (like Pamela's) with rigid absolutes would have been more likely to prevent the tragedy than to bring it on. Once again there is proof of the superiority of the artist over the didactic moralist.

For three days, now, Lovelace concentrates on making Clarissa happy. He arranges that she should overhear a conversation which will ease her mind about his feeling for her, the application to Lord M, and the delay over the Fretchville house; and at the same time ensure that she should not try to leave, by reminding her of the Singleton plot and threatening to confront the Harlowes immediately if she should ever be found missing. All seems much more tranquil. He even persuades her to go to the theatre with him. But he has not changed, in spite of further urgings from Belford and Lord M, and eventually his purpose becomes clear. The whole manoeuvre is designed to get her out of the house, while Dorcas and the prostitutes transcribe all of Anna's letters they can find in the closet, to which Dorcas has a key. Lovelace is determined to know what the opposing strategy amounts to.

Nothing could be more unfortunate for Clarissa, for Anna expresses just those elements of the feminine code that are both the counterpart and the natural target of the rake. We have seen how she shares Lovelace's view of the relation between men and women as a struggle for dominance. She is basically good, warmhearted and moral, but she is much less scrupulous and sensitive than her friend, and her morality is less entwined with her heartstrings. No absolutist, she is ready to adapt to circumstances and is something of a strategist, as her advice to Clarissa has shown. Indeed she is like Lovelace in many ways. Her strategy to make him speak out corresponds to his with Clarissa; her Mrs Townshend scheme pairs with his Singleton plot; she uses threats to make Clarissa continue a forbidden correspondence just as he had done; she propounds a scheme to get at *his* letters. She has a similar spirit and liveliness behind which, for all its charm, there is visible a slacker sense of responsibility than Clarissa's; and the epistolary style that creates her for us is a beautifully modulated female variant of Lovelace's. It is of course more playful; she is something of the allowed jester cheering up her graver friend, and her bark is far worse than her bite. Nevertheless her style shares Lovelace's volatile changes of mood, his sharp and witty argumentativeness, even the predilection for animal anecdotes and images – and the implications that go with these. She too is a lover of power as her treatment of Hickman shows; and she too is corrupted, and rendered more arrogant and unfeeling, by her success in playing with her victim. She is, finally, as arrogant in her female pride as Lovelace in the male variety. Behind her vocabulary is a basic contempt for men.

Consequently she seems to fit, exactly, the rake's definition of woman. Her past affair with Sir George Colmar proves to Lovelace that sex is the reality, morals merely the veneer of custom and education. A passage in one of her letters confirms that women cannot help being attracted by rakes. Her female tyranny, strategy and pride seem wholly to endorse his view of the sex-war and justify his behaviour as merely meeting women with their own weapons. Her contempt, as he broods on her language, is bound to lacerate his pride and instigate revenge. Her basically moral nature he can no more understand or accept than Clarissa's.

There is another irony of fate in his capture of just *this* bunch of letters; any other would have had a less disastrous effect. The situation they cover is the one most calculated to anger Anna on her friend's behalf, starting from Clarissa's acceptance of Lovelace and dealing (with the single exception of the 'last chance' scene) with a period in which he seems wholly to blame. Again, Anna has undertaken to write as seldom as possible in order to reconcile Clarissa to the forbidden correspondence, so that, for example, she never discusses the 'last chance' scene. She is also enraged by three outside factors: her mother's treatment, her discovery of two shabby affairs in Lovelace's past, which she only hints to Clarissa, and a nasty letter from Uncle John Harlowe, of which again she gives only the gist. The prostitutes naturally extract from her letters the passages most likely to enrage Lovelace and serve their ends. Finally, from the brief mention of Morden's letter there is no indication for Lovelace of what it was about; still less of the reason why it upset Clarissa so much – that is, the one factor that would have done her some good in his eyes, the evidence of her love for him.

In fact the letters encourage him to suppose just the opposite, and worse still, to assume that Clarissa's must have been in the same vein, and would have revealed her also as a proud and scornful beauty, and a schemer. 'Well might her saucy friend', that is, Clarissa, '(who has been equally free with me, or the occasion could not have been given) be so violent as she lately was, at my endeavouring to come at one of these Letters' (IV, 185; *II, 362*). It is true that if Lovelace had got hold of the corresponding batch of Clarissa's letters, they would have revealed her as more angry than ever before; but the contrast would have shown up the whole difference between the two girls and their attitudes. Clarissa herself admits one contrivance to Lovelace, but her letters would have shown how incapable she is of Anna's strategies. Just twice, at her angriest, she falls into Anna's 'wretch' vocabulary, but the word immediately stands out as not her kind of language.

The greatest distortion of all comes through extraction and selection. Lovelace still smarts from that disdainfully refused kiss. '*It is the cruellest of fates for a woman to be forced to have a man whom her heart despises*' is what the prostitutes transcribe from Anna's letter about that scene. 'That', cries Lovelace, 'is what I wanted to be sure of . . . I was afraid that she *indeed* despised me, – And I cannot bear to think she does. But, Belford, I do not intend that this lady shall be bound down by so cruel a fate. Let me perish, if I marry a woman who has given her most intimate friend reason to say, *she despises me*! – A Lovelace to be *despised*, Jack!' (IV, 198-9; *II, 371*).

The assumption that Anna is simply reflecting Clarissa's view seems reasonable, especially without our knowledge of why Clarissa was annoyed. Yet if we turn back to Anna's letter itself, and replace the extract in its context, the impression is very different. 'But, as matters now stand betwixt you, I am very unseasonable in expressing my resentments against him. – Yet I don't know whether I am or not, neither; since it is the most cruel of fates, for a woman to be forced to have a man whom her heart despises. You must, at *least*, despise him; at times, however' (IV, 119; *II, 317*). The word and the feeling are Anna's and she is manifestly unsure that Clarissa shares them. Clarissa's language indeed has never gone further than 'dislike', and even that in a context where much of her feeling is directed against herself. She has grown more aware of the mismatch in their minds, but by the same token is just beginning to see that he may have a different point of view. If he does not know what delicacy is 'and yet thinks himself very polite, and intends not to be otherwise, I am rather to be pitied, than he to be censured' (IV, 112; *II, 312*). This is not to be despicable, though he has sunk greatly in her opinion. Indeed her letters would have shown him that she loves him enough in the face of his character and behaviour, to despise herself for doing so. She may have been guilty of some 'conscious superiority', but her letters show her worrying about this herself.

If we put ourselves in Lovelace's position, then, separating the extracts from their context, and Anna's letters from the complex experience of the whole instalment, it is easy to see how they must affect him. Yet we must remember what distortion is involved: she is not a 'scornful beauty' or a schemer, and it is not Anna's instigations that have made her act as she has done.

Nevertheless, after her three happy days in which she has behaved with great complaisance, she suddenly faces a Lovelace angry and violent for no reason she can think of, unless it be that she has been too obliging. One stormy scene on Sunday night is followed by an even stormier (and splendidly dramatised) one the next morning, in which he accuses her of hating him at Anna's instigation, and they both flame out (IV, 212 ff.; *II, 380 ff.*). In her rage she tells him that she does hate him 'with my whole heart', and that her 'soul is above thee, man!' As she tries to rise from the chair in which she has thrown herself, 'crimsoned over with passion', Lovelace clasps her knees and pulls her down, to her absolute terror. He lets her go immediately, but the tussle over the letter at the end of the first phase has been succeeded by a personal liberty at the end of the second. It is minor enough, and Lovelace tells us that he was as much moved by admiration as anything else. Yet, another Rubicon has been passed. As soon as she is gone the effects are visible in his mind. 'But how do I know till I try, whether she may not by a less alarming treatment be prevailed upon, or whether (*Day*, I have done with thee!) she may not yield to *nightly surprises*? This is still the burden of my song, I can marry her when I will. And if I do, after prevailing (whether by *surprize*, or by *reluctant consent*) whom but myself shall I have injured?' (IV, 217; *II, 383*). Having tried intimidation, he will try first what gentleness, and then a 'night surprise' will do.

The third, halcyon, phase opens with a real attempt to communicate. There is a little truth, as against Clarissa's view that he must deserve tokens of value before he expects them, in Lovelace's argument that he could have been more open with her had he been 'encouraged by such a share in your confidence and esteem, as would have secured me against your apprehended worst constructions' (IV, 223; *II*, *387*) – though only a little. He is genuinely affected, almost to tears, by what she says about her father's curse and the sufferings he himself has caused her. When she begs him to release her from all obligation to him he knows real conflict – until Dorcas tells him that they are transcribing one of Clarissa's papers, and he collects himself. He twits her deftly about Anna's opinion of him, but Clarissa confesses with more sincerity than prudence that Anna has advised her to marry him. But she now says that her 'Day' is 'Never'; that she *thinks* she hates him; 'And if, upon a re-examination of my own heart, I find I do, I would not for the world that matters should go on farther between us' (IV, 229-30; *II*, *392*). Yet we should be able to suspect from this formulation (even without the third edition's insertion here) that she is far from hating Lovelace, and so indeed it proves.

The paper the women have transcribed is Clarissa's answer to his proposals for the marriage settlement; ripped almost in two in her anger on the Sunday night. Once again Lovelace is much affected, by her view of the obligations of a wife, her concern for her future husband's honour, the lack of recrimination, the obvious sincerity of what she says about her family, and the fairness of her view of the quarrel. He tries hard to talk himself out of this by casuistry about the torn paper and the possibility of artfulness, and by reminding himself of Anna's letters and the severe things Clarissa has said recently. There is a real struggle between his pride and his conscience in which his conscience very nearly triumphs. But at the centre of it all is a cry from his innermost antipathies. 'O Belford, Belford! I cannot, cannot (at least *at present* I cannot) marry' (IV, 240; *II*, *399*); and by way of a little self-dramatising and unrealising allegory, he succeeds in talking himself back into the old Robert Lovelace, with a flourish.

His next letters are back in his best rakish form. He sets about constructing a tranquil situation as deftly as he had built up the stormy one, obtaining letters from his cousin Charlotte and

Lord M to reassure her of his family's interest in the match, dropping the Fretchville scheme as likely to cause suspicion, arranging for the settlements to be drawn up by a lawyer, producing patterns for wedding clothes. Clarissa responds immediately, behaving with great sweetness and on one occasion – it must be the first in the novel – actually allowing him to get away with a little provocation (IV, 261; *II*, *413*). Then, after their pleasant coach ride round the environs of the City, Lovelace makes himself ill by taking ipecacuanha, to test her feeling for him. He gets his answer quite unmistakably. She does love him, in spite of everything, and she confesses as much to Anna, if not with the openness he sees in her face and eyes.

There follows the *pièce de résistance* of his plotting, when he produces 'Captain Tomlinson' as a supposed emissary from Uncle John Harlowe, seeking to explore the possibility of a reconciliation. She will not admit marriage to Tomlinson; (Lovelace fails to distinguish tacit acceptance of deceit in front of the inhabitants of a temporary lodging, from active deceit to an emissary of her family); but in every other way the plot produces a revolution in Clarissa. She is radiant, her reserves banished, her whole behaviour gently deferential to her future husband, happiness in every gesture and word, as she dreams of a family reunion and even of Lovelace's complete reconciliation with them. With a fine flourish he has promised to meet the Harlowes '*all the way*', and she can hardly find words to express her delight and obligation (IV, 329; *II*, *460*). As she retires in embarrassment at her emotions Lovelace actually sobs with feeling of his own, for the first time in his life. Having brought himself in his previous battle with his conscience, to have a glimpse at last of how Clarissa's virtue may be rooted in her, he begins to doubt the rakes'-creed explanation of how a woman 'so capable of delicate transport' could be so cold. 'Can *Education* have stronger force in a woman's heart than *Nature*? – Sure it cannot. But if it can . . .' (IV, 332; *II*, *462*). If it can, or if as Clarissa will argue, it can produce a 'second nature' no less deeply rooted, Lovelace's gentle methods will be no more successful than his boisterous ones.

The Tomlinson scheme is a turning point for Lovelace, and indeed for our understanding of *his* tragedy, for it demonstrates what he has rejected and is rejecting by his plots. The culmination of his world of lies finally clarifies what could so easily have become the truth after the abduction: a Clarissa made happy and easy by a move to reconcile her with her family, clearly in love with him, treating him with wifely deference, and with only the memory of her fault and the mismatch of their minds and temperaments to give cause for concern within the love that is clearly there. 'Why', Lovelace himself exclaims 'had not this Scene a real foundation!' (IV, 329; *II, 460*). As always with his deceptions, part of him knows how to behave to achieve those results, and part of him wants to be like that. The suspense in our reading experience (since we only find out for certain that it *is* all lies after the two Tomlinson scenes are over) ensures that we too should have a full imaginative realisation of what might have been, and a deep sense of loss when the idyll is exploded by the truth about the genteel crook.

There is a deeper significance however: the Tomlinson plot is also a point from which there can be no turning back. All his other plots, and this is their strength, could be discarded without difficulty, like the Fretchville house scheme, and with every hope that Clarissa need never know anything about them. Lovelace could balance, with freedom to go one way or another. But this plot is different. She must eventually discover it, and she could never forgive the abuse of the family feelings that lie closest to her heart, with such cruelty and cynicism, and in a way only explicable as deliberate design against her honour. He could marry her before she found out, but he might never know again the radiant Clarissa he knows now; and if he cannot marry 'at present', only tragedy lies ahead. He doesn't of course realise this, but we do, because we know Clarissa as he does not.

Indeed we now also begin to discover the full extent of his rapacious pride and realise that he can never be satisfied by anything short of the complete subjection of Clarissa. All this time he is being hardened by the taunting of the prostitutes, and steeling himself by constant reference to Anna's letters, but the real trouble lies deeper. 'I would have the woman whom I honour with my name, if ever I confer this honour upon any, forego even her *superior duties* for me. I would have her look after me when I go out, as far as she can see me, as my Rosebud after her Johnny; and meet me at my return with rapture. I would be the subject of her dreams, as well as of her waking thoughts. I would have her think every moment lost, that is not passed with me: Sing to me, read to me, play to me when I pleased; no joy so great as in obeying me. When I should be inclined to Love, overwhelm me with it; when to be serious or solitary, – if apprehensive of intrusion, retireing at a nod; approaching me only if I smiled encouragement: Steal into my presence with silence; out of it, if not noticed, on tip-toe . . .' (IV, 264; *II*, *416*). The adolescent quality of this only covers the real paradox: the very things, apart from sex, that demonstrably make him love Clarissa most – her nobility, integrity, moral courage – are also the things which make him feel unbearably inferior. When he reacts with childish dreams of a woman who will be a mere cipher to feed his pride, what he in fact reveals is an inability to form any maturely satisfying sex relationship; since for the women he has succeeded in subjecting he feels nothing but contempt, or, if they happen to have died in childbirth, a maudlin sentimentality.

This helps to explain why, when he has consistently argued that it is Clarissa's refusal to acknowledge her feelings that inflamed his pride, her open show of love fails to mollify him. The Tomlinson plot shows that he cannot be satisfied with the best he could possibly hope for. His will be a tragedy wholly different from Clarissa's, because brought on entirely by himself, yet there is a human waste. 'Do not despise me, Jack, for my inconsistency – In no two Letters perhaps agreeing with myself . . . But I am mad with Love, – Fired by Revenge, – Puzzled with my own devices, – My Invention is my curse, – My Pride my punishment – Drawn five or six ways at once, can *she* possibly be so unhappy as *I*?' (IV, 329; *II*, *460*).

The aftermath of the Tomlinson scheme is also significant

because it shows that gentleness is no better than intimidation as a means of seducing her. She tells him that the sign of true love is respect not freedom, and that she conceives marriage as a state of purity not licence. She firmly resists one or two preliminary attempts to take advantage of the new situation. Finally Lovelace takes a chance, twists her kerchief aside, and kisses her breast. The tranquil phase ends with a physical liberty more personal than the other two. It is not disastrous, for the Tomlinson scheme ensures that she will not break with him now unless she is forced to, but her anger shows that he cannot hope to succeed in this way. By modern standards Clarissa's outrage is excessive, and many readers might agree with Lovelace that it is 'a shame to be ashamed to communicate to her adorer's sight the most admirable of her personal graces' (IV, 355; *II, 477*). Indeed Richardson himself, for all his horror of predatory sex and his inclination to support Clarissa's judgement, will be forced to explore this further, but for the moment we should realise that it is not the act itself which matters so much as the attitude it symbolises. What Lovelace is in danger of proving is the failure of his 'love' to respect her personality, and if this were to be proved, 'Far as matters have gone, I will for ever renounce you' (IV, 354; *II, 476*).

The last phase of the instalment proves just that, and its effect is as she threatened. Having tried the tactics of both Boreas and Phoebus to smuggle his traveller out of her cloak he cannot resist his third possibility, to see what surprise can do. He does not hope to seduce her by consent, but hopes at least for 'yielding reluctance' in an attempt for the first time to force her.

Richardson ensures that he should be warned, at this crucial point, of his misreading of her character, and should have at least a chance to see that he could be wrong to suppose that marriage will be still in his power if it came to the worst. The warning comes from Belford just before the 'fire-plot' is mounted.

Belford has been changing, though the wide separation between his letters masks the change unless we read carefully. His first pleas for Clarissa are easily countered because they are still made on the whole within the assumptions of the rake's creed, and come somewhat awkwardly from him when they are not. But when he watches his uncle die, and has to cope with Belton's suffering in the collapse of his relationship with his mistress, Belford's letters begin to acquire a new perspective and resonance. He begins to detect the posturing of the rake; to see, for example, that Lovelace's pride makes him far from a god-like figure dangling human puppets, makes him indeed little more than James Harlowe's instrument in the ruin of his sister. Belford no longer cares to be 'in character', or worries 'whether my past or future actions countenance my preachment' (IV, 124-5; *II, 320-1*). He begins to argue seriously on grounds of moral sensibility and compassion.

Yet, ironically, the effect of his later letters is as unfortunate as that of the first had been, with its assumption that she might be overcome. His picture of the insecurity and degradation of a relationship outside marriage has a certain bite, but when Lovelace sees a witty way of turning the argument inside out, the effect is merely to make him more pleased with himself than ever. Then, in Belford's last letter before the fire-plot, he turns from argument to entreaty. Though he has only met Clarissa once, he sees her more truly than Lovelace, for he foresees that only tragedy can result from what Lovelace is doing (IV, 363; *II, 483*), and suspects that the effect may be either to make Clarissa think of suicide, or at best to break the mainspring of her life. He argues acutely that any sensual wench would be more sexually satisfying; that it is precisely Clarissa's moral and spiritual qualities that make his friend love her, and yet it is just those qualities that he is seeking to degrade in a way that must make her hate him. Unfortunately, he throws in a taunt about the staleness of Lovelace's devices; and predictably this, and not the rest, is what fixes Lovelace's myopic gaze. It is a huge affront to his pride; he becomes more and more determined to *show* Belford, and succeeds in talking himself back into his most rigid Restoration pose. When he does try to justify his actions the mask has once more wholly hidden his face. He can damage nobody's 'property' in seducing Clarissa (IV, 377; *II, 492*); her sufferings are no plea since they are not for his sake; she has been a rebel to love; her resistance and her virtue are the stimulus to the rake's 'imperial' motives of conquest and revenge. He even succeeds in projecting himself back into the mood of the coppice-letter in the first instalment; giving us a glimpse we never had at the time of his rage and humiliation, culminating in the vow never to rest till he had got Clarissa to co-habit with him (IV, 379; *II*, *494*). In this frame of mind he is totally blind to Clarissa's nature. Belford has affected him, as he confesses in the next letter when his plot is actually under way; but the challenge to his pride has enabled him to write himself back into being 'my own man again' (IV, 385; *II*, *498*).

The plot also releases all his actor's volatility and sense of drama. As he sits writing a 'to the moment' letter to Belford, all prepared in gown and slippers for Dorcas to give the fire alarm, he is vividly and enjoyably aware of the drama he is creating – though if we are unsuspicious we may not realise this until afterwards. It is not that he does not actually feel the nervousness, the tenderness, the tension; yet he is playing them up, watching himself doing so, teasing Belford with suspense, posturing. One moment he is clinical, 'coolly enjoying thy reflections in a hurricane!', the next, working up his part with high enjoyment. 'What! where!—How came it! – Is my Beloved safe? – O, wake not too roughly my Beloved! (IV, 387; *II*, *499*). It is not the least acute perception of the 'Shakespeare of prose' to measure the way that acting gets in the blood and makes it difficult for the born actor to be sincere.

The fire-plot is the first 'warm scene' in *Clarissa*, and duly came in for moral objection,[1] which Richardson seems to have anticipated after the fate of *Pamela*, for he makes Lovelace warn Belford not to allow free rein to his imagination. The scene is indeed more sexual and less mechanical than the ones in *Pamela*, but no more prurient, because of the way Richardson changes the focus.

[1] Richardson printed an *Answer to the Letter of a Very Reverend and Worthy Gentleman*, dated 8 June 1749, to defend the Fire Scene. The gentleman was probably the Rev. Philip Skelton.

The opening is perhaps mildly erotic insofar as it is dramatic and experiential but very quickly the narrative breaks off short, and the action becomes wholly indefinite. What moves into focus instead is the terror and grief of Clarissa and the reality of her humiliation as she begs him to 'permit her to hide herself from the light, and from every human eye' (IV, 391; *II, 502*). The suspense ceases to be sexually emotive (How will he touch her? Is he going to tear her clothes off, take her?) and becomes moral (Why is she reacting like this, how will he react to her distress?).

Already prurience is banished for us because of the reality of her aversion. For us – but not for Lovelace: 'I besought her pardon, yet could not avoid offending'. The indefiniteness blocks the imagination; what remains is the brutality, the inability to realise that his hopes are already defeated. Even her hysterical attempt to stab herself with the scissors does not convince him. When the sexual detail now returns, with a half-glimpse of Clarissa naked beneath her 'scanty coat', it is immediately fused with her overflowing grief and anger.

As she slips through his arms to fall on her knees at his feet, we watch a tableau charged not with sex but with moral symbolism. It is a grotesque inversion of a proposal scene, in a way that insists on the humiliation of the 'goddess' Lovelace purports to love, crumpled weeping at his feet. This kind of scene was to become a cliché in Victorian melodrama, but here it is imbued with our whole experience in the novel of the significance of 'decorum'. (We remember the related scene with James Harlowe.) The parody of a proposal is insisted on with a kind of grim humour in the context of the marriage-danglings that have preceded it: 'I mentioned the morrow as the happiest day of my life' (IV, 393; *II, 503*). It is also like a scene from a saint's life, where the posture makes the point. Richardson is so far from a *Perils of Pauline* exploitation that he insists on how, in dishevelment and distress, she remains beautiful and ordered.

Lovelace however cannot take in the reality of her aversion, or realise that he can only make himself hateful, and her vile in her own eyes. He is blindly obsessed, trying again and again.

When the sexual action does come – 'I hope I did not hurt the tenderest and loveliest of all her beauties' – it would be hard to conceive an imagination prurient enough to be stimulated by the indefiniteness. The focus is on the coarse brutality masquerading in the would-be tender accent; the sexual meaninglessness. When Lovelace eventually gives up, he has no idea what he has done, and his later reaction to his failure is predictable. As soon as he has let her go he is aware of 'the ridicule I should meet with below'; and goes back to her locked door determined 'to execute all my purposes, be the consequence what it would' (IV, 397; *II*, *506*). The next morning he is cheering himself up with superior worldliness: she is 'a little silly Soul' to have been upset so much by 'a *frolick* only, a *romping-bout*' (V, 1; *II*, *507*). He plans to enjoy her confusion when they meet again. In better moments he realises how he has trapped himself by the Tomlinson scheme; he even thinks of visiting Belford to ask his advice about marrying, if she will only forgive him in a way which mingles love and confidence with her anger. Yet his pride is always welling up, he cannot forgive her superiority, cannot bear to think of marrying a bourgeois daughter of the Harlowes who would excel the last of the Lovelaces. Even at his best, when he cannot see how she can feel degraded in her own eyes since she has so exalted herself in his, there is a kind of moral stupidity. He cannot imagine what the experience of having her whole being, mind, heart and spirit, reduced to her body would be like for Clarissa.

He is consequently enraged at her escape. The grief he had witnessed at her keyhole becomes 'False, devilish grief! *not the humble, silent grief, that only deserves pity*! – Contriving to ruin me, to despoil me of all that I held valuable' (V, 20; *II*, *520*). The formulation is ironic. It is not virtue that has made her fly from 'the charming prospects that were before her', but 'Malice, Hatred, Contempt, Harlowe-Pride' (V, 24-5; *II*, *523*). (He has convinced himself that he was 'conditionally resolved' to marry her, a phrase as self-deceiving as Clarissa's 'conditional liking') When he finds her letter, renouncing him for ever, it is 'for what? Damn'd confounded Niceness, Prudery, Affectation . . . But if ever again I get her into my hands, *Art*, and more *Art*, and *Compulsion* too, if she make it necessary (*and 'tis plain that nothing else will do*,) shall she experience' (V, 29; *II*, *526*). His gaiety and exultation are infectious when she is discovered at Hampstead, but we need to measure the irony when he sets off to recapture her, 'dressed like a Bridegroom' (V, 66; *III*, *26*).

The structure of *Clarissa*, then, shows a broad similarity to that of *Pamela*. Once again the focus has narrowed appreciably from the first movement to the second, while the probing of the heroine has become correspondingly deeper. The dominant conflict in the first instalment between socio-economic and power values, and moral values, has given place in the second to a conflict about the nature of love. In the process we not only measure the full contrast between Clarissa and Lovelace, but discover much more about the particular drawbacks and dangers of the values Richardson himself holds dear.

There is also a parallel between the endings of the first and second instalments. This is more than a device to inflame curiosity and help the sales of the last instalment however, for in fact the narrative die is cast. The fire-plot casts a long shadow ahead. It has been, in its proof of Lovelace's obsessiveness and his total ignorance of the nature of what he is doing, a miniature of what is to come. The only really new theme awaiting exploration is the nature of Clarissa's agony and its implications; and also the question-mark that is posed by her suicidal impulse in the fire-plot scene. The instalment may end with another 'escape', but its immediate issue is not in doubt.

CHAPTER SEVEN

The Inquisition

(*The Final Instalment*)

I

Once more, Richardson's first audience had to wait, this time for seven months, before the final instalment appeared. The news leaked out, however, that there was to be a tragic ending, and there was a spate of appeals for mercy. They came from young ladies and gents and clergymen, writing under flowery or classical pseudonyms. Lady Bradshaigh threatened: 'If you disappoint me, attend to my curse:—May the hatred of all the young, beautiful and virtuous, for ever be your portion! may you meet with applause only from envious old maids, surly bachelors, and tyrannical parents! may you be doomed to the company of such! and, after death, may their ugly souls haunt you! Now make Lovelace and Clarissa unhappy if you dare.'[1] A more practical threat lay in the promise of many correspondents not to buy the last volumes unless Richardson changed his mind, and as a businessman he must have known very clearly how much better a happy ending would have sold. Moreover the appeals also came from authors like Fielding, Thomson, Lyttleton and Cibber.[2] Many of the objectors invoked the theory

[1] 'Mrs Belfour' to Richardson, 10 October 1748; Barbauld, *Correspondence*, IV, 181.

[2] Richardson to Hill, 7 November 1748; Carroll, *Letters*, 99; and additionally for Fielding, Richardson to Stinstra, 2 June 1753; William C. Slattery (ed.), *The Richardson-Stinstra Correspondence* (London and Amsterdam, 1969), 33.

of 'poetic justice', and theoretical considerations would have their due weight with a novelist pledged to moral instruction. But to his lasting credit Richardson remained unmoved, though passages in the novel itself are directed at the objections, and his efforts to write a postscript and get his friends to help him answer them, show how seriously he took it all.

Yet anybody who had really responded to the novel should have known that tragedy was inevitable, for all the surface suspense. In the fourth volume the shadows had begun to close; in the fifth the actors become fixed in the parts of a play which both have written but neither understands. There soon begins to be something of the inevitability of nightmare, where human actions hold the attention, yet at the back of one's mind seem curiously stylised, because the outcome already exists in one's apprehension and cannot really be affected by anything that happens.

Briefly, in Hampstead, the action takes place on a social stage again, after the prolonged single combat of Clarissa's captivity. She seems to have escaped from Lovelace's power, yet it is not so. For we are made aware once more of the capitulation Richardson saw everywhere in his society to rank, influence, and wealth. The moment Lovelace arrives in Hampstead all citadels fall before him. The people he has to deal with are not Harlowes obsessed by greed or pride, the innkeeper and his wife, Mrs Moore, Miss Rawlins, even the jolly widow Bevis, are all kind, respectable, middle-class folk. But Will has only to mention that his master is 'one of the finest gentlemen in the world' for the innkeeper and his wife to pity Lovelace before they see him, and to be 'ready to worship' when they find his 'person and dress having answered Will's description' (V, 73-4; *III*, *30-1*). He goes off in his chariot the short distance along the Heath to Mrs Moore's because 'What widow, what servant, asks questions of a man with an equipage?' (V, 78; *III*, *34*). In the first stormy scene with Clarissa he has only to insist on his letters from *Lord* M and *Lady* Betty and *Lady* Sarah to have the women half on his side, and when he finally puts the 'ostentatiously coroneted' letter from

Lord M into Miss Rawlins' hands it 'clench'd the nail. Not but that, Miss Rawlins said, she saw I had been a wild gentleman' (V, 119; *III, 62*).

Lovelace now begins to reap the benefit of his previous plots to make her seem to have consented to pass as his wife. He manages to shout her down several times in the first stormy scene when she is insisting that he has no right to persecute her; but he is also able to say himself, uncontradictably, that Tomlinson has reported their marriage. Behind this is a clear power situation. He can produce nine witnesses to swear that she has passed as Mrs Lovelace, and if he has legal rights as her husband, the people at Hampstead have to be very careful how they go about offending a man of his status and influence. Clarissa's character also plays into his hands again, particularly her delicacy and to some extent at the back of it her pride. She is obviously ashamed to tell a story which in outline, without the complications, which do – heaven knows – take a long time to make clear, shows her to have run away from her family with Lovelace, to have lived with him for some time, and to have left him because of an attempt her modesty makes it impossible for her to describe. Richardson steers dangerously close to disaster when Clarissa, in her first private conversation with the women, does not categorically deny Lovelace's well-tried stories about the unconsummated marriage – though she expresses her scorn. Yet when she does, immediately afterwards, publicly challenge him to declare that they are indeed married, the strength of his position is clear. All he has to do is to be sweetly reasonable: 'But, my dear, will you be pleased to consider what answer half a dozen people whence you came, could give to your question? And do not now, in *the disorder of your mind*, and in the height of passion, bring into question before these gentlewomen a point you have acknowledged before those who know us better' (V, 131-2; *III, 71*). She may cry out 'I own no Marriage with thee! – Bear witness Ladies, I do not', but she cannot deny what her heart has already reproached her for. The fact that she cannot, with the 'explanation' of the unconsummated marriage and the confirmation of Tomlinson's carefully doctored letter, is enough to ensure that she gets no help from women already overawed by Lovelace's rank, and ensnared by his charm and plausibility.

Richardson again risks improbability, but is perhaps just saved by the consistency with what we know of his heroine. There is a familiar double criticism. Lovelace remarks on 'that Security which Innocence gives, that nevertheless had better have in it a greater mixture of the Serpent with the Dove . . . A dear silly Soul . . . to depend upon the goodness of her own heart, when the heart cannot be seen into but by its actions; and she, to appearance, a Runaway, an Eloper, from a tender, a most indulgent Husband! – To neglect to cultivate the opinion of individuals, when the whole world is governed by appearance!' (V, 122; *III*, *64*). The criticism of a world so governed is clear enough, but the criticism of Clarissa is plain as well. It is not enough for her to wrap herself in her own innocence; in the world as it is, Clarissa is betrayed not only by her physical cowardice but by the theoretic and idealistic nature of her views. She is betrayed also by her good qualities: her modesty, her unwillingness to speak at all if she cannot speak the whole truth, and by her self-reproach for having already lent herself to deception. Once again the art exposes the uncomfortable fact, for its author, that Clarissa's moral nature unfits her to cope with situations that less admirable characters would have made short work of.

On the other hand, though we can appreciate the masterly psychology of Lovelace, and the clever way he plays on the romantic susceptibilities as well as the self-interest of the women, we should notice how his strategy has become purely a matter of keeping Clarissa in his power. He is being forced out of 'appearance' himself. He can prevent her escape by hedging her about with servants, keeping the women perplexed by his tissue of lies and half-truths, tampering with Anna's correspondence, and finally forging letters from her and his relatives, but the tactics that serve him best for retaining power are those which serve him worst if he should hope again to convince her of his love and penitence. When he starts out of his old man's disguise at Mrs

Moore's, like Milton's Satan touched by Ithuriel's spear (V, 88; *III*, *41*), the scene is not only Lovelace-theatrical but symbolic. His 'own form' is not yet clear to Clarissa, but it begins to be clearer from that moment. The 'fire-scene' has been a turning-point for her willingness to trust him, and the more he surrounds her with deception and force, the less likely it is that she will ever trust him again.

Even Tomlinson cannot help now. He and his master may bring all the familiar big guns to bear: the 'fact' that reconciliation can only be undertaken by her uncle if they marry, the threat from James Harlowe and the threat to him if she renounces Lovelace, the hopes of Lovelace's family, the whole allure of their relationship and the resulting ease of social re-acceptance. Clarissa shows how much these can still move her, but she can no longer be persuaded. She is ready now to confess that she could not have agreed to marry him if she had not loved him, and that she would have shown her feelings more clearly if she had not been driven back into her shell when she needed encouragement. Her obvious difficulty in sustaining her decision to give him up shows the continuing power of those feelings, and the pain of renouncing her happier prospects. But she cannot trust him now; indeed, begins to be ominously suspicious of Tomlinson. The fire-plot has shown her that Lovelace does not respect her personality, 'he could not love the creature whom he could insult as he has insulted me' (V, 230; *III*, *138*). He cannot make her happy, nor she him, and to marry him might cause her to fall into error. It is not the physical attempt itself that matters but its implications, especially the fact that the complicity of the women at Sinclair's suggests deliberate design. The fact that she still cares for him in spite of it makes things worse, not better. 'If I had never valued him, he never would have had it in his power to insult me; nor could I, if I had never regarded him, have taken to heart as I do, the insult (execrable as it was) so undeservedly, so ingratefully given' (V, 228; *III*, *137* – omitting Richardson's italics.). The counters of value may change with the centuries, but the relationship between them does not, and we should have no difficulty in understanding the accuracy of Clarissa's diagnosis of the meaning of the fire-plot, even on the facts she knows. She is brought to agree to see Lady Betty when she arrives, but that is all.

The pain this costs her shows, however, that even now there might have been some hope for Lovelace if he had been able to be open, and to put his trust in her own decision and her generosity. When, with another of his momentary bursts of sincerity, he wholeheartedly begs forgiveness (with real tears!), and whispers to Tomlinson 'By my Soul, man, I am in earnest' (V, 234; *III*, *141*), he actually produces a moment of indecision in Clarissa. But Lovelace is now the trapped one. He is still under pressure from his old obsessions, but what has finally trapped him is the net of his own contrivances. He has put it 'out of my *own power* to be honest. I hate compulsion in all forms; and cannot bear, even to be *compelled* to be the wretch my choice has made me! – So now, Belford, as thou hast said, I am a machine at last, and no free agent' (V, 241; *III*, *146*). If, as the now squeamish Tomlinson urges, he gets 'Lady Betty' to persuade Clarissa to marry him, and gets Tomlinson accepted as her uncle's deputy, he can be 'honest' to the extent of marriage. Yet the revelation of the extent of his designs must finally come; and how will she take that, when she has reacted so strongly to the little she knows already? The risk of losing her love seems almost as great with honesty as with dishonesty, though Tomlinson for one can now see that only violence will serve if Lovelace does mean to go on with his plans. Lovelace at last begins to realise that if she really finds him a villain she may refuse and abhor him. He is plagued by conscience and begins to see that even 'victory' will undo him. He reflects how happy he could be 'had it been given to me to *be* only what I wished to *appear* to be' (V, 242; *III*, *146*). He begins to sense that his love may not be of the '*Right sort*', though he has little enough idea of what the right sort might be (V, 225; *III*, *156*). But it is too late to turn back.

At this point the 'garden scene' (V, 245 ff.; *III*, *149* ff.), the last oasis of calm, allows us to see just what Lovelace has lost.

Clarissa speaks to him quietly and much more openly than ever before. She sums up the evidence she has of his premeditated plots, and insists that she cannot marry where there is such disunion of minds. Yet her feeling for him is quite apparent now in her face and eyes, she lets him hold her hand, she openly shows her distress at the loss of relationship with his family and she confesses, with hesitation and embarrassment but unmistakably, that she still cares for him and finds it painful to renounce him now. But she will not err 'wilfully and against the light of my own judgement' (V, 251; *III, 153*). If she can acquit herself of this she will be 'more happy than if I had all that the world accounts desireable'. As Lovelace listens, it seems to him that 'Her whole person was informed by her sentiments. She seemed to be taller than before. How the God within her exalted her, not only above me, but above herself!' Yet she will not be called 'Divine creature'. 'All human excellence, said she, is comparative only. My Mind, I believe, is indeed superior to yours, debased as yours is by evil habits: But I had not known it to be so, if you had not *taken pains* to convince me . . .' (V, 252; *III, 153*).

This, in its way, is an extraordinary achievement; the modern reader is aghast that Richardson should think of taking such a risk. Yet he succeeds triumphantly here as he had so consistently failed in *Pamela*. The thing is said quietly, as the fact it indeed is. It is said in rebuttal of praise. And it is said curiously without personality, and wholly without animus or conceit. Lovelace has many times accused her of 'conscious superiority', meaning a synonym for arrogance, an indication of the proud and scornful Beauty. It is Richardson's achievement now to transform the phrase. This is superiority in an absolute sense; and it is conscious without hypocrisy, circumlocution, or disguise. Yet it is at this moment wholly insulated from self-applause and indeed from self. She is superior not because of her basic nature nor even because of his – Richardson has none of Fielding's oddly Calvinist assertion of good and bad *nature* – but because of the effect on him of what he has chosen to do. She is superior, as

Lovelace himself can see, because she allows the God *in* her to exalt her, and we shall find this formulation significant.

That Lovelace should see all this; and yet feel that he has created a situation where he is likely to lose her love whatever he does, and even if he should succeed in marrying her, is the foundation of his tragedy. Yet he prevents us from feeling it as we might because he manages to prevent himself, eventually, from feeling it at all. His characteristic response is to clamp the rake's mask back more and more firmly on to the human face, in order to hide the truth from himself. There is now however a certain awareness and admission of what he is doing. He tells Belford how Tomlinson's opposition (like Belford's earlier) served to confirm the very purposes it set out to change. 'Had he left me to myself, to the tenderness of my own nature . . . had he sat down, and made odious faces, and said nothing; it is very possible that I should have taken the chair over against him . . . and have cried and blubbered with him for half an hour together. But the varlet to *argue* with me! – To pretend to *convince* a man, who knows in his heart that he is doing a wrong thing! – He must needs think that this would put me upon trying what I could say for myself; and when the excited compunction can be carried from the *heart* to the *lips*, it must evaporate in words' (V, 218-9; *III*, *130-1*). Verbalisation is a kind of anaesthetic. So he converts his battle with his conscience into a humorous stagey knockabout; and his thoughts about love into a 'debate' in which debating points score. He relapses into his gayest and most cynical vein on hearing Belford's news of the death of his uncle, but we can see that the cynicism is being used to escape facing the situation it so splendidly verbalises as 'the necessity I am under of committing either speedy Matrimony, or a Rape'! (V, 244; *III*, *148*). When he succeeds in capturing the vitally important letter from Anna that Clarissa has been waiting for, we can watch him using it to whip himself up to vengeance as he had used its predecessors. Finally he succeeds in recapturing his old persona, in convincing himself in the old rake's way that she is ruled not by virtue but pride. 'She cannot bear to be thought a *woman* . . .

And if, in the last attempt, I find her *not* one, what will she be worse for the trial? – No one is to blame for suffering an evil he cannot shun or avoid' (V, 284; *III, 175-6*). He gives way again to the gratification of his 'predominant passion' because it is in his power; and argues with his old whole-hearted levity that he is conferring a benefit on her by procuring her the penitential life she seems to want – at the expense of which he waxes very witty. If we should wonder at this success in clamping the mask back so fully – 'Why, Jack, I cannot but say, that the Westminster Air is a little grosser than that at Hamstead' (V, 288; *III, 178*). He is back in the brothel, and in the attitudes the prostitutes so sedulously foster. He gives way again to his full aversion to marriage in sporting with the wording of the marriage licence which has now arrived, and in outlining his grand proposal to reform the marriage laws to permit an annual change of partners. Finally he gives rein to his immense delight in acting and intrigue as he coaches his two high-grade tarts for their impersonation of Lady Betty and Charlotte, in order to decoy Clarissa back to town.

What we watch is the deliberate self-blinding of an intelligence; the fixing into the rake's persona of a man whose experience and understanding had been enlarged well beyond it, but who refuses to face the facts of his situation or the truth of his emotions. Once this has happened, Clarissa never stands a chance. She has no reason to distrust his 'relatives', or imagine that he could descend to using their reputations to despicable ends. It is easy enough to get her into the coach for the expedition to 'Lady Betty's' lodgings. It is harder of course to get her back into 'Sinclair's' on their 'accidental' passing there; but when we get the whole story nearly a volume later, it is clear that the drugging begins in the coach, with the hartshorn and water she is given for her faintness and her near hysteria.

Lovelace's letters describing the scenes that follow are only seen in their full repulsiveness afterwards, when we know the whole story, but even without this they are repulsive enough. He never seems shoddier than when he rehearses, to extinguish the last possibility of pity, the old gramophone record of his reasons for vengeance; or resolves not to be made a fool of before the prostitutes; or pleads, after his stagily protective show of indignation when Sinclair has been allowed to terrorise his victim, that 'her coming in was without my orders' (V, 313; *III*, *196*). But what is finally ugliest about Lovelace now is his tone. For what his 'to the moment' letters (composed retrospectively, though just before the rape takes place) reveal above all, is his savouring enjoyment. He is taken up with his own suspense as the sadist is. He enjoys replaying the part of not knowing what is happening – 'What shall we do now! We are immersed in the depth of grief and apprehension!' (V, 306; *III*, *191*) – significantly identifying himself with his victim to share for the moment the flavour of her terror. He obviously loves the scurry, the hectic emotions, the part-playing; he revels in his starring role in his own dramaturgy. Richardson may perhaps be releasing through Lovelace something in himself, something that probably exists at the back of the mind of any dramatic artist; and something which in this hectic form looks forward in particular to the sentimental excesses of the latter part of the century: what Richardson himself called 'sporting with distress'. But the important difference is that Richardson is showing how far Lovelace has succeeded in blinding himself so completely to the meaning, and even curiously to the reality of what he is doing. He is 'quite astonished' at 'so sincere, so unquestionable a repugnance' (V, 309; *III*, *193*), but it makes no difference because the reality of Clarissa's feeling never locks home in his mind. The strength of his self-obsession is shown by the flimsiness of his excuses: 'Yet how should I know that it would be so till I tried? – And how, having proceeded thus far, could I stop, were I *not* to have had the women to goad me on, and to make light of circumstances, which they pretended to be better judges of than I?' He can achieve moments of absolutely blank calm because of his ability to unrealise: 'Dreading what might happen as to her intellects, and being very apprehensive that she might possibly go thro' a great deal before morning . . . I humoured her' (V, 311; *III*, *194*). Language could hardly be more anaesthetised.

There is sadism behind his delight in playing with his victim. But at the very heart of Lovelace, as deep as one can go, what Richardson succeeds in showing is the inability, finally, to believe in the reality of other people, their personalities, and their emotions. Behind the Restoration playacting, behind the rake's ideology, behind the power-urge and the sadism, is an obsessive egotism so complete that nothing else exists for it.

After the rape, with Clarissa deranged and insensible, he half glimpses that it is what *she* feels about her virginity that matters, but with horrible obsession he still cannot see what he has done, and can still occupy himself with thoughts of his darling notion of cohabitation. At the moment which moved Fielding so much, when Clarissa half comes to, and holds up the licence 'in a speechless agony' Lovelace's language again expels reality. 'She seemed about to call down vengeance upon me; when, happily, the Leaden God, in pity to her trembling Lovelace, waved over her half-drowned eyes his somniferous wand, and laid asleep the fair Exclaimer, before she could go half thro' with her intended imprecation' (V, 323; *III*, *201*). He can speak of the '*little* Art' that has been used, and of its '*generous* design (if thou'lt allow me the word on such an occasion) in order to lessen the too quick sense she was likely to have of what she was to suffer'. It was a 'little *innocent* trick', and 'Who the devil could have expected such strange effects from a cause so common, and so slight' (V, 325; *III*, *202*). It is not finally the rape itself, nor even the utter obsessiveness, that makes one feel as though one is moving through some nightmarish quagmire. It is the fact that Lovelace can succeed to the extent he does in dehumanising his own reactions.

We must however be clear about the significance of the rape, and why it happens as it does. How can Lovelace go through with a sexual act from which he can gain no possible sexual satisfaction, since he is not a sex maniac, and admits himself with characteristic brutality that 'there is no difference to be found between the skull of King Philip, and that of another man'? (V, 318; *III, 199*). It cannot be a trial of her virtue either, in the sense of finding out whether she can be seduced, for the same reason: her will is paralysed. We discover later that she is already 'stupid to their hands' from the first dose of the drug in the coach (VI, 185; *III, 368*), before she is given what turns out to be the overdose in her tea. The drug makes her alternately drunken and numb, but not unconscious. She remembers vaguely seeing the women moving about while she is being raped, but goes into fits and a coma thereafter.

Yet the rape is, precisely, a trial of virtue itself, in that it is an attempt to disprove the existence of a moral *nature*. It is a last desperate effort to prove the rake's creed true, and preserve Lovelace from having to give up his whole idea of himself. The blind obsession, the mind forever tramping the treadmill of its own assumptions and seeking feverishly to force down any glimpses of a different truth, are an index of how crucially Lovelace's ideology is tied up with his deepest psychological needs. What is at stake is the mainspring of his life, what makes life worth living for him. He *must* go on, to stake everything on a last desperate throw to prove he is right about her, and himself. He cannot make her consent, but if his basic assumptions are right that doesn't matter. For he knows that she loves him, and if he can only reveal to her what she 'really' is, even without her consent, everything else will follow as of course. If the basic nature of woman is sexual, and her morality is only a veneer of custom and education reinforced by pride, then the physical violation which puts her at a stroke beyond the pale of custom, and is a complete humiliation, will allow her 'true' nature to emerge. The experience of sexual penetration itself should result in an irreversible change; hence 'once subdued, always subdued'. (There is a modern analogy here with Terence Rattigan's *Ross*, where the experience of rape reveals T. E. Lawrence's homosexuality to him, wholly outside any question of consent.)

The most agonising question Richardson can ask about his heroine is whether her virtue is real or not, and the rape is the beginning of his inquisition. Each of Lovelace's basic assumptions will be tested against her reactions to her violation. Again, and very curiously, the rape in *Clarissa* is like the half-attempted rape in *Pamela* in being 'sexual' only in a rather peculiar sense. It takes place in public, in the presence of Mrs Sinclair and probably Sally and Polly. This is partly because of Lovelace's need for an audience to play up to, to the bitter end. It is also partly because Richardson's whole concept of morality and immorality is public. But the central reason is that the rape is a public trial in the strict sense; the first stage in proving a hypothesis about the true nature of Woman. If we want an analogy we should think of a scientific experiment carried out in front of an expert audience. It is the most extraordinary climax of any novel in English. Yet it is not so for any desire to shock, let alone titillate, by the *outré*. It is because, for Richardson, the rape of his heroine enables him to expose her innermost nature. It is the beginning of his answer to the most basic of all questions: the Psalmist's 'What *is* Man?' – or Woman?'

2

He begins to open up Clarissa's mind by using derangement as Shakespeare had done, to reveal the unconscious. Indeed, since the ravings of later tragedy are little more than emotional indulgence, this is the first honest attempt to deal with the unconscious since Lear and Ophelia. Richardson clearly understood how much lay hidden in the mind that the daylight consciousness either repressed or failed to understand . . . but which dreams, or derangement, could reveal.

Clarissa's nightmare in the first instalment, if we look back at it now, reveals its full significance. She dreams that 'my Brother, my Uncle Anthony, and Mr Solmes, had formed a plot to destroy Mr Lovelace; who discovering it, and believing I had a hand in it, turned all his rage against me. I thought he made them all fly into foreign parts upon it; and afterwards seizing upon me, carried me into a church-yard; and there, notwithstanding all my prayers and tears, and protestations of innocence, stabbed me to the heart, and then tumbled me into a deep grave ready dug, among two or three half-dissolved carcases; throwing in the dirt and earth upon me with his hands, and trampling it down with his feet' (II, 283; *I*, *433*).

This is obviously a product of its circumstances. She has just heard from her aunt and Betty about the plans for the fatal Wednesday; has overheard her brother and sister exulting in the success of their plans; and, spurred on by her apprehensions and by a wholly new rancour, has written her letter agreeing to use Lovelace's help to escape. But immediately afterwards she is seized by deep misgivings, she cannot get to sleep, and when she does her nightmare expresses her fears, in a significant form. In her unconscious mind she clearly perceives that she is only a pawn in the struggle of Lovelace and her family to destroy one another, in which the destructive urges of pride and revenge dominate, and do indeed drive her family to 'foreign parts'. Her dream separates out this truth from the complications of her duty, her love for her family, and her dawning love for Lovelace which inhibit her daylight understanding, so that in the dream she can see the subterranean motives clearly. They are by no means the whole truth, but they are true. Unfortunately, the daylight Clarissa thinks very slightly of dreams, for if she had managed to lock home in her mind what part of it knew, her subsequent behaviour might have been rather different, and wiser.

Further beneath the surface however, the nightmare clearly has sexual significance too. An anticipatory irony manifests itself when the rape is over. The rape is what stabs her to the heart; the grave is the pit he digs for her and the bed in which she experiences the 'death' of drugs and sex, and the annihilation of her previous life and reputation. (This will of course ultimately become a literal death too.) The two or three carcasses are the women she is levelled with, whose flesh is already corrupt, and the dirt and the trampling hardly require a gloss. At the moment of the dream however, all we need say is that Clarissa already unconsciously perceives the character of the 'love' that will eventually lead to the rape and prove the dream prophetic. In realising his darker motivation, she sees that his 'love' is something desecrating, hence the churchyard, and destructive of her personality and her purity. One must sound a note of caution here: this is a perception about Lovelace, not necessarily about sex itself, though clearly her fear of sex would enter into it. When we remember what Lovelace hopes to prove by the rape, however, it enables us to predict the way she will regard it, and the impossibility that it could have the effects he hopes for.

Her derangement allows us to test the prediction. The most obviously striking thing about her first few 'papers' is however something unexpected. Clarissa in our experience has developed a real intellectual stature; we think of her as an analytic *mind*, collected, firm, penetrating. We forget her age. And there is about her emotional life an aura of reserve. We have seen a good deal into it in crisis, but have also seen how blind she can be to the state of her own heart, and how her feminine code has encouraged her to conceal many of her feelings and emotional problems not only from others, but from herself. It is against the background of this experience over four volumes of the novel that her first few papers gain their touching quality. It is as though we had never really seen her before; for the derangement shows itself less in her lack of connection, though that is there, than in the childlike tone. The first few papers are written by her emotions. The educated, highly developed mind, the self-sufficiency, the analytic intelligence, suddenly drop away. What we see is a lost and bewildered teenage girl, confused and grief-stricken, all assurance and sophistication gone, seeking desperately for reassurance and love in the only direction she can, and failing to find any. Anna, we remember, has not written (as far as Clarissa knows) since before the escape to Hampstead. Her father has cursed her to perdition, both here and hereafter. Her life-lines of affection are cut, or lead nowhere. She tries to believe that they still exist to be laid hold of again. But she cannot – and here we see the first effect of the rape – not only because she cannot communicate, but because the 'self' of her past relationships is gone. She cannot focus on what has happened; she 'cannot tell' the 'dreadful, dreadful things' (V, 327; *III*, *205*) that have been done to her, partly because she cannot bear to think of them, and partly because she doesn't yet fully understand. 'But I am no longer what I was in any one thing – In any one thing did I say? Yes but I am; for I am still, and I ever will be, *Your true* – '. But she cannot sign the name that should have followed, and the paper is torn in two and thrown away. For a moment she can assert continuity with the past, since her love for Anna is unaltered; but it breaks down, for the self that feels now is not the same as Anna's friend. Similarly, in the second paper, her love for her father remains real and because of it she asserts that the bond between father and child cannot be broken. 'Yes, I *will* call you Papa, and help yourself as you can – for you are my own dear Papa, whether you will or not – And tho' I am an unworthy child – yet I *am* your child – ' (V, 328; *III*, *206*). But again she cannot go on, and the paper is scored across and discarded. For, once more, 'I don't know what my name is! – I never dare to wish to come into your family again!' The rape has damaged her sense of her own identity, her sense of herself as a continuous personality, and with that, the relationships nearest her heart. Lovelace seems to be right. Her first reaction is indeed to feel that an irreversible change has taken place. We are however being made to realise imaginatively what sort of experience this is in its agony and confusion, and to measure the disorientation that can convert the Clarissa we knew into this stricken child – it already seems unlikely that it could issue in the slick conversion of Lovelace's brutal theory.

The third paper is written very simply, but after its first sentence it is wholly coherent and ordered, and in it she does begin to understand. Having reached for help outside herself, and failed, she is forced to seek a foothold in her own being, and she finds one. Her moral nature (be it 'original' or a 'second nature') is still real to her, its values apply, and it gives her a language she can use to understand what has happened: the language of moral fable. Lovelace is hopelessly wrong after all. Her moral nature is no sham veneer; it is authenticated by her suffering because it is the only bedrock reality that remains. The first thing she understands by its aid is inimical to his hopes of a change in her nature, for it is an assertion that her nature is utterly different from his. In her fable the young girl is savaged by the tiger she has fed and loved since infancy; but 'who was most to blame, I pray? The Brute, or the Lady? The Lady, surely! – For what *she* did was *out* of nature, out of character, at least: What *it* did was *in* its own nature' (V, 329; *III*, *206*). This is admittedly a crude and immature view of another human being (and it is not Richardson's, as we have seen), but it is natural enough at this point. Yet it is not the view of Lovelace that matters so much as the insight into herself. Far from revealing a 'real' sexuality that her morality has glossed over, the effect of the rape is to enable her to see that it could never have happened if she had not betrayed her real nature, or at least the 'character' that re-formed whatever nature she had to start with. What happens is the opposite of what Lovelace expected. It is not her morality which is false, but her love which was wrong. She sees, behind that love, something in herself which courted disaster, which was blindly prepared to ignore the 'hungry maw' and the brute nature she had to deal with, which even boasted her own power to subdue. *That* was finally to blame. Lovelace was right to believe that the rape would show her what she is 'really like'. But we can already guess what the something laid bare inside herself is; or at any rate we can see that it isn't the sexuality Lovelace expects.

The fourth paper identifies it beyond question: it is spiritual pride. The paper is couched in the language of puritan introspection this time; the 'thees' and 'thous' indicating a necessary objectivity. 'How art thou now humbled in the dust, thou proud Clarissa Harlowe! Thou that never steppedst out of thy Father's house but to be admired! Who wert wont to turn thine eye, sparkling with healthful life, and self-assurance, to different objects at once, as thou passedst, as if (for so thy penetrating

Sister used to say) to plume thyself upon the expected applauses of all that beheld thee! Thou that usedst to go to rest satisfied with the adulations paid thee in the past day, and couldst put off every-thing but thy Vanity! – ' (V, 329; *III*, *206*). By the light of this self-arraignment, in the fifth paper, she is even able to reach out to Bella in the understanding that however much her sister's penetration was owing to her jealousy, what she saw was true. 'I was too secure in the knowlege I thought I had of my own heart. My supposed advantages became a snare to me. And what now is the end of all?' This is of course to some extent unfair and exaggerated, as the experience of remorseful introspection usually is. Yet the rape has enabled her to see deeper into her heart than ever before, and to detect for herself something that Richardson has already clarified in the experience of his fiction.

The sixth paper is interesting because it confirms the analysis in the way it most needs confirmation: by showing at the moment of her greatest insight that she remains ensnared by what she has seen. She thinks that the rape has put marriage forever beyond her reach. But in bringing this home to herself pathetically – indeed with sentimental indulgence – she reveals that her thoughts of marriage, religious and responsible though we know them to have been, are also intertwined with pride and vanity. 'No court now to be paid to my smiles! No encouraging compliments to inspire thee with hope of laying a mind not unworthy of thee under obligation! No elevation now for conscious merit, and applauded purity, to look down from on a prostrate adorer, and an admiring world, and up to pleased and rejoicing parents and relations!' (V, 330-1; *III*, *207*). One can imagine the tear-ducts of many of Richardson's first feminine readers beginning to work overtime at this point, but the tears would surely have been thrown away. We have only to remember the 'garden scene' to make a placing comparison. What is giving its last spasm here is the product of those aspects of the feminine code which fostered the very pride and vanity she has taken herself to task about. The paper is a farewell to something whose falsehood she has just revealed, yet whose power over her she cannot help reinforcing by the syrupy sweetness of her last indulgence of it.

Again Lovelace has been right about her pride; but the next three papers turn to him, and the first, paper seven, is the knell of his hopes from the rape. For, however, one might interpret it in detail, it expresses the most powerful revulsion against what he has done to her. The mode this time is poetic image, partly because Clarissa cannot confront her sexual experience directly, and partly because of the intensity of her feelings. The indirection does however cause a certain difficulty, especially since this must be the crux for interpreting her attitude to sex. The simplest way to read the paper is as an expression of revulsion at sex itself, by way of Lovelace. In this reading the ambiguity of the 'Thou' which is the first word – is the caterpillar an image of sexual appetite? or is it Lovelace? as indeed it turns out to be – is unimportant. I used to read in this way, making rather unfavourable comparisons with the treatment of worm, storm, and rose in Blake's great poem of Experience, which may well derive from it.[1] But I now think such a reading would be both superficial and significantly mistaken. For what it leaves out of account is just the most striking feature: that from the first image onwards, the emphasis is not on violation or desecration of purity, but on the destruction of potential fertility, growth, warmth, and colour. 'Thou pernicious Caterpiller, that preyest upon the fair leaf of Virgin Fame, and poisonest those leaves that thou canst not devour' – the second clause surely says something different from and deeper than the first? (V, 331; *III*, *207*). What Lovelace has done is not simply to desecrate her virginity, but to poison or kill a vitality his 'love' is incapable of making its own. A caterpillar's petty gnawings spoil a leaf that a man could enjoy in its entirety. This is not sex seen as desecration like the first apostrophe, but *rape as seen as a desecration of true sex*, and the difference is crucial. Moreover the point, once taken, is confirmed and strengthened by all the images that follow. The 'fell Blight', the 'Eastern

[1] Blake said Richardson 'won his heart'; see Geoffrey Keynes, *A Bibliography of William Blake* (New York, 1921), 64.

Blast', the 'overspreading Mildew', not only destroy 'the early promises the shining year' (which are already a potentiality of growth and fertility, not a state), but they also mock the toil and blast the joyful hopes of the 'Husbandman' – and it is not fanciful to see a grim pun. The crops don't exist for their own sake and beauty; they do exist to be harvested, and so enrich the life of man. But they demand laborious pains and toil to cultivate them to fullness of growth, and to harvest them at the proper time and in the proper way; they are not to be snatched or spoilt, blighted, or made to decay before they have reached their full ripeness. Similarly the crime of the 'fretting Moth' is to corrupt the 'fairest garment' which is meant to be worn, not just to be beautiful in itself. And the crime of the 'eating Canker worm' in the opening bud of the rose of love, is that it prevents the rose from reaching its full rich red (which is not the colour of virginity), but turns it to 'livid yellowness', the colour of disease and pallid unfulfilment. I labour the point, but it is there, it is far too easily missed, and without it the full irony of Lovelace's 'proof' is lost. He is, as we have been noticing all along, so curiously near the truth in his predictions; but the narrow margin of error makes a world of difference. Clarissa does feel that an irreversible change has taken place which has revealed her true nature to herself. She has been proud, and the experience is indeed one of utter humiliation. But each of these means something quite different from his expectations. It is her moral nature which is the reality to her, and her love for him the aberration. Her pride lay in believing in her own power, believing that her love could overcome his destructive brutality; her new humility will renounce all such hopes in victory over herself, not abasement before her 'conqueror'. She does indeed admit her sexual nature, if only under the cloak of image; yet, if I am right, her idea of sex is deeper and more human than his, in its insistence that sex should be growth, fertility, harvest, warmth, richness – and by these values his idea of sex as ego-endorsement can only be seen as poisonous, corrupt, and diseased.

Now in her eighth paper she can speak to Lovelace simply and directly about the way she had looked at him at first, and had allowed her love to grow through her readiness to find in him the qualities she wanted to find. 'But, Oh! you have barbarously and basely conspired against that Honour, which you ought to have protected: And now you have made me – What is it of vile, that you have *not* made me? – Yet, God knows my heart, I had no culpable inclinations! – I honoured Virtue! – I hated Vice! – But I knew not, that you were Vice itself!' (V, 332; *III*, *208*). The strength of the grasp she has regained of her moral nature can be gauged now. She has come out of derangement, from the emotions of the lost, hurt child, through the languages of moral fable, puritan introspection, and the intensity of image, to a point where she can write with clear and ordered simplicity. She doesn't name what he has done to her but she does try to face it. Having condemned herself for pride and blindness she now finds nothing culpable in her love itself, apart from these. Her view of her own vileness, and of him as 'Vice itself', are less than satisfactory, but even here she qualifies still further in the ninth paper. The essential difference between them is the difference between their hearts. 'Had the happiness of any the poorest Outcast in the world, whom I had never seen, never known, never before heard of, lain as much in *my* power, as my happiness did in *yours*, my benevolent heart would have made me fly to the succour of such a poor distressed . . .' It is quite clear that Lovelace has entirely misread her, and that the effect on her of what he has done can only be to make her condemn and despise him beyond recall.

The last of her papers is scrawled over with quotations from the poets; from Otway, Cowley, Garth, Dryden, Lee and Shakespeare (V, 333; *III*, *209*). Having searched herself for the meaning of what has happened, she finally uses the poetry of others as an emotional catalyst and relief. So Hamlet's horror at his mother's lust is an index to her feelings; Cowley's *Despair* helps her to express her own at being forced back from insensibility into the cage of a conscious body; and several others bring out the longing for death which (as we have seen before) is her immediate emotional reaction to the hateful prospect of her life.

What such use of quotations makes one suspect, however, is confirmed by what three of them say: she is still afraid of her feelings. The first shows her longing to escape from consciousness and memory; the other citation from *Hamlet*, the Ghost's 'I could a Tale unfold / Would harrow up thy soul! – ' is chiefly remarkable for the dash; and the adaptation to Anna of lines from *Venice Preserved* speaks of the divided soul warring within her. She has always been emotionally reserved; has always had difficulty in seeing into her own heart. Her moral insight may have become clearer and clearer, but her emotions are still turgid, confused, and terrifying. Yet the quotations help her to begin to get them outside herself and look at them; and at the end of the paper she finds some words from the *Absalom and Achitophel* of Lovelace's favourite bard, which help her to sound a note of acceptance that will become the novel's dominant chord:

> For Life can never be sincerely blest.
> Heav'n punishes the *Bad*, and proves the *Best*.

What we have been watching is a personality disintegrated and remade; a successful search for reorientation after what Richardson clearly thought was the most damaging and challenging blow a woman could suffer. Only now does he show us the real derangement which these ten papers have brought her out of: her letter to Lovelace which, apart from its ordered postscript, probably antedates them all and represents the last stage of her delirium. It is really disordered. She cannot keep her mind at all on what she writes, for 'My head is gone. I have wept away all my brain' (V, 334; *III*, *210*). She thinks Lovelace may have poisoned Anna, may be in Faustian league with the devil. She is incoherently terrified of Mrs Sinclair, and desperately pleads to be sent away from her hateful house to some private lunatic asylum where she can be hid forever from the world. Mixed up with this is the dawning insight into her own responsibility, and pride, which her suffering reveals to her. But at the heart of the letter is a moment of sheer self-revelation, of what it *feels* like to know that she has been raped; and there is no moment like it in the eighteenth century novel. 'O Lovelace! if you could be sorry for yourself, I would be sorry too – But when all my doors are fast, and nothing but the key-hole open, and the key of late put into that, to be where you are, in a manner without opening any of them – O wretched, wretched Clarissa Harlowe! For I never will be Lovelace – let my Uncle take it as he pleases' (V, 335; *III, 210-11*).

As soon as one realises what this is about, the maidenly groping for language becomes deeply moving. The whole of her upbringing, her feminine code, and the ethics of her age, have inhibited all thought or mention of sex; have encouraged her native reserve; have taught her to think of her body as a fortress locked against attack; have made her regard any sexual approach before marriage as an encroaching liberty, to be resented as an insult. The experience of rape is the agony of knowing that the opening in her body, in spite of the fact that her senses and her intellect have been wholly unmoved, has enabled Lovelace to 'be where you *are*' – not 'were' – to be always part of her inner consciousness, having touched her most private being. There is a deep psychological truth here; and not for a hundred and fifty years could the English novel begin to approach again a 'new way of writing' which could probe its characters as deeply as this. Clarissa could only make such a self-revelation in derangement, but to bring it off at all is an astonishing feat in the mid-eighteenth century.

Richardson has moved behind sex, behind 'character', behind morality. His imagination told him here that what was really the issue in the situation he had created was the sacredness of a human being's innermost self – whether we use the new word 'psyche' or the old word 'soul'. What is really unforgivable about Lovelace is not the raped virginity, the ruined reputation, the moral turpitude. It is that he cannot conceive or respect the essentially private inner core of personality that each individual has a right to dispose of as only he or she may wish. He has not treated her as a human being but as a mere object, a function of his ego, and this she will never accept. We can now see that this also lay behind the Harlowes and Solmes; that it is what the whole novel has been about. Yet to answer his ultimate question, what is 'Clarissa' *essentially*? and to prove the existence of that inner core, Richardson has had to challenge himself to disintegrate his heroine, to break her down to the last possible distillation before her personality disappears into the mechanism of madness. No novelist better earns his right to his ultimate beliefs by his courage in putting them imaginatively to the test – not even Henry James, whom he resembles in so many respects, though James is a much more accomplished artist. It does not matter whether one agrees that a moral nature may be innate; or whether one simply sees Clarissa remaking her personality into the shape she wishes it to have. It doesn't even matter, in the last analysis, whether one admires or detests that shape. At the heart of Richardson's novel is the assertion of her right to be what she wishes to be, and one is bound to respect the integrity that drives him so far, in order to earn the right to make it.

3

In the scenes that follow her recovery, Richardson confronts persecutor and victim in a last mutual judgement.

It is not to be expected that Lovelace should understand the import of the papers he can describe as 'whimsical'. He is still justifying his mercy in using '*somnivolencies* (I hate the word opiates . . .)' (V, 340; *III*, *214*); trying to escape from himself by outlining a plot to Belford for a joint seduction of the Hampstead women; consoling himself by the thought that when Clarissa's intellects return, as her first attempt to escape suggests they are doing, his conquest will be vindicated by her shame and confusion. 'Sweet Soul! methinks I have her before me: Her face averted: Speech lost in sighs – Abashed – Conscious – What a triumphant aspect will this give me, when I gaze in her downcast countenance!' (V, 345-6; *III*, *218*).

Instead he meets a Clarissa with the fullest sense of what he has done to her, but strengthened by long hours of prayer for self-control, wholly in command of herself, and perfectly coherent. She seeks him out herself to demand in the clearest terms 'what *further* I am to suffer from thy barbarity?' (V, 349; *III*, *220*). Her 'majestic composure' is Lovelace's first indication of how hopelessly he has misjudged, and how contemptible he now appears in her eyes. He is utterly confused, and for the first time in the book can think of nothing to say. Richardson catches, with the true dramatist's ear for the inflections of the human voice, the hopeless long-drawn-out stutter of a suddenly emptied mind, the playactor who has 'dried' and for whom there are no cues (V, 350; *III*, *221*). Clarissa's language is won by suffering, introspection and prayer. Lovelace's no-language represents the collapse of a confident volubility built on ideas now revealed as wholly inadequate, even to him. The stutter comes about because every potentially slick formula is evacuated of meaning as it begins to leave his mouth; he has no language, faced with her, to use about what he has done or what he can do about it now.

It is clear that there are no 'amends' that he can offer. Clarissa's delicacy is gone. She makes no pretence of not understanding, and cuts right through the further stutterings about marriage with a whiplash contempt for the idea that marriage can put right such a wrong. It is probably still one of the clearest moments of rejection in fiction: '*the man who has been the villain to me you have been, shall never make me his wife*' (V, 352; *III*, *222*). The conviction that it carries, the sense that it *must* be so, is Richardson's answer to the objections of the sentimentalists who had written to him, and to a whole world of sentimental fiction. Marriage is no formula for patching up happy endings; to him and to his heroine it is a serious sacrament before God. It remains to be seen whether Lovelace has 'sinned beyond the *possibility of forgiveness*', but there can be no doubt about marriage: 'it would be *criminal* in me to wish to bind my Soul in covenant to a man so nearly allied to perdition' (V, 353; *III*, *223*).

Lovelace's voice, one is made to feel, now comes from another world of space and time. Knowing him as we do, we can see the significance of the illumination that suddenly strikes him: 'such irresistible proofs of the Love of Virtue, *for its own sake* – did I never hear of, nor meet with, in all my reading' (V, 352; *III*, *222*). But the spectators at a chess championship cannot be excited by a tyro's discovery, after watching long days of play, that it is the nature of a castle to move in certain straight lines. The perception is a world too late, and what he builds on it he has himself devalued too often for it to have real significance now. Even if he is in earnest, his kneeling in penitence, his vows of reformation, his appeals to heaven to witness his sincerity have been too often debased to count. We watch unmoved the replaying of an old scene which, despite its new meaning, can only seem tiresome in the aftermath of what we have been watching. It is Lovelace's tragedy that these new intimations in him should fall dead upon our sensibilities. And he cannot sustain them, cannot realise how hopeless it is to imagine he can palliate, let alone falling back into lies which could not help him even if they were true. After she has left him he peers through her keyhole, watching her asleep in her chair. Her symbolism is reversed: he can intrude on her privacy, but the tiny opening in the locked door allows only a glimpse of another world beyond, and only by emphasising the barrier between.

Immediately after this she tries to escape again, is foiled, throws open a window to scream for help to passers-by, is overpowered, and carried bodily upstairs again in hysterics. The power situation still seems watertight; the language of force still works; and Lovelace has little difficulty in disposing of the constables who come to inquire. Yet his understanding of the limits of power is dawning too. 'I thought to have had one trial (having gone so far) for *Cohabitation*. But what hope can there be of succeeding? – She is invincible! – *Against all my notions*, *against all my conceptions* (thinking of her as a woman, and in the very bloom of her charms) *she is absolutely invincible*. My whole view, at the present, is to do her legal justice, if I can but once more get her out of her altitudes' (V, 362; *III*, *229*). Yet the 'dawn' is still foggy: 'The *Consent* of such a woman must make her ever new, ever charming'. This bears only on his own psychic aversion to shackles – as far as any relevance to Clarissa is concerned, it is as remote as another planet. 'But, astonishing! Can the want of a Church-Ceremony make such a difference!' A world of incomprehension is bared in a sentence.

Any attempt to enter Clarissa's world moreover, must mean the destruction of the whole personality he has built for himself. 'I am confoundedly out of conceit with myself. If I give up my contrivances, my joy in stratagem, and plot, and invention, I shall be but a common man: Such another dull heavy creature as thyself. Yet what does even my success in my machinations bring me, but disgrace, repentance, regret? But I am overmatched, egregiously overmatched, by this woman. What to do with her, or without her, I know not.' Even the words of the last phrase are reminiscent of B; but the enormous difference between the novels is the depth and inwardness of our knowledge of what the world of Lovelace looks and feels like from the inside, and what the gap between it and 'common humanity' entails. Lovelace is just beginning to glimpse this final knowledge, but the gleams of light serve mainly to emphasise the darkness of his ignorances. She can have no interest in his 'legal justice'. He can never hope for 'consent' to anything less than a complete surrender to her world of values, and in the light of what he has done it might, even then, be too much to hope. It is crass moral stupidity to put her revulsion down to the lack of a 'church ceremony', or to imagine that she can be influenced by prospects of 'grandeur' now that Lord M is dangerously ill. But underlying all the vapourings, the rationalisations, the twistings and turnings, is his stubborn unwillingness to give up his own idea of himself. We are watching, we ought to realise, the distorted mirror image of Clarissa's struggle; distorted, not because his is a 'wicked' image while hers is a 'good' one, but because he can only retain 'himself' by bending or breaking her to his will, while she requires no more than freedom to choose. He *cannot* leave her alone while there remains a spark of hope, however wild or misconceived. He has to go on and on trying to balance an equation that will never balance, bending and bruising her in the impossible attempt to shape her into a component of his own self-design.

So the hopeless scenes go on. In the next one, we are left in no doubt of Clarissa's reaction to the 'shape' he has already fixed on her. To his attempted plea that if they marry now, he will only have 'anticip—', she retorts with another whiplash of revulsion: 'thinkest thou, that I will give a Harlot-niece to thy honourable Uncle, and to thy *real* Aunts; and a cousin to thy Cousins from a Brothel?' (V, 365-6; *III, 231-2*). Lovelace puts our own first reaction to this: 'You know *better* than to think the *worse* of yourself for suffering what you *could not help*' (V, 367; *III, 233*). But Clarissa's words only appear to be a moral argument; they are really a spasm of physical and psychological self-disgust at his classification of her. She knows she is not a harlot, but that is how Lovelace has regarded her. He has put her in what he regarded as the proper place to bring out her real nature, and treated her as merely flesh for the gratification of his needs and his will. She has known what it is to be seen through such eyes and the experience has left an indelible psychic stain. She is careless about hiding it from the world because he has ruined her in her own eyes, and that is what matters. Because of this he is 'Abhorred of my Soul!', totally renounced, for ever. So much for any hopes of bending her, but the scene further clarifies the impossibility of bending himself. He urges her to imitate her God, who requires only that a sinner should repent; she replies by testing his repentance. She asks him to swear solemnly before God to the truth of 'Tomlinson' and the overtures to her uncle, and to the genuineness of 'Lady Betty' and 'Charlotte'. It is a moment of sheer self-determination, but his instinct to lie is pathological, and he solemnly perjures himself. Even so she doesn't believe him; but the point is that he has shown once again his total inability to meet her on her own ground and in her own language. The only language he can use sincerely is the language of force and possession. 'Yet, if you think yourself in my power, I would caution you, Madam, not to make me desperate. For you *shall* be mine, or my life shall be the forfeit!

Nor is life worth having without you! – ' (V, 367; *III*, 232). This sort of thing he can manage, and it rings true for him. But it is also meaningless, since there is no sense in which 'mine' could mean anything.

As he finishes describing the scene, moreover, there is a moment of psychological revelation quite as significant in its way as the ones we have noticed with Clarissa. He is shocked and shaken by her threats of suicide, but he cannot face his feelings, and tries to pass them off in song. He fails, falls to croaking, 'And at last I ended, like a malefactor, in a dead psalm melody'. Then, however, the feelings do pass off, and in a highly significant way. There can be no doubt about it. *He yawns.* 'High-ho! – I gape like an unfledged kite in its nest . . . What a-devil ails me! – I can neither think nor write! Lie down, pen, for a moment!' (V, 372; *III*, 236). This is a psychic boredom, an instinctive withdrawal. We shall recognise it again in Mowbray, the coarsest of the rakes, when confronted by any humanly moving situation. Lovelace is more complex but not essentially different. He cannot feel anything, as a repeated phrase has it, 'for half an hour together'. He can be temporarily moved by Clarissa, but the instinctive reaction of his whole being to the challenge of human feeling is withdrawal. He will not play a role in her version of the drama for any length of time. He gets bored, and the exterior yawn is the symptom of a rejection taking place far inside himself. This is in some ways the most revealing of all Richardson's touches in the portrait of his villain-hero. He knows and understands him quite as well as Clarissa; knows in his imagination the true inner response of the ego trapped into listening to an unfamiliar language and made to cope with emotions it cannot really share or understand. He bodies it forth, one suspects, with the real artist's delight in all truly created things.

Clarissa tries to escape a third time, and Lovelace's response is to resort again to violence or the blackmailing threat of it. He comes back to life; but his dramas are fated to anticlimax now. A terrified Clarissa, on her knees in a corner, bangs her nose on a chair, blood pours down her bosom, and Lovelace, fearing she has stabbed herself, is as terrified as she. Richardson is very sure of himself to write this scene, for I don't think there can be any doubt that it is a corrosive kind of comedy. Apart from Lovelace's compulsive need to dramatise himself, to acquire face in his own imagination, the terrorising is pointless. The compassionate intervention of Dorcas scrabbling at his feet is a bogus set-up, and our whole response is governed from the start by the knowledge that the scene is a sham that cannot possibly avail him anything. The woman who has been raped and has reacted as Clarissa has done may be terrorised and humiliated again and again; may be raped again; but she cannot be changed. With this sense of pointlessness and sham once established in our response, the scene's farcical conclusion can make its true effect. When Lovelace, blending 'heroically' his Restoration and his Roman or Imperial personae, draws his sword to make away with himself, only to discover the considerably less than epic truth, what we watch is surely comic, though it is too acrid to be funny. 'What an unmanly blockhead does this charming creature make me . . .' – but the creation is Lovelace's own (V, 378; *III*, *240*). The scene is a parody of Lovelace-melodrama, because the force Lovelace relies upon can only be self-defeating, and because while Clarissa will not and cannot play the game, Lovelace can only parody himself.

He inevitably sinks back into the morass of his blindness. He confesses that he cannot even now keep steady about marriage. Back come the rake's mask, the unrealising language, the impossible fancies. Perhaps the reason for her oversensibility is that she is pregnant? He would give up an imperial diadem to his enemy 'to have one charming Boy by this Lady', and if she escapes him without this, 'my Revenge on her family, and, in *such* a case, on herself, would be incomplete, and I should reproach myself as long as I lived'. He cannot doubt 'to have her still . . . on my own conditions' if she is pregnant, nor 'question that *revived* affection in *her*, which a woman seldom fails to have for the father of her first child, whether born in wedlock, or out of it'. With a flourishing animal image, that both proclaims his affinity with the 'strutting villain' of a rooster pursuing his imperial pleasures 'from feathered Lady to feathered Lady', and his superiority in that he cares about the 'genial product', his recovery is almost complete (V, 382; *III*, *242-3*).

Intrigue follows immediately. His style comes back to its old gay, teasing life as he seizes on Clarissa's pathetic attempt to win over Dorcas as a justification and opportunity for a plan to get her into bed with him again. This is to be alive: to allow his freewheeling fancy full play once more, starting with cold facts and careful planning, but soon soaring away with all the old compulsion. His vision of both Anna and Clarissa consoling themselves by comparing notes over their illegitimate babies has the full humorous flourish; but it has an emotional truth for him, and the steps by which he reaches it are the genuinely characteristic movements of his mind. It is his humour to outline the plot as a dream, but as usual his author's point is there as well. Lovelace cannot live in the real world. In the depths of his mind his psyche merely lies in wait for a chance to escape into its own proper fantasia. He cannot engage with truth.

It keeps presenting itself to him. 'I never, never *will*, never, never *can* forgive you! – And it is a punishment worse than death to me, that I am obliged to meet you, or to see you... Compulsion shall do nothing with me' (VI, 26-7; *III*, *260*). For a moment at a time he can see. 'By my Soul, Belford, this dear girl gives the lye to all our Rakish Maxims. There must be something more than a *name* in virtue! – I now see that there is! – *Once subdued*, *always subdued* – 'Tis an egregious falshood!' (VI, 28; *III*, *261*). But he cannot change, cannot stop tormenting her pointlessly. He can use her situation to 'infect' her conduct: she is forced to try to bribe a servant; to feign sick; to give an assurance, which she knows will be misconstrued, that she will try to make herself easy till her uncle's birthday, in order to save herself from a gloating and hot-breathed sexual blackmail. He forces her out of her moral absolutism. 'Twenty and twenty low things, that my soul would have been above being guilty of, and which I have despised myself for, have I been brought into by the infection of thy company, and by the necessity thou hast laid me under, of appearing mean.' (The full improvement on *Pamela* locks home again.) Yet, 'I thank God, destitute as I am, that I am not, however, sunk so low, as to wish to be thine' (VI, 25; *III*, *259*). But Lovelace cannot accept the evidence of his own eyes and the four-times-repeated desperation of her attempts to escape; cannot accept the freedom of her will against his 'princely offer'. As few other novelists would do, Richardson allows his heroine to be humiliated over and over again. Her physical and emotional cowardice enable Lovelace to terrorise her, tease her, blackmail her, play with her at will. Yet, when all the trappings of normal human dignity are ripped away, she retains her power to move us because beneath it all her will remains indomitable. She remains a human being, while he becomes more and more a sort of frenzied automaton.

One scene is, admittedly, never enough for Richardson when there could be five. Yet the repetition has its own logic and power, for it emphasises as nothing else could do the real extent of Lovelace's obsession. It also reminds us, in so prolonging Clarissa's persecution, that convictions are only convincing when they can stand up to the same pressures day after day. Finally these scenes are like watching a battle between two sea monsters. The surface of the water boils again and again, in different patterns and places. It conceals however, while it implies, what is really happening far below: the inexorable advance on each other's throats. Lovelace is fighting for the life of his world and the personality he has chosen; Clarissa for hers. In a psychological sense it is indeed a fight to the death.

This, I think, helps us to understand the melodrama of the last of these scenes: the Lucretia-like 'penknife scene'. The women have been telling a Lovelace eager to listen, that his difficulties are really owing to the fact that she was *never* subdued, because of the drug. '*Had* she been sensible, she *must* have been sensible. So they say. The methods taken with her have augmented her glory and her pride. She has now a Tale to tell, that she *may* tell, with honour to herself. No accomplice-inclination. She can look me into confusion, without being conscious of so much as a *thought*, which she need to be ashamed of' (VI, 54; *III*, *279*). The drug may have inhibited either the tell-tale sexual reaction itself, or her consciousness of it. The logical step then is to rape her again, in full possession of her faculties. The opportunity is carefully engineered. She had not fallen into the trap of trying to escape through Dorcas; but now her 'bribing' letter is to be 'discovered', she is to be confronted with a jury of the prostitutes, and 'judged'. If Lovelace does decide after all not to rape her again, at the very least he will give himself an excuse for tightening her imprisonment while he goes down, as he must do, to Lord M's deathbed. The street door is double-locked, and all the shutters bolted so that no sound of screaming shall be heard outside the brothel.

The melodrama, again, is of Lovelace's making. The preparations are grimly practical, but when the action starts the atmosphere is deliberately overheated with shouts, execrations, tears, screams, Lovelace's sword out again, hysteria. But being bogus, the effect is of a monstrous charade, a horrible farce. Yet it is indeed a 'judgement' scene in ways that Lovelace hadn't anticipated. It allows him and the women and us a final judgement of the nature of the struggle, its inevitable outcome if continued, and an unmistakable public verdict. When Clarissa comes in voluntarily, and confronts them with open-eyed detection and contempt of their shoddy contrivances, the farcical uproar is cut short and absolute silence falls. Once again the false stagey language which is for Lovelace a much more real and vivid world than any other, and the only one in which he can be the self he most wants to be, falls apart at the sound of Clarissa's voice. His only resort is to rape her again; he advances . . . but she has the penknife. It becomes starkly evident that she will indeed kill herself rather than submit. Yet, as her derangement answered the questionmark that hung over her ultimate attitude to sex, so this scene deals with her ultimate attitude to suicide. She is perfectly lucid about the sin involved for herself as she calls down the law of man and of God on them; 'My heart from *principle* abhors the act' (VI, 69; *III*, 290). She may have been facile before, but she is not now. Yet she believes in the mercy of God, and what might have been her last words implore it.

In a melodrama of his own contrivance, using his own language of power, Lovelace is made to judge the implications of his obsession in terms he cannot misunderstand. Below the melodramatic surface the scene is deeply thematic. What the penknife gives her for the first and last time is a command of the only currency Lovelace deals in. It is the one thing which allows her, as a woman in her situation, to express her will, to show (in terms that later melodrama was to devalue almost irrecoverably) that she genuinely would rather be dead than be 'his'. There is also a sardonic comment on the rape. As she is to tell Anna later, he has seen her 'as dead' through drugs. If he wants her this time, she will really be a corpse. Finally, what has been submerged comes to the surface and he can no longer escape the real terms of the equation he has tried to balance. He wants her, the person she is; but he wants her consenting, which would be the death of the person she is. He cannot combine irreconcilables: he must choose between Clarissa alive, and rejecting him absolutely, or face in cold fact the total extinction of her by his will that he has been trying, psychologically, to bring about. There is an end of delusion.

The scene is, then, another of Richardson's extraordinary achievements. It is a farce with the most serious undertones and symbolic meanings. What is farcical is the last implosion of the Restoration-dramatic world of Lovelace's imagination, and of the theories underlying it. What is grim and serious is the revelation of how wholly and solely it has rested on power, but also its revelation of the limits of power where there is real will to resist. The effect is to superimpose upon our existing sense of Lovelace's evil, the completed sense of his shoddiness. It is indeed a judgement which he cannot escape.

From M— Hall he presses her to marry him, with increasing desperation, in four messages whose carriers meet each other at four-hour intervals. The language is almost pathetic now in its attempts to palliate, its deceptions, the old gramophone record of familiar pressure-points, the fictions about her family. What is most obvious however is the growing realisation of the hopelessness of expecting her language in reply. The first letter begs for 'a line' (VI, 76; *III*, *295*) to signify her willingness to meet him at the altar on her uncle's birthday. The second letter shows him no longer asking for love, only to 'do you all the justice I can now do you' (VI, 77; *III*, *295*); but the expectation has shrunk to four words, the name of the church and the day, without inscription or signature. The third letter asks her to send a message through Belford if she won't write the four words herself. At last, after Belford's refusal to act without an assurance of Lovelace's intentions, he is driven to try to use Tomlinson again. The lies about her family reach their peak with the pretence that her mother is being won round, but his expectations of reply are at their nadir. 'Tell but the Captain, that you *forbid me not* to attend you . . .' (VI, 88; *III*, *303*). But there is complete silence. There are no words to be spoken, for as Belford says, four would be as much as forty if their import was that she could meet him on any terms. Only in the language of truth, honesty and freewill could she speak, and then it would be merely to renounce him again.

The silence is broken only with the news that she has succeeded in escaping, this time (it turns out) never to be recovered.

4

Clarissa is in hiding for a little over a fortnight. She uses her time to discover the full truth at long last, and to clear away the misunderstanding with Anna. She finds out how Lovelace intercepted and faked Anna's letters; learns about the forged letters and the faked Ladies from the real Lady Betty; exposes through Mrs Hodges and Mrs Norton the whole fraud of Tomlinson. Richardson also needs to 'hark back to make up', so only now do we get Clarissa's narrative of how she was decoyed back to the brothel, and what she can remember of the nightmare scenes before the rape. In the meantime, Lovelace convinces his family that he is serious about marrying her, and they enlist Anna to persuade her to agree. Before Anna's urgings can reach her, however, she has disappeared again; imprisoned for debt at the suit of Mrs Sinclair.

The prison episode is the novel's last turning-point. On the surface it is an accident, brought about by the women on their own initiative, and responsible for a serious deterioration in her health. After her escape from the brothel she had been so disordered again that she wrote to Anna at home; and it seems possible that only the shock-therapy of a wounding reply from Mrs Howe prevented another nerve storm. Now however the far deeper shock of her public disgrace and imprisonment, the hysterics produced by the tormentings of the prostitutes, her inability to eat, and her refusal to go to bed in a room she cannot lock, complete the damage that the rape and the drugs began. This is only the surface, however, not the real significance of the prison scenes. They must be read on two other levels, and these direct our response to the remainder of the novel.

We should recognise the ways in which her imprisonment, though Lovelace did not intend it, is a logical extension and a concentrated image of what he has been doing to her all along. The sordid walls in High Holborn are only the most tangible of her enclosures by force and fraud. She is imprisoned for 'debt'; but from the beginning he has been imprisoning her in order to exact what he feels she owes, without any need for him to earn or justify what he demands. When Sally suggests a gentleman to bail her, we are left in no doubt by Belford that this was a well-known avenue to prostitution. Lovelace too has tried to level her with harlots, to make her one of Sally's 'US'. The chair which removes her from the door of her heavenly Father's House to the squalid court in High Holborn, re-images the chariot which took her from the door of her earthly father's house on her way to the brothel. The social disgrace, the wounding imputations from the bystanders in Covent Garden are, if anything, only the palest reflection of what she might expect from an ignorant society because of Lovelace. Indeed, this puts us on to the last ironic twist of this imaging. We watch a reorchestration of what we have watched before, stripped of its gildings and revealed concretely for what it really was – but there is one crucial difference. What is happening to Clarissa now is infinitely better.

The sponging house may be physically vile, but though Belford may dwell on the details, in every important sense it is infinitely less vile than the 'very handsome apartments' Sally tries to blackmail her back to (VI, 280; *III*, *432*). Its owners are relatively humane and treat her with a degree of sympathy. The tauntings of Sally and Polly are vicious enough, but their treatment of her is far less so than Lovelace's. Richardson reveals again, as with Bella in the first instalment, his dramatic ability to capture the flick and sting of the human voice intent on inflicting pain. Their motives reflect Lovelace's low pride and callousness, and the desire to reduce the victim to the level of the persecutor; and the tormenting is pursued (by, we remember, women who have watched her being raped) further than we actually experience in Belford's second-hand re-creation, until Clarissa is hysterical again (VI, 294; *III*, *442*). But Sally and Polly are merely jealous, callous, and spiteful. They do not pretend to love her; their terrorising has limits, for they at least keep Mrs Sinclair away; and it is not directed obsessively to the breakdown of her whole personality. The social disgrace, the physical hardship, the mental torture, are real enough and made so to our experience – but they are far less than Lovelace had made her suffer. There should then be an extra sting in our response to his distraction over what 'they' have done to her: ' 'Tis impossible that Miss Harlowe should have ever suffered as thou hast made me suffer, and as I now suffer! That Sex is made to bear pain . . .' (VI, 305-6; *III*, *450*).

Clarissa herself is in no doubt of her preference. She refuses to be released by Belford; and is only persuaded when he guarantees that she will be safe from Lovelace at the Smiths'. In this way the lesser evil becomes a means of release from the greater one. At last she is really free: free to see whom she wishes, to send and receive letters in her own name, to dispose of her own future. The whole novel has been a series of imprisonments: by her family, by Lovelace, by the women; by a world of people who insist that she owes them something and that they have the right to make her a passive object of their wills and of their power. Release from the prison becomes, then, a release from the confinement of the world – though not yet from its pressures.

Yet the prison is also a turning-point in a more significant inward way, though we may not recognise this unless we read with the closeness Richardson demands. The key section of her correspondence in her fortnight of freedom is no longer with Anna, with whom she is mainly concerned to clarify the past. It is with her old nurse Mrs Norton, it concerns the future, and it has to do only indirectly with Lovelace's plots and hopes. Mrs Norton's letters come like a breath of fresh air in a fetid room, reminding one that one had almost forgotten what it is like outside. This is because her voice is the first human utterance we have heard for a very long time that is genuinely compassionate, does not set itself up in judgement, is quietly convinced of Clarissa's basic integrity without needing detailed proof, and breathes real feeling for her sufferings. By contrast Anna comes off very badly indeed. We are forced to recognise the other side of her wit, her vivacity, her sharpness. Her first barbed letter, as Clarissa has cause to notice (VI, 159; *III*, *350*), is written in a deliberately wounding style reminiscent of Bella. There has been room for misunderstanding, but she has willingly occupied it. She repents immediately, but we shall never again be unaware of the limits of her understanding, faith and compassion. More significantly still, Mrs Norton's letters announce a new perspective: a call to recognise and submit to the workings of providence in a tragic world. Her own unhappy life, and the fact that her beloved only son is dangerously ill as she writes, makes it possible for her to speak without hypocrisy or empty preaching. She is concerned to persuade Clarissa to have faith, to reject despair, to be patient, to think beyond the perspective of time: for 'what, my dear, is this poor Needle's point of NOW to a *boundless* ETERNITY?' (VI, 149; *III*, *344*). Clarissa responds at once, and one can see why she should fancy that Mrs Norton must be her real mother, and she a changeling in Harlowe Place. Yet it is one thing to respond and quite another to achieve the values she is responding to. She has to begin forcing herself to stop calling on God for vengeance and vindication; to try to think in terms of forgiveness. She has to recognise how much her impatience under her wrongs may be founded on 'self-partiality, that strange misleader' (VI, 142; *III*, *339*). We watch the beginnings of her last struggle; and we should recognise how it follows the pattern of Pamela's in that the final 'agon' is a spiritual one, only occasioned by her persecutors.

The deepest significance of the prison scenes lies in her acceptance of humiliation, her achievement of patience and resignation. She will not answer the tauntings of the prostitutes, will not recriminate or denounce. There is a marked change here from Bella's adversary and from the girl who used to flay Lovelace at the slightest provocation. Some may not like the change, but there should be no doubt what it signifies. It is not the result of being cowed by ill-treatment and grief; it is willed, with great effort. Belford may not know whether she is 'mortified into meekness' or whether she 'has made a resolution not to be provoked' (VI, 276; *III*, *430*), but we should be able to read the answer and the effort between the lines of his already second-hand account, as he cannot. 'Am I not worth an answer, *Miss Harlowe*? I would answer you (said the sweet Sufferer, *without any emotion*) if I knew how.' Or again: 'She would trouble nobody; she had no friends; was all they could get from her, while Sally staid: But yet spoken with a patience of spirit, *as if she enjoyed her griefs*' (VI, 276-7; *III*, *430*). My italics show where Belford's understanding and ours separate, for knowing Clarissa as we do, we can measure the strain of her self-control, spot the occasions on which it wavers, and detect the irony of Sally's taunting advice to behave '*as a good Christian should*, comporting herself to her condition, and making the best of it' (VI, 283; *III, 435*). Clarissa herself tells the Rowlands what great difficulty she has 'notwithstanding the seeming composure you just now took notice of, to bear, as I ought to bear, the evils I suffer' (VI, 286; *III, 437*). Richardson not only poses the question-marks, he shows also that self-partiality and indulgence do not quickly disappear. We can detect the false notes easily enough: 'A shower falling, as she spoke, What, said she, looking up, do the Elements weep for me?' (VI, 287; *III, 437*). But for the most part she really does succeed in holding down her resentment, recrimination, impatience, and self-pity.

Moreover she begins to struggle to forgive. She starts in prison with bitter sarcasm: '*Now*, Lovelace! Now indeed do I think I *ought* to forgive thee!' (VI, 275; *III, 429*), but the irony reverses itself. By the time of her release she has started on the spiritual path towards forgiveness. 'Let him know, Sir,' she tells Belford, 'only one thing, that, when you heard me in the bitterness of my spirit, most vehemently exclaim against the undeserved usage I have met with from him, that even *then*, in *that* passionate moment, I was able to say . . . 'Give him, good God! Repentance and Amendment; that I may be the last poor creature, who shall be ruined by him! – And, in thine own good time, receive to *thy* mercy the poor wretch who had *none* on me!' (VI, 310; *III, 453-4*). This is only a beginning, as one can see from the sliding into recrimination in the act of prayer; but by the same token there can be no doubt of the effort it costs her. Her imprisonment does begin to bring about, through effort and self-discipline, an important change. The accent is already very different from the impassioned vigour of 'I never, never *will*, never, never *can* forgive'.

Lastly there are one or two important hints of another change – in her attitude towards death. We have seen how, from quite an early stage, a longing for death has been an immediate (and questionable) emotional reaction to the hateful prospects of her life, growing stronger as those prospects became more hateful. Writing to Anna just before her imprisonment she notices the first symptoms of 'decline' in herself, and welcomes them, regretting the naturally healthy constitution that makes the process slow. During her imprisonment she shows a tendency to dramatise and indulge her death-wish. But at calmer and more self-controlled moments there is the beginning of a less questionable tone and attitude. She tells Sally that she will not live long; but she also tells her that her future will be 'as it shall please God' as well as 'those who have brought me hither' (VI, 281; *III*, *433*). And when she agrees to Belford's release she tells him 'that she did not expect to have lived till now: That therefore all places had been alike to her . . . But that, since she feared she was not so soon to be released, as she had hoped', she will go to the Smiths (VI, 311; *III*, *454*). She is beginning to learn that death cannot be had by wishing, that it is not an easy and emotionally satisfying way out. The last of her imprisonments will turn out to be her own body, and on the physical level the sponging house is the beginning of her release from that too. Yet it will not come until she recognises that it is not a right but a priceless gift, that must be earned; and the start of that recognition is here too.

5

The prison scenes are almost the last dramatic action in the novel. In any other writer it would be impossible to imagine that such a long drawn out, slow-motion, wholly undramatic movement of fiction should still have to intervene before the moment of her death. Tension drops, tedium may mount. Yet it is possible to see what Richardson thought he was doing if we allow the last of the action to show us how to respond to the inaction . . . that is, if we wish to understand. We have just seen how the significance of the prison scenes lies not in the surface action, but in two levels of meaning underneath. On one hand we have to realise the nature of the pressures on her from the outside world; on the other, to read between the lines to detect the nature of her inner response, her spiritual 'agon'. Similarly, in the inaction that lies ahead, we must see behind the surface in the same two ways. She is surrounded by people who do not understand and cannot share what is happening to her. She is filtered to us now through Belford, whose awakening to what she is, is gradual. Her own letters are mainly concerned to resist various pressures from a world that is now thoroughly alien to her, or to make practical preparations for leaving it. We have first of all to see what those pressures are and why she resists them. And only by reading between the lines (though then, clearly enough) will we glimpse the real 'action' going on deep within her being; and be able to answer the psalmist's other great question, not only what is man, but is God mindful of him? Or is Clarissa merely morbid, as one may have suspected?

This inner 'agon' cannot be dramatised. It will be, has to be, a painfully slow process far within. There are no crises, nothing to seize and exploit dramatically. Indeed it is anti-dramatic by definition, since drama is concerned with living, or at least with the protest of life against death. The willing cessation of response to life, the deliberate stilling of conflict, is the most undramatic subject one could imagine.

In our predominantly irreligious world, where death is almost the only obscenity, this conclusion to the novel has met with a total lack of understanding and response. This is hardly surprising, especially since there are artistic reasons for it too. We are deliberately removed for the most part from immediate experience of Clarissa's mind. Where we occasionally get more than a glimpse, in her Meditations for example, her consciousness is expressed in the words of the Bible and it may not occur to us to read between the lines. This means that she grows away from our imagination; becomes someone we cannot know, and whose experience we can only infer, no longer share. She becomes an increasingly distanced saint-like figure – and we don't care for those. We seem occupied almost wholly with the impedimenta that delay her journey, while the experience that is really meaningful to her is closed to us. A St John of the Cross might have been able to make us imagine it, but Richardson seems to have known his limits. We can hardly blame him for the tact he chose. Yet, unquestionably, there is a great experiential loss in reading this extraordinary conclusion to an extraordinary novel. Only, we can at least try to grasp what can be grasped.

Before we left the prison scenes we might have noticed, for example, that we *are* let into her mind, some time afterwards, when Belford gives Lovelace the first of her Meditations, written in the sponging house (VI, 426-7; *IV*, *6-7*). It is taken from the part of the Bible Sally noticed fell open at the touch: the Book of Job. There are obvious ways in which Clarissa duplicates Job's situation. Her worldly prospects, wealth, and happiness have been destroyed. Her nearest and dearest have been taken from her. Her body has been defiled. The wicked prosper. The righteous are brought low. So, on the Saturday, the day after her arrest, Clarissa concentrates Job's poignant outcries into ten of the Book's most powerful verses, to express the agony of her own spirit, her own immense impatience. 'Wherefore is light given to her that *is* in misery; and life unto the bitter in soul? Who longeth for death; but it cometh not; and diggeth for it more than for hid treasures? Why is light given to *one* whose way is hid; and whom God hath hedged in?' The forced composure and patience before the prostitutes is one thing; these hints of the private agony behind are quite another; for it is not just the misery, it is the questioning of God and his Providence, in redoubling suffering upon the already crushed. 'I was not in safety; neither had I rest; neither was I quiet. Yet trouble came.' But she does not respond to Job's protestations of his own righteousness; nor to the full grim grandeur of the unsearchable Jahweh in the whirlwind. Her composure comes from accepting Elihu's view: 'But behold God is mighty, and despiseth not any. He giveth Right to the Poor – And if they be bound in fetters, and holden in cords of affliction, then he sheweth them their works and their transgressions'. She longs for death; she battles against impatience; but she is making herself realise that affliction does not separate her from the love of God, but is actually a challenge to look into the transgressions of her own heart.

The symbolic centre of the prison episode, then, which provides the key to the remainder of the novel, is the moment when Belford finds her asleep kneeling against the table, with her fore-finger in the Bible (VI, 298; *III, 445-6*). The world keeps breaking in on her with suggestions about what she must do, but they can only be an intrusion even when kindly meant. Her real concern lies where she points, hidden in the pages of that closed Book.

First, however, let us look at 'the world'. What will be the reaction to her tragedy of Lovelace's aristocratic relations? And of Clarissa's circle? And of the clergy with whom her family has been connected? And of her grasping materialist family themselves? Clarissa is free at last and can no longer be made to do anything. What would her society think she should do?

If Lovelace is a throwback to the Restoration aristocracy, the reputation of his family suggests that they share respectable middleclass standards, and this impression is endorsed as we meet them for ourselves. Lady Betty quickly collects the family together to bring pressure on Lovelace to make amends, and they put him to a family Trial (VI, 222 ff.; *III, 393 ff.*). His 'playbook' account of the proceedings puts a lens of mockery between us and them, and brings out his quick wit, strategic cunning, and sheer audacity. He partly succeeds in turning the trial to jest, but it is only partly; we never lose our sense of the seriousness of the issue, and though he often runs rings around his family, they never forfeit respect for their basic good nature and morality. And yet – Lovelace could not succeed as far as he does if his family did not ultimately fail in their own trial. They never manage the heartfelt condemnation he deserves, and he can therefore make too much play with his readiness to repair by marriage. The older ones are too easily diverted by 'tub to the whale' attacks on feminine pride; the younger ones and Lord M cannot help being amused by his audacity and levity. Lord M's 'wisdom of nations' shows his sense of basic human standards, but his magpie mentality and garrulousness not only make him comic, but suggest a lack of real seriousness and discipline. He is a relic of an older age: the great feudal landlord with his dream of bonfires and rejoicings over the birth of an heir to the last male of his family, his pocket boroughs, his urgings that his nephew take his rightful place as a public man and a peer. But Lovelace sees him as a fossil collecting fossils, and so to an extent do we. Recovering from a dangerous illness, Lord M can both pray with the chaplain and make his nephew entertain him with his rogueries. The Montague girls can also blame the facts while they are entertained by 'my manner, my invention, my intrepidity' (VI, 217; *III, 389*). They are not really horrified by what he has done, they regard marriage as a suitable atonement, and it is an article of faith that Lovelace's reformation will follow. While they eventually accept Clarissa's rejection, and applaud it, it is clear that none would have made it in her place; and their final ostracism of their kinsman *after* her refusal is curiously pointless.

Anna is much taken with their grandeur and their talk of settlements, and agrees with her mother for once that Clarissa should marry. 'If you would not have the wretch for *your own sake*; have him you must, for *mine*, for your *family*'s, for your *honour*'s sake' (VI, 258; *III, 418*). Hickman agrees too, but in his 'ludicrous' encounter with Lovelace there is also an unpleasant hint that he and Anna (like Charlotte Montague) are more squeamish about Clarissa than about Lovelace, and would not press so strongly if they did not believe her 'faultless in every particular' (VI, 365 (c.f. 241); *III, 491 (c.f. 406)*). (We have already noticed the limits of Anna's faith and compassion.) For the middleclass, the counterpart of the aristocratic Trial is Colonel Ambrose's Ball, on Clarissa's birthday, when the intrepid Lovelace tests the depth of the revulsion that Clarissa's own circle might be supposed to feel. Anna comes off much the best in showing anger and contempt, but she seems as conscious of the eyes of the assembly as of her own feelings; and though she can see and condemn 'how pleased half the giddy fools of our sex were with him' and that it is to this that the Lovelaces 'owe much of their vileness', whereas they should be 'shunned, and despised, and treated as beasts of prey' (VI, 451; *IV*, *23*), her own behaviour is a little theatrical, and she never manages the quiet, icily convincing revulsion that cannot be turned aside. Most of the company however are half won over by Lovelace's intrepidity, his mixture of seriousness and gaiety, his bland assurance and address. When he does finally urge on Anna and her mother the seriousness of his intentions, Clarissa's closest friends Miss Biddulph and Miss Lloyd join the Howes in 'opinion that you should be his' and so, having satisfied himself that Lovelace is serious, does Colonel Morden (VI, 455; *IV*, *26*). Anna will not even send Clarissa's decisive rejection to Lovelace's family until she consults her friend yet again. Once more there is admiration for Clarissa's decision afterwards; but with the best of the middleclass as with the aristocracy it is clear that marriage would have been regarded as amends, and that more attention is paid to Clarissa's and her family's honour than to the seriousness of the sacrament. The contrast is with Clarissa's carelessness about revealing what has happened to her; and with her determination not to 'sanctify' Lovelace's crime at the altar, or take vows of love, obedience and honour, before God, which might hazard her 'future happiness' both here and hereafter. Richardson's judgement of his society, confirmed by the outcry about the 'unhappy ending', is unmistakable.

The worthiest clergyman Clarissa has known, Dr Lewen, has heard that she has refused Lovelace, and will forgive him, if only she is left alone. For him, also, there are but two ways to repair honour, and if she refuses the one she must adopt the other. It is true that he is under pressure from the Harlowes, but equally clear that his letter represents his own opinion too. He writes in his last illness to urge Clarissa 'That your Religion, your Duty to your Family, the Duty you owe to your Honour, and even Charity to your Sex' (VII, 225; *IV*, *181*) oblige her to prosecute in the Courts, and that this will prevent further mischief. (This had already been proposed by Mrs Howe.) There can be no proper pardon 'till we have it in *our power to punish*' (VII, 227; *IV*, *182*). Clarissa allows much of this argument, and clearly neither she nor her creator believe that maidenly modesty should stand in the way of law and justice. The real point however is not that her health forbids a prosecution, or that her case would be shaky because of her own fault in leaving her father's house and living with Lovelace so long; it is that Dr Lewen, on what turns out to be his death-bed, should be so concerned with worldly matters and verdicts, whereas Clarissa is thinking in what seems to her a deeper dimension.

The worldliness is magnified in the activities of the other extreme of the clergy, the insufferable young pedant Brand, who is sent by John Harlowe to make inquiries about her. Regarding the Smiths as biased, he prefers the gossip of the milliner and the mantua-maker about the rake Belford's daily attentions. He makes little of her illness, but much of bad appearances, moved not only by his self-seeking ambition and his sense of what the Harlowes want to hear, but also, as his imaginary discourse to Clarissa shows, by a real incapacity to think in other but worldly, and hence essentially pagan terms.

The Harlowes magnify both Brand's myopia about her illness and his willingness to believe the worst, and barb it with characteristic cruelty. It is not that they cannot feel; but what they feel most is their own suffering and the ostracism they are beginning to experience from their neighbours. They are misled by Brand and inflamed by Anna's blistering correspondence with Bella, but they never themselves inquire into what really matters: the truth of what happened, and the state of Clarissa's mind and body. They simply cannot imagine her response to her experience, and crush any belief in her illness by reminding themselves of her 'moving ways' (VII, 105; *IV*, *100*). Mrs Harlowe echoes Lovelace in refusing to believe that Clarissa could be suffering as much as she (VII, 33; *IV*, *51*). Mr Harlowe lifts the second part of his curse, but 'will never own you, nor forgive you; and grieves he has such a Daughter in the world' (VII, 40; *IV*, *57*); he would rather she died a hundred deaths than become

Mrs Lovelace (VII, 374; *IV*, *281*). When she begs only a last blessing, her uncles reply with wounding questions about whether she is likely to perpetuate the stain on the family honour by having a child, and insist on knowing before they do anything. Anthony and Bella, as always, respond to incipient feeling by lashing out the most viciously. Anthony cruelly assumes that she 'has lived several guilty weeks . . . at bed as well as board, no doubt' (VII, 112; *IV*, *104*), and half-promises money 'after you have smarted a little more'. Bella implies that Lovelace must have got tired of her because she wasn't very good at it (VII, 41; *IV*, *57*), and tauntingly conveys an ultimatum, either to fulfil the family's revenge by sending Lovelace to the gallows, or to emigrate to Pennsylvania (VII, 235-6; *IV*, *188-9*). But it is young James, as ever, who holds them rigid, and who finally declares, when Morden calls the family conference that looks like ending with permission for Mrs Harlowe to go and see for herself, 'that if ever my Sister Clary darkens these doors again, I never will' (VII, 375; *IV*, *282*). When Morden angrily breaks off relations – which will have financial repercussions, as Bella fears her sister's death, unreconciled, will also do – the uncles think again; and when they hear Clarissa's 'noble' letter to Morden, Brand's recantation, and Morden's own news of her dangerous state, the Harlowes at last bestir themselves – too late. Clarissa dies before their letters can reach her.

So much for the pressures of the world, but where exactly does Clarissa's index finger point? In the first place, the rest of her life is a struggle for true forgiveness. This takes two forms. As far as Lovelace is concerned she must banish personal recrimination and forgive sincerely from the heart. As far as the Harlowes are concerned the challenge points interestingly in the other direction; forgiveness is too easy when it glosses over the fault, as we have consistently seen her do. Both Lovelace and Anna accuse her of double standards, and are right. It is one thing to imagine the Harlowes' suffering and to try to see from their point of view, quite another to argue that their resentments are 'just to them if they think them just', or that their cruelty is excess of love, or to paint portraits of their suffering that resolutely repress their baser motives (VII, 44 ff.; *IV, 59 ff.*). Gradually, and painfully slowly because each change is costly, we watch her learning to ally forgiveness with justice and justice with forgiveness. She also learns to be just to herself. She must see, irrespective of others' faults, how her transgressions opened the way to theirs, and must be quite open about her story and her faults, banishing the last pride; but she must also be quite clear about the limits of her guilt, and see that she is '*entitled*' to the blessing she demands (VII, 81; *IV, 84*) and indeed to the forgiveness she never receives.

Yet, curiously, we cannot altogether explain in moral terms the position she finally reaches in her deathbed letters to those who have wronged her. Her last struggle is only part of her weaning herself from the world, and her resolution for death. It is perfected only when she dies. It is here that the difficulties really begin for most modern readers. For why *does* she die? Is her death not a morbid indulgence in both her and Richardson?

Christopher Hill, in an otherwise excellent article,[1] is certainly quite wrong to claim that she dies because she no longer has value in the marriage market. (The *jeu d'esprit* is a telling example of the dangers of purely social criticism.) Quite apart from the pressure of almost the whole of her society to persuade her to marry Lovelace, Richardson specifically blocks such a reading by having her old suitor Wyerley propose again, showing that he thinks as highly of her as ever, and that Lovelace is not the only man who would marry her if he could. Yet the purely physical explanations do not account for her death either. Even allowing for the rape, the after-effects of drugging and derangement, the breaking of her health in prison, and the final blow when she spends two days, in spite of extreme weakness, escaping Lovelace's final persecution, the medical men cannot explain her case or treat it. Yet she cannot be accused of mortifying herself; she does her best to eat, sleep, and obey her doctor. It seems that it is her will to live rather than her body that has broken down

[1] Christopher Hill, 'Clarissa Harlowe and her Times', *E. in C.* (1955) 331-2.

irrecoverably. Hence we seem driven to a psychological explanation, and with it, the question of morbidity. Only, how are we to answer that question? We are cut off, as I argued, from direct experience of Clarissa's mind. The reforming Belford changes before our eyes, but though he admires her more each day he learns only gradually to understand her. Even Mrs Norton is limited here, for her last letters show that she too doesn't understand how far the process of 'decline' is going, or why. We are left (I believe) with only three kinds of evidence: Clarissa's Meditations (using the words of the Bible both by inclusion and omission); her purchase of her coffin; and certain significant hints of a struggle in which she is not the main actor.

Perhaps we should look at the coffin first (though the Meditations come earlier) for here Richardson raises the question himself. The modern horror at the obscenity of death, and the charge of morbidity, are openly voiced by the reactions of Belford, the Smiths, and Morden, to her buying the coffin, decorating it with emblems, and using it as a writing desk in her bedroom. There is no point in the whole of Richardson where one is so likely to be wholly out of sympathy. It is true that Donne, on his deathbed, had himself dressed in his winding sheet to pose for his effigy; but this was not quite so bizarre in the author of *Death's Duell*, still so closely in touch with the Middle Ages, as in this sensitive and delicate girl in the so-called Age of Enlightenment. Yet Richardson is at least perfectly aware of how extraordinary it is. Clarissa herself admits there may be 'too much solicitude for this earthly part' (VII, 335; *IV*, *255*) and sees a touch of pride in the coffin's expensiveness (VII, 339; *IV*, *257-8*). Belford asks whether a coffin is 'a proper subject to display fancy upon' (VII, 337; *IV*, *256*). Yet the whole point of the episode seems to be its matter-of-factness, the attempt to familiarise the horrific. Clarissa makes a practical point: there is nobody close enough to her to make arrangements, so she does it herself. There may be a suspicion of indulgence in the interest she takes in the emblems, but as with her Blakean paper on sex, we must be careful to look at the whole context. The broken lily, apparently connecting with the sentimental image Lovelace had used of her earlier (V, 309-10; *III, 193*), could easily be self-pity. If however the other emblems define this one, the lily is no longer a lachrymose symbol of desecrated innocence untimely cut off. For the theme of them all is the comment of eternity on time, and the lily is the psalmist's emblem of the transitoriness of *all* human life. 'The days of man are but as grass' the inscription reads, 'he flourisheth as a flower of the field: For, as soon as the wind goeth over it, it is gone; and the place thereof shall know it no more'. When Christ recalls this, and the same image in Isaiah, in St Matthew's Gospel, it is to speak to men of little faith about God's providence. On the coffin, too, the God who clothed the lily, though it be cast into the oven tomorrow, rewards the faithful: 'Thou hast delivered my soul from death; mine eyes from tears; and my feet from falling' (VII, 338; *IV, 257*). Time, the winged hourglass and the urn, is set against the crowned serpent, D. H. Lawrence's 'him with his tail in his mouth', the emblem of eternity and fulfilment, completion. The date is not that of her death but of leaving her father's house, when both her transgression and her spiritual journey began. The last anti-sentimentality is the matter-of-fact comment on the white satin lining, 'soon, she said, to be tarnished by viler earth than any it could be covered by' (VII, 339; *IV, 258*). She confesses: 'I dwell on, I indulge (and, strictly speaking, I enjoy) the thoughts of death'; but this is because 'there is such a vast superiority of weight and importance in the thoughts of death, and its hoped-for happy consequences, that it in a manner annihilates all other considerations and concerns' (VII, 340; *IV, 258*). The Clarissa who speaks this is surely no longer the girl who indulged herself with thoughts of death as the easy and emotionally satisfying way out? There is again the factuality, and an assurance that can also be seen in the past tense of the inscription: 'Thou *hast* delivered my soul'. We need to know where that came from.

It is partly earned by the struggle for composure and forgiveness, whose cost in anguish the Meditations alone allow us to glimpse. The second, third and fourth are occasioned by wounding letters from her family; the fifth is 'On being hunted after by the Enemy of my Soul', when Lovelace breaks his promise and drives her from the Smiths. Again however, though the heart-rent verses allow us to guess at what is happening inside her, what she leaves out is as important as what she puts in. There is none of Job's self-justification or his questioning of God, and none of the Psalmists' vindictive self-righteousness or cries for vengeance. Moreover the anguish she uses to define her own, especially from Psalm 102 and the seventh chapter of Job, is no mere self-expression. Belford reports her as trying 'to regulate her vehemence by sacred precedents' (VII, 135; *IV, 120*), making herself remember that the verses she copies were written by people better than herself, who yet were even more afflicted. Her own 'edition' is significant too. The first part of Meditation Two, 'Poor mortals the cause of their own misery' (VII, 99-100; *IV, 96*), sounds like Elihu but is in fact her own, and represents a victory over her tendency to resent. Meditation Four interpolates a sentence of her own with an important distinction: 'There is a shame which bringeth sin, and there is a shame which bringeth glory and grace' (VII, 136; *IV, 120*). Meditation Three, which suggests her nightmares, also places her death-wish by picking out, for conclusion, that very patient sentence from Job: 'Yet all the days of my appointed time will I wait, till my change come' (VII, 107; *IV, 101*). Meditation Five must be seen alongside the allegorical letter she writes the next day, with its 'overjoyed . . . assurance of a thorough Reconciliation' (VII, 189; *IV, 157*). All the Meditations are an attempt to control her feelings within the word and the design of God, which is the basic theme of both Job and the Psalms.

If the state of mind in which she buys the coffin is partly earned by her struggle with herself, however, we shall not understand it fully until we see that it is mainly *given*, the most precious grace of all. For by that time the use of God's word in the Old Testament has given way to the actual presence of the Emanuel of the New, the 'God within her' first hinted at in the garden at

Hampstead. Whatever our own views (or lack of them), we are bound to see that Richardson's novel has finally shifted from the psychological to the directly religious. The self-indulgent morbidity and self-pity of her death-wish has been abjured. She has learnt that death cannot be had by wishing, and is a hard struggle with a body that clings and encumbers. Victory is not won, but given, and God is the protagonist. We see this first, pointedly, on her final birthday. 'Nor let it be imagined' she distinguishes to Mrs Norton, 'that my present turn of mind proceeds from gloominess or melancholy; For altho' it was *brought on* by disappointment . . . yet I hope that it has obtained a better root, and will every day more and more, by its fruits, demonstrate . . . that it has'. By the time she goes to the undertaker she has had 'such joyful assurances . . . that she could hardly contain herself' (VII, 269; *IV, 210*). She remarks on the serenity and clarity of mind God has given her, and how gradually and happily 'God *dies away in us*, as I may say, all human satisfaction, in order to subdue his poor creatures to Himself' (VII, 401; *IV, 299*). She tells Mrs Norton of her 'charming forebodings of happiness already!' (VII, 404; *IV, 301*). She no longer cares as she would otherwise have done about her cruel family, or about seeing Anna. '*God will have no rivals in the hearts of those he sanctifies.* By various methods he deadens all other sensations, or rather absorbs them all in the Love of Him'. Dying might have been even easier had she had the Harlowes' pardon, 'But God Almighty would not let me depend for comfort upon any but Himself' (VII, 459; *IV, 339*). The death-bed scene itself juxtaposes tear-jerking with this other view. The 'lamentable' is Belford's, indulging what Lovelace has called his talent, but tears are reproved by Clarissa as 'blameable kindness' (VIII, 3; *IV, 346*). Her own emphasis is on happiness ('you know not what *foretastes* – what *assurances* . . .') and her last cry is the bride's 'come – O come – Blessed Lord – JESUS!' Only now can she manage the full forgiveness and even gratitude for her affliction, that her deathbed letters partly express; for that victory too is ultimately the gift of God.

It is peculiarly unfortunate that Mr Richardson should then return, with a tedious attempt to exploit the death both in lachrymose sentimentality and in exemplary rewards, punishments, and moralisings, which deny the achievement I have attempted to describe, and also defeat their own object by the directness of the onslaught. In my experience, the only moment where one may experience a chokiness is the reaction of the poor, where at first there is some indirectness, but it soon vanishes. The third edition, as I have argued elsewhere, makes things worse by trying to turn Clarissa, retrospectively, into an ideal maiden's compendium, whereas her stature had been established in quite other terms. Yet the lapse cannot seriously damage the achievement – for that rests on the brave self-challenge of the dramatic artist in his inquisition into her being, and his willingness to ask the really awkward questions himself.

Finally, moreover, that kind of integrity expresses itself again in the treatment of the hero, where Richardson remains true to his dramatic imagination.

When Clarissa's letter to his family, and their ostracism, finally bring her rejection home to Lovelace, he becomes ill, but this shows not only the extent of his feeling, but also his inevitable reaction – the psychic withdrawal again. He has been capable of seeing that the forgiveness of his victim may be necessary for the forgiveness of God; but he still confuses forgiveness with marriage, unable to accept that he has lost her; and his final effort is as much a self-recovery as an attempt to win her over. When he breaks his promise and hunts her out of her refuge, we see again, in his cavalier treatment of the Smiths, his aristocratic high-handedness at its worst, and the essential compulsion to convert reality into playacting which allows no dignity or humanity to others. He goes back to the brothel, where he allows Sally to parody Clarissa. In the context of Clarissa's agony and illness, his brutal humour loses its last appeal. His reaction to the death of his friend Belton, and his refusal to attend the funeral, show the same withdrawal from the challenge of feeling as Mowbray's. As the rake's mask is clamped back, however, there is the most open confession yet that 'it is to *deep Concern*, that my *Levity* is owing: For I struggle and struggle, and try to buffet down my cruel reflections as they rise; and when I cannot, I am forced, as I have often said, to try to make myself laugh, that I may not cry' (VII, 346; *IV, 262*). Yet if he is '*Inexpressibly miserable*', it is partly because he hates to express.

As *his* 'agon' then moves to its climax, we should see that it is a death struggle between two possible selves. There is an inner being which expresses itself in dream, in the frightening and prophetic vision of Clarissa's 'assumption' and his own annihilation. There is the answering impulse to mock, as, disappointed by the discovery that Clarissa's letter about her 'Father's house' was allegorical, he turns to ridicule the idea of reformation by imaging it in terms of a ludicrous monument in Westminster Abbey (VII, 331; *IV, 252-3*). This is directed at Belford's account of Clarissa's effect on him, but it has an obvious extension to her effect on Lovelace too. As she grows worse however, the seriousness that seemed more a product of his inability to have her than of genuine understanding, is replaced by real grief and remorse, and a final insight into his own criminal folly and incredulity, as he prowls the highway, waiting for news.

Her death causes a mental breakdown analogous to Clarissa's after the rape, since what has happened strikes at his very being. It takes the form first of a violent 'Restoration tragedy' frenzy. His incapacity to confront the fact of death is shown, like that of Tamburlaine and his seventeenth-century derivatives, in his 'mad' insistence that she should not be buried, that she belongs to him, and he must have her heart. Yet the real significance lies in his response to the experience of derangement, which we are bound to compare with Clarissa's. He diagnoses the source of the derangement in the nature of his upbringing, which led him, because of his mother's banishing of control and contradiction, to believe in a world shaped to his wishes, and made him unable to cope with inescapable frustration. (The portrait is wholly consistent; the excessive reaction to his first jilting falls into place.) Even more important however is his absolute horror at the threat to his intellect, which makes him the Lovelace he wishes to be. His 'brain was on fire day and night . . . I had no distinct ideas, but of dark and confused misery: *It was all remorse and horror* indeed! . . . My lucid intervals still worse, giving me to reflect upon what I *was* the hour before, and what I was likely to be the next, and perhaps for life' (VIII, 144; *IV, 441*). He cannot bear to think of himself in a lunatic asylum – to be afraid of being beaten – to be an object in the power of others. (This is not the first time we have seen his outrage at what he himself has meted out to other people.) Yet the real horror is that his very life, as it seems to him, is bound up with his quick mind, the cleverness wit and invention, that make him superior to common humanity in his own eyes. To lose *that* is unthinkable. His doctors warn him to expect recurrences, but what is most significant is his own diagnosis that the main threat is allowing himself to feel. From the first, as we saw, his obsessiveness sprang from a subterranean awareness that he must either break Clarissa to his will or cease to be himself. Now that she has gone, the threat to 'himself' is located in his own heart and conscience. What he says flippantly, that he 'must either get a train of cheerful ideas, or hang myself' (VIII, 145; *IV, 442*), is true at a deeper level. Inevitably he *will* not remember, feel, or go on struggling. He makes a choice in the depths of his being, as Clarissa had done, and recovers the Lovelace he wishes to be. Richardson's imagination allows his villain the same right to self-determination as his heroine, and challenges himself as deeply to inquire into the ultimate springs of the self.

Once restored to himself, moreover, Lovelace's end is also certain. He cannot help acting up to his persona in seeking out Morden, and pays his last tribute to his idea of himself with his life. Richardson's final ironic twist is also truly imagined: the obsessive certainty that he must win, and his outrage when reality again refuses to shape itself to the scenario he devises. On his deathbed, as we read between the lines, the struggle between the two selves is reassumed. In his delirium his imagination veers between Clarissa as frightful spectre and as blessed spirit. As he dies, the latter predominates: his last words are 'Blessed', and 'LET THIS EXPIATE!' Yet there may well be a doubt whether the final words are addressed to Clarissa or to God, and whichever it may be, they show pride and self-dramatisation, not remorse[1] (VIII, 277; *IV*, *530*). It is a dramatic, not a religious end.

Colonel Morden's part in the final catastrophe also completes Richardson's attack on Clarissa's society. For only Belford, of all who have known, admired and wept for her, is radically changed by Clarissa. The sentimentality of dwelling on their grief is implicitly shown by Richardson's awareness that they too will go on being themselves. Morden is a 'good' man, but his affinity with Lovelace has been hinted in certain remarks that suggest a low opinion of women, in suggestions that he has been a rake himself, and in his first encounter with Lovelace when it would be hard to distinguish whose allegiance to false honour and proud persona is the stronger. Now, for all his morality and his admiration of his niece, his solemn engagement to her to abjure vengeance is shown to be less important to him than his worldly honour. He has not truly understood or responded to her.

The immense superiority to *Pamela* hardly needs underlining. It can be seen in the degree to which *Clarissa* clears itself of all the specific objections one made to *Pamela*: the waverings about vanity, snobbery, intrigue, the idea of virtue rewarded in worldly terms. Reformation and forgiveness no longer come easily. It can be seen more powerfully in the way that formal development, the multiplication of correspondences, not only avoids the central flaw of *Pamela* by creating a hero we experience in the same way and to the same depth as the heroine; but also ensures, by forcing the author to examine them through their friends as well as each other, that he probes them to the limit of his imagination.

[1] Richardson remarked to Edward Moore (Carroll, *Letters*, 122) how Lovelace's last words 'with his wonted haughtiness of spirit' were 'all his apparent Invocation and address to the SUPREME' – yet the ambiguity seems equally apparent.

Lastly, the superiority is visible in the greater novel's exposure of the facile nature of its predecessor's hopes of the efficacy of example. Richardson finished *Clarissa* in a state of gloom about his society, as his postscript shows, because the misinterpretation of the first instalments and the outcry for a happy ending seemed to foreshadow society's reaction to the whole. Yet his novel's reception was to prove him wrong to some extent, and in reviving his idea of moral community, pave the way for *Sir Charles Grandison.*

PART THREE

Sir Charles Grandison

CHAPTER EIGHT

'Sir Charles' and 'Harriet Byron'

I

Sir Charles Grandison is one of those books that were greatly respected for a time, and are read by hardly anybody now. Yet it is not so much a bad book, as misguided. It contains Richardson's most likeable heroine and some of his liveliest writing. His technical artistry was at its height, and the novel has a curious energy that constantly surprises one, in the midst of irritations, with the knowledge that one is by no means as bored as one had thought.

What seems to face us is the odd phenomenon of a writer at the height of his powers, who yet so mistook their real nature, as to complete his work with a 'masterpiece' that only allowed those powers to operate now and then. He was betrayed, perhaps, by his own idealism; and by the degree to which a cherished dream had already come true.

It may be helpful, I think, to start by looking at a picture: a rather charming, if not very accomplished drawing by Susanna Highmore, which is reproduced in Mrs Barbauld's second volume of Richardson's letters.[1] In the 'grotto' of his country house at North End, we see the novelist 'in his usual morning dress' of gown and turban, reading aloud from the manuscript of *Grandison* to three young ladies and three young gentlemen, who listen with

[1] See also Plate II in Eaves and Kimpel, *Richardson*, which reproduces the sketch owned by the Pierpont Morgan Library.

graceful attention. The date is 1751, and the scene must have been reproduced over many a week-end, before the novel was eventually published between November 1753 and March 1754.

This begins to pinpoint the oddness of Richardson's last book, and the problem of coming to terms with it now, by reminding us that it sprang from and proceeded to explore an ideal of community that we can hardly imagine.

After *Clarissa*, Richardson was surrounded by a circle of admirers, many of whom visited him regularly at those weekends in Hammersmith, while he kept up a voluminous correspondence with the more scattered ones. There has been a tendency to wax humorous or supercilious about this 'dovecote' of maidens, matrons, and sober young men, and to see it as merely supplying the author with a diet of sentiment and flattery. There is some truth in this, but there is also something facile and snobbish. It is easy enough to establish the limitations of Richardson's coterie, especially when one remembers the nearly contemporary circles which centred on that other grotto at Twickenham, or at the dinner-table in Fleet Street. Having said this, however, one may have said less than one imagines. For what emerges is the lack of common ground for comparison. Richardson was a bourgeois 'Cit', not an Augustan of the Town; he was not an intellectual; and he had no deep interest in literature, or politics, or questions of the day. His painful diffidence ensured that he could never be a conversationalist, and having 'only common School-Learning', he was never likely to be comfortable in intellectual discussion. It ill becomes those who are more fortunate to sneer. His circle was not a literary one, for though the ticket of admission was an admiration of his books, this was not for their literary qualities; and unlike the circles of Pope and Dr Johnson, the habitués of North End were not admitted or valued for high talent or attainment. On the other hand, Richardson's circle was essentially a community of both sexes, as Pope's and Johnson's were not, and one in which the feminine contribution was vital. The equality of the sexes in Miss Highmore's picture is significant, and the very ordinariness of the people not less so. What we need to recapture first in looking at it, is some sense of the peculiar nature of the Richardsonian dream it shows to have come true.

In the last section of *Pamela*, after her wedding to Mr B., Richardson had imagined the growth of a moral community. As the happy pair tell their story again and again on their visitings, person after person, through voicing admiration, finds a truer self liberated, and becomes linked into a widening circle of community. Hearts are opened, values shared, deeper relationships are formed and confirmed. We smile at so transparent a revelation of the response Richardson longed for, but what imagination had seized as possible, experience brought about. The publication of his moral stories produced around him what he clearly saw as just such a moral community – not a 'fan-club' based on charisma, not a literary circle linked by taste or technical influence, not a fellowship of intellectuals devoted to the life of the mind, all of which seem familiar possibilities to us, but something different and difficult to imagine now. For we have to postulate not only a shared moral commitment, but also an appetite for elaborate moral casuistry in the old and unpejorative sense of the word. Seen from such an angle, the 'union card' of admiration for Richardson's work, however much it might also minister to his unfortunate craving for reassurance and flattery, could seem primarily a guarantee of the moral commitment of a good heart. The discussion of particular moral situations in the books became a springboard for the exploration and refinement of a detailed ethical code. Younger and shyer members were encouraged to become articulate, more confident ones were tempted into detailed discussion, the most assured were encouraged to engage in almost formal debate with the Master. Yet given this basis of shared value and interest, the relationship of the heart was just as important if not more so. Those moral discussions were clearly intended to produce, and to some extent actually did produce, a deepening personal relationship that required a language stronger than friendship: the language of family. *Grandison* itself, as we shall see, was much concerned to explore the idea of a moral and spiritual tie as deep as that of blood, but the Richardson circle was already long accustomed to this idea. He encouraged its younger members to think of him as a father and to call him 'Papa'; he treated the older ones as brothers and sisters of the heart. All six of the people in Miss Highmore's drawing married within the circle.

A. D. McKillop has suggested an analogy with the mediaeval 'court of love', and this is helpful.[1] There is the same feminism, the same insistence on the ethical and spiritual refinement of the sex which the world outside condemned to inferiority. There is the same curious exclusion of that world in all its workaday aspects, in favour of a private realm of feeling, and the meticulous adjustment of relationship and behaviour within doors. In both, there seems always time and to spare! There is, granted a shared basic code, the same genuine and now barely imaginable interest in casuistry: the discussion of particular awkward cases, the pursuit of increasing delicacy and elaboration. There is the same insistence on making a private world the subject of public debate. Yet the analogy is misleading in one essential direction. The 'Court of Love' *was* a court, and carried into the world of love a feudalism of sovereignty and service. Richardson's ideal was the extension of the family into a model of community, and the 'love' at the centre looked through 'courtship' to an extended brotherhood, sisterhood, fatherhood and childhood of the heart.

This is the world in which and for which *Sir Charles Grandison* was conceived. It was likely in any case that Richardson would have sought to place beside his heroines a picture of male virtue; in positive action, no longer on the defensive as Pamela and Clarissa had been; and given the scope and freedom of 'high life', high manners, affluence, and the free choice of life-style. He was also clearly irritated and disturbed by the success of Fielding, not merely in jealousy, but also with a puritan's contempt for what he understood of the permissiveness of his rival's idea of goodness. Sir Charles was to show a truer picture of what a good man's life should be, and rebuke the corruptions

[1] McKillop, *Richardson*, 198.

of a society that had found *Tom Jones* admirable, though it had partly redeemed itself with the relative failure of *Amelia*. Richardson understood nothing of Fielding's ironic art, and hence had no idea how close Fielding's vision of human goodness had come to his own, as Fielding lost confidence in the efficacy of founding virtue in the loving heart alone. Yet his puritan insistence that true goodness had to aim at being virtuous at every point and in the smallest detail, would always have made Fielding antipathetic.

Nevertheless Richardson was certainly encouraged by the demands of his circle, and particularly Lady Bradshaigh, that he should give them The Good Man, and perhaps even by the hope that their response might prove the nucleus of a wider one. We see in his correspondence an active sense of communication with the well-disposed who had urged him on. He made them feel part of the work in several ways. They might see reflections of themselves in the characters: Hester Mulso and Lady Bradshaigh both probably contributed something to the sharper liveliness of Charlotte and the gentler variety in Harriet, and something of Sophia Westcomb may have gone into Emily. Members of the circle were encouraged in playful identifications '(our good brother Jeronymo'[1]); and even to attempt letters 'in character'.[2] We have some evidence that he used details from real-life banter like Lady Bradshaigh's flippancies about old maids, and there may have been more of this than can be recognised now. The point is not one of serious influence, but simply to establish how Richardson felt his community around and with him as he wrote. So we see the extended family in action, in Susanna Highmore's picture, while the novel was being written, indeed, before the completion of the second volume of the seven.

The picture's most valuable evidence, however, has to do with the kind of response that Richardson sought. For though his ambition was to write a programmatic work, demonstrating in

[1] Richardson to Hester Mulso, 9 April 1753; Carroll, *Letters*, 225.

[2] Richardson to Hester Mulso, 21 August 1754; Carroll, *Letters*, 312, though this was when the novel was finished.

detail what the behaviour of a truly good man would be in a variety of situations and relationships, the picture nevertheless reminds us of the circle's commitment to debate. The young Rev. Duncomb and Miss Prescott look pensive, Edward Mulso reaches into his breast-pocket, perhaps for a handkerchief, and Miss Highmore bends over her sketchbook. But Miss Mulso looks appropriately quizzical, for 'Heck' was one of the circle's doughtiest debaters and got into print in her own right. Thomas Mulso, moreover, has clearly just made an observation or asked a question. And the Master, at first glance, seems about to call attention to a particular point in his reading with an admonitory tap of the foot, like the italics in his printed texts. This is fully in keeping with what Richardson said many times about the nature of his last work. 'Many things are thrown out in the several Characters, on purpose to provoke friendly Debate; and perhaps as Trials of the Readers Judgment, Manners, Taste, Capacity. I have often sat by in Company, and been silently pleased with the Opportunity given me, by different Arguers, of looking into the Hearts of some of them, through Windows that at other times have been close shut up.'[1] The connection of moral casuistry with the opening of the heart is very characteristic of Richardson and of his circle. But where a modern reader would be likely to concentrate on Richardson's interest in psychology, he needs to be reminded in reading *Grandison* above all that Richardson was also, perhaps even primarily, looking for another response, of a kind that has gone wholly out of fashion. Particularly in a novel where *all* the main characters are 'good', and where the main difficulties arise out of goodness, he expected his readers to examine their conduct in minute detail, and continually to raise the question 'Given the circumstances, did he (or she) *do right*?' He was of course likely to defend his work as stubbornly as ever, but what is new is the encouragement of questioning, in contrast with his irritation at what he saw as the misreading of *Clarissa*, and his consequent gloom and

[1] Richardson to Lady Echlin, 10 October 1754; Carroll, *Letters*, 315, see also 244, 257, 296, 311.

anger at the frivolity and corruption of the age. The difference is owing to the existence of the circle, to the dream of community come true. He was, it seems, encouraged to give the reins to Mr Richardson the Moral Casuist of Behaviour, rather than to the exploration of consciousness and inner being. This had happened before, in the special circumstances of the continuation of *Pamela*, but it happened now with a new confidence and zest. Only, the more they are indulged, the more difficulties arise for readers in our very different climate.

What really concerns us however are the points at which this zest for casuistry affects Richardson's imagination. The most obvious of these almost drives one to say that drama is the child of the devil – for the demotion of the devil in *Grandison* amounts to a severe limitation of the drama we can hope to find in it. Since Richardson's imaginative art at its finest had been essentially dramatic, this is a serious matter.

There are implied superlatives in the names of both Clarissa ('clarissima', the most excellent girl) and Grandest-son. Both are nearly perfect moral creatures in their conception, but there is a central difference in their imaginative treatment. From the beginning, Clarissa was conceived in a dramatic situation, hard pressed by the world and the devil in the shape of her family and her lover. This ensured that the idea of displaying virtue was overcome by something far more penetrating: an exploration of the nature of moral being. The challenge proved powerful enough, as Richardson's imagination began to grasp its implications in dramatic conflict, to expose the dangers of moral absolutism, and even to raise searching questions about the existence of a moral nature. The single dramatic situation, from which the whole complex tragedy emerged inevitably, gave the work great unity for all its length. The devil produced the drama, the drama produced the depth and unity. Sir Charles, however, was conceived as an ideal-in-himself independent of any situation. Richardson had to invent a method of 'producing' his hero; and it was just here that the appetite for casuistry made sure that it would be the urge to display, and not the urge to explore, that would predominate. With no built-in challenge to force him to probe inward, the casuist's interest in the elaboration of a given code, and its detailed application to a variety of cases, encouraged him to take his hero's integrity for granted, and to concentrate on finding as many ways as possible of putting him into exemplary action. So he was led to think in terms of a variety of situations rather than a single centrally demanding one, and to think in terms of behaviour rather than of consciousness. Already, as far as the hero is concerned, the imagination becomes extensive and circumstantial, rather than intensive and psychological. Moreover, the casuist's ambition for refinement, and his curiosity about minute detail, would further affect the *kind* of situation he would be likely to invent. I think we begin to see why one set of situations in *Grandison* should be 'easier' than the problems Clarissa faces; why another set of situations should be more 'tricky'; and in both cases, why there should be a tendency to banish the challenge of real evil. If one wanted to illustrate the style of an athlete as perfectly, as variously, and in as much detail as possible, one might well choose to photograph in the gymnasium and on the practice-ground, rather than when the man is really hard pressed in crisis. So Richardson seems to have conceived the progress of Sir Charles from situation to situation as a triumphant display of his ethical repertoire, rather than as a critical test of his ability to survive. Many of his challenges are far tamer than Clarissa's, he is given great advantages, and several situations are made easier for him than they might have been. The desire to set the story in 'high life' is, I believe, a phenomenon of this order, and not usefully to be discussed in social terms at all. The 'high life' of *Grandison* seems to me a dream-stage, on which the hero can be given free scope for elaborate displays of good behaviour – and it is beside the point to argue about Richardson's knowledge or ignorance of the actual manners of contemporary 'good families'. On the other hand, in another set of situations where he clearly does wish to drive Sir Charles into a corner, it is of a special casuistic kind. In a crisis of survival, the issues become more unmistakable as the pressure mounts. Conversely, to establish the most basic values, the challenge of evil is obligatory. But Richardson in his last novel is not so much interested in basic values, which are largely taken for granted, but rather in the awkward case, the delicate situation. And, as Sir Charles often ruefully suggests, the most awkward and delicate challenges come not from the devil, but from the conflict between equal 'goods' in special circumstances. The 'propitious' situations appeal to the casuist's delight in the effective illustration of his code, the 'awkward' ones to his interest in its delicacies and punctilios. The former satisfy his enthusiastic idealism, the latter supply a pleasurable challenge to his taste for moral debate, for in the collision of goods there is room for gentle readers to differ, where in the clash of good and evil there should be none.

What tends to be excluded, however, is drama. In a book whose hero (like Daniel Deronda a century later) is conceived as a nearly perfect moral creature from the start, and whose development to his pitch of excellence has taken place before the novel begins, there can be little inner stress. 'Character' is not the product of dramatic imagination working through conflict, but the illustration of moral habit in characteristically uniform behaviour. As the hero progresses through one set of actions, designed not to expose his inner being but to give him opportunities to display what the behaviour of a good man should be, there can be only difficulty, not crisis, or fundamental self-questioning. There will also be little excitement, uncertainty, or involvement. And even in the other kind of situation, where the duty of the good man is far from straightforward, and drama returns, it will be a drama of embarrassment not of being. The central situation in *Clarissa* calls her moral existence in question; the central situation in *Grandison* poses the problem of how to behave like a perfect gentleman when one is in love with two equally admirable ladies at once.

But the importance of drama in Richardson is not, as these points might suggest, a matter of the narrative excitements offered to the reader – for as Dr Johnson reminds us, a man who would read Richardson for the story were as well go hang himself. What one meant by saying that his imagination at its best had been essentially dramatic, is that only through the challenge of conflict had that imagination proved able to explore beyond the normal confines of Mr Richardson the bourgeois moralist. It has been my central concern in this study to show how, by being forced to project himself into modes of being very different from his, and fundamentally challenging to one another and to him, his imagination had proved capable of laying hold of insights quite outside his normal reach. To attenuate the role of drama in his work then, would seem to guarantee that he will be confined to the range of his normal vision – the vision, say, of his letters. It is to chain the daimon that had proved capable of transforming him . . . however unevenly . . . into a major artist.

We can see the difference in formal terms too. For where in his finest work the epistolary form is a means to a dramatic end, one of the features of *Grandison* is the extent to which the letters can become no more than a convenient packaging of straightforward narrative. Indeed, the first half of the book turns out to be structured very largely in alternating slabs of 'present tense' epistolary writing, and retrospective narrative. There are other factors involved but one significant reason is that where the attention has turned from inner exploration to the recording of behaviour, straight narrative is quite as satisfactory and far more economical than Richardson's 'new way of writing', whose cumbrousness can only be excused by its power to do what the stage can, involving one in a present action, and allowing direct access to the minds and hearts of the characters. Again, the interest in moral casuistry tends to break the epistolary convention in another way, by making the correspondence so public that the confessional possibilities of private letters are minimised. The habits of Richardson and his circle get inside the novel itself. Pamela's letters are only meant for her parents, and Clarissa's for Anna, but the correspondence of Sir Charles (and Harriet's too) is for a forum of judgement, and gets passed around a whole circle of readers, as the manuscript of the novel was to be. This is bound to affect the degree to which, in the case of Sir Charles particularly, the letters can probe into the recesses of heart and mind.

If the casuistic energy of *Grandison* inhibited many of the strengths of Richardson's imaginative art, it also unfortunately allowed him to indulge his worst weaknesses. He was always didactic, but in his best work the moral vision was a product of the drama. But in *Grandison*, as in the continuation of *Pamela*, there is a huge increase in the amount of preaching and moral argument. The commentary is often in danger of overwhelming the text, or indeed of becoming the text. And the fervour of the idealism encourages that even more irritating habit: the building of the moral applause he hoped for into the work itself. From the moment of his first appearance, Richardson's hero is accompanied where'er he walks with such a tizzy of admiration that any reader might be forgiven for developing an equally constant snarl. These are open irritations, but there is a more subtle and significant one too. The indulgence of Richardson's didactic urge means not only that 'what ought to be' always seems to take precedence over 'what is' in his hero, but also that there seems hardly any difference between them. Sir Charles *always* behaves ideally, so that we seem involved in a moral fairyland rather than a realistically human world; but even granting his special rectitude, the annoying thing is that it seldom seems to cost him anything or require any effort. There seems no gap between the moral demand and the instinctive response, whereas it is precisely in that gap (in our own experience) that we locate our fiercest struggles and our humanity.

At this point one seems to have outlined a fairly comprehensive recipe for artistic failure and a response of boredom and withdrawal. But it is just here that the real critical problem in coming to terms with *Grandison* poses itself, for we are only at the beginning of critical inquiry when we have got this far. We have somehow to account for the fact that all these irritations, these inhibitions of the kind of imagination that produced the Richardson one cares about, do not amount to the radical disqualification we might expect. The novel is not as boring as one's critical equipment suggests it should be. It has a curious kind of energy, an imaginative impulse, that has not yet got into one's account.

It is here too that one may reap a further benefit from pondering Miss Highmore's little drawing, with its action-picture of the casuist getting the response he was looking for. For it reminds us that we have been engaged in plotting the damaging consequences, for Richardson's art, of indulging a zest for moral casuistry in creating his hero, without allowing anything for the idealism that drove him in that direction, and collected his circle around him to listen. It is true that we may need some historical imagination to grasp this. Indeed, our own impatience with public morality and our fascination with private consciousness, are likely to predispose us in the opposite direction, to make us ignore what we find hard to understand, and concentrate on the absence of what would satisfy us. Yet there is something in the very energy with which Richardson gave rein to his idealism that may fuel our historical imagination – and even enable us to see that what confronts us is itself imaginative, though in an unfamiliar way. For what blinded Richardson to all else was the very strength of his desire to imagine beyond the normal horizon of human capacity. We have only to put positively many of the points already made negatively to cast a different kind of light. He wanted his good man to be, as it were, ready for take-off and capable of free flight. He was impatient to move beyond the stage of moral development to something more inspiring: the task of picturing the fuller humanity that might be possible for a man who had succeeded in overcoming his failings and who had trained himself to follow his conscience instinctively. He must have thought he could show how such a man could demonstrate his achievement by perfect behaviour in the whole range of duty, including the ability to rise to specially awkward occasions, and also how he would inspire virtuous emulation in all who came across him, and were at all capable of response. Most of all, such a man could begin to break down the barriers between human beings, and offer a new vision of human relationship. We come to see that what our distrust of public morality and our fascination with private consciousness blinds us to, is precisely the opposite nature of Richardson's feelings. If the focus on the hero of his last novel has shifted from 'private' to 'public', from the interior exploration of consciousness to the behaviour which produces the expanding family of the heart, it is because of the intensity of Richardson's drive to overcome human isolation, and to lay hold of an image of people bound together by stronger ties than blood.

Here what we have been calling 'casuistry', the moralist's interest in the elaboration and refinement of an existing code, has flowered into something more imaginative: the desire to give human shape to an ideal beyond what is accepted. There was always a direct connection in Richardson's mind between the casuistic interest in behaviour, and the opening of the heart. We saw this in the dream of community at the end of *Pamela*, and in the operation of the 'family'-circle that was the dream come true. We begin to see how the casuistry of *Grandison* could be a means and not an end. And we may need to look at Susanna's picture one last time, for it may be as important to see that the pensive ones are being stirred as that a moral argument is taking place. If Edward is reaching for his handkerchief, he is doing no more than respond as the characters within the novel do, in tears of moral joy as well as painful sympathy. If gentle 'Pressy's hand moves to her heart, and John Duncomb's gaze is rapt beyond this present, it is because the idealism they respond to calls heart and imagination to conceive a human potential greater even than perfected behaviour. Both the moral casuistry and the response of the heart that it awakens, bind the separate individuals into a circle, within the pages of the novel, and within the grotto where the novel is read. Perhaps this is fanciful as a response to the drawing, for Susanna's art is not expressive enough to make one sure, but that Richardson's own art drove in just that way *through* casuistry to the opening of the 'shut up' windows of the heart, and through shared admiration to the creation of a moral family, admits of little doubt. There is an excited imaginative energy at work which must at least get into our account.

To say this is not of course to explain away the consequences of Richardson's apparent turning aside from that inner drama which produced his greatest work, though it does put them in a more complex perspective. The question becomes one of the wisdom of his allowing himself to take so much for granted, and to forgo so much in doing so. Ought he not to have earned the position from which he started, by making Sir Charles credible in a process of realised and explored inner drama and development? It may well be so. But before we can be sure, it might be as well to make some further points about the method he chose.

It is at least arguable that the desire to imagine the possible, the ideal, is as valid as the desire to imagine the probable and realistic. If that is so, we have an argument for dream and vision, and a need for the freedoms of dream. The idealistic imagination soars precisely when the normal weight of human frailty and incapacity is removed. We may still be entitled to demand that the result should be tested against the normally credible. But to do so within a single character, and in terms of a fully realised development from the norm to the ideal, may not be the only way.

I have already suggested an analogy between Richardson's last novel and George Eliot's.[1] She had constantly concerned herself with the struggle of human beings to escape from egotism, so that only at the end of each book could there be a moment of freedom, a glimpse of truer selfhood, finer humanity. But in *Daniel Deronda* she clearly wanted, as Richardson had done, to ask the further question: What *then*? Suppose one allowed oneself to begin from such an achievement, instead of confining oneself always to the painful struggle towards it? What further life, what richer human potential, what ultimate aim in living would there be? George Eliot also found herself dreaming of a new brotherhood and sisterhood of the heart, which should

[1] For George Eliot's praise of the novel see G. S. Haight (ed.), *The George Eliot Letters* (London, 1956), I, 240; II, 65; VI, 320.

transcend the isolated individual and link him with others in a widening vision of human community. Once one has taken in this striking similarity, it is true that the visions differ markedly, and a comparative study would throw much light on the difference between the eighteenth century and the nineteenth. But the point here is to see how George Eliot confronted the problem of relating her dream to her vision of normality.

As Henry James observed,[1] her structure hinges on the irony that, though it has two apparently parallel stories, the heroine of one reaches the climax of her development, only to find that she has merely gained the point which the hero of the other began by leaving behind. In other words, George Eliot hopes by her method to achieve the benefits of both relation and separation. The two stories provide a continuous cross-commentary, a mutual perspective; each constantly reminds us of what is missing from the other. Yet the fact that they are separate, allows the freest operation of the very different kinds of imagination appropriate to each.

At once one is reminded, salutarily, that the whole discussion so far has been concerned with Richardson's hero. Yet the analogy with *Daniel Deronda* holds true, for in *Sir Charles Grandison*, there is also another story which we might call 'Harriet Byron', and it too springs from a different kind of imagination. If 'Sir Charles' is a novel of 'Ought', 'Harriet Byron' is a novel of 'Is'. There is not the fundamental contrast of *Daniel Deronda*. Harriet is not limed by shortcomings; she is in no sense an inferior moral being; and there will be no possibility of a similarly ironic ending. Indeed, hero and heroine are conceived as perfectly matched. We can nevertheless detect that they are imagined in markedly different ways. In 'Harriet Byron', the Richardson we find it easier to respect is at work, in a more genial frame of mind than ever before. Harriet is quite the most credible of his heroines, and though her essential goodness never wavers, she is allowed from the start to be less solemn and more

1 'Daniel Deronda: A Conversation' in Morris Shapira (ed.), *Henry James: Selected Literary Criticism* (London, 1963), 45-6.

subject to feminine foibles than Pamela or Clarissa. Much more important, in her 'novel' Richardson's essentially dramatic art operates confidently, if not at the tragic depth of *Clarissa*. We live into her consciousness as we never enter the inner life of Sir Charles, the art is exploratory, and what it seeks to explore is precisely the difficulty and the cost of moral aspiration.

Richardson seems to have anticipated George Eliot in trying both to allow his idealistic imagination free rein in conceiving a high human goal; and to test it in a more realistic inward context in a separate but related story, rather than within a single developing character. We cannot justly measure the effectiveness of this if we insist on applying the same criteria to both stories, for the method depends on allowing very different kinds of imagination to play against each other. We have to see Richardson's hero, and the kind of imaginative art which creates him, as merely one pole, whose *nature* it is to be qualitatively different from the other pole in a larger interaction, which is the life of the novel-as-a-whole. There has to be an imaginative criticism of 'ought' which differs from the criticism of 'is', in order to achieve a criticism of the whole. It may appear at the end that the novelist's method was badly misguided. Dr Leavis responded to *Daniel Deronda*[1] by arguing that the best and the worst of George Eliot lay side by side: the best, because 'Gwendolen Harcourt' is purged of the dreaminess that flaws even *Middlemarch*; the worst, because the 'Jewish' novel allows that dreaminess to run mad. But his eagerness simply to dismiss half the novel as unworthy of serious attention, and his unwillingness to allow for more than one kind of imagination, are suspicious signs of inattention to the structure of the whole. We must not hope for a just verdict at the end if we deny the novelist his basic gambit from the outset.

The critical problem, then, turns out to be the need to overcome predisposition and immediate irritation, to see whether one can find a criticism of 'ought' to play against the more familiar criticism of 'is', before one tries to judge the success of the novel

[1] F. R. Leavis, *The Great Tradition* (London, 1955), 79-84.

as a whole. Fortunately the immediate structure, which we have already noticed is an alternation of slabs of different kinds of writing, becomes an aid to us as it was to Richardson. Fortunately too, he chooses to begin where it is easiest for us . . . with Harriet.

2

There is a new geniality in Lucy Selby's opening sentence. 'Your resolution to accompany Mrs Reeves to London, has greatly alarmed your three lovers' – we see immediately how the book could have been a favourite of Jane Austen's. The girl from the country on her first visit to Town was a formula in which Fanny Burney and Jane Austen were to see sprightly possibilities; and the three lovers, the touch of excess, looks provocative too, since there are obviously several more to come. The aggressive lover's portrait of Harriet is spiced with enough gaiety to keep it human; and Richardson immediately shows himself aware of the problem of his heroine's attitude to praise and the repetition of praise as he had never been before. Harriet is no *ingénue*, as Evelina and Catherine were to be, but in her very first letter she is allowed to raise a smile against herself, and to do so by overpitching a moral sentiment, as she longs 'to be able to look down from the *elevation* of thirty years' (I, 14) safely past the dangers of being young and pretty. This is not Richardson being unconsciously funny, for he puts a jocular uncle in the novel to tease his heroine, and Uncle Selby takes up the opening immediately. Harriet is soon being witty at her own expense. Her little exercise in seeing herself as others see her, when she imagines what each of the people she has just met would write about her, and how they would write, shows intelligence, observation, pleasant good humour, and a mature ability to take herself down a peg. It is also entertaining, and an apt example in miniature of what the epistolary method can do in characterising both the 'writer' and the 'written about'.

It is a good start, better than ever before. The writing is lively;

it creates a girl we can respect without having to take her too solemnly, and there is room for a relaxed humour that comes from the author's confidence in himself and his art. Harriet is both credible and likeable – one is prepared to read on. Lady Bradshaigh, and perhaps Hester Mulso, may have suggested something of her liveliness; but it is also interesting to see how Richardson associated her 'serene-pertness' with her family background. For he said later[1] that he had tried to imagine what a Clarissa could have been like if she had really been loved, cherished and admired by all around her, happy and confident and trusted to make her own decisions. It may also be significant that this is despite being an orphan and an only child. She is related to Mrs Shirley and the two Selby families by the secondary family ties, but what has really bound them to her is the sweetness of her nature. Her circle, unlike the Harlowes, lives in terms of the heart's response to goodness.

Having brought her to London, what Richardson proceeds to do with her confirms that this, and not any social comedy of fashionable life or satire of manners, is the direction of his imagination. Harriet goes to plays, concerts, fashionable places, but we hear very little about them; and though she is not impressed by the manners she meets, Richardson's use of the country/city contrast is very different from the possibilities that suggested themselves to Fanny Burney and Jane Austen, as they exploited the vein he had opened. Harriet remains wholly open-eyed, assured, and socially competent; there is no rural innocence caught in the trammels of Town sophistications. Indeed, the main function of the set-piece discussion of education, which is the only 'social entertainment' we get at any length, is to reverse any expectation that a pretty young country girl need be an *ingénue*. Richardson saw no reason why she should not combine intelligence with modesty and good manners. She must not put herself forward, but if pressed she should be able to hold her own as a rational creature. The classical education of the gentleman, and the Grand Tour, may not be open to her, but

[1] Richardson to Lady Bradshaigh, 24 March 1751; Carroll, *Letters*, 179.

for Richardson, she can acquire the basis of all real education, the ability to read the best books in her own language, and make intelligent use of their wisdom and morality; and she will show to real advantage against the 'gentlemen' who have merely learnt Latin and Greek, or fashionable manners and tastes. On the other hand, Richardson clearly believes that modesty and gentleness remain essential to true femininity, and marks the point with a sketch of the kind of woman who would rather be a man. The suggestions of lesbianism in Miss Barneveldt are probably the first in fiction, and provide a comic moment, as she embraces his heroine, of an unusual kind for Richardson! (I, 81). What he does use the country/city contrast for is to present Harriet with two extremes of courtship, which are such obvious non-starters in themselves that they encourage us to look, not to the verdict, but to what its delivery tells us about the nature of her heart: the 'enthusiasm', and the 'frankness' which will be her central characteristics, and which entail breaking the forms of accepted behaviour.

Sir Rowland is a rural Mr Oddity, odder than anything she has known in Northamptonshire, and the nephew he courts her for is even shyer than Mr Orme; while the Town Beau Sir Hargrave can offer little temptation to the girl who has already rejected Mr Greville and Mr Fenwick. We are clearly not meant to take either courtship seriously. What is interesting is Richardson's attempt to show that the 'excessive' enthusiasm and generosity of feeling that make Sir Rowland comic, also have real value, and call out an enthusiasm from Harriet that also exceeds what the situation seems to require. She sees clearly enough how laughable he is in terms of the restraints of conventional manners; but this matters little to her compared with the source of his behaviour, the overflowing goodness of his heart. So she feels not merely embarrassment but genuine pain when a man old enough to be her father insists on kneeling for a favour she cannot grant. To be merely kind and courteous in refusing is not enough for her own heart, though it would be all that good manners require. Her gratitude is enthusiastic – we shall see the significance of this later – and it makes her respond with the first announcement of Richardson's ideal of the Family of the Heart, as she begs him and his nephew to regard themselves as Father and Brother to her, the father and brother she has not in blood. Too many tears of mixed pain and moral happiness may be shed for our tastes, but the element of excess that makes her a 'surprising Lady' (I, 136) has a serious basis in Richardson's feeling that goodness should open the heart to respond with more than the 'enough' of conventional behaviour. Only (and this is an important reservation), Harriet is made to see, just before the scene begins, the need for a distinction between virtue and nature. It is natural for her 'to pay civility for esteem. . . . There is no merit, therefore, in my behaviour, on such occasions. Very pretty self-deception! – I study my own ease, and (before I consider) am ready . . . to attribute to myself I know not how many kind and complaisant things, when I ought, in modesty, to distinguish between the *virtue* and the *necessity*' (I, 131). Her behaviour to Sir Rowland is more than 'civility', but the reservation shows Richardson not unaware that enthusiastic gratitude studies her ease, and hardly costs her anything . . . yet. The novel of 'is' already announces itself, however, in the distinction she draws, and it will begin to develop when 'ought' comes less easily than it does here, and starts to cost a good deal more.

As she peels off the external rusticity and oddness of Sir Rowland to respond to the goodness beneath, so she cares as little for the fashionable grandeur of Sir Hargrave, compared with his egotism and dark temper. Sir Rowland honours her, Sir Hargrave honours himself. And though the actual context of the remark about her own nature I have quoted is her inability to be *un*civil to those she dislikes, her response to Sir Hargrave when he demands her reasons for refusing him, shows another kind of frankness and readiness to break conventional forms. As she puts it: 'tho' I would not be thought rude, I value myself on my openness of heart' (I, 143). Once unavoidably challenged, she does not mince her words, but tells him bluntly that he does not hit her fancy personally (I, 124) and that she has no opinion of his morals (I, 142).

The antechamber to the novel, then, is concerned to use the epistolary method to open up Harriet's character, announce the theme of the Family of the Heart, and suggest a contrast between the restraints of conventional behaviour and the enthusiasm and frankness of the good heart, while reminding us that there may be, as there has not been yet, a question of inner cost. There is immediately an 'outer' cost to Harriet's blunt refusal of Sir Hargrave, since he revenges himself by abducting her from the masquerade, but this is more plot than theme, and is basically Richardson's device to introduce his hero. A slab of narrative replaces the genuine epistolary method, and though Richardson does what he can by way of suspense and narrative excitement, we may pass on quickly – for such things were not his *forte*. He was hardly over-inventive, since this is his fourth abduction, and though it is the most elaborate and detailed story of them all, with an attempt at forced marriage, an accidental injury to the heroine, and a battle of hero with villain, the narrative elaboration of external drama merely calls attention to the lack of any of an inner and psychological kind. It is Lovelace-and-water; for there can be no conflict within the heroine; nor has Sir Hargrave any of the charm, flair for playacting and disguise, or psychological insight of Richardson's more splendid villain. It is simple black-and-white, and resolves itself into a question of how Harriet will get away from so uninteresting a baddy, as we know she will. (The attempt to import a moral in retrospect also traps Richardson into a blunder. Uncle Selby and Harriet blame it all on the wickedness of masquerades, but she could just as easily have been abducted from an ordinary ball.)

Nevertheless the hero enters quite favourably, handsome and brave, resolute and kind. Moreover Richardson is able to merge the romantic kind of heroism into a real moral question as Sir Charles is forced to cope with Sir Hargrave's challenge. But I postpone this until we discuss the novel of 'ought'. Where the novel of 'is' resumes, is the re-orchestration in newly testing terms of the implications of Harriet's behaviour to Sir Rowland. Harriet, as her grandfather used to say, is 'an enthusiast in her gratitude', but if she was grateful for the honour Sir Rowland did her, what must she feel to lie under the real and unreturnable obligation she now owes Sir Charles? At the same time her serene-pertness begins to be undermined. She is in a position of some humiliation, ashamed at having gone to the masquerade, embarrassed by being found in extravagant fancy-dress, more embarrassed by having leapt into Sir Charles's arms, and upset by the fact that rescuing her has put him in danger. Her sense of obligation is overwhelming, but by a fine irony, it is increased by the turning of her response to Sir Rowland on her own head, as Sir Charles makes her his and Charlotte's new sister. Now we see an ironic development of the novel of 'is' out of the ideal of 'ought'. For we were not mistaken in seeing the offer of family as still too facile. There is a nice ironic moment now, when Sir Charles has to ask his new sister's Christian name (I, 219). And Harriet is sharply sensitive to the thought that the offer may have been no more than a gesture to tide her over her lowness of spirit. The more she sees and hears of him, the more her moral enthusiasm adds fuel to her gratitude and to the physical attraction which is there from the very beginning. ('How irresistibly welcome to me was his supporting arm, thrown round me, as we *flew* back, compared to that of the vile Sir Hargrave' (I, 254) – though she thinks she is making a contrast between the 'tenderness of a brother' and the brutality of a libertine.) So, letter by letter, she begins to betray what she does not yet realise, that gratitude has become only a self-deluding name for love. Once again, in the novel of 'is', the epistolary form is ideal for the purpose of allowing one into a mind beyond the threshold of its own conscious awareness, and because there is no moral inhibition to Harriet's feelings (as there was with Pamela and Clarissa) the development can go further and yield richer dividends. Yet this time Richardson is not merely seeking to do more elaborately what he had done before, nor even merely doing better what he had already done well. He is doing something different, for what is revealed is a blend of love with humiliation, that can only spring from loving someone genuinely admirable, and out of reach. Her slips of the pen show not only the enthusiasm of a good heart opened by gratitude and moral admiration, but also the cost that must now be paid in sensitivity; not only the frankness of that heart, but also its recoil in wounded modesty, and a resentment not wholly under control. The more she loves, the more unsatisfactory will she find the brothering and sistering she ought to welcome. And the more frank she tries to be, the more aware she must become of the humiliations of her position: hopelessly pining for a man she feels to be above her, who makes no sign of returning her feelings, and who, if he knew, would certainly be kind enough to *pity* her. Richardson proceeds to add to her embarrassment by having her assailed on three sides.

The Grandison sisters use their 'sisterhood' to offer confidences about Sir Charles, and to ask questions about Harriet's affairs, which continually rub salt into her wounds. If they do not know how she feels, the effect of several hints of how their brother is pursued by women who do not wait to be asked, is nevertheless upsetting. If they do know, the remarks become barbed, and their quizzing of Harriet's feelings seems almost cruel. (In fact they do suspect she is falling in love, and are very much on her side, though they can say nothing because of a previous promise to use their influence on behalf of their friend Lady Anne. It is she who hasn't waited to be asked. But Harriet does not know this, and neither do we.) The effect of 'sisterhood' is therefore double-edged. Mostly she feels strongly attracted to them and warmly grateful for the special relationship. Yet there cannot but be an underlying sensitivity to the possibility of patronage. She strongly resents the momentary suspicion that they may be thinking of their profligate cousin for her, and feels almost equally insulted by the thought that they may be regarding her as a lovesick girl in need of a sisterly warning.

Her slips of the pen are not lost on the 'venerable circle' at home in Northamptonshire, and they lose little time in telling her so. Their verdict that she is already head-over-heels is upsetting; their admission that at best 'our side must perhaps be the hoping side, the gentleman's the triumphant' (I, 325), and at worst that she may be 'entangled in a hopeless passion' (I, 326), cuts even deeper.

Moreover, they have been approached by the Countess of D on behalf of her noble son, to whom there can be no preliminary objection. Before there was any Sir Charles in the case, Aunt Selby had replied that Harriet's affections were disengaged. What is to be done now?

Harriet's frankness is put to the kind of test that costs a good deal in wounded modesty and pride. She has to bring herself to confess to her family that she is indeed in love without hope of return, but so much so that she cannot think of any other proposal. After a struggle, she manages to do so with dignity, encouraging herself with her family's admiration of Sir Charles, and the conviction (which Mrs Shirley had voiced) that it cannot be a disgrace for a woman of virtue to be in love with a worthy man. Next, she must undergo the further trial of having the Countess, whom she has never met, told frankly what the position is. Then Richardson piles on the pressure. Before Aunt Selby's letter could reach her, the Countess decides to visit the Reeves and meet Harriet. The irony of 'sisterhood' is rubbed in, as Harriet guesses that a private exchange between the Countess and Lady L must consist of an assurance that Sir Charles has no apparent intention of turning 'sister' into sister-in-law; and as Lady L calls on her 'sister Harriet' to say whether he is not the genteelest of men (I, 431). She must discourage the Countess's hopes, but to seem so set against a considerable 'catch' before she has even seen him, is bound to raise the eyebrows of not only his mother but of the Grandison sisters too. She escapes a full explanation then and there, but she cannot hope to go on doing so.

There is a postponement for the reader: another narrative slab of the novel of 'ought' intervenes, containing the history of the Grandisons and the revelation of Sir Charles's moral stature when he returns from his 'exile' abroad. But the first crisis of the novel of 'is' arrives, near the end of the second volume, in an extremely embarrassing scene for Harriet, when the Grandison girls determine to ferret out her secret (II, 199 ff.).

By this time we know enough of Lady L and Charlotte to see how Richardson uses them to set off Harriet. He divides her characteristics between them, in order to show the significant interdependence of the qualities for which he values her. Lady L is a Harriet in gentleness and good-nature though her virtue isn't quite so scrupulous, or her feelings quite as delicate; but she lacks Harriet's lively intelligence. Charlotte, conversely, over-develops that side of Harriet into a playfulness that can wound feelings and break decorum, because she lacks as loving a heart and as sweet a nature. She is not basically ill-natured or unprincipled, but she can betray dangerous potentialities in both directions. Though both sisters respond to goodness, they do so more slowly than Harriet and without her enthusiasm. And Charlotte has been secretive, where Harriet has struggled to be frank.

Harriet's 'trial' by her 'sisters' is brought on by the 'trial' of Charlotte by her brother. She has been accusing him of reserve, but finds the attack turned upon herself, for he has received some hint about Captain Anderson, and fears that he may have been misleading her suitors, by taking at face value her assurances that her affections are disengaged. Charlotte fights a stubborn rearguard action and has to be driven into the last corner before she will confess to anything at all. She does however redeem herself by being completely open and repentant thereafter, and it comes out that she has not, after all, lied to her brother about her affections. Yet she has kept the whole truth of her entanglement from him; her shame has led to disingenuousness; she has put both herself and Sir Charles in a false position, and has prevented him from helping to free her from an obviously unworthy man.

Charlotte bounces back – she cannot be dashed for long – and immediately sets out to revenge her own pulling-down, at

Harriet's expense, persuading Lady L to think that she has 'acquired a kind of right to punish those who affect disguises to their best friends' (II, 199). There is something less than good-natured in this, for neither has their brother's excuse for needing to know what they seek to discover; and there is an element of cruelty in their enjoyment of the teasing and trapping, whereas Sir Charles seemed sensible of the pain he had to cause. On the other hand their motives, though mixed, are basically good-hearted, for their ultimate aim is to assure Harriet of their love and support. The gentler one soon repents of their tactics, and Charlotte changes tone too. Nevertheless this is a hard experience for Harriet. Unlike Charlotte, she has no folly to be ashamed of, but she fears that they may despise her for the unmaidenly confession of loving before she is loved (which her brother had warned Emily against in the preceding scene); and she fears still more that if she has given herself away to them, she may have given herself away to him. She resents the abuse of the 'sisterly'; she makes the mistake of attempting evasion at first; but once the question is put on the right basis – 'They assured me of their love; and called upon me, as I valued their friendship, to open my whole heart to them' (II, 207) – she succeeds in speaking out.

What is interesting here is that Richardson is so willing to place his heroine in a situation where she cannot be heroic. Indeed, she is allowed to be 'silly' (a word she will often use of herself), *because* she feels more strongly and sensitively than those who tease her, and because she is no good at disguise; and because the frankness she values is really difficult now. There is a temptation to misread here, since there may be a response to the surface silliness alone, with no sense of its sources in the heart. We may perhaps need some historical imagination too, since the position of women has changed so much that there would be nothing like the same embarrassment in the same situation now. Yet Richardson's dramatic use of the letter form succeeds in bringing Harriet's feelings alive. Both 'trials' are done in dramatic dialogue, but there is a significant formal difference that amounts to a difference in psychological power. Whereas Charlotte's trial is merely described by Harriet-as-spectator, Harriet's is permeated by the rendering of her own agitated consciousness too. Even if one would not feel as she does, her state of mind comes over so genuinely that it would seem crass to dismiss it all as a pother over nothing. What Richardson seeks to do is no easy thing for a writer who very much wanted his heroines admired. But he was so determined to test his values that he chose to strip his heroine of glamour, exact a severe price for her dominant characteristics in inner turmoil, and even allow her to make a fool of herself. If those values come through basically unharmed (as I think they do), their metal must ring true. This new drama of embarrassment cannot achieve the depth and power of the questioning of ultimate being in *Clarissa*, but it takes even greater risks with the dignity of the heroine. And the determination to make 'ought' justify itself in terms of realised consciousness, and in the sharp difficulties of 'is', shows once again the imaginative courage and integrity which make Richardson valuable at his best.

3

Sir Charles enters as romantic hero, rescuing a maiden in distress, but is immediately involved with a moral question in the different mode of the novel of 'ought'. The *Spectator* had attacked duelling, and Richardson obviously felt that the good man and the Christian ought to have nothing to do with it. Yet there remained the problem of imagining in a concrete situation how a hero could refuse to fight without ceasing to be a hero.

We may now hope to reap the benefit of having thought about Richardson's basic method. For it is quite obvious that he did indeed imagine a hero whose development is complete before the novel opens. The dramatic potential of the situation is deliberately muted. The problem is not a new one to Sir Charles. He has been through it all several times before and knows exactly what he must do. His speech and behaviour are therefore not conceived dramatically, but in the terms appropriate to acquired habit and careful premeditation. There might have been inner conflict the first time, but there will be nothing of that sort now. Sir Charles's whole aim is to defuse the situation, lower the temperature, and avoid drama – and the same is true of his author. Since the main encounter in Sir Hargrave's house is cast in dramatic form, in the transcript of the hidden short-hand writer, we face the paradox of a normally dramatic writer, producing apparent drama, but with a basically anti-dramatic aim.

Richardson concentrates whole-heartedly on what ought to happen; not what could happen, or even what might be likely to happen in conditions of normal human frailty. So Sir Charles must show unflinching moral courage in confronting a social evil; he must be coolly reasonable; he must seek to convert his opponents rather than triumph over them. Yet how is he to retain a reader's sympathy, in the face of both the contemporary idea of the man of honour and the customary fictional idea of the hero? (Fielding simply funked this problem. It seems clear to me that he too opposed duelling – but he never allows a hero to refuse a challenge, and his attitude can only show itself indirectly, in terms of moral plot and ironic tone.)

The novelist of 'ought' has to tackle the problem head-on; and he does so by making some careful moral distinctions in the space he has made for himself by excluding inner conflict. The first essential is to distinguish the principled refusal of a challenge from cowardice. For the good man and the Christian, moral courage must come first, but it ought ideally also to be supported with spirit. In this respect the hero of 'ought' should behave just as a gentleman and a romantic hero should; and Richardson seizes every opportunity to make him do so. Further, since his aim is to convert, and since as we saw with Harriet, true goodness aims at doing more than enough, he ought to demonstrate a courage that banishes all question of cowardice. 'Something', as Sir Charles puts it, 'must be done by a man who refuses a challenge, to let a challenger see (such is the world, such is the custom) that he has *better* motives than Fear, for his refusal. I will put Sir Hargrave's honour to the fullest test' (I, 372). Here again there is a distinction. The good man must renounce the false terms of worldly honour, but he can ideally show his courage and spirit by trusting his life to those elements in worldly honour that he can respect. So Sir Charles goes alone to meet Sir Hargrave and his three friends on his enemy's ground. Moreover he takes his sword, so that he may not seem to make his safety depend on being unarmed, and this introduces the next distinction. The Christian must not kill, but he is not forbidden to defend himself or the cause of virtue by force of arms, providing he does not usurp the function of the magistracy if that is available. And Richardson goes a clear step further, this time in the face of one of the most difficult of Christ's behests, the one about turning the other cheek. Not only will Sir Charles defend himself with the sword against the sword, but he will meet physical insult with physical chastisement. So the hero is allowed to make it clear, with some emphasis, that though he is forbidden to kill, or engage in premeditated violence, he cannot be attacked or insulted with impunity. On such a basis the novelist of 'ought' can hope to carry his hero through his refusal to fight, without forfeiting respect for his manliness, and indeed with a certain verve and *panache*.

If we are to allow him (for the time being) the benefit of his 'ideal' mode, we cannot complain of the 'abnormal' absence of conflict, hesitation, or frailty which his method presupposes. If Sir Charles's behaviour is *right*, it must be conceivable, and the novelist of 'ought' has set out precisely to conceive the right rather than the normal. We have to look for different criteria. The first response that Richardson wanted was the response of casuistry in moral argument. The proper question to ask is not 'Could I or the kind of person I know behave like that?' but '*Did* Sir Charles do right?' It is true that any answer takes us out of the proper sphere of literary criticism (as happened in the Richardson circle), but the literary critic should at least formulate the issue. Thereafter the true pacifist must argue that violence should never be met with violence but absorbed in non-resistance, the non-pacifist must argue that the last resort to violence need not be limited to self-defence; and those in between must find the point at which they wish to draw the line . . . knowing that Mr Richardson in heaven is looking through the previously shut-up windows of their hearts.

Literary criticism returns however at the point where the moral case begins to shade into the question of imaginative rendering. I think this turning-point is reached when one suspects that Richardson makes things too easy for himself and his hero. But the nicety is to determine just where, and on what criteria, the idealistic imagination could be criticised for exceeding the licence of 'ought', without resort to inappropriate demands of 'is'.

We might begin in casuistic terms by pointing out that Richardson gives his hero advantages which are no essential part of the moral case at all, and belong to the romantic hero: a physical strength, speed of hand and eye, considerable skill in swordsmanship. These are only mildly apparent in this episode, and Sir Charles's success does not depend on them. Yet they contribute something to a reader's total response, since they were visible in the rescue of Harriet, are visible again in the disarming of Sir Hargrave in the garden, and are explicitly referred to in Sir Charles's account of himself when the crisis is past. They will come into full action subsequently in the fracas with O'Hara and Salmonet in Sir Charles's front hall. The question whether this isn't a kind of cheating seems to be a question of 'ought' as well as a question of 'is'. Richardson admits the objection in his postscript to the novel, but excuses himself by arguing that his purpose was to make the first breach in a wall of prejudice by showing that duelling *could* be refused with honour. 'And when it is once allowed that there are cases and circumstances in which these polite *invitations to murder* may consistently with honour be disregarded, a little attention will easily find others; vulgar notions will insensibly wear out; and more ground be gained by degrees, than could have been attempted with hope of success, at once; till at length all may come to stand on the firm footing of reason and religion' (VI, 327). Moreover he is quite prepared, once challenged, to make the case for the man without physical prowess, by drawing a firm distinction between moral courage in a good cause and physical bravado in a bad one. Undoubtedly some worldlings would despise such a man if he refused a challenge but he would be respected by every good man, 'and perhaps, inwardly, by many who are mean enough to join outwardly in blaming'. Yet the fact remains that Richardson chose, for the purpose of an ideal demonstration, to give his hero advantages that have no intrinsic relation with that ideal. I think it significant that he is driven, in Sir Charles's account of himself, to forge a particular and individual connection between moral attitude and physical prowess, to make up for the absence of any other kind. Sir Charles explains not only how his horror of duelling arose through the way his father's wounding in a duel brought on the death of his mother; but also how it drove him on to make himself master of both sword and staff, precisely in order to help him refuse challenges without risking his life or his dignity. That Richardson should be driven to make such a connection in the particular and individual terms of 'is'; when there is no such connection in the general ethical terms of 'ought', shows that his imagination has exceeded the proper licence of 'ought'. I think we can see that a hero who could refuse a challenge, with less calm assurance of the outcome of being forced to resort to violence in self-defence, would have been worthy of more and not less respect. The idealistic imagination, too concerned with playing to win, has failed to discipline itself in its own terms, and has produced a demonstration less admirable than Richardson thought. And the literary significance of this casuistic point emerges still more clearly, when we see how the over-eager playing to win has affected the rendering of the scene as a whole.

For the challenger does not really challenge, the opposition does not sufficiently oppose. A contemporary reader objected that, in life, Sir Charles would never have had time for all that talking.

He would have been pulled by the nose.[1] This is refreshing, but it simply misunderstands the nature of the novel of 'ought', and the need to make a moral case clear in detail. Richardson also covered the point in theory, since Sir Charles would then have beaten his assailant as he beat the man who boxed his ears in Italy – but that would have been a less ideal demonstration. Yet the criticism exposes a point it cannot make: that even in terms of 'ought' and without resorting to criteria of 'is', the imaginative conception of the scene is too facile. The three friends of Sir Hargrave become, almost at once, an admiring chorus – often excessively so – mainly anxious to placate Sir Hargrave and let his ego down lightly. This means that Sir Charles's control over his passions, on which he is allowed to be pleased with himself, is never tested as it would have had to be if he had been faced with a more critical, or even taunting atmosphere. The more awkward problem of complacency is barely raised. We may allow the absence of any inner conflict or hesitation, as a consequence of Richardson's chosen method; so that our criticism should not conceal a desire to see him revealed, within, as less perfect, more normal. But the overeagerness to play to win, which explains the absence of any real outer challenge too, means that the demonstration of what *is* ideal becomes less effective than the author supposed.

The effect of this is clear when we consider what has been the simplest and most immediate response in modern critics: that Sir Charles is a consummate prig, as Pamela is a hypocrite and Clarissa a prude. The charge contains two elements, for to call him a prig is first to assume that he cannot 'really' be so perfectly virtuous, and then to 'explain' the apparent virtue in terms of concealed ego and vanity. The prig puts on an excessively goody-goody show because it makes him feel superior.

Now the purpose of my argument has been to show that this response is simply blind to the whole method of the book, and hence to the real critical problem. The first element denies the

[1] A friend of Lady Bradshaigh's. See Lady Bradshaigh to Richardson, 11 December 1753; Forster, XI, fol. 57; also Carroll, *Letters*, 271.

author any right to imagine a character who is a fully developed moral being; and the second jumps to a moral conclusion on no evidence. One does not argue that a prig might not behave and speak as Sir Charles does. One argues that because the method will not allow us to 'get inside' Sir Charles, there can be no internal evidence of priggish egotism. Without this, the external evidence is unconvincing, because it could easily point either way. The formal rhetoric – would a genuine human being speak like that? – is just as readily explicable in terms of careful premeditation appropriate to the character as conceived. The criticism nevertheless points in the direction of Richardson's imaginative failure, albeit in wholly misleading terms. For if there can be no internal evidence that Sir Charles is a prig, there can be no evidence that he is *not*. The only effective way to demonstrate that he is truly virtuous, would have been to conceive a sufficiently testing external situation, which openly raised the problem, and have Sir Charles meet it convincingly. This is what Richardson failed to do. It is not that he himself mistook priggishness for virtue, but rather that he conceived virtue without perceiving the need to give it a chance to defend itself against the charge. At one point he seems on the verge of seeing the problem, and it is just there that we can hope to illustrate his over-eagerness. As Sir Charles warns Sir Hargrave of the consequences of insulting him, he suddenly sees that this may look like boasting. But when Jordan observes that for his part, he 'could not bear such an air of superiority' (I, 384), Sir Charles produces a clear moral argument that he must *be* superior, in not wishing harm to Sir Hargrave, to a man 'who can think of justifying one violent action by another' (I, 384), though his opponent can lessen the superiority any time he likes by behaving the same way. It is surely a good answer, and I see nothing unacceptable. Nor is it even difficult to imagine an 'ought' argument for a good man voicing it openly, for why should he be inhibited from speaking a truth or urging a moral point, because of an unworthy fear that he may be suspected of vanity? As Sir Charles will frequently say in the novel, the good man must live to his own conscience, not the opinion of worldlings. But the significant point is that Richardson, having raised the possibility of ego, does not allow the opponents of Sir Charles to press it, to ask the really awkward question whether the moral superiority may not be a trap for egotism also, to see if there might not *there* be an opening to provoke Sir Charles and play on his passions. So instead of Sir Charles being forced to confront the possible relation of virtuous ambition and self-pluming ego, or being made to show that he really has control over his passions when needled at a vulnerable point, his opening rejoinder is simply met by an effusive chorus:

Mr Bag.: By G— this is nobly said!

Mr Jor.: I own, Sir Hargrave, that I would sooner veil to such a man as this, than to a king on his throne. (I, 385.)

This is ridiculous, but it is also rather sad. For the fact that Richardson made his hero raise the question at all suggests how much better he might have done. Yet in his haste to make Sir Charles prevail he asks us, at the first testing time, and when the possibilities of the dramatic form for external challenge are still open to him, to take far too much on trust. Even in terms of 'ought' the effectiveness of a quite spirited and morally courageous stand is less than it might have been, though not I believe disqualifyingly so, as yet.

The next section of the novel of 'ought' is the Grandison family history, told by the sisters to Harriet at Colnebrook, and made into a connected narrative by her. 'Harking back to make up' is clearly the major function of this section, but Richardson also seizes the opportunity for a moral tryptych: on one side self-denying and suffering virtue in the death of Lady Grandison; on the opposite side a portrait of egotism in Sir Thomas maltreating his daughters; and, in the middle, the Grandest-son, combining his mother's virtue with his father's high spirit, in active benevolence.

The pathetic death-scene is not a genre we are likely to find congenial and the spectacle of Richardson pulling out all the stops reminds one irresistibly of Oscar Wilde's witticism about the death of little Nell, that only a heart of stone could forbear to laugh. Indeed, Richardson tries even harder than Dickens, for he makes three assaults on our heart-strings. The scene itself, the Grandison girls re-telling it, and also the audience at Colnebrook are all copiously tearful. Yet characteristically also, Richardson is not merely tear-jerking, and we might do well to ask both why we are expected to weep and why we so lamentably fail to do so.

The tears shed at the time are natural enough, perhaps, though one begins to find the scene objectionable when they are dwelt on with such relish: 'every feature of his face seemed swelled almost to bursting, and working as if in mortal agonies' (II, 38). The effect is grotesque, and this increases as the lachrymose fuses with the edifying. Rhetorical or formal language, which has point in moral casuistry, makes us laugh when it suddenly pretends to be the language of the heart. Lady Grandison exclaims that her son's tears 'embalm' her (II, 37); but we are more likely to be struck by the inappropriate rhetoric than impressed by its moral content. The young Charles beseeches his sisters to be comforted: 'But who can say comfort? – These tears are equally our duty and our relief' (II, 40). The moral sentiment may be impeccable, but the sententiousness is disastrous; two 'oughts' collide instead of supporting each other. Richardson seems to have felt that because it was morally good to feel deeply at such a time, and also morally good to edify, there could be no problem; but we can hardly feel it as an 'ought' that grief should be so collected in its phrasing or regard itself so solemnly as a duty.

The pietism is compounded as one broken voice succeeds another in the storytelling of the sisters. Indeed, Caroline excels her brother for once as she observes that 'Tears, when time has matured a pungent grief into a sweet melancholy are not hurtful: They are as the dew of the morning to the green herbage' (II, 37-8). Yet the phrasing that ensures we do not weep also begins here to tell us why Richardson wanted us to: not just because it is pleasurable, but because he believed it made the good heart grow. Behind the tear-jerking attempt is a moral theory.

So when he makes Harriet and Emily weep as copiously, merely hearing the story, there is a little more involved than his fatal addiction to building the response he wanted into the fiction itself. Here the objections of a modern critic come to a head. Richardson misunderstands the psychology of reading: the more overt the emotive design, the more stubborn the reader's resistance. And the scene reveals its full sentimentality (in the modern pejorative sense) because the grief is imaginatively unearned. The death of Clarissa can be meaningful, even in the face of Richardson's later exploitation, because of our deep inward experience of her; but we know Lady Grandison only by hearsay, and however worthy her deathbed piety may be, it can be no valid demand-note on our emotions.

Yet it is just here, too, that the gulf between our criteria of 'is' and Richardson's criteria of 'ought' appears in another form. This time I do not believe the critical verdict can be mollified, for whereas there is some continuity in ethics between Richardson and ourselves, there is a historical chasm in this particular dimension of feeling, which cannot be crossed in terms of response. Yet in fairness we should at least note its existence. Richardson writes in the tradition of 'the man of feeling', that new morality of the heart which had developed out of the latitudinarian answer to seventeenth century puritanism, and is in the process of turning into 'sentimentalism' when we meet it in Richardson (and Fielding). Virtue is founded in the heart, and the good heart distinguishes itself from the bad by its capacity to feel intensely for others. Its tears are ready, not only in compassion but joy, and not only joy but moral admiration. In weeping thus, moreover, the good heart not only shows but also exercises itself, and grows even better. So Richardson's defence against the charge that his tears are unearned would be that they are precisely earned by the moral significance of Lady Grandison. That is why it is a duty (not merely 'natural' in a son) for Charles to weep for her; why the tears embalm her, in recognising and seeking to preserve what is queenly, and why her daughters' tears will make their hearts grow. In our preconceptions of 'is' we demand that our tears be earned by our experience, of the inner life of the individual, and of naturalistically 'realised' circumstance and action. In Richardson's preconception of 'ought', tears are the due of general moral excellence in itself. (We shall find Harriet weeping simply that there should be such a man in the world as Sir Charles.) It is a strange theory, and made stranger by the fact that eighteenth century men and women did weep more easily and often than we do, and were encouraged by their moral ideas to weep morally. The difficulty is enshrined for us in the very word 'sentimental'. When Dr Johnson defined the word in his Dictionary, and advised that Richardson should be read for 'the sentiments', he thought in terms of moral significance, *sententiae*, not the exploitation of feeling, and meant a compliment. Richardson would have distinguished himself very sharply from the 'sentimentalism' of the later eighteenth century (and more justly from Fielding even, if he had understood him), because he descends from the puritans as well as the latitudinarians, and demands that the good heart be morally meticulous as well as feeling intensely, so that feeling becomes a response to morality and not merely a self-rewarding pleasure.

Nevertheless the link between morality and tears, if it once existed, has ceased to do so in us, and it is simply impossible to respond as Richardson wanted us to. The scene must remain a weird fossil from an unrecoverable world. Yet the value of trying to understand its origin may lie in the suggestion that we examine the moral significance of Lady Grandison, rather than simply dismiss the scene as a grotesque imaginative failure. We shall find it in the value given once again, to *excess*.

With both Harriet and Sir Charles we have already seen that Richardson's idealism reached beyond the limits of correct behaviour to a vision of goodness that sought always to do more than enough. So Lady Grandison is his patient Griselda, meeting unfeeling neglect and cruel folly with serene acceptance and unfailing forgiveness. For the puritan in Richardson, the failure in duty of one partner in a family relationship is no excuse for failure in the other; but for the man of feeling in him, this applies not only to duty but to love. It may be more difficult to love in such a case, Harriet comments, but it is 'indispensable' (II, 36). Lady Grandison not only accepts and forgives, as is her wifely duty, she offers her tiresome and contemptible husband an 'excessive' sweetness and love.

The opposite panel of the tryptych may well seem more to our taste, for with the return of the devil, our kind of drama comes back. Seeking his own ease and pleasure, Sir Thomas sets up with one mistress after another, symbolically banishes his conscience in the exile of his son, and when Caroline's affair with Lord L threatens his finances, he bans the match and torments both girls. Morally this demonstrates the opposite of Lady Grandison's selfless love, in the heartless egoism of the father, and in the partial failure of the girls to live up to the standards of their mother. But in imaginative terms we are bound to find it more satisfactory and entertaining. Harriet re-tells the central scene in dramatic form (II, 70 ff.), and the way the actors 'come alive' demonstrates again the difference between the art of 'ought' and the art of 'is'. Richardson captures remarkably well the flick of the human voice intending to hurt, and the sound of frustration when the urge to retaliate has to try for restraint in the cause of duty. We live into the consciousness of the girls, and one's moral judgement of the father co-exists with a sense of the vitality of his language.

The effect of this, emphasising the contrast to the left and to the right, is to make us see that there may be a double challenge in the centre panel of the tryptych. For the first time in the novel of 'ought' we are faced, not with right and wrong, but with an open clash between orthodox virtue (which Harriet calls 'goodness') and 'excessive' virtue (which she calls 'greatness'). But in the light of the sudden vitality of the art in the scene with Sir Thomas, the moral question is bound to contain a stylistic challenge too. What life-style 'ought' we to prefer?

Sir Charles's letters from abroad recall his mother, for he gives way to his father's will in every particular, unfailingly, and could not treat him with more deference and respectful affection if Sir Thomas really was what he ought to be. In the third edition the question of moral excess arises even for Harriet as she hears of this. She thinks that Sir Charles 'keeps clear of every extreme'; but she has just suggested that 'it would have been an excess of generosity, amiable indeed, but pitiable, as contrary to the justice that every man owes to himself, and to those who may hereafter depend upon him' if, in agreeing to his father's mortgaging the Irish estate, he had 'sacrificed to the unreasonable desires even of a father, the fortune to which he had an unquestionable right'. Now the casuist should spot the hairsbreadth that has saved Sir Charles from doing just this. His readiness to regard himself as wholly his father's, with his cry 'Leave me not any-thing!' (II, 60), is far from supporting Harriet's certainty that he would have refused if the estate had been entailed (his by unquestionable right), and not merely at his father's will.[1] The style of the letters is, moreover, the style of 'ought', the deliberate rhetoric that raises the now familiar question, not only ought he to feel as he does, but can he, really?

When the young man arrives home, however, we find that his morality of excess is fully intended, and we even get a psychological explanation of it. He has responded deeply to the element of excess in his mother's virtue; and has intensified it by trying to transform the characteristics he inherits from his father, redirecting them to moral ends. When the self-centredness of Sir Thomas is removed from his high 'spirit', it becomes moral courage, and a readiness to break through social decorum and orthodox morality, but for a moral not an immoral end. Personal and family pride, which Harriet still sees clear traces of in Sir Charles (II, 146), becomes a determination to be 'a Grandison' in terms of moral rather than worldly grandeur. He explains to his uncle how he has made his pride strengthen his determination

[1] This passage may have been inserted in response to a criticism of Miss Talbot's. I quote from the edition of Ethel M. M. McKenna, London, 1902, *Sir Charles Grandison*, II, 158.

to live within his means, and be just, and then to be generous if he can. 'I told your Lordship, that if I could not conquer it, I would endeavour to make it innocent at least' (II, 139). We now get the insight there could and should have been in the encounter at Sir Hargrave's: Sir Charles might have been made to admit an element of ego which is very close to priggishness, and yet firmly distinguishable, for the ambition to be superior is made the servant of morality, not the other way round. Lastly, Sir Thomas's 'magnificence' is made to heighten generosity into great-hearted munificence, well in excess of orthodox goodness.

So, in the disagreement of this 'Grandest-son' with his sisters over the treatment of his father's mistress, we get a contrast between two different conceptions of virtue, each containing an element of ego, but directed to very different ends. To the girls, still smarting from their father's maltreatment, Mrs Oldham is the woman who took their place with their father, and lived in state, while his financial embarrassments were made the excuse to keep them unportioned, and to veto Caroline's engagement to Lord L. It is wholly natural that they should hate her. Moreover she is a fallen woman, and they are the children of their mother, brought up to be virtuous, though without her 'excessive' power of forgiveness and refusal to criticise. It seems just, that Mrs Oldham should be made sensible of her crime. So their treatment of her shows resentment, distaste, and a conscious superiority that is both moral and egotistic. Sir Charles has been as much injured by Mrs Oldham, since his father's keeping of mistresses was the reason for banishing him from England for more than eight years. Yet he treats her with the greatest consideration from the beginning, and when she reveals a penitent heart he will take notice of nothing but the excellent housekeeper she should have remained. He tells her that if he learns of anything his father wanted to do for anybody, he will carry it out as exactly as if it were part of a legal will. 'Shall we do nothing but *legal* justice? – The Law was not made for a man of conscience' (II, 127). He insists that she keep all she has been given or has saved, assists her to set up a household, and pays her an annuity for her illegitimate children by his father, with a promise to help them further as they grow up. This is 'excessive' in that it is not only more than justice but more than forgiveness too; and it springs from his moral reorchestration of pride and magnificence, strengthening his mother's attitudes. To the objections of his sisters there are two kinds of reply. To treat persons who can claim only justice with such absolute forgiveness and generosity is a guarantee that he will treat better people even better. He rapidly proceeds to show his sisters what this means, and insists that his bounty, aimed at making them independent, be regarded as merely their due. And on the charge that his treatment of Mrs Oldham is 'an encouragement to a guilty life' Harriet comments: 'if it be not goodness . . . it is greatness; and this, if it be not praise-worthy, is the first instance that I have known goodness and greatness of soul separable' (II, 133).

Would we really (the question arises), with the Grandison girls at the time, have preferred a hero who behaved more naturally, normally, and within the ordinary understanding of virtue? And, interestingly, Sir Charles himself at one point makes this a question of language and style as well as one of manners and psychology. As he speaks of his father's funeral, out pops another ludicrously pompous piety, when he proposes 'to interr the venerable remains (I must always speak in this dialect, Sir) with those of my mother' (II, 110). We laugh, or snarl. And yet . . . if he had said 'I shall bury the body with my mother's', there would have been no laugh, but is one quite sure that it would have been so much more admirable? For it is because he so excessively insists that his father should *be* venerated, in spite of his misdoings, that he will also insist that Mrs Oldham should be treated as he treats her. The dialect of 'ought' is often excessively tactless, but the judgement of it may not be quite as simple as it looks, for the excess at this point seems meant to be challenging. And we can see a similar challenge being posed by the positioning of a break in Harriet's narrative. The sisters begin a scene with Mrs Oldham which has dramatic potential in the same genre as their scene with their father; and Harriet ends a letter, just before

Sir Charles enters, on their threat 'You'll soon know, madam, what you have to trust to from *him*'. Inevitably, the apparent suspense turns into anticlimax in the proportion of Sir Charles's ideal goodness. But the pause reminds us that there could have been a scene which heightened what we have already had: the flicker, thrust, and defence of ordinary human voices behaving naturally, in the drama of the normative. (How would 'realistic' characters, who have cause to feel as these four do, behave and speak? – the imagination of 'is'.) We have seen clearly enough by now what the art of 'ought' has to forgo: the wit and intelligence that can hurt, the feelings that are not ideal, the complex and natural prose of mixed motives, the drama of inner as well as outer conflict. Instead of drama, the staple becomes narrative interlaced with moral speeches. And the first response to Richardson's tryptych is bound to be an instant preference for the art of Sir Thomas's panel. Yet the challenge of the juxtaposition itself, Sir Charles's occasionally excessive language, and the poised moment when the scene with Mrs Oldham could have gone one way or the other, is to make us think about what it might mean to rest secure in our first judgement. I do not conclude that that judgement should be reversed, for the first response must be significant. But it does seem that there is more to the argument than one had thought. Indeed, a possible defence appears for an art of 'ought': that it forces us to examine the psychology of our reading, the nature of our preconceptions, and the possible facility and over-security of our initial responses. One sees here a deeper explanation of Jane Austen's admiration, and of Richardson's influence on her, than the appeal of the novel's opening. For in *Mansfield Park* she too opposed an art of 'ought' to a far more lively, realistic and appealing art of 'is'. Her most Richardsonian novel is less stark in its opposition, since the author's irony is allowed to play over both sides, but it offers many of the same challenges, difficulties, and rewards.[1]

[1] For her high opinion of the novel see J. E. Austen-Leigh, *Memoir of Jane Austen*, ed. R. W. Chapman (Oxford, 1928), p. 89, and Henry Austen's Biographical Notice, *Novels*, ed. Chapman (2nd ed., Oxford, 1926), V. 7.

As the 'Sir Charles' story intersects again with the 'Harriet' story in the present tense, Richardson proceeds to expand the implications of the morality of excess in a variety of situations.

Those in which Sir Charles is involved away from home are given to us, for the first time, in his own narrative. This presents an obvious formal difficulty, for as he had himself remarked in the scene with Sir Hargrave, stories which reflect credit on a man come ill from his own mouth. Richardson attempts to bypass the difficulty by again making moral habit and casuistry displace psychology. Sir Charles has been in the habit for years of submitting everything he does to the scrutiny of Dr Bartlett; so that the letters which recount his handling of his executorship for Mr Danby, his rescue of Lord W from his mistress, and the problem of Emily's mother, are meant to be taken as a simple continuation of that habit. They consist largely of narrative; they concentrate on what he does rather than on his consciousness; and, whenever he can, Richardson makes him disclaim credit. Yet there is always a risk, familiar since *Pamela*, that the formal difficulty will raise an unwanted question of conceit. The letter form is not suited to Richardson's purpose here, and he can only hope to get away with it by making the letters so straightforwardly narrative when they deal with action, that we may forget that they *are* letters; and by trying to ensure that when the personal voice is heard it should direct our attention away from the speaker and towards the moral significance of the action. Yet the form remains clumsy, and the clumsiness becomes worse when the pretence of a realistic correspondence raises the further problem of getting the letters to us. Richardson gets them to Harriet by making them the reward of her own communicativeness – she has allowed Dr Bartlett, as well as her 'sisters' and Lord L, to read some of her letters – but it is distinctly awkward that she should then send them away to her family. It would have been far better if they had not appeared; if, having created an opportunity for Harriet to read them, Richardson had made her tell the story and provide the commentary.

In the Danby affair (II, 246 ff.), Richardson expands the

generous element in the grandest son, and the distinction between law and conscience. Sir Charles refuses to profit by Mr Danby's legacy at the expense of the nephews and niece, who have been treated unjustly in their uncle's will because of their dastardly father's attempt on his life. As executor, Sir Charles regards it as his duty to preserve the memory of his friend's real benevolence by setting aside the defects of the will he made as a dying and embittered man. He does not presume to renounce the whole – he keeps nine of the twenty-four thousand, though he hopes to devote much of it to charity – but he does insist on adjusting the disproportion of his friend's gratitude for saving his life, to what he thinks that friend in happier days and health would have wanted to do for his young relatives. (With Wilson, the servant who had been the instrument of Harriet's abduction, there is a further repetition of the pattern of the treatment of Mrs Oldham. Because he repents, Sir Charles not only advises against a prosecution, but gives him enough money to marry and lead a virtuous life free from the temptations of dependence.)

In the rescue of Lord W (II, 335 ff.), Richardson develops the moralisation of pride. Only the mean pride of egotism has prevented Lord W from getting rid of his mistress, and Mrs Giffard from leaving him. Sir Charles's solution is to take the financial penalty for breaking the contract upon himself; and so shame his uncle for revealing that £100 a year means more to him than his own tranquillity and the prevention of any complaint of injustice. 'Greatness' of mind overcomes meanness; and once more the determination to do more than justice is enforced against any fear of 'rewarding' guilt. The moralised 'spirit' of Sir Charles also plays off against both the cravenness of his uncle and the shrewishness of Mrs Giffard. Lord W underlines the moral transformation of the qualities in Sir Thomas he disliked, by saying that now the name of Grandison is the first of names. And Sir Charles sets out to complete the reformation, and the opening of his uncle's heart, by finding him a virtuous wife whose circumstances are such that the marriage could be a real mutual obligation and a ground for secure mutual loyalty. (In doing this, of course, he is acting directly against his own worldly interests as Lord W's likely heir.) We notice with the Danbys, and Wilson, and Lord W, the way that Richardson saw his hero not only as an exemplar of good conduct, but as an opener of hearts and an inspiration for new and better relationships.

With the O'Haras (II, 373 ff.), Sir Charles's inheritance of characteristics from his father is shown in two lights. For the first time in the novel, he allows himself to be passionate; he is irritated enough by the blusterings and drawn swords of the two bully-boys to use violence in disarming them and thrusting them out of the house. With the moral defence for this we have already dealt, but the point to notice now is that Sir Charles is extremely dissatisfied with himself. The moral theory he had outlined at Sir Hargrave's is not, after all, sufficient for his ambition to behave even better than could reasonably be expected of a good man. One kind of 'spirit' is set off against a better kind. So, instead of allowing their behaviour to count against Emily's mother and her new husband, he persuades his ward to heap coals of fire by increasing their allowance in such a fashion that each is given a motive for behaving well to the other. As with Wilson, Lord W, and Mrs Oldham, he tries to hit on some way of liberating the potential good that may still exist in vice or folly.

Again, however, one may ask whether Richardson gives his hero undue advantage in his dream of 'high life'. All this generosity may be very well, but Sir Charles's behaviour is rendered distinctly easier by his affluence. Richardson the self-made man knew the value of money perfectly well, but there may have been all the more imaginative pleasure in allowing the thousands and the hundreds to trip off the tongue. On the other hand, the attitudes clearly do not depend on the affluence – by this time we can see that the young Charles in Europe would have treated the Danby legacy and his uncle just the same, and would have given the same advice to Emily. Nevertheless it remains true that the easier Richardson makes it for his hero in the interests of ideal display, the less truly meritorious, in a way he seems not to have noticed.

We now have a fair idea of the kind of overflowing benevolence, the ambition to be 'great'-hearted in doing much more than enough, that Richardson's idealism conceived, beyond the limits not only of normal frailty but also of normal goodness. It is not easy to learn to read in the terms of 'ought', while still concerned to clarify, fairly, the loss to the art in terms of 'is'. There are many difficulties in the way of a modern reader, which Richardson increased by a characteristic tactlessness, and some mistakes. Yet his hero cannot simply be dismissed as a prig, and the art of 'ought' contrives to mount a not despicable challenge that has an imaginative and stylistic as well as a moral aspect.

Significantly, however, there remain two scenes in which Sir Charles is pitted against Charlotte at home – and these begin to prepare for a crucial turn in the novel of 'ought'. These are dramatic scenes in the full sense, for unlike all the others in the 'Sir Charles' story, they direct our attention to his consciousness as well as his conduct, and imply very strongly the presence of inner conflict. For the first time we see him uncertain, hesitant, blushing.

Ostensibly, the moral concern is to develop the contrast between Sir Charles and his sister. Charlotte brings out a lighter side to him which both inherit from their father. Both have a quick intelligence, a kind of wit, and playfulness, but these qualities in Sir Charles are subject to a much more scrupulous morality. He is less lively and can be more sternly heavy-handed than a situation deserves. On the other hand, we have also to recognise a greater responsibility, an unwillingness to give unnecessary pain, a scrupulous discrimination of the point beyond which teasing and evasiveness must stop, and seriousness begin. In the first scene (II, 162 ff.), Charlotte has to be driven into a corner before she will tell her brother what he needs to know in order to be responsible to Lord G, and in order to free her from her entanglement with Anderson. In the second scene (II, 404 ff.), she has to be forced into a sense of responsibility about keeping a good man dangling about, as Harriet would never do. In both scenes there is the stylistic challenge we noticed before, as Charlotte's lively style reaches the point of collision with her brother's.

The new thing, though, is that Charlotte is also given a handle against her brother. The 'trial' arises out of her charge of 'reserve', which is turned against herself, but the charge is not fully answered. He says he prizes frankness and sincerity, and he clearly does. The 'distance' Charlotte complains of is not altogether his fault, since whenever he is asked seriously about his own affairs he does his best to answer, though he will not allow quizzing of himself to be a means of evasion for Charlotte. Yet when at last, and embarrassingly for Harriet, in her presence, the question is fairly put whether he has seen the woman he would wish to marry, he can only say that he has and then refuses to say any more.

'*Miss Gr.* . . . Is the Lady a foreign Lady?

'How every body but I looked at him, expecting his answer! – He really hesitated. At last; I think, Charlotte, you will excuse me, if I say, that this question gives me some pain – Because it leads to *another*, that, *if* made, *I cannot at present myself answer:* (But why so, Sir, thought I?) And if *not* made, it cannot be of any signification to speak to this.' A moment later, he tells Lord L, 'my peace has been broken in pieces by a tender fault in my constitution – And yet I would not be without it' (II, 401-2).

This is not the dialect we have become accustomed to, nor the man so 'complete' that he acts always with assurance. The frankness is far from matching Harriet's, yet it is obviously painful, and whatever his scruple may be, his scrupulousness is costing him something for the first time. The novel of 'ought' is no longer merely interweaved with the novel of 'is' . . . they have met. With this, we are prepared for the crucial scene, on which the whole novel turns.

4

In the library at Colnebrook, Sir Charles confers privately with Harriet – the first time since the rescue that they have been alone together (III, 2 ff.). Ostensibly he is out to discover from

Charlotte's ambassadress what he cannot get in plain English from his sister, but it soon becomes clear that he has also decided to clear up the mystery of his own situation.

The question whether Charlotte is to encourage Lord G is not, however, merely a pretext. Always with Richardson we have to look for a point in his juxtapositions, and here it is the problem of disappointed 'first love'. Charlotte's case has to be considered in the realistic terms of 'is'. She did not feel very deeply for Anderson, but her humiliation at his unworthiness, coupled with her hero-worship of her brother, promises little for Lord G. For she clearly feels that he, too, is her intellectual inferior; and on the other hand his good-nature and moral worth are not glamorous enough, in the face of an inevitable comparison, to capture a heart that has ventured once only to be humiliated. Yet both Harriet and Sir Charles think that Lord G would make a good husband, provided that she could learn to control her teasing. In realistic terms, such an open-eyed marriage seems the best available, since Lord G is not deterred either by his knowledge of the Anderson affair, or by her faulty temperament. It would be an unromantic union of imperfections, but it could be hoped that with love on one side, and the response of a basically good nature to good-nature on the other, a durable affection could ripen. Yet it is also clear from what Sir Charles says about Beauchamp, that there could be a more 'delicate' view. He himself has wholly forgiven Charlotte her error, and loves her for, as well as in spite of, her faults. But he would be uneasy about encouraging her to think of Beauchamp (supposing she had meant anything by mentioning him) because a man with 'nice notions' (III, 6), and without a brother's partiality, might feel differently about the 'first love' and particularly the degree of indiscretion involved. There is already a hint of the question-marks of 'ought' which will be in the air for Harriet as Sir Charles confesses his secret.

We shall hardly be surprised, however, as he tells the story of his involvement with Clementina and the Porretta family in Bologna, to find the question of indiscretion vanish. It becomes clear that he refused to take any advantage of the special relationship ('brotherhood' and 'sisterhood' again), to which the family admitted him in their gratitude for his rescue and reformation of Jeronymo. He even felt bound to uphold his honour by agreeing to sound Clementina on her refusal of the Count of Belvedere. (When a fuller narrative is supplied to Harriet by Dr Bartlett later, we shall find Clementina confirming our own suspicions that this is a point where discretion became excessive rather than defective.) Summoned back to Vienna, after Clementina had opened her heart to Mrs Beaumont, he continued to guard his behaviour when he met Clementina and her mother, before the conditions of marriage were proposed, because he suspected what those might be. When he had to refuse to renounce his religion and his country, he handled the unfairness and the resentment of the family with a necessary firmness of spirit, but with the greatest restraint. Indeed, if anyone was indiscreet, it was the family, in giving him such free access to their daughter, in asking him to discuss Belvedere with her, in arranging for him to see her before the conditions were proposed, and in summoning him back from Vienna at all, when his attitude to his religion had always been perfectly clear.

But the second question, the implications of 'first love' to those who aspire to the greatest delicacy, is rather more complex. What does Harriet feel? What ought she to feel? And the same questions have now to be asked about Sir Charles as well, questions of 'is' *and* 'ought', for he is visibly in difficulties too.

The story is bound to be a terrible blow to Harriet. The suspense that has tortured her is partly lifted – while we see how intensely felt it was as she nearly faints – but the problems it leaves behind are almost worse. To the humiliation of having had to confess to his family and hers that she has loved without real hope of return, is now added the certainty that the best she can hope for is 'half a heart': to be the second choice of a man disappointed in his first. And what is a lady of nice notions to make of that? Moreover, her suspense is not over, for she cannot understand the meaning of his incoherence as he breaks from her in the library. 'And now, madam . . . What shall I say? – I cannot tell what I should say – But you, I see, can pity me – You can pity the noble Clementina – Honour forbids me! – Yet honour bids me – Yet I cannot be unjust, ungenerous – selfish! . . . Allow me, madam, to thank you for the favour of your ear – Pardon me for the trouble I see I have given to a heart that is capable of a sympathy so tender – And, bowing low, he withdrew with precipitation' (III, 35). He speaks with the greatest tenderness and respect; and when the sisters hear the story, they tell her that his struggle is between his compassion for Clementina and his love for herself. Her godfather, too, had formed the impression, from hearing Sir Charles talk of her, that all was ripening for the best. Nevertheless, though there have been many signs in his behaviour of his high regard for Harriet (especially after she has allowed him to read her letters since Lord L had done so), his sisters have had to confess that they could not tell how much significance to read into those signs. He has spent so much of his time away from home; apparently far less eager than a lover would have been to seek the company of his beloved. And his words in the library are capable of a construction far less hopeful and more humiliating: that he has seen his effect on her, and in his brotherly tenderness and respect, has felt bound to make her understand that he was committed elsewhere, in order to help her overcome a hopeless attraction.

Much more significant for Richardson, however, than the romantic 'he loves me, he loves me not' of the 'love story', is the challenge to the quality of Harriet's own heart. In the section of the 'Harriet' story I have not yet looked at, between her 'trial' by the sisters and the scene in the library, she has discovered how love can subvert honesty and narrow the heart. What seems delicacy can turn out to be indelicacy. She is ashamed of having been pleased when the sisters pretended ignorance of her feelings, as they tried to get Dr Bartlett's assessment of the situation, for no true thing can involve deception (II, 275). There is a real temptation to read what Sir Charles said of her, in the letter Charlotte took from the Doctor's desk (II, 277 ff.).

And, alarmed by her godfather's hint that Emily may be falling in love with her guardian, Harriet gives way momentarily to impulses of petulance and jealousy before she pulls herself up. 'O how deceitful is the heart! I could not have thought it possible that mine could have been so narrow' (II, 313). In penitence, and real compassion for Emily's position and her sufferings over her mother, she responds with her characteristic frankness and enthusiasm to the chance to redeem herself, and to found a new sisterhood of the heart.

Yet, if it is possible to feel thus for a girl who, after all, has a good deal less hope of Sir Charles than herself, is it possible not to be jealous and narrow-hearted about Clementina? The pressure of potential feeling is just below the surface as she defends herself against a possibly adverse comparison, since Clementina concealed her love; and there is a revealing need to blame *someone*, in moments of petulance with Sir Charles, and the sharp edge to otherwise just comments on the indiscretion of the Porretta family (III, 73 ff.). But it is clear that her primary feeling is what it ought to be: a real pity and admiration for the Italian girl. Only, she yearns to be great, not merely good. So, in the library, while her pity is instantaneous and unforced, her 'enthusiasm' almost topples over into hypocrisy. 'Who, Sir, said I, knowing only so far as I know of the unhappy Clementina, but must wish her to be – Ah Lucy! there I stopt – I had like to have been a false girl! – And yet ought I not, from my heart, to have been able to say what I was going to say? – I do aver, Lucy, upon repeated experience, that Love is a narrower of the heart. Did I not use to be thought generous and benevolent, and to be above all selfishness? But am I so now?' (III, 34-5). 'Ought' and 'Is' come into a new collision in the Harriet story. As we read on now, there will no longer be only the questioning of the cost and difficulty of being and feeling what one ought to be and feel, but a real question how far the limits of 'ought' should stretch, and can stretch. Without ceasing to be explored in realistic terms of consciousness, the heroine has entered the arena of 'ought'.

Conversely, the new hesitations and confusions of the hero of 'ought' show that he is entering the other arena where the cost of 'ought' has to be measured in terms of inner conflict and disturbed conscience.

At first, as the fuller story of what happened in Bologna is unfolded by Dr Bartlett to Harriet, the familiar questions of casuistry will be uppermost. Was he discreet enough, or too discreet? Ought he to have got himself into that embarrassing position of examining Clementina about Belvedere with her mother behind the door? Ought he to have offered his compromise, to allow a Catholic wife not only her confessor but also to bring up their daughters as Catholics, though the sons would be raised as Protestants? (It is worth reminding oneself that Richardson was approaching rather more of a hornets' nest than the problem of duelling. The violent anti-Catholicism of the Sacheverell period lay many years in the past, but the '45 rebellion, which takes place in the novel while Grandison is in Bologna, had only been over for eight years when the book was published. Moreover, though Grandison argues that there would be precedents for papal sanction, his position is a good deal more liberal than the papal one now, over two centuries later, when the issue is still alive.)

But now that some of the Porrettas have begged him to return to Bologna, to help Clementina recover from the mental breakdown which followed their refusal to let her see him again, and their subsequent policy of harshness, there arises a very difficult question of 'ought' which must at the same time be a question of 'is' in a new way. If we have had to separate the two kinds of question before, in order to be fair to Richardson's chosen method, it would seem unlikely that they could be separated now. For the questions 'Ought he to go back?' and 'Ought he to feel bound by his previous offer?' would seem necessarily involved with the nature of his feelings for the two girls. In the library, we cannot be sure what he feels for Harriet. His incoherent words could suggest that he does indeed love her, but cannot feel free to say anything without being dishonourable and selfish, while he is still entangled with Clementina. But as we have seen, they could bear other constructions, and the nature of the novel of 'ought' has not permitted the inner knowledge of his mind and heart that would enable us to be sure. Yet the scene in the library must point forward to a clarification. On the other hand, Dr Bartlett's narrative to Harriet tells us far from enough about Charles's feeling for Clementina. Though there are extracts from his letters, the narrative is still too concerned with his conduct to allow us to be sure of the proportion of compassion to love in what he felt at the time. Yet now, as we wait to see what will happen in Bologna when he gets there, the 'ought' question about his obligation to the Italian girl would seem inextricably involved with the 'is' question of what he feels about her *now*, after he has met Harriet. The central drama of embarrassment, just opening out as the novel reaches the half-way stage, has contrived to pose so genuinely awkward a question, in the clash of opposed 'goods', and the competition of feelings about equally admirable women, that the two kinds of imagination seem bound to fuse.

There is also a second heroine now, and she too seems about to pose questions of both 'ought' and 'is'. English Protestant readers might be expected to endorse the rightness of refusing to renounce both England and Protestantism, even though the cost should be the loss of a girl he really cares for and admires. But Richardson shows the fairness and responsibility of his imagination of 'ought' by reversing the question with the Catholic girl. What ought Clementina to do when (as Harriet sees is already the case at the beginning), her religious fervour means that she loves Grandison in a real sense 'against inclination', granted the special feeling of Catholics about heretics? And this, because it must again involve a conflict between two 'good' feelings, must be a question of 'is' as well. Once more, the excessively narrative nature of our first acquaintance with her means that we do not get sufficiently 'inside' her mind and heart. But in her conversation with Mrs Beaumont, her slightly deranged secret letter, and her last interview with Charles, we get suggestive glimpses. Then the obduracy of her family closed the question as far as her own choice was concerned; yet we can foresee that the effect of Grandison's return to Italy may well be to open it up again. What ought she to do and feel? What will she do and feel? Richardson, with Clementina too, will have to face the challenge of reconciling his two kinds of imagination.

Half way through the novel, it appears that there may be real justification for Richardson's method. The 'Sir Charles' story has allowed him to liberate one kind of imagination in order to expound and explore an idealistic morality, with a freedom and variety that would hardly have been possible in realistic terms. The heavy loss of imaginative and artistic vitality, and the danger of losing a reader's sympathy and credence, have been very considerable; yet the imagination of 'ought' is able, once we are prepared to make an effort to understand it, to pose some not uninteresting challenges. On the other hand, he has also been able to explore the cost and difficulty of such idealism in the 'Harriet' story. And now he seems about to explode the two into one another. I think we can see that if he were to succeed in keeping both at pressure, the subsequent exploration might well prove worth the price of the initial separation.

CHAPTER NINE

Crisis, Resolution and the Family of the Heart

I

Richardson 'makes us wait' for Sir Charles to depart and arrive in Italy; but the rest of the fourth volume provides both a reprise of themes and problems and a new kind of perspective, bringing into focus a different conception of 'drama'.

Sir Charles ties up the loose ends of his various good works, and achieves a new one. A triple wedding, which he presides over as good fairy, completes the launching of the Danbys. He continues to try to influence Sir Hargrave and his friends. He finds in Miss Mansfield the wife he had sought for his uncle, arranges the marriage, and helps his new relations to regain the property and income they had lost through duplicity and miscarriage of justice. Lord W responds to the goodness of his nephew and his new wife by shedding his meanness. The O'Haras, too, begin to respond to the generosity of their treatment, and one source of heartbreak for Emily looks like being removed. Sir Charles receives Mrs Oldham and her children again, and procures a commission for her eldest son – in the face of the continuing objections of orthodox 'virtue' from Charlotte. Charlotte is persuaded to marry Lord G before her brother leaves; and though her behaviour is far from satisfactory in its levity and disrespect for her future husband, there is still the hope that this is a last fling of temperament before the serious vows at the altar sober her up.

The new undertaking is to persuade Sir Harry Beauchamp's second wife to allow her stepson (Sir Charles's closest friend) to come home (III, 253 ff.). She had made unsuccessful approaches to the young man herself, and married his father in revenge, which she carried out by securing his exile and keeping down his allowance. The technique Sir Charles chooses to overcome this old resentment is to adopt a playful tone, jollying her out of any excuse to lose her temper. Since she has been expecting a solemn young prig, she is jolted out of prepared positions and never allowed to recover. He insists on seeming charmed, pretending that every pepperiness and occasion for offence is an inaudible 'aside', keeping the tone light and teasing. Unwillingly she smiles where she meant to frown, and the ice is broken. It is deliberate playacting, but it begins to open up a new insight into the problem of reconciling 'ought' and 'is'. For the technique that creates a propitious atmosphere is only the first step; the real persuasion lies in offering Lady Beauchamp a developed role to play, which she can see will suit her and show her off to far greater advantage than her existing one. In *Clarissa*, 'acting' had been morally dangerous. Clarissa herself is incapable of pretence, and as the pressure on her mounts, the novel becomes more and more concerned with her integrity and sincerity. Lovelace, conversely, is an inveterate playactor; so much so that even when he feels deeply he can never be wholly sincere. He acts even to himself, his face is always wearing some kind of mask. He begins by acting out different sides of his personality, but ends by becoming so obsessed with his rake's script that he is wholly blinded to realities and destroys the only thing he has ever loved. But now, in the middle of *Grandison*, Richardson suddenly hits on a new moral application for his lifelong love of the drama. Not only does Sir Charles play-act for a moral purpose, but the role he offers Lady Beauchamp is a kind of moral engineering. It is nicely calculated to her own real character, her 'spirit', her pride, her love of power above all. He shows her how she can exercise power and satisfy pride in a way that will heap obligations on her husband and stepson instead of causing continual unpleasantness. He shames her into generosity as he had shamed his uncle. And the whole 'performance' is based on his insight into himself, and his success in moralising inherited characteristics. Richardson need not have got the basic idea of the relativity of the passions from Pope's *Essay on Man* (which he certainly knew) but there is a close resemblance to Pope's theory that the same passions can produce opposite results. 'Reason the byass turns to good from ill, / And Nero reigns a Titus, if he will.' Everything depends on how the passions are directed; and in the dramatic scene with the Beauchamps, Sir Charles becomes the player-director, 'producing' a 'performance' which lays the basis for moral change. Shortly afterwards, he will teach Emily to do the same, making her and the O'Haras act out a significant pretence as she hands over money to her stepfather to give to her mother 'as from' himself, and watching even O'Hara catch on to the spirit and meaning of the thing.

That Richardson is conscious of his new insight is made clear at the beginning of the fourth volume, immediately after Dr Bartlett's thirteenth and last letter. Harriet determines to try to behave 'with assumed bravery', but her cousins' 'kind concern for me looks, however, as if they thought me a hypocrite; and I suppose, therefore, that I act my part very aukwardly. But, my dear, as this case is one of those few in which a woman *can* show a bravery of spirit, I think an endeavour after it is laudable . . .' (III, 233). This is interesting because, while admitting the gulf between 'ought' and 'is', Harriet refuses to be deterred by what she considers misplaced notions of sincerity. If it is right to act in such and such a way, even though one can not yet do it sincerely, then it is right to 'act', to pretend; for right behaviour is more important than sincerity and 'acting' may generate the proper feeling. One must not be prevented from trying to do what is right by the possible impurity of one's motivation, one must seek to make it purer.

Consequently, what we see in the 'Harriet' side of the fourth volume is a deliberate attempt to drill herself, not only into behaving as she ought, but also into feeling as she ought. The wish that Sir Charles might marry Clementina, when she had begun to utter it in the library, nearly made her a 'false girl'; for it ran clean contrary to her heart. Yet even then she thought that she *should* have been able to be 'above all selfishness'. While she is reading Dr Bartlett's letters, we can detect a development: the half-suppressed irritation, injured pride, and potential jealousy we saw in her response to the Doctor's first packet, give way more and more surely to pity and admiration for the Italian girl. There is still the possibility of affectation, and she shows herself aware of it (as when she overpitches by exclaiming that she is not worthy to be the handmaid of either of them (III, 165)) but she comes more and more to feel that in reason and justice Clementina deserves Sir Charles. After the thirteenth letter she imagines Sir Charles returning with Lady Grandison: 'Surely I shall be capable, if she be Lady Grandison, of rejoiceing in her recovery!'... and a big tear blots her letter-paper (III, 236). Nevertheless, having chosen her role in terms of 'ought', she is beginning to live her way into it – as an actress lives into a part to make it real.

Her success is shown in two 'acts' with the Countess of D, and one with Sir Charles himself. She has been due for an *éclaircissement* with Lord D's managing mother ever since their first meeting; but now there is more than the mere drama of embarrassment there would have been if this had taken place at the time of her 'trial' by the Grandison girls. When the Countess asks if Sir Charles has made addresses to her, she answers quite straightforwardly; and though she is still embarrassed by the further question of whether she has any hope, she sheds all hesitation at the suggestion that she should allow Lord D to court her in case nothing comes of Sir Charles. She not only cannot but ought not to have any hope herself, she says, 'since there is a Lady who deserved him by severe sufferings before I knew him'; but she loves him in a way that will not permit her to think of any other man as she ought to think of a husband. She repeats, 'as the strongest expression I can use... That my heart is already a wedded heart' (III, 279). And there seems no more hint of affectation in the first statement than the second.

Then, as Sir Charles tells her of the latest news from Bologna, and of his plans, she confirms the role she has chosen. She takes an opportunity to be by herself for a moment, to control the conflict between her love and the impulse of justice and generosity to Clementina which 'pulled my heart two ways' (III, 296). She wants to make a deliberate declaration, and it must be clear both of 'precipitance' and of 'affectation'. She puts to herself, point by point, the justice of Clementina's primary claim. 'The struggle will cost thee something: But go down, and try to be above thyself'. The language is revealing; she 'intensifies' herself, as an actress might before a big moment: 'I attempted to assume a dignity of aspect, without pride, and I spoke, while spirit was high in me, and to keep myself up to it' . . . but it is herself that she raises. The realism of 'is' has not abdicated before the demands of 'ought'; but hypocrisy (false pretence) has given way to achieved role (the heightening of the self to carry conviction). She declares herself, as she urges him to go to Clementina, in a way that will help her 'to live up to it', and she subsequently does, though inevitably with many 'twitches' of the heart.

Sir Charles responds by fixing his role with Harriet too, by going as near as his delicate situation will allow him, to a declaration of his own feelings. 'From the first I called Miss Byron my sister; but she is *more* to me than the dearest sister; and there is a more tender friendship that I aspire to hold with her, whatever may be the accidents on either side, to bar a further wish: and *this* I must hope, that she will not deny me . . .' We must not allow changes in the language to obscure this development of the theme of the 'family of the heart', for Richardson is availing himself of an eighteenth century meaning of 'friend' (a blood relative) to continue the sense of unbreakable relationship, and also of a gloss Anna Howe had used when she refused to call the Harlowes Clarissa's 'friends'. Sir Charles's 'friendship' has to mean more than one feels for 'the dearest sister' and there is no English word for it now. Yet Harriet knows what he means when she talks about it to Dr Bartlett later. 'A *Friend* is one of the highest characters that one human creature can shine in to another. There may be *Love*, that tho' it has no view but to honour, yet even in wedlock, ripens not into friendship. How poor are all such attachments! How much beneath the exalted notion I have of that noblest, that most delicate, union of souls!' (III, 338). This is *agape* – not 'the love called Platonic', which Harriet understands in the debased sense of repressed *eros* pretending to be ordinary friendship, but the Christianised Platonic concept at full strength. *Eros* (Lord L had agreed with Sir Charles) can be selfish, 'Friendship' cannot, and in a pure love they cannot be disunited. (The position is identical with that of Fielding's famous Preface on Love in *Tom Jones*; lacking only his insistence that where the two are united, *eros* heightens *agape*.) Sir Charles cannot offer her Love; but he can offer her this kind of Friendship irrespective of what happens with Clementina.

Finally, Richardson proceeds to use the Countess of D once more, to clarify in a last retrospect the significance of Sir Charles's behaviour to Harriet, and his own position as he sees it. The Countess is a good comic creation, as she smashes through social niceties and roots into complicated feelings, like some sublime rhinoceros let loose in a formal garden, happily convinced all the time that her social standing and good character are such that she cannot give offence. But she is also very useful to her creator as a device for making explicit what would otherwise be hidden, as she is allowed to produce her greatest triumphs of embarrassment yet. Harriet listens in some horror (and lively interest) to the account of how this formidable woman set off to tackle Sir Charles, whom she had never met, with some devastating point-blank questions about his intentions. What are his expectations with Clementina? Sir Charles is going to try to restore the stricken brother and sister, if he can, 'without one selfish hope', and 'As generosity, as justice, or rather as Providence, leads, I will follow' (IV, 9). So, he cannot in honour be under any engagements with Miss Byron? However much he might have been tempted, and it is clear to the Countess that he *is* in love with Harriet, he could not possibly in honour have tried to engage her affections. He cannot, then, take it amiss if

Lord D should try? No, he cannot, in justice and honour. 'God forbid, that *I*, a man divided *in myself*, not knowing what I *can* do, hardly sometimes what I *ought* to do, should seek to involve in my own uncertainties the friend I revere; the woman I so greatly admire' (IV, 11). She is a beautiful girl, she deserves to be happily married, Lord D is a good man with great advantages. If there is something of fierce satisfaction for a modern reader, at the sight of Sir Charles at last impaled on the thorns of 'ought'; it is no less true that the promise of the end of the library scene is being fulfilled. Sir Charles is coming alive in the manner of the art of 'is'. (Even his language is becoming the complex prose of 'is'; there is a faint but real possibility of acid undertones as he lists Lord D's advantages.) And what if events in Italy should free him from uncertainties? He has no right to hope that Harriet should wait for him. This would be to offer indignity both to her and to Clementina. He thinks himself obliged in honour to go to Italy, but he makes no conditions for himself. He is fettered, but both girls are free. Then Lady D produces her masterstroke, though she tells Harriet it was only to test his heart. Will he then, since he claims Harriet as a sister, use his brotherly influence on behalf of her son? But Sir Charles controls himself, and manages a good answer. It would be presumption to imagine he had such an influence on her – and this reinforces another point he has already made, which may be significant later. We need to be reminded that, though he must suspect something of Harriet's feeling for him, he cannot know what we do because he has seen much less of her. He has told the Countess that she has such command over her feelings, that no man will ever have a share in them, until he has courted her in a way that convinces her she has his whole heart. Now Harriet knows, and we know, how far from the truth this is. Yet Sir Charles may be genuinely uncertain what proportion of the signs he has seen is attributable to gratitude, what to soul-affinity, and what to love.

The effect of all this is a considerable clarification of his past behaviour. Harriet can now interpret correctly the riddling incoherence of his words in the library. She can also see a new deliberate significance in his prolonged absences, and in the 'brothering' and 'sistering' which had annoyed her all the more, when she saw how he had used the same technique to control the situation with Clementina. At the same time, in the new kind of 'drama', Sir Charles too has fixed his role by explicit declarations. But by the time the Countess descends on Harriet and tells her all this, he has left for Italy – having had to spend his last private moment with Harriet, fulfilling the embarrassing promise to tell her of the Countess's visit, and that she must be prepared to be tackled about Lord D again.

No sooner has the Countess finished her story, than she begins to serve Harriet as she had served Sir Charles. 'Let me ask you, as if I were your real mother, "Have you any expectation that Sir Charles Grandison will be yours?" ' (IV, 12). Harriet rises to the occasion. She thinks, 'from my heart', that he ought to be Clementina's husband; hence she must try to conquer the 'particular' feeling she has for him. He has offered her Friendship and she must be satisfied with that. But she has not a heart to give to any other man (IV, 13). Then the Countess at last reveals her plan. Another proposal has been made for her son. She would never consider the kind of suggestion she is about to put, were it to anyone but Harriet, but suppose she let the other proposal lie? and suppose they all agreed to wait until the fate of Sir Charles was settled? and let Lord D have 'the *first* preference if Sir Charles engages himself abroad'? (IV, 14). But Harriet immediately sees the relevance of one of Sir Charles's answers: to keep one person in suspense while you wait to see what will happen to the other, is to offer indignity to both. The Countess is forced to admit that she has never been 'so effectually silenced by a precedent produced by myself in the same conversation' (IV, 15). One is sorry her work is done.

The other main devices to fill the interval before Sir Charles's second Italian campaign are the marriage of Charlotte, and the arrival from Florence of Olivia. Yet that is a false way of putting it, for we can be sure we are looking from the right angle when we see how Richardson could claim, in his preface, that every scene in the novel was relevant to his design. In fact, Charlotte and Olivia present the contrast of two other kinds of drama, to set off the new kind that Richardson is developing. As against the drama of 'living-into' a role of 'ought' by raising one's heart, Charlotte and Olivia are trapped in defective roles, extremes of heartlessness and emotional extravagance, of their own devising, but not ultimately true to themselves.

Charlotte sees herself as Queen of Comedy, and will not give up the role even after she has promised to love, honour and obey Lord G. We need, however, to understand the psychological basis of her behaviour before we can grasp either the form her 'playfulness' takes or its moral significance. With Anderson, she had 'played with her passion till she lost it', and his unworthiness gave her 'an indifference to all men'. Moreover, she is in love with her brother, and can only see Lord G as infinitely inferior. (There is nothing as strong as 'incest', but Richardson's psychological insight is acute, as we shall see later on.) She prefers Lord G to all the other men she has known, but she over-values her own intelligence, and he is undoubtedly far from equal to her in that. She has no respect for his virtuoso interests. She hasn't the naturally loving heart of Harriet or Lady L; and because she does not feel anything deeply and is not in love with Lord G, she cannot enter into his feelings. She finds his demonstrativeness embarrassing and irritating; sees his pride in her as possessive; and cannot understand how much she wounds his self-respect. Because her own feelings are untouched she can remain calm in the tempests she stirs up, which gives her great advantage. This is an acute study of a certain kind of temperament in a loveless marriage; and it is important that we see how Charlotte's behaviour is partly a matter of her own nature, and the particular kind of strain put on it by her circumstances.

Nevertheless the way she behaves, if it has a psychological basis, is primarily a matter of the role in which she chooses to cast herself. Unlike Harriet, who perceives a role of 'ought' and struggles to raise herself to it, Charlotte chooses a role for her own amusement. She is 'playful' by nature, but in many ways it has been bad for her to discover how easily she can be forgiven by her sister, her brother, and Harriet, who preach at her, but never really threaten to withdraw affection. (Sir Charles, who comes closest to doing so, has the greatest power over her for just that reason.) She has been encouraged to regard herself as a privileged joker, and the 'play' she proceeds to cast herself and her husband in is a deliberate 'Comedy of Errors'. She exaggerates each of the things that irritate her, so that Lord G is cast as Clown: now foolish, childish and doting, now ridiculously overbearing and irate. The role has a basis, but she knows she is exaggerating. She perversely mistakes everything he says and does in order to fit them to some aspect of his role and, with her quicker intelligence, ties him in knots as soon as he tries to protest. Either she feigns displeasure, or casts herself in the infuriating role of sunny-tempered long-suffering wife. Because she feels nothing herself she can always stay calm while, more and more frequently, she goads him into losing his temper – and then she will smile sweetly, chat serenely, or play her harpsichord. The ease with which he forgives her prompts her to abuse her power over him still more. Though Harriet sees quite clearly that it is an act, a game, she also sees how dangerous it is because Lord G takes it so seriously. 'I now see it is and will be, his misfortune, that she can vex him without being vexed herself: And what may he expect, who can be treated with feigned displeasure, which, while it seems to be in earnest to him, will be a jest to his wife?' (III, 342). But Charlotte will listen to no warning that she may be wrecking her own happiness, for the simple reason that she playacts because she enjoys it. She cannot apparently grasp, for all her intelligence, how much she is hurting his feelings and damaging his self-respect, because she does not feel enough. Indeed, the pleasure of playacting is as ingrained in her as in Lovelace. It is the greatest pleasure of her life, and she shares Lovelace's tendency to obsessiveness, so dominated by her role that she cannot see what she is doing. But after two months of marriage Lord G is showing that his love itself may not be joke-proof, and Charlotte begins to come to her senses, before it is too late. She had told Harriet not to blame her heart, only her head, and she turns out to be capable of feeling, though it requires a threat of withdrawn affection to make feeling more important to her than self-amusement.

Olivia, on the other hand, is a Tragedy Queen. Vastly rich, 'Italianately' proud, she has unusual freedom to make her life what she would have it because of the way that great estates have devolved upon her. Her name may have been suggested by Shakespeare's heroine, but she chooses a role and a style more reminiscent of heroic tragedy. She sees herself as the magnificent woman, free to break through the confines of social convention and degree, and to give her heart grandly to a man capable of acting in an equally grand style. Though we do not yet know her full story, the hints we have are suggestive enough: that the relation began, appropriately, at the Opera, where Sir Charles's heroic behaviour in saving a lady from insult touched Olivia's heart, that she took the initiative in offering herself to him, making it clear that barriers of class, religion and nationality were nothing to her, that she was even prepared to cohabit with him and leave marriage in his power. The other side of the grand passion however is of course an 'Italian' impulse to revenge when her offer of herself is politely refused. She threatens to have him beaten up or assassinated in Florence (and an attempt is actually made on him later). Hearing that the hated Bolognese family have rejected him, she comes to London to offer herself again, only to find him on the point of setting out to Bologna once more. She then tries to stab him in his study. The 'revenge tragedy' however inevitably ends in anticlimax, not only in the obvious physical sense of her failure to kill him, but also in the more interesting psychological fact that the real Olivia, subsequently revealed to Harriet, is not tiger-hearted at all. Consequently the 'staginess' is not a failure of Richardson's art but part of his design; Olivia's melodrama is as deliberate as the unpleasant aftertaste of Charlotte's liveliness. Moreover, if our criticism had been that the art of 'ought' debarred the kind of drama we expect from complex characters in an art of 'is', Richardson pushes the question to 'comic' and 'tragic' extremes. Once again there is a tryptych; only this time the 'middle' panel is not simply 'ought', but an attempt to reconcile 'ought' and 'is' in a drama of moral role; while the outer panels show extremes of willed self-satisfaction, where the drama can be seen to arise from the characters' need to shape themselves and their circumstances to the image of their desires. Yet, though both women are sincere, in neither case does the self-chosen role correspond to the whole truth of their natures. The contrast is between an apparent insincerity in Harriet, which changes into a greater truth as she painfully struggles to achieve a selfless moral role; and an apparent sincerity, which leads Charlotte and Olivia in their different ways to falsify their situations, and ultimately their real selves.

With this, we are ready to judge the challenge Richardson posed himself, to reconcile 'ought' and 'is' in the far more testing circumstances posed to Sir Charles by the Porretta family in Bologna.

2

This is the central crisis of the novel as a whole, because 'ought' and 'is' have been brought together in a highly challenging situation. The more one has been prepared to make allowances for Richardson's chosen method, and to try to read the 'Sir Charles' story in terms of its own criteria, the more important it will be now that Richardson should justify that method by a convincing testing of 'ought' by 'is'. In the interval between the library scene and the arrival of Sir Charles in Bologna, he has produced a way of reconciling the two kinds of insight and imagination. Harriet's moral drama established a clear grasp of what she ought to feel as well as do, without in any way excluding a realistic exploration of the cost in conscious struggle, of trying to raise herself to her chosen role. Now, in Italy, Richardson poses his hero with an even more awkward problem; the most delicate he could devise – so difficult, indeed, that the normally assured moral paragon has to confess to the Countess that he hardly knows what he ought to do. Instead of a clash between right and wrong, or even between the 'great' and the merely 'good', he is caught at a cross-roads with no clearly marked route. In the situation itself there is room for considerable disagreement among equally moral judges; and Richardson invites the response of serious casuistry more strongly still by deliberate delaying tactics. While the crisis is taking place we are given a number of clues to the hero's thinking, but no full-scale discussion of the problem as a whole. Only after it is all over and he has returned to England will Sir Charles be allowed to argue a full case for his conduct, to Jeronymo and to Harriet. There is little doubt that this is because Richardson was determined to test his readers as well as his hero. So the problem of 'ought' itself is more awkward than ever before. On the other hand, in the library, and as he faced his grilling by the Countess, Sir Charles's very uncertainties have begun to bring him alive in terms of the art of 'is'. Expectations of a wholly new kind in his story have arisen: and because there is no straightforward 'ought', only a collision of opposed impulses and loyalties to two excellent women, the crisis seems bound to be one of consciousness at least as much as conscience. Whatever role Sir Charles chooses should hardly be less painful and costly than Harriet's, and will have to be convincingly earned in terms of inner conflict, and psychological as well as ethical 'delicacy'. 'A man divided in himself, not knowing what I *can* do, hardly sometimes what I *ought* to do' . . . the confession to the Countess of D holds inner conflict and problems of principle in a newly exacting tension; and the treatment and solution of the crisis will have to satisfy us in the same double way.

Richardson's preparation for the crisis, the treatment of achieved role in Harriet, suggests a suitable critical method: to establish first the nature of the role Sir Charles chooses to play, then the nature of his feelings, and finally a judgement how far there has been a reconciliation of the demands of 'ought' and 'is'.

The crisis falls into four distinct phases, marked by separate batches of letters to Dr Bartlett. In the first (IV, 112 ff.), the real concern is with Clementina's prospects of recovery under the influence of Grandison's return. The question of marriage is left deliberately open. In the second phase (IV, 222 ff.), the family is won over to the belief that she must be indulged in all her wishes, and the decision is left entirely to her. In the full expectation that she will choose to marry her chevalier, the terms are finally agreed, on the basis he had originally proposed. The last letter of this batch is sent away the day before he goes to hear her answer. In the third phase (IV, 279 ff.), Clementina astounds everyone by refusing him on religious grounds. At first both sides agree not to try to influence her; but after the Bishop and her Confessor have broken the conditions by responding to her appeal to them as Catholics, Sir Charles makes a final effort to persuade her that her faith would not be at risk if she married him. In the final phase (IV, 363 ff.), he has accepted her decision, and waits only to make sure that she will hold to her resolution. He urges her, as a brother, not to think of taking the veil.

What did Sir Charles mean by telling the Countess that his journey to Italy was 'indispensable'? 'As generosity, as justice, or, rather, as Providence leads, I will follow.' He obviously thinks it would be unjust and ungenerous to allow the Family's rejection of his terms to prevent him offering his help in the recovery of the stricken brother and sister, even though only some of the Porrettas have asked him to return. But when he told the Countess that both girls were free, while he was bound, he clearly meant that he felt bound not only to try to restore Clementina from her mental breakdown, but also to marry her if she and her family wish it. (There is in any case a direct connection, since the implicit assumption is that he can help precisely because she loves him so much.) He makes it clear to the Marchioness that this must be so in justice: 'I never yet made an offer, that I receded from, the circumstances continuing the same' (IV, 123). Harriet had made the same point long before. Since the very obligation of the terms he had offered, which Clementina had never refused, made it impossible to make any move toward Harriet, he feels that the only circumstances that have changed are his accession to the title and to his father's estates – and if the terms were just when they were offered, his new wealth and position cannot be allowed to make any difference. If justice requires him to be ready to stick to his offer, however, generosity demands that he should put self-interest out of the question. So he assures the Marchioness that the family are free from obligation; he overcomes the general's hostility by insisting that he will accept no decision in his favour that is not endorsed by all the Porrettas; and when the bright hopes of Clementina's recovery cause a change in her mother's behaviour, because she fears he may take advantage, he proves his disinterestedness by himself suggesting that he should try the effect of short absences. He goes to Florence for a fortnight, then to Naples for three weeks, to see whether her recovery is as dependent on him as it appears. If this 'justice' and 'generosity' put him in the hands of the Family, he also insists that he is in the hands of Providence above all. He must have no wish for himself; if Jeronymo can be restored physically and Clementina mentally, may 'Providence dispose as it pleases of me!' (IV, 139).

The interesting point about this chosen role is its *passivity*. Whatever we may have thought of Richardson's hero up till now, he has been a remarkably active moral agent. Yet the essence of his solution to the dilemma he is in, seems to be that he has no right to make any decision.

But as the first phase becomes the second, with the family's conviction that Clementina must be allowed to choose for herself, the role acquires more initiative. The discussion of terms calls on him to suppose Clementina his, and to make a series of decisions on that assumption. Here there was much room for contemporary controversy especially over his compromise about possible children, that the sons should be brought up as Protestants, but the daughters as Catholics. What seems most important however is simply to establish the careful balance in this, and all Sir Charles's thinking. If it is just that Clementina should be secured in her faith, with her own confessor, and her own personal attendants to provide a Catholic circle around her; it is no less just that Sir Charles should protect his household against zealous attempts at conversion, and should refuse to compromise his rights as its head. He clearly attempts a meticulous even-handedness. But generosity is also guaranteed, in his attitude to his wife, her servants, and his 'in-laws', and in the whole range of the financial settlements, where he makes it clear that self-interest has no part. For the mid-eighteenth century, his proposals strike one as notably liberal.

As the third phase opens, moreover, there seems to be a temporary change from the passive to the active. Just before he leaves to see Clementina, Sir Charles adds an interesting gloss to his trust in Providence, but he tells Count Belvedere that his attitude must change now. 'I have been willing to consider the natural impulses of a spirit so pure, though disturbed, as the finger of Providence. I have hitherto been absolutely passive: In honour I cannot now be so' (IV, 283). Once the objections of the family have been removed, it no longer seems just or generous to be a passive 'offering' to Clementina. But then she gives him her famous paper, beseeching him to be great enough to help her follow her conscience. He is dumbstruck at first: 'Never was I so little present to myself...' (IV, 297). The Porrettas underline what Clementina had made clear, that it is wholly in his power to make her surname what he pleases. They consider themselves still bound to him, and offer congratulations on her confession of her love. But Sir Charles himself is sure that he ought to revert to his previous passivity, and that her plea of conscience must override all others. 'God only knows, whether the ardent heart would be punished or rewarded, by the completion of its wishes: But this I know, that were Clementina to give me both her hand and her heart, and could not, by reason of religious doubts; be happy with me, I should myself be extremely miserable; especially if I had been earnest to prevail upon her to favour me against her judgment' (IV, 310). He readily consents to his part of the bargain that no effort to persuade her be made from either side; but when her brother the bishop and her confessor break the conditions, he does feel that honour obliges him to make one matching effort. But it is strictly circumscribed both in motive and point. The only valid motive is his concern for her female delicacy. When Clementina has the original conditions put to him for the first time as from herself, he is anxious, in refusing them, not to seem to refuse *her*, and allows it to appear that the family have merely sounded him out. Now the same concern for her delicacy prompts him to argue that a woman has a right to expect the man who claims to love her, to make one effort to assure her that she could be happy with him. At worst this will test her resolution, and they will both be easier in their minds afterwards. But he must not argue the merits and demerits of the two Faiths, and he must respect her conscience throughout – all he can and should do is make a last effort to assure her that her conscience has nothing to fear from marrying him. He fails, because the very effect of his tenderness seems to justify her distrust of her own power to hold out for what, when she is not with him, she knows to be the 'irresistible impulse' of her conscience (IV, 334). From this point Sir Charles accepts her decision absolutely. He must become her brother again, and it can only be in that capacity that he can urge her not to think of becoming a nun.

Richardson's first surprise for us at the crisis, then, is that the role of 'ought' his very active hero chooses, is a role of extraordinary passivity. It might therefore seem that the less Sir Charles can act, the more important it will become to show us the inner struggle of consciousness in the strong man who can hardly lift a finger in the circumstances he finds himself trapped in. But Richardson's second surprise is that, while he makes it perfectly clear that a severe struggle is taking place, we are only allowed to see the ripples on the surface of his prose to Dr Bartlett. The conflict in the depths is unexplored.

Sir Charles in his first two letters only mentions Harriet to congratulate himself on not having tried to involve 'that loveliest of women' in his difficulties (IV, 123), and to say that he is 'ready to think' that she will not be able to resist the persuasions of the Countess and her noble son (IV, 133). But between the two letters he has been taken ill, 'by a hurry of spirits; by fatigue; by my apprehensions for Jeronymo; my concern for Clementina; and by my too great anxiety for the dear friends I had so lately left in England. You know, Dr Bartlett, that I have a heart too susceptible for my own peace, tho' I endeavour to *conceal* from *others* those painful sensibilities, which they cannot relieve' (IV, 132-3). I think there is no doubt that we are meant to read between the lines here. The phrasing of both mentions of Miss Byron has the air of a man repeating a lesson to himself of which he has some need; and the 'sensibilities' and the 'too great anxiety' clearly spell 'Harriet' at least as much as anything else. At the same time we are given his motive for not opening his heart in his letters. After his first visit to Clementina and his quarrel with the general, he is taken ill again, badly enough to need to be bled. To his worries about Harriet and the stricken brother and sister has to be added a growing resentment of the Porrettas' failure to match his own attempts at justice and generosity.

In the second phase, Richardson allows his hero a momentary slip, but so ambiguously that we cannot be sure what it means. Mrs Beaumont has been telling him that 'there is a man whom she wishes to be Clementina's', and Sir Charles goes on, 'There is a woman – But – do thou, Providence, direct us both! All that thou orderest must be best!' (IV, 225). This looks like the first indication that Sir Charles's heart is really with Harriet all the time; but it is broken off before we can be certain. There is however a further hint in the next letter to keep suspicion alive; when the fancifulness of Clementina's dress, hinting the disorder of her mind, also brings the contrast with Harriet home to him. He is careful to equate the two girls, remembering the 'unaffected elegance' of Clementina as she used to be, but the reservation has its significance all the same (IV, 229).

But if at first we are only given this kind of hint, after the second phase even less is available. As the apparent certainty mounts that he will marry Clementina, hints of what he actually does feel are replaced by statements of what he ought to feel. The conclusion of the last letter of this batch, which leaves everyone in England in such cruel suspense, shows very clearly the switch to the language of ought and ought not. 'What, my dear Dr Bartlett, would I give, to be assured, that the most excellent of English-women, could think herself happy with the Earl of D.— ... Should Miss Byron be unhappy, and through my means, the remembrance of my own caution and self-restraint could not appease the grief of my heart. But ... What are these suggestions of tenderness – Are they not suggestions of *vanity* and *presumption*? They *are*. They *must* be so. I will banish them from my thoughts, as such. Ever-amiable Miss Byron! friend of my Soul! forgive me for them!' (IV, 248). We have the exact equivalent here of Harriet's 'wish' in the library that Clementina might marry Sir Charles. But the idea that it would be presumption to worry about Harriet's happiness would seem to lock the door on any hope of our witnessing the inner struggle, which alone could validate the wish and remove all hint of hypocrisy.

And so indeed it proves. From now on there is no mention of Harriet in connection with himself. After Clementina's refusal Sir Charles is indisposed again, but there is no hope of knowing whether feelings about Harriet still play any part in his sufferings. Indeed, when his last attempt to persuade the Italian girl fails, the evidence seems to be that his emotions are concentrated on Clementina. He is 'greatly dissatisfied with myself, yet hardly knowing why. I thought I wanted somebody to accuse, somebody to blame – Yet how could it be Clementina? ... It is difficult, my dear Dr Bartlett, at the instant in which the heart finds itself disappointed of some darling hope, to avoid reflexions that, however, can only be justified by self-partiality' (IV, 336-7). The 'darling hope' seems to indicate that Harriet is no longer in contention in his heart, and that the 'greatness' of Clementina's refusal has also been the moment when Sir Charles fell wholly in love with her. Yet the next sentence is suspicious, because it is framed so completely in the language of 'ought'. 'What must I be, if, led as I have been, by all her friends to hope, I had not been *earnest* in my hope!' The assumption that he could not feel anything besides the 'right' feeling is one that begs all the important questions. Now he has not only closed the doors of his heart to us, he has closed them to himself as well.

At the crisis then, Richardson not only makes his hero choose an almost completely passive role, but also allows him to prevent us from discovering what really goes on in his heart and mind. At best we are given only veiled hints and guesses by implication; but then even these are obliterated by his determination to admit only what he ought to feel, not what he actually does. Instead of the equivalent of Harriet's struggle to earn her moral role, and to learn to feel as she ought by overcoming other feelings, we are confronted with a closing-off of consciousness, leaving only 'public' words and behaviour to judge.

We have yet, of course, to hear Sir Charles's final confession of what did go on in his heart and mind, in those accounts to Jeronymo and Harriet that Richardson held back until after his return to England. But since Richardson went to such lengths to test his readers, it might be valuable to take up the challenge on the basis of what we know now. My readers might like to examine their own responses at just this point, and formulate what they would like to have said at one of those gatherings in the grotto at North End . . .

The main objections of Sir Charles's handling of the crisis are likely to concentrate on three points. The first of these is put by Uncle Selby, and even more strongly by Olivia, writing before Sir Charles leaves Italy. 'Unworthy Grandison! . . . You who could leave her', (i.e. Harriet), 'and, under colour of honour, when there was no pre-engagement, and when the proud family had rejected you, prefer to such a fine young creature, a romantic Enthusiast . . .' (IV, 423). This is to question whether Sir Charles need have felt bound to Clementina at all. The second objection would allow some obligation, but sees a gross oversimplification in the notion that circumstances have not changed. For Harriet has fallen in love with him, and he cannot be wholly blind to the signs of this, even if he cannot know it as surely as we do.

What about his obligation to her, then? Thirdly, it can hardly be questioned that his own feelings have been engaged, as they were not when he proposed terms to the Porrettas. Is not this a change of circumstance of the most crucial kind?

If we imagine the debate at North End, however, and a reply from the kind of reader the Master longed for, one can conceive answers on the basis of what we already know, without needing to appeal yet to whatever Sir Charles may have to say for himself.

The crucial point in answering the first objection is that Clementina herself has never been given the chance to say 'yes' or 'no' to Sir Charles's proposal. *That* is why he cannot consider himself released by the family's rejection of his terms, especially since her mental breakdown was obviously connected with her love for him. The answer to the second objection is that he could not possibly be held responsible for Harriet's feelings in the same way, since he has, wholly honourably, done everything in his power to avoid engaging her affections. Moreover, possibly the clearest single piece of evidence we have of his thinking at the crisis, was concerned precisely with Harriet's happiness. But that reminds us, not only that he cannot know what we know about her heart, but also that he has to guard against the vanity and presumption of even suspecting she could have fallen so deeply in love, when he had made no move. To the third point, about his own feelings, the answer would be that if it were right to believe that only Clementina could release him from his proposal, and that he was responsible for her mental stability and happiness as he could not be for Harriet's, then it would be right to suppress whatever he felt for Harriet if Clementina accepted him.

It is at just this point however that the argument becomes more subtle and more interesting. For if the last point be granted, and Sir Charles's problem became that of reconciling a principled decision with his conflicting feelings towards the two girls, it would seem as important for his integrity that his feelings for Harriet should be proved delicate, true and tender, as that they should be convincingly overruled. Now how could this be proved unless they *engage* with his feelings for Clementina; unless the pain of their suppression guarantees their genuineness; and unless the question of whether they *can* be effectively overcome is openly raised and resolved? For this affects the delicacy and tenderness of his feelings for Clementina too. If we are expected to admire Clementina for facing up to the question of whether she could make Sir Charles happy in the light of her religious scruples, can we admire Sir Charles for never apparently facing up to the question of whether he could make Clementina happy in the light of his feelings for Harriet? Lastly, ought there not to be at least a question of whether the existence of those feelings should be confessed? – whatever the decision might be in the light of Clementina's precarious stability.

What is significant about this development of the argument is the way that questions of 'ought' have become utterly inseparable from questions of 'is': the need to know what Sir Charles actually does feel, at the time. If he is to convince us imaginatively of his ideal goodness, it cannot be sufficient to judge on the basis of his actions alone, or his feeling for Clementina alone. He is under no 'obligation' to Harriet; but the integrity of his behaviour to *Clementina* is inextricably bound up with the conflict between his feelings for the two girls. Moreover the obvious danger of the passivity he chooses, even if it be judged right, is that he will seem to have become merely a creature of circumstance and not a moral agent at all, unless we can be convinced of the integrity of his heart. And what have we to go on, since Richardson has allowed him to close the door on that heart, and firmly avert his own eyes from introspection?

The signs begin to point to a crucial and damaging miscalculation at the heart of the novel; for the only possible rescue will lie in Sir Charles's own retrospective self-justification, and there may well be a doubt as to whether this could be a really effective substitute for convincing experience of his consciousness at the time.

The letter to Jeronymo is no help at all. It confirms that

Clementina was his first love; that he imputed her sufferings to her love of him; and that consequently he felt his honour involved in keeping himself free until her destiny was decided. But when he met Harriet, this obligation caused him 'uneasiness' for the first time, though he was not sure of succeeding with the English girl even had he been free. So much we already knew . . . the only interesting thing is the hint of evasiveness in the word 'uneasiness'. But as Sir Charles goes on to give us the first new insight, the evasiveness becomes even more marked. 'Shall I, my dear Jeronymo, own the truth?—The two noblest-minded women in the world, when I went over to Italy . . . held almost an equal interest in my heart' (V, 40). Which was more equal than the other? The fact that he is writing to Clementina's brother makes the evasion suggest that it must have been Harriet. This would make it all the more important that Italian delicacies should be satisfied about the rightness of his then coming within an ace of marrying Clementina; but Sir Charles continues overly diplomatic. As Clementina's recovery confirmed her feeling for him and the importance of his attachment to her, he says that he 'contented' himself with wishing the English lady a worthier husband than he could be in his embarrassed situation, and when the whole family wished their daughter to be his, 'I had not a wish but for your Clementina'. But this is to beg precisely the real question of the *nature* of the resolution of conflicting feelings, and the conviction it can carry. It is not enough to think one ought to feel something, and then assume that every other feeling is banished – if this could be done, it would say very little for the integrity of the heart that could manage it. On this interpretation of 'almost equal', the best that could be said for the diplomacy of the letter is that it succeeds in blurring the issue for Clementina. When she reads and comments on it some time later, (V, 273 ff.), she reacts to Sir Charles's confession of his feeling for Harriet by a spasm of outraged delicacy, that he remained tied to her only through compassion. But when she comes to 'almost equal', she construes it in her own favour, and the further question vanishes. But even so, in the rarefied atmosphere of delicacy in which we are moving, it should not vanish quite so easily – one would expect her to ask searching questions about the nature of 'contented' and 'not a wish' that she does not ask – or at the very least to wonder why Harriet was never mentioned to her at all. And, in any case, which *is* the right interpretation of Sir Charles's riddling phrase? The only thing we can be certain of, is that he has not owned the whole truth.

We are left then with his very last chance, his statement to Harriet – and it is left exceeding late. But it starts well: 'altho' what I have to say, may, I presume, be collected from what you know of my story . . . something, however, may be necessary to be said . . . of the state of my own heart . . . And I will deliver myself with all the truth and plainness which I think are required' (V, 106). At least there should be no ambiguity now. He confesses his attraction to her from the first moment, but that it was his growing knowledge of her mind and behaviour that led him into a 'gentler, yet a more irresistible passion', especially since there seemed 'no *probable* hope' of Clementina (V, 107). But because of his obligation to the Italian girl, he took himself to task, and saw as little of Harriet as he possibly could. He detected the wishes of his sisters and Lord L, and sometimes thought that he could hope for Harriet's love by their interest, but he would not permit himself to hope, and resolutely made himself ascribe all signs of Harriet's favour to her natural goodness of heart, and to her powerful sense of gratitude. But, finding that his feeling for her continued to increase, he had no way left but 'to strengthen my heart, in Clementina's cause, by Miss Byron's assistance' (V, 108). *That* is why he told her the story in the library, knowing that this would deprive him of any hope of encouragement to break his obligation, and that it would engage Harriet's generosity on Clementina's behalf.

So far, this is distinctly good. We could not have inferred the motive with absolute assurance, but it is wholly convincing, because with it all the signs of Sir Charles's feelings for Harriet fall into place alongside the strength of his sense of obligation to Clementina, without either weakening the other. His behaviour in the library, and his incoherence at the end, also become even more poignant and understandable, and for perhaps the first time in the novel Richardson's hero can command undiluted sympathy. Moreover this is increased, as we learn for the first time what happened as he left the library in high discomposure. He asks Dr Bartlett to advise him, and help him compose himself, and he tells the Doctor three things we have never seen clearly (V, 109). He has no hope of conquering the opposition of all the Porrettas. He cannot help resenting the way they have treated him. And above all, he has no doubt that even were they to comply with his terms, he would be happier with Harriet because of the differences in nationality and religion. Moreover, though Dr Bartlett admires Clementina and is very sorry for her, he 'next to adored' Harriet... and he advises Sir Charles accordingly.

This makes the question whether or not to continue to feel bound to Clementina even more agonised than we knew, and brings the first stage of the moral argument to the sharpest possible focus. But Sir Charles meets the challenge admirably. He reminds the Doctor, and himself, not only that Clementina never refused the proposal, but that the terms were acceptable to her and 'she even besought her friends to comply with them' (V, 109). If he was determined to await either her recovery or her release before he met Miss Byron, 'will Miss Byron herself, if she knows that, forgive me (the circumstances not changed) for the change of a resolution of which Clementina was so worthy?' (V, 110). The repetition of the phrase about circumstances in this new context removes the objection to it. It clearly means only his change of rank and fortune, and it does not mean that he ignores the difference that meeting Miss Byron has made. Only, he sheds on it a new light that is genuinely delicate and tender to Harriet: the question of whether she would be happy to know that her courtship was based on a broken obligation? The way that Clementina has been treated, for his sake (as she wrote in her disordered letter); the fact that she still wants to see him; the possibility that he could restore her to her right mind; surely these things confirm that he should not try to engage Harriet's affections? 'Could I be happy in my own mind, were I to try, and to succeed? And if not, must I not be as ungrateful to her, as ungenerous to the other?' *This* is the real core of the problem: that to break the obligation to the Italian girl is to offer a flawed relationship to the English one. Harriet would not be happy in herself if she knew; and Sir Charles's unhappiness would be bound to affect the relationship still further. Moreover, as things stand, he cannot be responsible for Harriet as he is for Clementina.

Harriet and her friends at Selby House have nothing to say to this; and nor, I believe, have we. It seems to me a complete defence of Sir Charles's behaviour, a satisfactory answer to the whole first part of the moral argument, and the only trouble about it is that it has been left so late that it can no longer inject into the whole of the Italian crisis the inner life and imaginative sympathy that there might have been at the time.

But the second half of the moral problem remains: the question of Sir Charles's conflicting feelings in Italy, and the nature of their resolution. If anything, it is rendered more challenging by our new knowledge that he would have preferred Harriet before he arrived in Bologna, so that our reading of his letter to Jeronymo was right, and Clementina's was mistaken. Most important of all, his defence of himself has now seized on the crucial point that he can only offer a valid relationship to one girl if he has come to a satisfactory resolution of his feelings towards the other. What was delicacy on Harriet's behalf must be delicacy also on Clementina's, even if there is no 'obligation' to Harriet.

Alas – the second half of Sir Charles's self-defence evades the issue in the familiar way. It is little more than a summary, half a page as against the four and a half devoted to the conflict before he left for Italy. He says that Clementina on her restoration, 'shone upon us all even with a brighter lustre than she did before her disorder', and that 'what was before *honour* and *compassion*, now became *admiration*; and I should have been unjust to the merits of so excellent a woman, if I could not say, *Love*'

(V, 111). But the question of love is not and cannot be a question of Clementina's merits alone. We can accept that he now cared more deeply for the Italian girl than ever before, but this does nothing to clarify the nature and the resolution (for both their sakes) of the conflict of loves, unless the answer be that he now genuinely found that he loved Clementina so much more, not than he had loved before, but than he had loved Harriet. But that could not be expressed in terms of 'justice' to Clementina. He goes on, that now, concluding himself already the husband of Clementina, the welfare and happiness of Harriet were 'the next wish of my heart', and that he rejoiced that he had not entangled her. But he then 'devoted myself wholly to Clementina – *I own it*, *Ladies* – And had I thought, Angel as she came out, upon proof, that I could not have given her my heart, I had been equally unjust, and ungrateful'. Again circumlocution and fudging blur the question, by seeking to make love an 'ought', a question of justice and not of fact. There could only have been three possible resolutions after a fully honest and searching examination of what he actually felt for both women. He could have decided that he loved Harriet too much to make an honourable husband to Clementina. Or he could have decided that he now loved Clementina so much more than Harriet that the question no longer arose. Or he could have decided that he could not love Harriet so much that it became possible for him to break both his obligations and his new feeling; and that, having proved by painful struggle that it was possible to overcome his feelings for the English girl, he could conscientiously hope to make Clementina an honourable and loving husband. But that would not be loving in 'justice' to Clementina's merits; it would be loving despite Harriet's, and his own feelings for her, because his heart and conscience could not be easy over broken obligation. Now Sir Charles's formulation will not allow us to clarify which of the last two of these was the case, since the language of 'ought' allows him so easily to sidestep the question of what he actually felt for Harriet at the time. And it is surely very important that Harriet, and we, should know? For the essence of the novel has been Richardson's determination to imagine an *ideal* goodness, even excessively ambitious to overcome, not only normal human frailty and conflict, but also normally sufficient ethics. It might be very human and natural to seek to draw a veil over the actual situation for a normal hero, situated as Sir Charles is situated and speaking to Harriet. But if we have been prepared to repress criticisms based on the normative and the natural, in order to give Richardson's idealism a chance to justify itself, he cannot be rescued by appeals to such standards now. Sir Charles for the one and only time is supposed to be speaking with full truth and plainness about the state of his heart. If the second possibility was the case, then Harriet is his second choice, not a true love barred only by circumstances which have now been removed. If the third possibility was the case, then her delicacy surely might like to pose the question of how much of a struggle it was for Sir Charles to come to his decision. And we have only to reverse the position to see that the same would hold true for Clementina; while the question of whether it was right that she should never know a syllable of the matter until after she had made her decision, is never even raised.

There is perhaps one last gloss that we should look at, before deciding the significance of all this. Clementina was allowed to comment on the letter to Jeronymo, albeit deluding herself over its ambiguity; but Harriet is not allowed to comment on Sir Charles's account of himself to her. What we get instead is a full-blooded endorsement in every detail from Charlotte, in what can only be described as a curtain-lecture. 'The Lady's merits shine out with transcendent lustre in the eyes of every one... Must they not in *his*, to whom *Merit* was ever the *first*, *Beauty* but the *second*, attractive? He had no tie to any other woman on earth: He had only the tenderness of his own heart, with regard to Miss Byron, to contend with. *Ought* he not to have contended with it? He *did*; and so far conquered, as to enable himself to be *just* to the Lady, whose great qualities, and the concurrence of her friends in his favour, had converted Compassion for her into Love . . . But with what tenderness, with what politeness, does he . . . express himself of Miss Byron! He declares, that if *she* were not to be happy, it would be a great abatement of his own felicity. You, however, remember how politely he recalls his apprehensions that you may not on his account, be altogether so happy as he wishes, as the suggestions of his own presumption; and censures himself for barely supposing, that he had been of consequence enough with you to give you pain' (V, 128). One fears that this disposes of the last possibility that Richardson may have been challenging his readers to surpass his hero in delicacy, by finding the right criticism. The thumping italics sound unmistakably like the Master's foot tapping the floor, and suggest that this is to be taken as the official summing up.[1] And if Charlotte's hero-worship of her brother is always irritating, as providing the first violin in that orchestra of praise which has bespoken our response from the start, it is even more irritating than usual when it betrays the author's miscalculation. For even if we were to grant that love should follow merit so obediently (which is questionable enough), one need only riposte that Harriet too had transcendent merit to show that the real question is being fudged. It may well be that he ought to have conquered his feeling for Harriet – the suggestion is that the third possibility was the right one – but the crux for Harriet's delicacy would be the knowledge of how painful and difficult it was to do so, and that would be important for Clementina too. Lastly, the argument of presumption is just too easy an escape from *all* thought of Harriet. To put oneself in Harriet's place would I think be to prefer his anxiety for her to his 'politeness', because it is a truer indication of his love. But even if that were not so, it is precisely the strength of his love for her, and not his responsibility for her happiness, that is the real crux. The too-easy escape about presumption allows all eyes, including the hero's and

[1] Richardson told Lady Bradshaigh (14 February 1754, Carroll, *Letters*, 285) that one of his 'great views' in the novel was to show the 'Vincibility' of Love; but Eaves and Kimpel have a right to their irony when they suggest that Sir Charles is 'convincingly vincible'. (*Richardson*, 392.)

apparently his creator's, to be averted from the area of consciousness where the real conflict, and hence the real justification, could be found and proved. On the evidence we have, the most charitable account of the hero's behaviour might well be that he simply decided his obligation could not be broken, trusted to luck or providence in complete passivity, closed his eyes to everything but the welcome fact that he found himself feeling more for Clementina than he had done before . . . and was lucky. Yet that is hardly an account of ideal goodness and integrity. Ethical mountains have laboured and produced, alas, a moral mouse – to unmerited fanfares of applause.

I do not myself think that Richardson cheated, though one can see that in some ways his task of bringing Sir Charles and Harriet together might have been made more difficult by greater explicitness about Sir Charles's feelings at the crisis. Rather the evidence seems to suggest that he was uneasy about something in his treatment, yet unsure where that something lay. The close of the last of the second batch of letters, when Sir Charles seems certain to marry Clementina, says simply: ' "In the highest of our pleasures, the sighing heart will remind us of imperfection." It is fit it should be so' (IV, 249). And though Harriet is not permitted to comment on Sir Charles's final statement – a fact that could point either to deliberate evasion, or to obscure unease – she is allowed one remark that seems to indicate the latter. 'But still . . . something sticks with me (and ought it not?) in relation to the noble Clementina!' (V, 138). On the surface, both remarks arise from the awareness that a resolution is being achieved at the cost of others; but both seem to have wider reverberations too. The most interesting evidence of all, however, is Harriet's earlier reactions to the last letter Sir Charles writes in the third phase, when he is fairly certain that Clementina will hold to her resolution not to marry him, but is waiting to be quite sure. He has had letters from England, and has something to say about all the people he cares about, with the careful omission of Harriet. And noticing this, she comments also on the absence of any mention of her in all the letters of the third phase – but she praises him for his justice and delicacy: 'For, could Sir Charles Grandison excusably (if, on *other* occasions he remembred the poor girl whom he rescued; could he excusably, I say) while his soul was agitated by his own suspense, occasioned by the uncommon greatness of Clementina's behaviour, think of any other woman in the world?' (IV, 360). It becomes clearer than ever how consistently Richardson the imaginative artist has been blinded by Richardson the didactic moralist. The central miscalculation comes from a moral dogmatism, that insists his character must only think what he feels morally authorised to think. But the true artist in Richardson then produces a psychological rebellion of a significantly subversive kind. At the end of the letter, Harriet goes on to draw an apparently complimentary contrast between Sir Charles and Adam, which converts itself in the act of voicing it, to a curious kind of involuntary sarcasm. 'But is not his conduct such as would make a considerate person, who has any connexions with him, tremble? Since if there be a fault *between* them, it must be *all* that person's; and he will not, if it be possible for him to avoid it, be a sharer in it? Do you think, my dear, that had he been the first man, he would have been so complaisant to his Eve as *Milton makes Adam* ... To taste the forbidden fruit, because he would not be separated from her, in her punishment, tho' all *posterity* were to suffer by it? – No; it is my opinion, that your brother would have had gallantry enough to his fallen spouse, to have made him extremely regret her lapse; but that he would have done *his own duty*, were it but for the sake of posterity, and left it to the Almighty, if such had been his pleasure, to have annihilated his first Eve, and given him a second – But, my dear, do I not write strangely? I would be chearful, if I could, because you are so kind as to take pains to make me so. But on re-perusing what I have written, I am afraid that you have taught me to think oddly' (IV, 362).

It would not be too much to claim, I think, that its 'oddness' makes this the most crucial passage in the novel. For it is not only psychologically acute, as only Richardson could be in the eighteenth century, it also implies a radical diagnosis of what has gone wrong, that would have enabled Richardson to rewrite the crisis and turn disaster into triumph, if he had really understood and trusted what he had been imaginatively driven to make Harriet write.

In the first place Harriet reveals that curious trait of the psychology of reading that makes good characters so hard to draw sympathetically in fiction: the instinctive rebellion of flawed humanity against the depiction of a character who is set up to be better than one is oneself; and the instinctive impulse to find fault. Yet Richardson obviously embodied this without understanding it,[1] or his entire work would have been more tactful. For no human being, least of all the 'common reader', only thinks what it is right to think. Secondly, in producing a staggering example of absolute rectitude of *conduct*, that is at the same time intolerable inhumanity, Harriet unconsciously places her finger on the gap between 'ought' and 'is' that Richardson has allowed to be reopened at the crisis. For if we really think about the Sir Charles/Adam, the point is *not* that his conduct could be faulted, and that he would be a better man to behave as the Adam of Genesis did. A. J. A. Waldock, writing not about Richardson but about *Paradise Lost*, cites the passage as part of his argument that the story of the Fall is 'a bad one for God'.[2] But no Christian or Jew could accept that. Theologically, it can only be a bad story if there is no belief in God's love for man, or man's ability to love God. And imaginatively, in fictional terms, it can only be a bad story for God if there is a failure to make love between man and God as real in terms of consciousness as love between man and woman. If we could be imaginatively convinced of the reality of Sir Charles/Adam's love of God, and just as convinced of the reality of his love of Eve; if after experiencing a really painful inner conflict that guaranteed

[1] He came closest, after his novels were written, in a letter to Lady Echlin, 10 October 1754 (Carroll, *Letters*, 315), 'A good Character is a Gauntlet thrown out. As some apprehend, it reflects upon themselves, they perhaps think they have a Right to be affronted.'

[2] A. J. A. Waldock, *Paradise Lost and its Critics* (Cambridge, 1947 reprinted 1961), 18, 53.

the power and integrity of both feelings, we were then to see him agonisedly deciding that his obligation to God was the greater, and that his love for his woman must be suppressed, the hatefulness of his conduct would totally disappear, and we would be left with a kind of tragic grandeur. What Harriet puts her finger on, without understanding it, is the intolerable complacency that comes from the absence of realised inner conflict and torn consciousness; the insensitivity not only to what humans are, but also to what they should be, of the idea that rightness of conduct is all, and that the good man is he who feels only as he is authorised.

But this is the single spasm of Richardson the imaginative artist at the crisis, and it remains a sad might-have-been in the Pyrrhic victory of Richardson the moralist. Yet Harriet's *jeu d'esprit* also enables us to see how close the disaster at the heart of *Sir Charles Grandison* was to becoming a triumph, and to make a critical and not merely a moral diagnosis of what went wrong. For just as the fault does not lie in the rectitude of the conduct of Sir Charles/Adam, there is no real objection to the conduct of Sir Charles in Italy. What went wrong is that Richardson failed to hit on an artistic way of probing his hero's consciousness. Throughout his work, as it is the purpose of this study to show, Richardson's greatest achievements came when his *form* enabled him to free himself from his moralistic straitjacket. Clarissa, too, deluded herself that to say she should not feel something, was to say that she did not feel it. And Richardson the didactic moralist never budged from his heavy insistence that she felt only 'conditional liking' for Lovelace: that is, that her feeling was conditional on his moral reform. But the art of Clarissa is far deeper and more subtle than its author in his everyday didactic self, and it is so because his dramatic form allows him to probe Clarissa's heart, and reveal that she is indeed in love with her tormentor. The fact that her letters are scrutinised by Anna, who continually questions what she says, picks up implications, and insists on her examining herself more closely, means that she is driven (and her creator is driven) deeper and deeper into her consciousness. Now it is clear from our analysis of the hints in the first and second phases in Italy, and from the evidence of Sir Charles's illnesses, that an inner conflict *did* take place, and that he was indeed deeply disturbed about Harriet, and not like Sir Charles/Adam in his complacency about Eve. What went wrong, therefore, was that the absence of a formal equivalent of Anna meant the absence of stimulus to Richardson to probe that conflict, unsatisfied by arguments about presumption and rectitude, when the time came for Sir Charles to face the implications of marrying Clementina, and of being refused by her. Doctor Bartlett could have fulfilled such a function, particularly since he 'next to adored' Harriet (V, 109) and could have been vigilant in upholding his end of the argument he and Sir Charles had had in the library. But the correspondence would have had to be confidential. As things are, Sir Charles is clearly aware that his letters will be read by his sisters and their husbands, and that they are also likely to be sent to Harriet, as indeed they are. No baring of the heart is possible under such conditions – but it need not have been so.

If there had been a probing of Sir Charles's heart and mind, as deep as Anna's probing of Clarissa, I think it is possible that *Grandison* might have become an impressive novel of a very unusual kind. It would never have been as powerful as *Clarissa*; but the battle between a double love and a double conscience might have been explored with the subtlety and psychological depth that Richardson at his best could undoubtedly command. The recoil of turbulent emotions when the apparent resolution was overthrown by the surprise of Clementina's refusal, could have provided possibly the greatest psychological challenge in the whole of his work to the 'master of the heart'. In such a case, I believe the drawbacks of the art of 'ought' in the story of Sir Charles up to the library scene would have fallen into place as a necessary part of the total strategy. For the freedom to explore his idealism would have established the 'excessive' criteria against which Sir Charles would have to measure himself, while the new conflict between equal 'goods' would have ensured that he continued to come alive as he had begun to do in the library. Our objections to the unnatural ease of Sir Charles's conduct, when confronted only with the choice of right against wrong, or the great against the merely good, would have disappeared when we experienced the pain of his struggle between opposing 'greatnesses'. 'Ought' could have been reconciled with 'is'; and though the novel would always have had the rarefied atmosphere of Richardson's high conceptions of 'delicacy', it could have been an achievement to anticipate the subtleties of James or Proust.

As it is, however, the novel fails at the crisis, and because it fails, the allowances that one had been prepared to make in the first half, are betrayed. The method Richardson chose, the separation of 'ought' and 'is' in the two stories, could only justify itself when the two were brought into effective and illuminating mutual challenge. When, after careful preparation, Richardson failed to make and meet this challenge, the obliteration of 'is' by 'ought' means that the whole novel collapses into the mode of didacticism, and an unacceptable morality at that. The Harriet story of the first half remains a considerable achievement, and the temporary flickering of Sir Charles into psychological life an unfulfilled promise. Yet the book is broken-backed in the middle, and it must be doubtful whether it could hope for much life in the concluding volumes.

3

Before we proceed, however, Richardson's second heroine deserves to be considered in her own right. In seeking to treat the conflict between her love and her Catholicism Richardson was proposing an original challenge at a time when the '45 rebellion was a very recent memory. The nearest analogy is probably *Eloisa to Abelard*, forty years earlier – from which Richardson may have borrowed the 'tutorial' relationship – but Pope's story was an old one, safely cushioned in its pre-Protestant setting; and its author was himself a Catholic. Moreover Pope's poem sets extremes in collision, illicit love warring against divine dedication; while Clementina's crisis is like Grandison's, essentially a conflict between two undoubted 'goods', where the issues are made as arguable as possible. We have to ask whether the treatment of Clementina seeks to reconcile 'ought' and 'is' like the treatment of Harriet, or whether it is open to the same objections as the treatment of Sir Charles. Moreover, Clementina's derangement invites comparison with Clarissa's. In the earlier novel, the exploration of madness became not only the most honest treatment of the subject since Shakespeare, with genuine insight into the unconscious; but it also had a deeply functional purpose. Only by probing behind the consciousness which could be explained by environment, upbringing and custom, could Richardson hope to probe the moral integrity of his heroine, and disprove Lovelace's theory about the nature of the female heart. Consequently the madness of Clarissa is no sentimentality, but perhaps the novel's greatest imaginative success, and the guarantee of its author's integrity. Can the same be said of Clementina?

Richardson's first difficulty was the formal one: that in treating Clementina through Grandison's letters, there could be no straightforward access to her mind. But though Richardson begins narratively, with a run-through of the whole story in Grandison's account to Harriet in the library, we can then see, in the 'extracts' from his letters by Dr Bartlett, an interesting attempt to make the treatment more dramatic than is really credible. When Sir Charles tackles Clementina about Belvedere, there is little attempt at the epistolary. The scene is printed in fully dramatic form with the names of characters heading their speeches – and it is difficult to imagine Sir Charles writing it like that. All his other letters have been uncompromisingly narrative even when they contained dialogue. The two following scenes, the one in the garden when Sir Charles tries to discover the reason for her melancholy, and Mrs Beaumont's account of her success in doing so, are also given largely in pure dialogue. Richardson seems determined to give us direct access to Clementina herself at this early stage, as far as he can. As we read between the lines, therefore, Clementina's irritation when Sir Charles speaks on Belvedere's behalf, and the movement of the conversation in the garden from her 'secret' to his heresy, create a convincing sense of her love for him in terms of the art of 'is'. And the scene with Mrs Beaumont allows Clementina to speak out in her own words, confessing both her love and her apparent determination never to marry a heretic.

This is quite a good beginning. We see Clementina under several kinds of pressure and should have no difficulty in feeling for her. She loves Sir Charles. But to do so is to go against the desire of her whole family that she should marry Belvedere, and to raise the familiar Richardsonian problem of filial duty. Meanwhile her confessor, alarmed by her attraction to her Protestant tutor, has been terrifying her about the consequences of entanglement with heresy. She feels that she cannot confess to her love, yet she is everlastingly being pestered to explain her rejection of Belvedere, and her melancholy, which she cannot do without admitting that she has loved (like Harriet) before the man has made any move, and has also loved (unlike Harriet) where neither her family nor her confessor would approve. The nagging voice of Camilla is forever in her ears; and when we remember how little privacy was available to an eighteenth century girl, and especially an Italian, there is no difficulty in understanding why she should feel low spirited. The more this is so, the more she is upset by appearing obstinate and ungrateful to her parents and to her faithful servant.

Her explanation to Mrs Beaumont also enables us to take the comparison with Harriet a step further, in an interesting variation of the drama of moral role. Sir Charles, increasingly uncomfortable in a household filled with excitement by the success of Bonny Prince Charlie, decides to leave for Vienna. Clementina raises herself from her melancholy, and bids him goodbye with an apparent cheerfulness, and a sisterly affection, that for the moment fool her family and herself. Like Harriet, she is trying to raise herself to a heroism of 'ought' – but she cannot sustain it, and collapses afterwards into deeper melancholy than ever, but with the first hints of derangement. This is not because she is a weaker character than Harriet, but rather that Harriet seeks to intensify genuine impulses whereas Clementina seeks to deny her true feelings.

Richardson begins from the 'lover's melancholy' of *Twelfth Night*, a famous quotation from which she repeats to Sir Charles in the garden. She broods, is silent, seeks solitude, sighs, and the worm of concealment feeds on her damask cheek. But Richardson strengthens and de-sentimentalises his portrait through the religious element in the conflict; and begins to develop it into derangement with an astuteness worthy of the 'master of the heart'. For he sees in Clementina's melancholy the seeds of what we might now call a schizoid state. The day after Sir Charles's departure, having nobody to confide in, and no privacy, she shuts the door of her room, places a chair with its back to Camilla, and talks earnestly to an empty closet (III, 27-8). She is not talking to Sir Charles, as a merely romantic heroine would, but to her alter ego: the part of herself which insists that he is lovable; which must be hidden because of the terrors with which Father Marescotti had filled her, but which demands a kind of utterance her own lips cannot speak, only answer. Unfortunately Richardson makes no more than a beginning with this, and her mother's entrance breaks it off; but it is an interesting beginning.

We may however notice one essential direction in which Richardson has not yet managed to probe. We have been *told* that her confessor has terrified her and made her feel guilty, but we have experienced neither the harangues themselves nor, more important, the nature of their impact on her consciousness. Richardson has not created the specifically Catholic sensibility he is required to create if her derangement is to be convincing. We need to know the arguments; but we need even more to know the way they are taken home to her imagination and her feelings, and how they play against her love in the depths of her being. Without this the treatment is bound to be superficial compared with the real breakthrough into inner being that we experience with Clarissa. Protestant readers (for whom, after all, Richardson was mainly writing) will remain imaginatively unconvinced of the intensity of her trouble and there may be a danger that the failure to earn her derangement will make it seem overdrawn, or sentimental. Since Richardson is creating her in terms of the art of 'is', this may become serious, though it is not yet too late.

After Mrs Beaumont's discovery, the family proves less radically opposed to the alliance than Clementina expected, though they will insist that Sir Charles change his religion and live in Italy. He is summoned back from Vienna, and a meeting with Clementina is arranged before he learns the terms. At first she is too embarrassed to speak, but when they meet in the orange grove there is another convincing scene in terms of the art of 'is'. She is clearly ashamed of having taken the initiative, but she is also afraid, knowing the terms, that she may be humiliated by their rejection, and prickly about that too. Yet she is also ashamed of her petulance, and Camilla is 'afraid of her elevations' (III, 106). Pride allows her to assume a dignity that refusal will obviously demolish; and in her dissatisfaction with herself the seeds of her melancholy still lie dormant. 'If I hated the bitterest enemy I have, as *much* as at times I hate myself, I should be a very bad creature. This was spoken with an air so melancholy, as greatly disturbed me' (III, 110).

The inevitable happens. Her pride helps her to take the first news with dignity, but Father Marescotti – the Catholic equivalent of the Countess of D in his indelicacy and his blindness to sensitive feelings – insists that now is the time to press Belvedere on her. He is allowed half an hour with her, after which she is found to be as bad as she had been before, though this soon takes the new form of extreme restlessness. But once more we are not allowed to discover what he has said, or what really goes on in her consciousness. We get only hints. A few sentences addressed to Camilla show that her confessor has 'inveighed against' the heretic; Camilla's guesses that her dialogue with herself, which has started again, is concerned with what the Father had said; and a single outcry voices the pain of rejection, '*Jesu . . . To be despised!* – And by an English Protestant! Who can bear that?' (III, 119). Yet the turbulence of her heart remains unexplored.

It is the greatest pity that Richardson did not pursue the method he had begun, of allowing her deranged argument with herself to be overheard. This was the one way that the conflict between her love and her Catholicism could be tapped. Indeed, this turns out to be the moment at which the treatment of Clementina is poised between imaginative enquiry and emotional exploitation. If the opportunity had been taken to probe into her being, a great deal might have come of it, and further ways of overcoming the formal difficulty might have emerged. Indeed the obvious formal solution appears later, in the papers (like Clarissa's 'mad' ones) which her aunt takes away from her, but whose contents we are never shown, except for the quotation from the *Song of Songs*.

Instead, Richardson was fatally tempted by the siren call of pathos. The 'bleeding scene' (III, 126 ff.) is quite the most sentimental in the book – worse even than the death of Lady Grandison, which at least had a function in the novel of 'ought' – and it damages the dignity of the heroine. As she rushes into her brother's room, escaping from the doctors who have been trying to bleed her and appealing for protection, she is converted in an instant from a sympathetic young woman in the grip of a torturing situation, to a frightened and spoilt child, only pitiable with a mixture of contempt. When she compares herself to Iphigenia (III, 131), the effect must be mock-heroic – the disproportion deflates. One laughs; and when one finds that the response from Sir Charles and Harriet is wholly broken-hearted, the whole basis of the admiration and sympathy Richardson sought for his heroine is called in question. It seems, in both senses of the word, merely pathetic.

One can perhaps detect the vestiges of a more interesting idea. A comparison with Clarissa absolutely confirms the failure, but it also suggests that there might have been something in Richardson's mind besides the yearning for pathos. In treating Clarissa's derangement at its worst, Richardson had made her, too, seem childlike, to some effect. He wanted to peel her whole conscious mind away and reveal, behind the poised absolutist with her keen intelligence and self-assurance, an intensely vulnerable girl; and the contrast with the Clarissa we have known over four volumes is shocking and genuinely pitiable. We can believe in so terrible a derangement because it is the outcome of rape, under drugs, and before witnesses. The very intensity of Clarissa's moral intransigence prepares us to expect a very powerful reaction to the rape; and though she is physically timorous, we have been left in no doubt of her moral and spiritual courage. In the case of Clementina, however, the substitution of doctors wanting to bleed her for the experience of rape makes a similar response impossible, and the attempt to secure it sentimental. Only if Richardson had already succeeded in creating her derangement with convincing power, could this melodramatic extension of it seem at all convincing, and that is what he failed to do. Her morality has not been outraged; and we have had no experience of her courage, so that she seems simply cowardly. Consequently we respond not to the childlike but the childish, and the possibility arises that this is what she is 'really' like. It is just here, however, that we may see what Richardson may have had in mind besides his emotionalism. For perhaps he was indeed trying to show the heroine's most basic feelings, beneath the level of consciousness. He may have meant us to see how much her whole being is involved with her longing to reconcile her love and her religion, and save her lover from perdition. Her behaviour becomes a symbolic metaphor of blood-sacrifice. She can be serene because for a moment her love of her man and her love of God can be reconciled in her deranged mind. For his sake she is ready to bleed, and her tenderness of voice and hand as she strokes his cheek expresses her love as she cannot consciously do. The hint about Iphigenia suggests that she thinks of herself as offering her blood symbolically to appease the wrath of her God against the heretic. And Grandison exclaims that he would gladly offer *his* life for her restoration, though neither will sacrifice their religion. I think the following phase will show that this was indeed in Richardson's mind. Yet the scene itself can hardly be said to clarify its symbolic hint, which remains hidden beneath the gush of melodrama and unearned pathos.

After the blood-letting her 'delirium' is succeeded by a 'sedateness' as excessive as her restlessness had been. Camilla catches her stealing out of the house in disguise to visit Grandison, but she is dominated now by the desire to save his soul. She has convinced herself that she has been wholly rejected, because the family have not told her of Grandison's proposal to let her keep her religion and live in Italy. So she is going to him as a 'simple girl' on 'God's errand' (III, 145), to beseech him to become a Catholic for his own sake, not hers. When her mother allows Grandison to be summoned, to quiet her, he is able to tell her about his offer, and the knowledge that she has not been despised or rejected has its effect. Yet she tells him what she had been going to say: she is willing that he should hate and detest her, willing even to lay down her life, if he will only save his soul (III, 160). Her mother however, fearing too favourable a reaction to his proposals, cuts the interview short, and this is the last time that he will see her until he returns to Bologna after meeting Harriet.

We are however permitted one last direct experience of her in the slightly deranged letter she sends to warn him of the general's hostility. Most of the family have decided to have nothing to do with Grandison's offers, and a sterner treatment of Clementina has begun. The letter is deranged because she can hardly distinguish between what she is saying to herself as she writes, and how much she actually puts down, so that her disguised statements are transparently obvious, and her love very clear. The letter is quite moving, yet that seems again to be its only purpose: the last opportunity of entering into a direct experience of her conflict, in this first phase of her relationship with Grandison, is gone. 'Ah, Sir! they are very severe with me! Pity me: But I know you will; for you have a tender heart. *It is all for you!*' (III, 176). The letter is not a failure in itself, but in its context it is one, for it was a last chance to show us her basic conflict, and reverse the subjection of imaginative inquiry to pathos. As it is, however, the letter merely confirms Richardson's vision of her as hurt child, and the urge to exploit this.

Our last glimpses of her in Jeronymo's letters, after Sir Charles has left, pathetically looking for him in a crowded room, confessing her dream of a dead body in the garden, appealing for the love and sympathy she feels have been withdrawn, are still of the same kind; and after this the treatment becomes narrative. Richardson pulls out more and more stops: the fear of suicide, the binding of her hands, the fruitless journeyings, the final giving her over to Laurana, her cruel and jealous cousin, who beats her, taunts her with being crazy, and punishes her with a straitjacket. Yet narrative of 'what happens' can never analyse, or move, as Richardsonian drama can do. Thus, though the treatment of Clementina in this first phase began well, and contains promising psychological insights, the central conflict is never adequately explored or realised, and her stature is badly damaged by her creator's sentimentality. To compare Clementina with Clarissa is to judge that the family persecution is Harlowes-and-water, and that the madness remains merely pathetic, because we see too superficially. Moreover the failure has effects that must spread beyond itself, for one is likely to substitute for the response Richardson's basic design requires, Harriet's deep admiration and tragic pity, the rather more patronising 'poor child' – and this is to call in question the justness of Harriet's response, and Grandison's, and *their* conflicts.

When we meet Clementina again, on Grandison's return, she is in a state of fixed gloom (IV, 130 ff.). She often fails to recognise people, and is liable to starts of terror, though at other times she remains insensible. She can be frightened to hear Grandison named, because of what this has led to with Laurana, but Camilla cannot excite her at the prospect of seeing him, for she has been deceived too often. When she does recognise her mother, her dutifulness and the natural sweetness of her temper still show through her gloom, but the shock of catching sight of Grandison brings on violent weeping, followed by hysterics (IV, 144). The next day, seeing him again, she doubts his reality, and after beginning to talk to him suddenly recoils in terror (IV, 151). She shows later that she has still some vague notion of danger to him from her brother the general, but she is radically confused and her memory is gone. As she leaves the room she asks Camilla to tell Father Marescotti that she has seen a vision, and that he is to pray for them all. Yet the effect of calmer moments, when she realises that Grandison is actually there, reconciled with the general, and that she and he are being treated with affection, is to bring the first returns of reason and coherence.

As with her deranged letter before, we can diagnose her condition as the inability to distinguish actuality from her own mental landscape. So visitations of gloom extinguish the external world, and impulses of terror transform well-known faces into spectres. Conversely, her mind translates the actual reconciliation into something visionary. What is not yet clear is whether Richardson sees any causal connection between this condition and her basic conflict; or whether he derives her mental state purely from the continuous deception about seeing Grandison in the past, and the terrorising by Laurana.

When she gets better, however, signs of her basic conflict return, with interesting hints that the collision between love and religion has taken the shape of guilt. In the middle of coherent speech, the entrance of Father Marescotti makes her suddenly exclaim that she is an 'undone creature', a 'lost soul', and burst into tears (IV, 162). When Camilla uses the word 'innocent' she cries 'No, Camilla! – No', and first kneels in a corner, then to her mother, and then to Grandison, to beg forgiveness. Recollecting herself, she is immediately ashamed to have 'kneeled to a man' (IV, 165).

In the second batch of Grandison's letters, however, there is a change: her feeling for him can now be openly shown, and guilt has been replaced by the conviction that she can be grateful without being immodest. Significantly, on the other hand, her religious fervour is increasing too (IV, 225). She has also become more sensible of her ramblings, but this makes her feel them more, and she is liable to veer between emotional extremes: 'Her eyes had then lost all the lustre which had shewn a too raised imagination: But they were as much in the other extreme, overclouded with mistiness, dimness, vapours; swimming in tears' (IV, 230). And before the family and Grandison talk terms again, she tells him that she is burdened with a sense of unreturnable obligation. '*I* cannot reward you . . . I have high notions – My duty to God, and to my parents; my gratitude to you – But I have *begun* to write down all that has occurred to me on this important subject. I wish to act greatly!' (IV, 234). So, though the current of the situation seems to be setting firmly towards their marriage, in retrospect we can see her already thinking of rejection.

Quite the most significant thing here, however, is that we are at last given a hint that could link Clementina's mental breakdown with her basic conflict, and could also provide the basis of the final resolution. (It might even have made a great difference to our response to the 'bleeding scene' if it had been clarified at the time.) 'A too-raised imagination'; 'I have high notions' – it seems that Richardson is suddenly beginning to grasp something that has been lurking at the back of his mind for some time. (We remember Camilla being 'afraid of her elevations', but in context this referred to the high *feelings* of her pride. There have also been odd statements from Sir Charles and Charlotte about poets, pointing to the dangers of imagination, but in no context to make them significant.) It now becomes possible to see how Richardson might have explored the conflict between love and Catholicism, if he had probed as he should have done, and if he had grasped his guiding thread earlier. The unimaginative Father Marescotti could have been shown to have had so great an effect on Clementina, not merely because she was a Catholic, but because she was a Catholic with a 'raised imagination', for whom the horrors of sin and perdition, both for her beloved and for herself, could have been made vivid and real. We might have had an experience of a peculiarly Catholic sensibility to rival Pope's Eloisa, or even perhaps Joyce's Stephen. The same imagination, expressing its high notions in enthusiastic gratitude for what Grandison had done for her family, and in moral admiration, would have made suitably intense the conflict between 'goods' that are normally reconciled. Her idealism could have been further underlined in the elevated role she chose at his departure, and the recoil of self-hatred at her failure to sustain it. In such a context, the symbolism of the 'too-raised imagination' in the 'bleeding scene' might have meant more and have bulked larger than the appeal for tears. In her melancholic self-communings, the self fatally divided between opposed intensities of imagination might have become genuinely pitiable, psychologically fascinating, and fictively convincing. The psychosis that develops out of the original derangement might have been firmly related, not only to deception and cruelty, but also to the basic conflict; for the raised imagination would also be a convincing cause of the breakdown of distinction between outer reality and the inner world of the mind.

It is of course too late to recover these lost chances in terms of fictive experience; though it would have been very helpful if Richardson had seen clearly enough himself, to have made Sir Charles analyse the consistency of her mental processes as well as the moral consistency he remarks on later. It is at least clear however, that Richardson now sees Clementina's raised imagination as not only the source of her malady, but also the basis of her final 'greatness', through its reorchestration into moral role. She failed to sustain her first attempt at heroism, because her chosen role denied her real feelings. Now however her 'wish to act greatly' inspires her to imagine a role which can express all her conflicting feelings together, though it can of course only gratify those her Catholic conscience approves. Whatever changes she finds herself making in her frequently rewritten 'paper' always point in the same direction, and she takes this as a sign of divine prompting, clarifying the 'lines' of her part (IV, 306). When Grandison hears of her desire for more time before she sees him, he fears 'an imagination too much raised for the occasion (important as that is)' (IV, 285). But for Clementina, the occasion of rejecting him must be the greatest act of her life, and the imagination that can cause mental breakdown, can also 'raise' or 'heat' itself enough to elevate her acting to the 'sublime'.

Clementina's paper is therefore necessarily an essay in a kind of High Style, still faintly related to the mode of puritan introspection we first met in Pamela by the pond, but closely related now to the *Song of Songs*, as we see from the continual refrain: 'O thou whom my soul lovest'. Its theme is that of the fragment she had transcribed long before (III, 215): 'Look not upon me' – but not, as before, because she is black, and has not kept her own vineyard. And though she would still not write 'Let him kiss me with the kisses of his mouth: / For thy love is better than wine', and is anxious indeed to declare that her physical attraction to him was soon transformed into love of his mind and especially his soul, nevertheless she writes a love-letter, though very different from the Shulamite's song. The role her imagination has conceived, must freely declare both her love, which she cannot overcome by herself; and her firm resolution not to be his, precisely because she loves him too much to be sure she could remain a Catholic if she became his wife. The role also expresses, though it cannot satisfy, her gratitude. She knows that he is magnanimous enough to find his goodness its own reward, and that she could not make him happy because of her invincible doubts and her wounded mind and health. Yet her gratitude is as powerful as her love, so she cannot refuse him outright, but must leave the final decision to him. This also encompasses her duty to her parents, for she is doing what they want her to do in their hearts, while at the same time, in leaving the decision to Grandison, she is safeguarding their honour and formal consent to the marriage. Other feelings can also find expression: her determination that Grandison should not marry someone unworthy of him, like Olivia; and her desire to take a noble revenge on Laurana by taking the veil and giving up the estate her jealous cousin wanted so much. But above all, the reconciliation of her major feelings, her religious fervour, her love, her gratitude, her filial duty, is such that they can all be compressed into a single line:

'do God and thou enable me to say, Not my will, but his and theirs be done!' (IV, 296).

I think that one can claim on this basis, that 'ought' and 'is' are reconciled to some extent in the treatment of Clementina. The letter is still open to the objection that the Catholic attitudes to heresy and their operation in her consciousness, remain unrealised – but this should have been done long before, and if it had been done, we would be satisfied now with the simple reminder of the issue that we get: 'And shall I bind my Soul to a Soul allied to perdition'. To some degree, too, the formal 'theeing' and 'thou-ing', and the rhetorical high style, will put off modern readers. Yet the letter contains, as well as a firm grasp of 'ought' from Clementina's point of view, an ability to relate principle to the facts of her own nature. She sees quite shrewdly how hard it would be for a woman like her to have to deal continually with a suspicious confessor. Jealousy of Olivia, and resentment of Laurana, are intertwined with more selfless attitudes. And there is a steady awareness of the immense cost and difficulty of the role she has chosen. Moreover the paper does not have to achieve the relation of 'ought' to 'is' by itself. The dramatic situation when she hands it to Grandison, her total inability to speak what she has written, and the piercing sobs he hears from her closet after she has thrust the paper into his hands, shows us how hard she finds it to act up to her ambition. Even Richardson's incorrigible attempts to bespeak response cannot destroy, though they do distract us from, a convincing portrait of a woman under almost intolerable strain. Camilla may be like some ridiculous sentimental Pandarus: 'O madam! . . . – *Such* a scene! Hasten, hasten up. They will faint in each other's arms. Virtuous Love! how great is thy glory' (IV, 298). But I believe the basic integrity of Richardson's resolution can survive even this absurdity. Perhaps one can prove it by observing that Clementina has chosen precisely as Harriet made her Sir Charles/Adam choose. 'And shall I bind my Soul to a Soul allied to perdition? That so dearly loves that Soul, as hardly to wish to be separated from it in its future lot' (IV, 292-3). Yet the horrible complacency, the inhumanity, is quite gone, because one is convinced of the human cost of the decision, that she acts (as she says later, IV, 306) '*against my own wishes*' in human terms, and that no other man could compensate for what she is renouncing for the love of God.

Moreover, Clementina takes a leaf out of Sir Charles's playbook by offering him a role (as he did to Lady Beauchamp) that is totally suited to his character. She insists indeed that it is a greater role than her own, for he must take on his shoulders the decision she cannot make alone. Sir Charles thinks her claim to serenity 'too high set' (IV, 307), and this is true of her over-reaction when her mother takes both their hands, and she fears they may be joined. He is determined to wait and see whether she can hold her resolution after the 'heat' of her imagination subsides. Yet he can hardly fall below the magnanimity she attributes to him. His last effort to assure her that there is no need to fear any erosion of her faith, is doomed, because it is not his behaviour she fears, but her own susceptibility. Her role has already made full allowance for her love; and the greater the power of his tenderness, the more support for her argument.

Her 'heroism', however, has one more scene to play. She feels she must test his resolution against his tenderness as he had tested hers, and make a similar last effort to see whether his love will not overcome his Protestant obduracy, at whatever cost to her own modesty. She is 'dissatisfied and perplexed' by the failure of her first attempt to put the old conditions to him again, through her mother (IV, 323). But she sees her way: nothing will do but the open offer of herself in a dramatic fashion, that will be the same sort of immediate challenge to his feelings as his final courtship of her. So she will not allow her mother to speak for her again. 'False shame, I despise thee, said she: Yet, covered with blushes, she turned her face from me. – *That* hand, as *this* heart, putting her other hand to her throbbing bosom, is yours, on that one condition . . . But fear not to tell me (it is for my own future peace of mind, that I ask it) that you cannot accept it on the terms' (IV, 343). This seems melodramatic again, but it is not really so; for in eighteenth-century conditions it represents an extraordinary breach of custom, education, and modesty. She is in fact doing what Olivia has done, with a very different motivation.

The last phase is concerned with the attempt to reconstitute their brother-and-sister relationship on a new footing of intimacy, earned through the pain of renunciation. 'I will suppose', she says in her first letter after he has left for his month's trial by absence, 'that I am writing . . . to my Brother, and best friend. And indeed to which of my *other* brothers can I write, with equal freedom? . . . My heart shall be as open to you, as if . . . you could look into every secret recess of it' (IV, 366). She ruefully confesses the danger of a girl trusting 'herself with her own imagination' when she thinks with pleasure of the qualities of her beloved (IV, 367). And indeed the letter is perhaps less interesting in what it says than in its illustration of a mind coming back to the same place whatever subject she starts: to him. Her second letter makes two requests: that he will use his influence to persuade her family to let her take the veil, and that he will marry himself, so that there can be no looking back. (She even overcomes her jealousy of Olivia enough not to stand in the way if she would make him happy, but it is an Englishwoman she wants for him.) Sir Charles refuses the first request, since he has no belief in celibacy for its own sake, (though he had put to Dr Bartlett the interesting idea of setting up 'Protestant Nunneries' for lonely gentlewomen, run on faintly socialist lines – but inmates would be free to join or leave whenever they liked). He urges her not to set up a new conflict 'in supposing, that the will of God, and the will of your parents, are opposite' (IV, 381). He clearly has his thoughts about the second request, but 'I tell you not what I hope to be enabled by your noble example, in time, to do, because of the present *tenderness* of your *health*', only, she must not expect of him what she is not prepared to imagine for herself (IV, 380). When he returns to Bologna, she insists that she is in earnest about his marriage, and though she admits, as Harriet had admitted, that she is 'chargeable with affectation' (IV, 397) in imagining a future when she can be visited by his wife, she points out that his marriage would make it possible for her to go to England. And she makes as formal and deliberate a declaration as Harriet had done. He must cease to feel responsible for her health, and to try her resolution by '*officious* absences'. She is not insulted by his compassion; she will be grateful all her life, and hopes that he will remember her with tenderness until the end of his. But he must now name his day for leaving Bologna. 'I will hope to see you (in the happy state I have hinted at) in England, and afterwards in Italy. I will suppose you of my family. I will suppose myself of yours. On these suppositions, in these hopes, I can part with you.' The 'Family of the Heart' is now formally established in a dimension very much deeper than before, as she solemnly dedicates the garden seat they stand beside as a memorial of their love, which she will visit every day. She can only just sustain her role when he actually leaves, supported by his declaration that his happiness and tranquility are dependent on hers, but she 'assumes greatness' enough to make that motive suffice for bravery.

The treatment of Clementina as a whole, then, seems to exist at a point on the scale of success somewhere between the failure to create Grandison's conflict and the integrity of the treatment of Harriet. During Sir Charles's first visit, Clementina's conflict is not truly created or explored, and our response to her is seriously damaged by Richardson's sentimentality. With the second visit, however, there is a marked improvement. There are still sentimentalities, but Richardson begins to hint at a psychological diagnosis which would have made a great deal of difference if he had grasped it earlier; and which allows a resolution that no longer subordinates consciousness to principle or to pathos. We are left then with a curious paradox: that though the attempt to create the conflict itself is a failure, the resolution is a success, though Richardson can never retrieve the chances he has squandered. The failure to make us experience her Catholic imagination, means that we can never be convinced of the inevitability of her decision and its absolute rightness for *her*. Her madness also remains exploited rather than explored. Yet by the end she has regained a great deal of lost respect, because the role she finally chooses is convincing both in terms of argued principle, and experienced suffering and struggle.

4

With Sir Charles back in England and free to court Harriet the final resolution can begin, with only a minor crisis of delicacy to be overcome. He must both remain true to his feeling for Clementina, and be truly sensitive to Harriet's awkward situation, but he shows that he is not unbecomingly sure of her by choosing to approach her grandmother first. He secures Mrs Shirley's opinion that he may in delicacy try his fortune, since his letters from Italy show both that he is free, and that the Porrettas themselves want him to lose no time in setting Clementina an example. Yet his main problem is largely solved for him, since, as Mrs Shirley tells him, the whole 'greatness' of Harriet's role has been precisely its attempt to banish selfishness, in admitting Clementina's prior claim. Nevertheless Harriet still has the problem of coping with delicacy and pride in accepting 'a double, a divided Love' (V, 54) – and something of Richardson's strength returns in an art concerned once more to clarify the difference between what one ought to feel and what one cannot help feeling.

For it is perfectly clear how touchy her pride remains. Again and again, when it is possible to imagine a slight, she cannot help leaping to the conclusion that he is cocksure of her, and then realising with a spasm of self-reproach that the trouble lies in her own heart. She is also embarrassed by her good impulses, for her very success in persuading herself of Clementina's excellence makes her feel inferior, and so does her love. 'True Love will ever make a person think meanly of herself, in proportion as she thinks highly of the object. Pride will be up, sometimes; but in the pull two ways, between that and mortification, a torn coat will be the consequence; And must not the *tatterdemallion* . . . then look simply?' (V, 210-11). Yet the drama of embarrassment that allows its heroine to look foolish is an art of greater integrity than Richardson had managed at the crisis. In spite of embarrassment and wounded pride Harriet does manage to live up to her role. She insists that there shall be no inhibition in talking of Clementina, and that neither she nor Sir Charles can hope to be really happy if Clementina is not. She struggles hard against affectation and for her customary frankness. In answer to Grandison's first declaration she openly declares that her greatest difficulty lies in her own feeling of inferiority to the Italian girl (V, 144-5), and it is a mark of Richardson's success in creating her eddying feelings that this should be wholly convincing. Yet the experience of courtship must raise her in everyone's opinion, and gradually reassure her that she is indeed the beloved of Sir Charles – but what is most notable is how long her insecurity lasts. When the elaborate formalities, so necessary to Richardson's idea of female delicacy, have advanced as far as an argument about whether the great day should be in a month or a fortnight, Harriet has nightmares which show how little she still believes in herself or her luck (V, 257 ff.). The context is her renewed fear of danger to Sir Charles from the jealous Greville, and part of the nightmare is that he may be murdered, leaving her neither bride nor widow; but mostly her dreams reveal the depths of her self-doubt. She is scorned for presumption, and tries to hide herself in a subterranean cavern, made by a sea that has burst its bonds, and where winds howl and conflict. Yet even when she is dragged out, and instead of being punished is changed into an angel, she cannot believe that the baby in her arms is hers – it must be Lucy's or Emily's, or more significantly, Clementina's. She dreams again that she is married, but Sir Charles is disappointed in her, and accuses her of keeping him from Clementina; and again, that though he loves her, he turns into a ghost whenever she comes near.

It is this insecurity, not only psychologically but morally, that lies behind her resistance to the pressure of Sir Charles for a quick marriage, despite her uncle Selby's scorn of 'femalities'. The rarefied delicacies of Richardson's feminist idealism may seem merely tedious. Charlotte probably speaks for most of us in criticising them, and even Harriet is allowed to question, while she defends, the tyrannies of custom (V, 180). Yet the major reason for delay is not, after all, mere formal punctilio. Harriet insists on waiting for letters from Italy because her conscience continually upbraids her with being 'an invader of another's right' (V, 239), and because she must know that 'my happiness will not be the misfortune of a more excellent woman' (V, 182). She and Sir Charles match heroisms: Harriet insisting that she must still be prepared to give him up if Clementina changes her mind (V, 252); Sir Charles insisting that if she did, he would never marry anybody (V, 182); though it is typical of the different operations of Richardson's imagination that only Harriet confesses how much the self-denial would cost. Not until Clementina's own blessing arrives can Harriet be convinced that she may marry and rejoice; though even then the happiness of Clementina will be necessary to complete her own.

The long 'to the moment' descriptions of the marriage, the first public appearance of the happy pair, their settling in at Grandison Hall, and the perfection of their behaviour throughout, may be passed over here. The female members of Richardson's circle must have loved it all, but a mere modern male may perhaps be forgiven for not being enthralled. It is doubtless just as it ought to have been, and that is the trouble.

Yet it is not only in Harriet's struggle with herself that Richardson's imagination returns from 'ought' to 'is' in this last phase. There are other welcome signs of a willingness to count the cost of idealism in psychological terms.

Richardson himself is led into a limiting criticism of his own ideal of the Family of the Heart, in his treatment of jealousy in Emily, Charlotte, and Greville. Greville's attempt to beard Sir Charles on his first arrival in Northamptonshire, and the hero's disarming of his would-be rival, are unfortunately predictable, and there is the familiar objection to solving the physical challenge by Sir Charles's advantages of strength and swordsmanship. The provision then of a face-saving role for Greville and the overcoming of his hostility by elaborately acting it out are also familiar. What is new and salutary is Richardson's sense of the limits of acting above oneself. Greville is allowed to surprise everyone by ending his formal renunciation of Harriet with a genuine-sounding blessing and prayer for her happiness, which moves himself more than anyone (V, 162-3). Yet the episode does not end, as one might then have expected, with the permanent elevation of Greville; for he lapses back into conflict and threatenings, and though Sir Charles helps him through once more, Richardson is clearly aware that idealistic roles can impose intolerable strain. Moreover this is true also of better people: the sisterhood of the heart has lapses too.

Emily's infatuation with her guardian has been obvious since Harriet's heart-to-heart talk, after Emily's mother tried to claim her, which also sealed the special 'family' relationship between the older and the younger girl. Now that Harriet is no longer in Emily's hopeless position, but is actually going to marry Sir Charles, there are tears as well as happiness for her 'sister' (V, 58-60). Even more significantly, the letter from Charlotte that tells of the pangs of jealousy in the *ingénue*, betrays Charlotte's jealousy too. Her gratuitous harping on the fear that Clementina may recede comes from an impulse to hurt the 'sister' who will now unquestionably supplant her in her brother's heart; and though she does not admit the motive, she does afterwards confess the impulse to 'teaze a little' (V, 69). Emily finds that the granting of her wish to live with the newly married couple imposes a strain she cannot manage. She is quite pert when Harriet tries to repeat their heart-to-heart, and even accuses Harriet of jealousy (VI, 72-3), but she comes to see that her chosen role can only make her miserable as her feeling for her guardian grows (VI, 93-101). She herself decides to take up Mrs Shirley's offer, and supply Harriet's place in Northampton. Richardson has not lost his idealism, but he is costing it more realistically.

This, finally, is the point of reintroducing Clementina. Her family keep pressing her to marry Belvedere, and though this is now by persuasion rather than compulsion she finds it hardly less intolerable. She begins to show signs of wildness again, and before her family wake up to the danger, she has fled to England. She believes that she is merely escaping the family pressure and furthering her darling hope of becoming a nun; but as she herself will recognise later, it would have been more logical to fly to a Catholic country if that were all. It is not that she has any idea of recanting her 'heroic' decision, but clearly her love is stronger than her wisdom in the impulse to seek the protection of her 'brother'.

Sir Charles takes her under his wing with the full approval and enthusiasm of Harriet, and the sister-souls instantly take to each other. The Porrettas brave a winter crossing to come after their daughter, with Belvedere in their train, and Sir Charles undertakes a formal reconciliation. If Clementina will finally renounce the veil, her family will leave her entirely to her own choice thereafter. Clementina recovers her 'greatness' in tearing off their signatures to the formal 'articles' and binding only herself. Rejoicing is unconfined – except of course for Belvedere. Yet though the Family of the Heart is established at Grandison Hall, with Clementina and Harriet devoting themselves to each other and Sir Charles to both, Clementina does not get any happier.

There are two points at issue here. The first is the strain on Clementina's feelings, which completes the analysis begun with Charlotte and Emily. She is partly outraged by discovering the verdict of Italian society, as instanced by Olivia's reported bitchiness (VI, 248). She has not come chasing to England to offer herself to Sir Charles, as Olivia had done, but there is enough in the parallel to be wounding. Even more upsetting is Mrs Beaumont's drawing of the parallel with Emily, for though Clementina is outraged by being compared with 'a girl', the comparison is just. Her love for Sir Charles can only increase; she has come to love Harriet too; what can be the end? The sudden illness of Harriet is a symbolic turning-point. It is only a feverish chill, brought on by walking too far with Clementina and being caught in a thunderstorm, but the degree of responsibility that Clementina feels suddenly opens her eyes to what she would feel, if anything happened to mar Harriet's happiness through her fault. The conclusion is inescapable.

Only, what is she to do? The second issue is broached when she re-opens, with Harriet and Sir Charles, the question of becoming a nun. For they lead her gently but firmly to see that the desire to abandon the world is also open to misconstruction, and a 'sighing heart' in a convent is no real solution. The basic question is whether she will live for herself, cherishing her love for Sir Charles; or whether her duty to her family (and the Grandisons), and her own eventual happiness, point towards marriage, albeit to a second choice. A number of threads in the novel come together here, all concerned with the question of how a woman disappointed in her first love may best fulfil her life.

When it seemed certain that Sir Charles would marry Clementina, the Dowager Countess of D had written a cogent criticism of Harriet's 'bright fairy schemes . . . of living happy in a friendship with two persons, . . . the very thought of whose union makes your cheeks fade . . .' (IV, 264). She does not attack Harriet's idea of friendship itself, but she does seek to purge it of romanticisms: especially the belief that a first love makes it impossible to think of marrying anybody else. What one vows at the altar is not an absolute choice but a preference; and it is marriage which calls forth a woman's talents. How much more happiness Harriet would give her Friends, and how much more active good she could do, 'by permitting yourself to be called out into active life, with all its variety of relations, than you can while you continue obstinately in a single state, on purpose to indulge a remediless sorrow' (IV, 266). Given the status and opportunities of women in the eighteenth century, it is a good argument. Charlotte recognises at the time that it applies to Emily as well as Harriet – and now it applies to Clementina too. In the final volume the argument is re-urged by Mrs Shirley (VI, 218 ff.), and by Charlotte in judgement of the Northampton girls (VI, 233 ff.).

Mrs Shirley will have none of the mockery of old maids which has been such a speciality of Charlotte's; but she agrees that the life of a single woman is bound to be a limited, and often a souring one. The story of her friend Mrs Eggleton may be a portrait of an old maid who did not allow her disappointments in love to embitter her life or make it useless, but its real point is how her friend disabused Mrs Shirley of ideas drawn from romances, and helped her to choose what became her long and happy life with Mr Shirley. Charlotte, too, can not only argue that Harriet was a 'romantic' girl in refusing to think of anyone but Sir Charles (VI, 233), but more to the point, can also illustrate from her own case how a 'second choice' marriage has at last come to real affection and happiness, even though it had more to overcome than the absence of romantic feeling on the woman's side. For Charlotte has finally learned to value her husband's love more than her own independence, intellectual superiority, and mischief. Surprised by Lord G with their baby at her breast, and by the strength of her husband's feeling, the experience of intimacy teaches her the meaning of tenderness (VI, 230-2).

Though Richardson probably meant the debate to provide yet another casuistic challenge to his readers, and though Harriet is still partly on Clementina's side, there can be little doubt of his own view. Belvedere is a man Clementina can respect and esteem as Charlotte never respected Lord G. Marriage on that basis will give her the greatest fulfilment she can have, both in itself and in the joy of her family; it will also be the real fulfilment of the Family of the Heart, since it will secure the happiness of the Grandisons, and bind all the conjugal families more securely together. Clementina decides she needs a year to think it over, and make sure that she is well enough in her mind to marry, but all the signs are that she will.

It is then not on a basis of romantic idealism that the Family of the Heart is finally founded. Psychological insight, and the moral belief that happiness comes from active benevolence, duty, and the kind of intimacy only possible in the conjugal family, lead Richardson to avoid any 'platonic' idea of a love superior to mere worldly ties. Harriet had attacked the debased idea of 'platonic love'; and Sir Charles, while continuing to love both girls, makes a necessary distinction between his wife and his friend (VI, 279). Yet Richardson merely rebuilds on securer foundations his basic idea of the extension of the Family, in ever widening circles, till it becomes a moral community knit by indissoluble ties. As Clementina bids farewell, the spot where the Temple of Friendship will rise, will symbolise a wider and a safer bond than the garden seat in Bologna (VI, 312-13).

5

The faults of the novel are glaring enough. Its excessive formalities of behaviour and style, and the rarefied delicacies of Richardson's idealism, will ensure that even at its best it must remain an oddity. There is something to be said for the idea of pitting an art of 'ought' against an art of 'is', but the failure at the crisis to hold the challenge true means that the novel is broken backed, and the hero can never come alive as he had once promised to do. Yet it is a pity that *Grandison* should be so neglected. Harriet is a fine creation, and her side of the novel is a real achievement which has been lost to sight. Despite the failure at the centre, there are many ways in which the book does achieve a fruitful interplay between its two kinds of imagination. In the theme of role-playing, particularly, the moralist meets the dramatist in an interesting fashion, and 'acting' is given a new kind of significance. If there had only been some formal stimulus to the dramatic imagination at the crisis, the didactic Richardson might well not have overcome the dramatist, and we could have had a curious kind of masterpiece.

PART FOUR

Master of the Heart, Shakespeare of Prose

CHAPTER TEN

The Novel as Drama

I

The idea of writing fiction in letters was not new, nor did Richardson ever claim to have invented it. What he did invent was the idea of using letters, along with other techniques, to achieve the equivalent in the novel of the experience of drama. His 'new Manner of Writing – to the Moment'[1] was essentially the creation of a fiction which could seem to be happening 'now' rather than recollected in tranquillity; and to be shaping itself from moment to moment, rather than to a pattern perceived and articulated with hindsight and by an author. As in drama one must seem to experience directly for oneself rather than through an authorial filter.

What may prevent us recognising his art as dramatic is the commonsense association of drama with the stage. It is obvious that the novel can only approximate to the condition of the theatre; and has to do 'conventionally' what happens as a matter of fact between living actors and an audience. It is less obvious, but equally true, that not all plays are fully dramatic, and that the essence of the dramatic form does not depend on a stage, but lies in a distinctive process of imaginative creation. Dryden placed the essential distinction between epic and drama in the fact that the former is told by an author, the latter 'viva voce',

[1] Richardson to Lady Bradshaigh, 9 October 1756; Carroll, *Letters*, 329.

in the living voices of the characters.[1] The paradox then is that it is Richardson not Fielding who is the dramatist, although Fielding spent years writing for the theatre before he turned to fiction.[2] For Fielding's successful plays depend on having commentary between the audience and the action; his imagination was essentially epic in its operation; and like the early Ben Jonson he can usefully be described as an epic playwright. A twentieth-century critic who compares Richardson with Milton and Fielding with Shakespeare[3] shows less formal understanding than contemporaries, who were in no doubt that Richardson was 'Shakespearian' and a dramatist – though like Henry James, and for similar reasons, he could never have written a successful stage-play.[4]

Conversely, Richardson's 'letters' are in many ways unlike letters that people actually write, and unlike other epistolary fictions also, to the extent that they are to the moment dramatic narratives, attempts to catch living voices in a dramatic present. *Clarissa* produces a different effect from that of *Les Liasons Dangereuses* because, although the 'letters' in both cases banish the author, Laclos takes his convention more literally than Richardson. His letter-writers write letters, not dramatic narratives and dialogues, they write at moderate length and with a formality of style that acceptably imitates contemporary correspondence, and the experienced 'tense' of the action is always

[1] Dryden, *Of Dramatic Poesy: An Essay*, Everyman edition (London, 1962), I, 87-8. (He is building on Aristotle, see *Poetics*, Everyman edition (London, 1953), 8.)

[2] See also Claude Rawson, 'Fielding and Smollett' in the Sphere *History of Literature in the English Language*, IV, R. Lonsdale (ed.), *Dryden to Johnson* (London, 1971), 259-61.

[3] Walter Allen, *The English Novel* (London, 1954 reprinted 1963), 40.

[4] e.g. 'Of *Nature* born, by *Shakespeare* got' – David Garrick, 20 April 1751 – the first line of a poem inscribed on the flyleaf of *Clarissa*, quoted McKillop, *Richardson*, 161. See also Thomas Edwards, quoted McKillop, *Richardson*, 163. Among many comments on the dramatic nature of Richardson's work see Aaron Hill on first reading *Pamela*, S.H. ed. I, xiii; and John Read on first reading *Clarissa*, Forster, XV, 2, fol. 28. The *Monthly Magazine* in 1813, introducing the Richardson-Young correspondence, called Richardson 'the Shakespeare of Romance'.

past, although only recently. Where there is so much in common, the difference is all the more striking. If the emphasis is on the epistolary, Laclos is much the more successful, if it is on the dramatic, Richardson is more powerful, immediate, and exploratory. Similarly, Pamela's Journal does not break Richardson's form, since the experience of living from moment to moment, day by day, is more important than the letter convention. Characters can also be created in dramatic dialogue and action without themselves writing letters – though, as with B, this may place a strain on the reader's ability to separate his impression from those of the letter-writer who presents them to us. One of Richardson's best comic characters, Harriet's Uncle Selby, never writes a letter, but is no less successfully created than Clarissa's uncles, who do.

Richardson is an 'epistolary novelist' certainly; but to lay the emphasis there is to mistake a technical means, however central, for the formal end itself: the novel as drama. Richardson not only wishes to produce an experience that is 'like' drama; he creates by the imaginative process that is characteristic of the true dramatist, whether it be in verse monologues, stage plays, epistolary novels, or any other convention.

The forming vision, the 'shaping spirit of imagination',[1] is the process of dramatic projection, where the author formally banishes himself, and creates by becoming each of his characters. He tries to see through their eyes, and use their distinctive voices. He cannot be identified with any of them, and is not formally responsible for anything they may say. It can be a matter of some difficulty to establish what he himself 'thinks'; and this can only be done in the light of the complex creation as a whole. For, 'how can it be said I and not Charlotte dressed Aunt Nell? – Here I sit down to form characters . . . I am all the while absorbed in the character. It is not fair to say – I, identically I, am any-where, while I keep within the character'.[2] Richardson is the pioneer of 'point of view' fiction. In reading him, as we

[1] Coleridge, 'Dejection'.

[2] Richardson to Lady Bradshaigh, 14 February 1754; Carroll, *Letters*, 286.

have seen, we have to enter the points of view of *all* his characters, to form an overall comprehension that is greater than any possesses; and we have no obvious authorial presence to help us. By formal definition, no single point of view is 'reliable'. Where there is only one narrator for a given action, we may have to accept the narrative of speech, gesture and action, but it is always dangerous to accept the interpretation the narrator puts on these, and always necessary to read between the lines of the other characters, to discover their points of view.

Nevertheless Richardson does not banish himself entirely. He may be present as 'Editor' in footnotes, index, linkage, and summary, though I have argued that in such cases he is often 'unreliable' too, if not deliberately so as in the form itself. More significantly, as A. M. Kearney has argued,[1] we need to be aware of a controlling technique within the fiction, that plays across the dramatic projection and the 'characteristic' voices. The letter-writers themselves mime the process of authorship; they both experience, and shape their experience into commentary. Consequently they speak in two voices: one 'direct and spontaneous', experiential, subjective; the other 'more deliberate', distanced, analytic, objective. The second voice is always available to Richardson himself, and may speak for him. With the opportunity, of course, goes the danger of abuse: of breaching characteristic decorum locally, so that one hears the author himself and the illusion of living in a character's mind is snapped; or of so turning a character into a surrogate for the author that individual characterisation is blurred. In *Pamela*, the transition from one voice to another can be so abrupt and the contrast so extreme that unwanted psychological inferences arise; and the terminology and style can be so inappropriate to the character that one may sometimes feel that it is Richardson whom one is hearing, not the girl. Opinions may differ on where exactly the

[1] A. M. Kearney, 'Richardson's *Pamela*, the Aesthetic Case', *Review of English Literature*, 7 (1966), 78-90; reprinted in John Carroll (ed.), *Twentieth Century Views of Samuel Richardson* (Englewood Cliffs, N.J., 1969), 28-38; and Rosemary Cowler (ed.), *Twentieth Century Interpretations of 'Pamela'* (Englewood Cliffs, 1969), 78-88.

line is to be drawn.[1] Yet the whole art of dramatic projection depends on not allowing the question to arise at all, and Richardson was often tactless in his first novel. As the social status, and hence the style of his characters is raised, there is less danger of this particular gap; and the multiplication of letter-writers allows the commentary to be divided among them, so that the diverse opportunities open to Richardson take off the pressure to break in. Elevation of style can however increase the danger of using characters as author-surrogates. There is truth in Kearney's suggestion that Pamela virtually becomes Richardson in the continuation, and that Belford is used as his mouthpiece. It is not, I think, the whole truth. The continuation also contains the final proof of Pamela's unreliability, and there are two 'Richardsons' at work in it; while Belford's commentary is not ultimately Richardson's either, since his understanding of Clarissa is demonstrably limited. Nevertheless the danger is real, and I would agree that the borderline is crossed with Pamela in her exalted condition, and with Sir Charles, precisely because the didactic urge in Richardson overcomes the dramatic imagination. What I think happens in Richardson at his best, however, is both the dramatic diversification and the analytic convergence of the 'second voice'. As characters grow, their 'second voices' get nearer to the author's. All the four main letter-writers in *Clarissa* are capable of serious commentary; springing from appreciably different experiences and temperaments however, and representing different capacities. Where they ultimately converge, an approximation to 'Richardson' can be discovered. Yet the strength of the dramatic art is that the reader still has the responsibility

[1] For instance, Kearney's example of a lapse so extreme that it becomes 'unconscious parody', Pamela's comparison of herself to Queen Hester at the height of the misunderstanding in the continuation, could easily be defended. It is one of a number of biblical comparisons (which are more conceivable in terms of Pamela's likely reading than her occasional literary allusions), and – more important – the note of parody is appropriate in terms of her excessive, and mistaken, frame of mind. It occurs at the height of her unreliability, and B marks its exaggeration in calling it a 'tragedy-speech'. I should be far less certain that the touch of absurdity is Richardson's mistake.

of achieving a comprehensive vision that no single character can utter – and it is a vision that Richardson himself could only reach towards by transcending his ordinary capacity, in a process of dramatic projection and exploration.

It is indeed the exploratory challenge of the dramatic form that has been the central argument of this book. Even in the single-focus of *Pamela*, the effect of dramatic projection is to enable Richardson to reach out imaginatively beyond himself, in exploring, criticising, and transcending the attitudes from which he may have started. When the dramatic imagination lapses, the ordinary self comes back with sadly limiting effects. As the points of view are multiplied in *Clarissa*, however, the pressure to test them against one another is increased. The effect of really sustained projection into several points of view is to force Richardson to probe deeper and deeper, until his hero and heroine have to be taken to the point of disintegration in order to come at their innermost selves. Though the convergence of 'second voices' thereby takes place on a more challenging plane than ever before, the imaginative exploration cannot be contained within or limited by the commentary. No 'second voice' within the novel can account for the full significance of the conflicts in the three instalments, let alone for the derangements of Clarissa and Lovelace, and their deaths. The 'Richardson' one struggles to comprehend is the product of an enormously long and challenging process – it is scarcely surprising that Richardson himself could never do it justice afterwards, and I will not have done so either. On the other hand, *Grandison* shows that Richardson's 'second voice' can have its own imaginative, if anti-dramatic, quality, interestingly pitted *against* the dramatic imagination. Though at its centre the former overcomes the latter and the novel fails to fulfil its promise, we can still find, in the best of it, the power of the probing dramatic imagination to explore and criticise.

Richardson's name for his invention insists, however, on the importance of aiming this basic imaginative process at the creation of a dramatic 'present'. In the Preface to *Clarissa* he points to the '*instantaneous* Descriptions and Reflections'; and quotes

Belford on how 'Much more lively and affecting . . . must be the Style of those who write in the height of a *present* distress; the mind tortured by the pangs of uncertainty', than 'dry narrative' (I, xiv; *I*, *xiv-xv*). In Warburton's Preface the emphasis is less on the power to move than the power to penetrate. Writing to the moment afforded Richardson the only 'natural Opportunity' of representing 'those lively and delicate Impressions, which *Things present* are known to make upon the Minds of those affected by them. And he apprehends, that in the Study of human Nature, the Knowlege of those Apprehensions leads us farther into the Recesses of the human Mind, than the colder and more general reflections suited to a continued and more contracted Narrative'.[1]

It is obvious of course that even epistolary fiction can only partly imitate stage-drama, since actions are always past before they can be written down. Richardson has to rely more heavily than he admits on the reader's assent to a convention, to be able to do it at all naturally. Fielding made easy sport of Shamela scribbling in bed as Booby climbed in beside her, and the attempt to write 'instantaneously' creates difficulties of length as well as credibility. Of course 'omniscient' writing depends just as much on convention too; and 'to the moment' writing in Richardson covers a whole spectrum from literally present tense narrative, through a past re-created dramatically as though it were present, to a past treated as past but in the process of evaluation 'now', so that it is not the action but the response to it that is 'to the moment'. Epic and omniscient narratives can also contain dramatic scenes vivid enough to seem to be happening as we read, in spite of the clear 'past' context; but what is important in Richardson is the imaginative effect of his continuous and sustained effort to make the experience 'present'. We are made to feel that we are living through it as it happens.

[1] Richardson thought of working this passage into his revised Preface, see *Preface, Hints of Prefaces, and Postscript*, ed. R. F. Brissenden, Augustan Reprint no. 103 (Los Angeles, 1964), 6. Warburton's Preface, which originally appeared in volume 4 of the first edition, has been reprinted in *Prefaces to Fiction*, ed. Benjamin Boyce, Augustan Reprint no. 32 (Los Angeles, 1952).

Richardson only uses strict to the moment *narrative* to create suspense. 'But, mum! – Here he comes, I believe...' (I, 51; *I, 33*). In fact, however, there is not a great deal of this. (My example shows Richardson's own awareness that it has comic possibilities, since it turns out to be Mrs Jervis as we turn the page. The close of Letter 24 was also comic.) In *Pamela* the technique creates suspense just before the ill-fated attempt to escape; while she waits for B to arrive (I, 247; *I, 158-9*); and (less acceptably) on her wedding night (II, 155; *I, 316*). But it is inevitably Lovelace who provides the best examples, before the fire (IV, 386-7; *II, 498-9*), and just before the rape (V, 301 ff.; *III, 188 ff.*).

It is doubtful however whether one can separate 'the story' from the response to the story by the characters here, or anywhere in Richardson. What gives the really continuous impression of a present-tense experience is our sharing the response of the recorders as they record. That is what happens 'now' and makes one feel that one is living inside a mind from moment to moment. It happens on every page, and though the events described are over, they were over only 'just now' – a repeated phrase – and it is only now that they are being taken in. The past is continually made over into a present, that can be occasionally held in suspense by unexplained breakings-off.

Perhaps the most significant drive in Richardson's development, however, is the attempt to remove the past tense from the recorded actions too. Here the dramatist comes into his own, in a more obviously recognisable sense, in 'Conversations... written in the dialogue or dramatic way' (I, xiv; *I, xiv*). In the recording of scenes of conflict, the staple of *Pamela* is that of such scenes in novels in general: the tense is the past, but the voices can be done vividly enough to make it seem dramatically present. Actual intonations can be caught, but the linkage is by 'he said' and 'I replied'; and settings, gestures, and expressions are described. The more dialogue there is, and the less interruption by the narrator, the more dramatic the scene becomes and the nearer to experience in the theatre. (The high proportion of this already marks the degree of convention in the pretence that these are 'letters', and the difference from Laclos.) In the finely sustained scene with Lady Davers, however, there are the first signs of an ability to do without connectives. Every now and again there is a snip-snap of pure dialogue, though never for long (II, 197-8; *I, 343-4*). In the continuation this is taken a good deal further; particularly in the scenes with Swynford (III, 306 ff.; *II, 157 ff.*), Polly (III, 363 ff.; *II, 186 ff.*), and the Darnford sisters (III, 337 ff.; *II, 175 ff.*); and (with longer speeches) in the Trial scene. It is in *Clarissa* however that Richardson's confidence grows. The big scenes between Arabella and Clarissa (I, 317 ff.; *I, 216 ff.*) sustain almost pure dialogue for pages, with only occasional and tactful notice of gesture and expression. They are wholly absorbing, not only in their command of pace, but in their mastery of the intonation and expressiveness of the human voice, and their capture of the flick and sting of the tongue. Often expression and gesture are implied in the dialogue itself with no further need for notation: Bella's taunts tell us exactly how Clarissa speaks and looks. Dash and fullstop are all the pause marks we need. In reading these scenes one entirely forgets that they are technically 'past'. They happen while we read, and they cry out (as several of the book's first readers exclaimed) for the stage. In the equally sustained dialogue with Sally and Polly in the prison (VI, 279 ff.; *III, 432 ff.*), even the dash disappears, and Richardson captures an even harder effect: the pressure of the voice on silence. The dialogue is extraordinarily monosyllabic, and as far as Clarissa is concerned apparently expressionless; but it holds our attention precisely because of the silences: the suffering, aggression, or despair that lie between the words. It is a very long road from Richardson to Beckett and Pinter, but the eighteenth-century novelist is further along it than any eighteenth- or nineteenth-century playwright. In the rest of Clarissa he uses several varieties of dialogue between 'he said, I said' and pure drama. In the interests of economy he develops a mixed mode where condensed third person narrative is interspersed with speech. Where the situation is complex and delicate, there may be more need for interpreting;

where the emotional temperature rises, connectives and commentary tend to fall away. But now, infinitely more than in *Pamela*, it is not only the response to events but the events themselves that become effectively 'present' to a considerable extent. The effectiveness prevents one questioning the convention: one does not inquire how it is that Clarissa and Lovelace can remember every word, or how Belford can give us a fully dramatic scene at which he was not even present. Nor are we necessarily aware, in the most fully dramatic scenes, of a letter-writer at all, let alone of Richardson. Moreover, though Richardson thought of 'familiar letters' as a species of conversation on paper, so that there is already a connection between the 'speaking' and the 'writing' voice; in his most dramatic scenes the speaking voice reigns supreme.

In *Clarissa* also, there are two further developments. In Anna's humorous account of Uncle Anthony's courtship of Mrs Howe, there is a dialogue with her mother that is set out like a play (IV, 172 ff.; *II, 353 ff.*). The interesting thing here is the association of play-book with playfulness. Richardson seems well aware that, whereas the increasing dramatisation and the removal of connectives increases the reader's involvement; the imitation of a playbook within a prose fiction creates distance, and with distance may come comedy. This is of course a comic scene in itself anyway – but Richardson then pursues the idea by allowing Lovelace to distance and thereby mock a serious scene, by providing a full script of his Family Trial (VI, 226 ff.; *III, 395 ff.*). He does it again with the peppery occasion when Colonel Morden comes to demand Lovelace's intentions (VII, 280; *IV, 219 ff.*). The effect is peculiar: it is as though we are both in and out of the scene at the same time. The involvement allows the seriousness (indeed the dangerousness, in the Morden episode) to come through. Yet the distance allows us to glimpse comedy with the other eye, the 'artificiality' rubs off on the characters, we see them playing parts, fussy or touchy, with Lovelace as stage-manager. The effect is analogous to mock-heroic in Pope or Fielding, where situations can also be seen as both serious and comic. Richardson's command of his medium is very sure and subtle to be able to play with it like this.[1]

In *Grandison* he begins more varied experiments with this new technique. There is an interesting paradox in using formal drama to defuse the 'dramatic', in the use of the short-hand writer to record Sir Charles's discussion with Bagenhall (I, 338 ff.) and his visit to Sir Hargrave (I, 380 ff.): the avoidance of the duel. In the first scene the scribe is openly present, so that the writing-down is built into the interchanges. The effect is to formalise: Sir Charles makes formal statements, 'Repeating what he said to the writer, that he might not mistake' (I, 339). In the second, potentially very 'dramatic' episode, the scribe is hidden but the distancing effect is even more deliberate. The action is distanced for *us*, and style reinforces form as Sir Charles expounds and lectures. The 'dramatic' potentialities of the situation beat in vain against our sense of an action held at arm's length, and against the hero's measured tone.

Richardson then tries to build the 'script' technique into the fabric of the whole. 'By the way, Lucy', writes Harriet, 'you are fond of plays; and it is come into my head, that, to avoid all *says-I's* and *says-she's*, I will henceforth, in all dialogues, write names in the margin: So fansy, my dear, that you are reading in one of your favourite volumes' (I, 419). The distancing effect has depended on rarity, on our sense of contrast with what we are used to. How would it be if the reader grew accustomed to the technique as a convention which, with a little practice, could cease to obtrude? It would have the advantage for Richardson of extending the variety of his techniques, and allowing him to sustain the dialogue longer and with more speakers, without danger of confusion. Success will depend however on the reader's facility in translating dramatic script into a theatre of the mind, and taking in the attributions without really seeing them or

[1] On the other hand, in the scenes with the women and Tomlinson at Hampstead, the technique reminds us that the scenes are *staged*, with Tomlinson and Lovelace playing parts, though the situation is too serious to allow this to be funny.

interrupting the flow. Soon Harriet betrays her author's uneasy feeling that the technique is too 'formal' for mere conversation: 'As I think these conversations characteristic, I hope the recital of them will be excused. Yet I am sensible, those things that go off well in conversation, do not always *read* to equal advantage' (II, 13). The trouble is that this technique, where the others are still in use as well, does tend to draw attention to itself, and remind us that we are indeed *reading*. It is most successful where there is some additional justification. In the 'trials' of Charlotte by her brother (II, 163 ff.), Harriet by the Grandison sisters (II, 200 ff.), and Sir Charles by Charlotte (II, 398 ff.), the technique is acceptable not only because the scenes are long, but also because they are meant to have the flavour of public trial, the touch of something staged. The good scene between Sir Thomas and his daughters also works well, because we are meant to see it not merely as it was, but with Charlotte acting it out in three voices (II, 70). The scene in which Sir Charles sounds Clementina about Belvedere is also 'staged', in that her parents are listening offstage (III, 54). (But Richardson is on dangerous ground here, not only in the ethics of eavesdropping, but also because the gap between the letter convention and the stage-form opens too wide. This is supposed to be Dr Bartlett's recension of Sir Charles's correspondence from Italy, 'thus far, my patron' (III 59), but the form is utterly uncharacteristic of both of them.) The technique works best, then, when there is meant to be a staginess as part of the effect. Yet the scene where Sir Charles play-acts with the Beaumonts doesn't use it, and Richardson drops the idea.

Letters can also be regarded as extensions of dramatic soliloquy, though the mind's communion with itself is directed to a reader within the book as well as to an audience outside. It is already, and naturally, to the moment, and hence is the simplest way of making the past present on every page.

As there is little use trying to separate 'the story' from the response to the story, so there is hardly any hard and fast separation between moral analysis, self-examination, and self-revelation. We can distinguish shades of emphasis: there are 'sentiments' (in Dr Johnson's sense of moral reflections) which are formulated with a crispness no longer mainly personal, and which could be extracted into a collection of maxims like the one Richardson made from *Clarissa* and *Grandison*; there is personal self-analysis; and there are moments when consciousness is caught on the wing in ways that link Richardson with twentieth century fiction; but in practice these constantly shade into one another. The 'sentiments' on the relation of love and hate in Letter 23 of *Pamela*, and on descending with ease in Letter 24, are obvious examples of this. Both could be extracted, but both are integral parts of a personal self-scrutiny, and both in context reveal more about the character than the character knows. Just as our own letters can contain all three elements and yet remain distinctively *us*, the essence of Richardson's to the moment form is to make us feel that we are living in a mind whose characteristic activity and tone are recognisable; and which is constantly occupied in assessing experience, turning life into consciousness, and creating personality from moment to moment, as we watch. Having noted the danger of authorial breaking-in on the character, it seems less helpful to attempt to distinguish 'commentary' from 'revelation', than to appreciate again the creative interplay between dramatic techniques of involvement and distance.

The main technique is the creation of a distinctive mental voice, speaking on paper to its correspondent, analysing, commenting, arguing. In general terms, the greater the uncertainty or conflict, psychological or moral, the more likely it is that the voice will resemble the speaking voice, and the greater the reader's involvement. On the other hand, the more impersonal and crisply formulated moral conclusion, the 'sentiment', is most likely to occur when a tract of behaviour has been reviewed and a certainty reached. (So the first obvious 'sentiment' in *Clarissa*, Anna's conclusion about Avarice and Envy, comes at the end of Clarissa's first eight letters (I, 59; *I, 40*).) In practice however the interplay is again as important as the distinction. In *Pamela*,

Richardson uses a technique of distance for the mind in conflict, as well as a technique of involvement, and interestingly combines the two. When Pamela re-creates her crucial debate with herself in the first pond scene (I, 233 ff.; *I, 150 ff.*) there is no attempt to overcome the past tense, and still further distance is created by the use of 'thee' and 'thou' as she argues with herself. Consequently Richardson fails to create the experience of despair – yet I think the attempt to push the self to arm's length, to talk to oneself as though one were someone else, is significant. On the other hand, Pamela's self-colloquy after the second pond scene, on which the original first volume closed (I, 301; *I, 194*), is a good example of the involvement which springs from the same technique of to the moment dialogue that we discussed in relation to scene. Richardson anticipates Sterne in capturing the quick movements of the mind by the use of dashes; the first stream of consciousness in fiction, though it works by impulses of emotion rather than association. The reveries on her journey home, which Hazlitt so admired[1] and which finally reveal her to herself, interestingly combine the two. She finally understands the past, how love has crept 'like a Thief upon me', and castigates her 'treacherous Heart' as 'thou' (II, 8-9; *I, 220-1*); but when B's second letter arrives the insistence of the heart actually throbbing in her bosom breaks the distance down, the rhetoric disappears, and the past becomes the present in a sentence. 'Thus foolishly dialogued I with my Heart; and yet, all the time, this Heart is *Pamela*' (II, 13; *I, 223*).

In *Clarissa* the multiplication of foci creates the interplay between objectivity and subjectivity in a new way, since as one correspondent analyses another, the analysers come into focus subjectively while the analysed are seen objectively as they can never see themselves. It is by getting both inside and outside his characters that the important question-marks pose themselves to Richardson and drive him to probe further. There is also a much greater sense of self-analysis proceeding by actually arguing with somebody whose 'presence' is felt, as their responses, questions and objections are imagined. The 'soliloquies' become

[1] 'On the English Novelists', *Works*, ed. Howe, VI, 119.

dramatic monologues with the other half of the 'dialogue' more continuously implied than Pamela's parents had been. Hence Richardson's dialogue techniques are further developed for introspection as well as scene. At moments of pressure there is a great deal more of the quick movement of the mind and the use of the dash, and very effectively. What is interesting again, however, as playing against this increasing involvement, is an increase in the use of distancing techniques too. For, crude though the first pond scene in *Pamela* had been, it showed awareness of the mind's capacity to distance reality by stagey self-dramatisation, as well as of the mind's need to get itself at a distance to see clearly. In *Clarissa* Richardson develops both of these with considerable artistry, often playing the same technique both ways. Clarissa seriously debates the case for and against Lovelace in her midnight reverie; Lovelace uses debate to muffle the issue in debating points. Clarissa uses 'thee' and 'thou', image, and allegory in her desperate attempt to understand and rebuild herself in her deranged papers. Lovelace uses 'Imperial' 'thees' and 'thous', image, and allegory, to unrealise; to convert reality into the indulgent scenarios of his fantasy. With Clarissa, the present and the past move slowly but surely to increasing distance and moral summary, while the future is hinted at in mysterious moments of illumination. Lovelace refuses to remember, and continually escapes from present and past by his habit of fantasising about the future. Clarissa is gradually de-dramatised, Lovelace never ceases to dramatise himself to the very last moment.

Though we are finally debarred from Clarissa's consciousness at the end, the new feature of *Grandison* is that there is no experience of self-colloquy in the hero from the start. Over great stretches of the novel, moreover, his conduct is also reviewed as past, and he tends to talk in a formal style of moral summary. What is also interesting, but difficult to demonstrate, is the tendency even in the 'subjective' side of the novel for Harriet, Clementina, and Emily to think of themselves in the third person. This is in keeping with the novel's interest in serious role-playing for moral purposes, and though one can only point to the cumulative effect of numerous tiny instances, this plays some part in making the whole novel more public, 'formal', and objective than *Clarissa*. The fact that the letters, though addressed to one correspondent, are usually meant to be passed around a circle, means less intimacy too. Within these limits, however, the techniques of *Clarissa* are employed again, though Harriet can be more playful than Clarissa had ever been, and Charlotte is allowed to go a little beyond Anna in the direction of Lovelace. There is the hint of a new possibility in the 'schizoid' dialogue of Clementina with herself, but unfortunately Richardson failed to develop this.

His greatest artfulness, however, lies in his perception of how writing to the moment could be used to reveal things about the characters that they do not know themselves. Precisely to the extent that they write or speak 'in the heat', they are liable to give themselves away to a reader who pays close and sensitive attention to minutiae. The art is one of the most subtle implication, and requires continual reading between the lines. This is true of scene, where the smallest details of speech, gesture and behaviour are tell-tale indicators of the state of mind and heart. It is true of epistolary style, though I reserve discussion of this until later. It is true most of all of introspection, where we have to be especially alive to slips of the tongue, and to remarks pointed in one direction that may be very suggestive of another. Even the most collected analysis can say more than the writer meant. Unfortunately Richardson might have said of his twentieth-century readers what he did say of his contemporaries: 'But a great deal in charity to them, I attribute to their inattention. Ye World is not enough used to this way of writing, to the moment. It knows not that in the minutiae lie often the unfoldings of the Story, as well as of the heart'.[1] The most obvious examples are the tell-tale signs of dawning love in Richardson's heroines; but we should be no less alive to the signs of conflict in B and Sir Charles whose hearts are otherwise closed to us; and above all to the slipping of the rake's mask in Lovelace to allow us glimpses of the increasingly tortured and desperate face behind. The flippancies

[1] Richardson to Lady Bradshaigh, 14 February 1754; Carroll, *Letters*, 289.

and theatricalities of Anna and Charlotte can also show us their fear of emotional commitment, and their subterranean impulses to hurt the friends they know to be so much better people than themselves. There is always much more than meets the eye in 'the master of the heart'.[1] If the dramatic form, the expansiveness, the elaborate and rather Byzantine delicacies remind us of Henry James, so too do the subtlety and deviousness of the art of implication, and the challenge to the reader's sensitivity to nuance.

Writing to the moment also implies writing from moment to moment, and my whole interpretative method has insisted on the importance of trying to follow the twistings and turnings as one situation creates the next. Whereas epic art depends on a complex and worked-out plot; and so, for economy's sake, does the three hours traffic of the stage; Richardson allowed his characters to create their own developing situation, within only a general story-outline. He says consistently and explicitly that he wrote without a plan, even in *Clarissa*, and there is every reason to believe him.[2] (There is some ambiguity about the very first 'version' of *Clarissa*, finished before 24 July 1744, but the plan he sent Hill was I think, almost certainly a compendium drawn from the first draft rather than an elaborate preliminary to composition).[3] One must of course distinguish *Pamela* and

[1] The phrase is Thomas Edwards's, and gained currency because of the opening lines of his dedicatory sonnet, first prefixed to the second edition.

[2] e.g. Carroll, *Letters*, 71, 182, 194, 235.

[3] Hill speaks of 'that good and beautiful design I send you back the wide and arduous plan of', but also of his astonishment 'when you tell me you have finished it already' (24 July 1744; Barbauld, *Correspondence*, I, 101). McKillop deduced from this, and the fact that Hill was only sent the opening letters in December, that Richardson 'blocked out his plan before writing any of the letters' (*Richardson*, 121). Yet Richardson's answer to Young's letter of 8 December (Carroll, *Letters*, 61) seems to speak of the work itself, which Richardson is already trying to prune. In September 1746 he sent Hill a very detailed compendium, and in speaking of it in October (Carroll, *Letters*, 71) nevertheless refers to the diffuseness of his 'No-Plan'. It seems very likely therefore that what he had sent Hill in 1744 was a less detailed compendium, and what was 'finished' already was not a preliminary plan, whose completeness could hardly be astonishing, but a first draft. Eaves and Kimpel share this view: see *Richardson*, 206; and 'The Composition of Clarissa and Its Revision before Publication', *P.M.L.A.*, 83 (1968), 416-28.

Clarissa from *Pamela in her exalted Condition* and *Grandison.* The central story-line in the first pair is simple and tight enough to give a far greater unity; while in the others diversification means a real loss of the power that comes from concentration and inevitability, and there is evidence that Richardson was at times uncertain about which way *Grandison* might go.[1] Always, however, writing to the moment means that the central structure is not the author's epic design and analysis, articulated by plot, and elaborated *through* characters-in-action; it is the reorchestration *by* the characters of a basic situation again and again. The novel may indeed appear unstructured, but 'ars est celare artem': the organic appearance depends upon the convincing inevitability of each development, given the characters. Moments like Clarissa's two abductions and the rape are moments of danger for Richardson precisely because they are the 'turns' which might most easily not have happened, and yet are demanded by the story. He has to make them credible in terms of the characters or his own hand will be fatally revealed, whereas an epic artist can produce all sorts of accidents by plot. Richardson succeeds triumphantly with the rape, I believe; but only just with the abductions, and only because Clarissa is Clarissa. But because the structure works by constant repetition, it is revealed by the continuous comparison it demands. 'Shape' appears as we compare viewpoint with viewpoint, situation with situation, phase with phase. Each scene is structured by the conflicting attitudes of the protagonists; giving it both 'form' and 'meaning'. We have to measure the points of view against one another to understand how things happen and what will happen next; and the measuring process is also, as I tried to demonstrate in Letter 24 of *Pamela*, a structure of critical evaluation. Then, as scenes are repeated with variations, Richardson keeps giving his characters the freedom of another chance, which they use increasingly to determine themselves. Inevitability of event, and crystallisation of character and meaning go on together. Scenes become linked

[1] Richardson to William Duncombe, 22 October 1751; Carroll, *Letters*, 194, see also 198.

in chains, where apparent repetition points up significant differences and reveals development: the 'attempts' in *Pamela*, the 'marriage dangles' in *Clarissa*, for example. Or they divide into phases with clearly marked turning-points, like the deteriorating phases in London, each concluding with a more serious attempt on Clarissa. Overall structure may be marked by the chiming of scenes across wide intervals. The gift of clothes on which *Pamela* opens, is related to Letter 24, parodied by B in Letter 27, redeveloped in the Bundle scene of Letter 29, given a new symbolic twist in Pamela's clothes floating on the pond, another reorchestration when she repossesses her 'two bundles' (II, 85; *I, 270*), and a final pointing in the last journal entry (II, 359; *I, 449*). As Clarissa is taken to prison, we suddenly become aware of the thematic 'chime' with the abduction scenes that close the first two instalments, and of the whole theme of 'prison' that ends with Clarissa's escape from her own body. Similarly the three 'pond scenes' are the heart of *Pamela*, as the 'dedication scenes' are of *Grandison*. In comparing points of view we not only measure differences, but likenesses, often in unexpected places, like the full revelation of Lovelace's link with both Anna and James Harlowe, and the links between Clementina, Olivia and Emily, or Charlotte and Olivia. Examples could be multiplied, but in all this it is the apparently artless, organic, and inevitable development from moment to moment that is important. Richardson uses reorchestration to give shape and meaning, but at his best we never feel his manipulating hand . . . as is obvious by the fact that the structuring has passed virtually unnoticed.[1] It is the inevitability that gives his work what Coleridge called its 'dreamlike continuity'[2]: the powerful sense of something that

[1] I hasten to except Frederich W. Hilles, 'The Plan of *Clarissa*', *Philological Quarterly*, 45 (1966), 236-48; reprinted in John Carroll (ed.), *Twentieth Century Views*, 80-91. Hilles is particularly good on the 'symmetry of the plot', and its relationship to what Coleridge called 'The common end of all *narrative* . . . to make those events, which in real or imagined History move on in a *strait* Line, assume to our Understandings a *circular* motion – the snake with its Tail in its Mouth'.

[2] *Biographia Literaria*, ed. J. Shawcross (London, 1907 reprinted 1949), chapter 23, II, 183.

cannot be stopped or changed. Yet it is by giving his characters freedom that their self-determination becomes so convincing.

Two of the novels however again share a great advantage over the other two in that they contain plotters, who can import into the fiction some of the excitements of intrigue, suspense, and sheer activity that belong to plot. This function is shared between B and Pamela and, as we noticed, gives rise to some interesting moral difficulties, because the novelist in Richardson loved intrigue while the moralist began to see its human implications. When it stops, most of the 'story' excitement goes out of the book, and only when it reappears for a while in the Swynford episode and the affair with the Countess is there any 'story' life in the Continuation. With Lovelace, however, Richardson both gives full rein to the plotter in himself, sometimes for the sheer joy of it as in the plot to kidnap Anna; and, at the same time, confronts himself more fully with the implications of the urge. For Lovelace's plots not only destroy Clarissa, but also trap and destroy himself. Lovelace, along with James Harlowe in the early stages, is responsible for nearly all the narrative excitement and suspense in *Clarissa*; and one of the great losses in *Grandison* is the absence of such a figure. For while plotting is in 'life' terms a moral evil, robbing people of freedom and treating them as puppets; in 'art' terms, it is a 'felix culpa', a satanic temptation of the good to see what they are and what they can do.

Writing to the moment has certain implications for fictive 'time'. In the first part of *Pamela*, chronology is relatively indefinite. One is surprised to hear in Letter 4 that Lady Davers has been in the house for a month, and in Letter 20 that fourteen months have passed since the death of B's mother. Gradually, however, we begin to experience chronology.[1] Letter 23 is marked 'Thursday' – the key day in *Pamela*[2] – and she is to

[1] See also John Samuel Bullen, *Time and Space in the Novels of Samuel Richardson* (Logan, Utah, 1965); an extract from which is reprinted in Rosemary Cowler (ed.), *Twentieth Century Interpretations of 'Pamela,'* 108–11.

[2] And throughout Richardson – it was Mrs Richardson's lucky day. See John Carroll's 'Introduction', *Twentieth Century Views*, 4. Examples could be multiplied.

leave a week later. Though the days in this week are not explicitly marked, the letters do begin to make us feel that we are living from day to day, and not at interesting points separated by indefinite intervals. Then, in her captivity, Pamela's journal marks the days of the week, counts them, and sometimes marks the hour of day. We share the girl's awareness of the passing of time and of the way it slows or intensifies. After the wedding, chronology becomes more indefinite again, and remains so as a rule in the Continuation, with the exception of the affair with the Countess.

In *Clarissa* however, at great trouble to Richardson as he confessed,[1] the letters are carefully dated throughout, and we can be exact about chronology. The tragedy takes place between 10th January and 7th December (18th December, New Style). Clarissa leaves her father's house on 10th April, escapes to Hampstead on 8th June, and is raped on the night of 12/13th June. She dies on Thursday 7th September at 6.40 in the afternoon; Lovelace dies at about 10.30 on the morning of December 16th N.S. At the beginning and end only the dates are given and the letters are more widely spaced, but through most of the novel Richardson gives us the day of the week and often the hour of the day. The effect is to make us feel that we are fully experiencing time; that it is being enacted both chronologically and psychologically. Sterne was to note that the way we feel time depends on our mental and emotional state, and was to play with time wittily and seriously in his treatment of the human mind. But Richardson is the first novelist to make his readers experience the full interplay of 'personal' time and clock time. We wait suspended while the characters wait, or time fills with crowding conflict, but we also live from hour to hour, and day to day, and month to month, aware of morning, noon and night. This is clearly a major factor in the book's verisimilitude. Not only did the Richardson who so lived with his characters, and knew to the hour what they were doing, come to think and feel about them as though they were real people, but his readers do the same. Indeed some things would be incredible were it

[1] Richardson to Hill, 20 January 1745/6; Carroll, *Letters*, 63.

not for our experience of passing time. Clarissa dies about three months after she is raped, but unless we felt something of the passage of those months – and the dragging-out has a part to play here – we could not give it the kind of assent Richardson needs on the plane of verisimilitude, through which the deeper reasons for the death can be glimpsed.

Yet again the 'naturalness' conceals an artistry, both in itself and in the manipulations it allowed. After the long-drawn-out conflicts, Clarissa's two escapes create both surprise and suspense, heightened in the case of the book's first readers by making them end the first and second instalments, so that they had to wait months to find out what had happened. (One of the advantages of a return to the first edition would be to restore a very little of these 'gaps'.) Richardson also achieves a considerable impact by playing off a brutal closure against the expansiveness and suspense that preceded the rape and the death. The two 'fatal breviates' (Belford's a deliberate retribution for Lovelace's), the curt notes that mark the two climaxes, only gain their full effect because of the dense experience of time before them.[1]

The chronology of *Grandison* is also elaborate. Now, moreover, we can date the whole action. Richardson wanted the action of *Clarissa* to be thought of as having taken place some years before, but would not commit himself further. Eaves and Kimpel note[2] that the first day given is Wednesday 1st March, the date must be after 1720, and in 1721, 1727, and 1732 March 1st fell on a Wednesday. In *Grandison*, however, the '45 Rebellion takes place while Sir Charles is with the Porrettas, and it is to escape the continual arguments about the Jacobite successes in 1746 that he

[1] Other effects are obtained by disrupting chronology. Understanding is always delayed until we have more than one account of a given situation, but the effect of the long delay before we get Clarissa's account of the trick at Hampstead and the rape, is to achieve a stark juxtaposition. By moving the explanation out of its natural order, Lovelace's brutal posturings before the rape, and its terrible effect on Clarissa, are thrown into high relief against one another. Clarissa's collected account can then make its full impact, in retrospect. Richardson is also, of course, 'making 'em wait'.

[2] Eaves and Kimpel, *Richardson*, 239

leaves for Vienna and precipitates the discovery of Clementina's feelings. After the breakdown of the match, he returns to Paris 'not long before his father's death'. Eight months after that death Lord L takes his bride on a visit to Scotland, and it is to prepare for their return that Sir Charles is on his way to Colnebrook when he rescues Harriet. (Thursdays are significant again: Harriet is abducted on Thursday 16th February; Sir Charles is accepted on Thursday 19th October; and they are married on Thursday 16th November. The dates fit 1749 O.S.) The novel then is probably set between 10th January 1749 and 14th July 1750, though only the days and months are given.[1]

The experience of time is never as intense as in *Clarissa*, but it is still important, and many of the same techniques are used. What is new, however, is the simultaneous experience of different time schemes, which Sterne again made explicit in *Tristram Shandy*. When Harriet retells the Grandison girls' account of the history of their family and their brother, we are aware of Harriet writing 'now', of the week-long conversations behind, and of the narrative itself made to the moment at its best, so that three time schemes coincide; 'in the present'. Harriet later sends to Northampton Dr Bartlett's edition of Sir Charles's correspondence from the first visit to Italy, and her comments remind us that we should be reading with her eyes as well as our own. Later still, Charlotte sends her sister the four batches of actual letters from Italy as they arrive, and her comments and account of their impact on Harriet, and Harriet's own letters, make a curiously spectroscopic effect. We live in several time schemes simultaneously and have something at least of the experience of imagining several readings at once. The experience is more complex than *Clarissa*, and not uninteresting, though it forgoes the concentration and involvement with the one main action, that gave the experience of time such intensity there.

1 C. R. Cheney (ed.), *Handbook of Dates* (London, 1945). See also however, Richardson to Lady Bradshaigh, 25 February 1754; Carroll, *Letters*, 296, where he speaks of the marriage taking place in '1750, or nearer still to the present year, as the Reader should be disposed to calculate'.

2

The price we pay for the new way of writing is of course its length. Nobody could have been more acutely aware of this than Richardson himself, after his attempts to prune *Clarissa*; and he also knew very well that shorter novels would have sold far better.[1] *Pamela* is relatively slim, but its single focus is its major flaw, and every development that made *Clarissa* better, also made it longer. The multiplication of sustained points of view means more bulk in itself, and also that many scenes have to be gone over twice at least. Richardson cut some repetition by doing part of the second point of view narratively, leaving only the important impressions to the moment, but they have to be there. Increased dramatisation also means more bulk: dramatised conversations take longer than narrative; introspection done to the moment needs much more space than straightforward analysis. The complicated twistings and turnings of the exploration from moment to moment which make the fiction so inevitable and lifelike, and the continual reorchestrations which crystallise structure and meaning, continually expand the length. Yet Richardson insisted that anyone who tried the same method would produce the same luxuriance,[2] and conversely, attempts at abridgement merely prove how the length is identical with the strength. The more one tampers with the method, the more one destroys what the method was *for*. The epistolary convention has disappeared from fiction because the cost was felt to be too high. Shorter (and powerful) epistolary novels are possible, like *Les Liaisons Dangereuses*, but they cannot do what Richardson did. On the other hand, the essence of Richardsonian dramatic fiction can be compressed into non-epistolary forms: *The Awkward Age*, *As I Lay Dying* and *The Sound and the Fury*, the novels of Ivy Compton Burnett. Yet the compression also pays its price in much greater difficulty. We have to weigh the subtlety, complexity, depth and balance against the length; the exhaustive clarity against the exhaustion.

[1] Richardson to Hill, 5 January 1746/7; Carroll, *Letters*, 75, see also 158, 329.
[2] Richardson to Lady Bradshaigh, 9 October 1756; Carroll, *Letters*, 329.

There is also a problem of relevance. In speaking in his Postscript of 'the History (or rather Dramatic Narrative) of *Clarissa*' (VII, 309; *IV*, *554*) Richardson became more formally precise, but there is a significance in 'History' too. For there seems to me a useful distinction between History, Fable, and Myth when we seek to describe certain dominant orientations of the imagination in all kinds of literature. I have argued this at some length elsewhere,[1] so will be summary here. In Myth, an author presents a lifelike world, but does so in order to discover and reveal behind it, a hidden structure of 'truth', in a different and deeper dimension. In Fable the author constructs an artefact, a confessedly 'made-up' world, in order to be able to analyse certain features of 'reality' more freely and more precisely. But in History the author explores the contingent and phenomenal for its own sake, and is most concerned to create a world which can imitate 'reality' as fully as possible; refusing to impose shape or authorial vision on multifarious experience. The aim is to include everything, cheerfully accepting 'bagginess' and 'monstrosity' in the service of faithful representation. History as fiction begins with historians filling in lacunae between facts, writing scene or dialogue by inference to lend plausibility to 'what must have been', while remaining true to the facts as they have found them. Fiction as history half persuades us that its persons and places are empirically 'real', even though we know it is fiction. These terms are not of course intended to be evaluative. In any given literary work, moreover, two or more of them are likely to coexist. Yet one will always dominate. I think it is Myth in Defoe, Fable in Fielding, and History in Richardson. *Robinson Crusoe* has a strong element of History and some tendencies to Fable, yet its major impulse is to discover a deeper structure hidden beneath the surface of its 'realistic life', and its protagonist is an Archetype. *Tom Jones* has a strong element of History and some element of Myth, yet its major impulse is to manoeuvre its Types within, and for the sake of, an analytic design; it is marvellously

[1] Mark Kinkead-Weekes and Ian Gregor, *William Golding: a Critical Study* (London, 1967 reprinted 1970), 241-7.

'artificial'; and the dominant presence is that of the 'author'. *Clarissa* contains elements of Myth and Fable, but its main impulse is to create the character herself, to get her completely 'there' for us, to capture the quality of her life in its fullness.

The point is, then, that whereas Myth and Fable are radically selective and hence exclusive, using only what verisimilitude and detail they consider necessary for other ends, History aims at inclusiveness, yet can never tell all there is to be told. Where it sets out to be the history of an epoch, like *War and Peace*, it must be the intersecting histories of many lives and is theoretically limitless. Even when it sets out to be the history of an individual, it must be the history also of those lives which immediately bear on that person. And where, as Tristram Shandy comically laments while he shows the impossibility of writing a 'Life', can it truthfully begin and end? and where is the limit to its context? Beginning is arbitrary – procreation? birth? the start of the most formative phase? – but the History always 'really' begins before the 'beginning'. Ending is equally arbitrary – a wedding? a death? – but the History always 'really' stretches after the 'end'. Theoretically a *full* presentation goes on infinitely before and after and roundabout. Practically, Richardson chooses a starting-point *in medias res* as he must, but he has intense difficulty knowing where to end, and criteria of relevance are highly debatable. There is a definite sense in which he can say of *Clarissa*: 'Judges will see, that, long as the Work is, there is not one Digression, not one Episode, not one Reflection, but what arises naturally from the Subject, and makes for it, and to carry it on'.[1] (He makes a similar claim in the Preface to *Grandison* (I, ix).) To take anything away is to lose something. And yet, why should the work not be still *more* baggy and monstrous? The History of Clarissa would be even better history if we understood her upbringing in relation to her parents' marriage, for Mr Harlowe isn't fully 'there' now, and to her brother's and sister's developing personalities. The History of Harriet and Grandison would be better history if we saw them in bed, and as parents, and grandparents,

[1] *Preface, Hints of Prefaces, and Postscript*, ed. Brissenden, 4.

and dying. And the same is true of every character who impinges on the main ones, and helps to make them what they are. It is not only the literary form, then, that causes the length, but also the kind of imaginative drive that chooses the form, and commits both itself and its critics to highly insecure and arbitrary criteria of relevance. We easily detect the unfortunate consequences, which ensure that Richardson should be so little read nowadays. Yet at least we should also recognise the difficulties that will beset a critic who wishes to argue exactly where, and how, and on what grounds the works should have been shorter.

There are also disadvantages which spring from the letter-convention rather than the form or the kind of imagination. The correspondents have to be kept static, and apart. Whereas the protagonists in Fielding and Defoe can move freely, the main characters in Richardson have to stay put in order to write and receive the letters. The result is a curious effect of stasis, which Tennyson probably had in mind in telling Fitzgerald of his love of 'those large, still books'.[1] Richardson is driven (sometimes to awkward lengths) to find explanations why Pamela cannot be allowed to get away, or Clarissa to get to the Howes, or Anna to join her friend; but the real reason is that if Pamela reached her parents or Clarissa joined Anna, the letters would stop. The main characters have to be kept still, under the microscope, the letters must keep flowing. It is pointless to complain – yet at moments the plausibility can be strained. *Grandison* partly solves the problem by directing much of the correspondence to minor characters, with Harriet and Sir Charles together – but this means that the effect of interchange and interanalysis is lost.

Richardson also invites mockery because of the credibility gap between the bulk and frequency of the letters and our own experience as letter-writers. It is of course silly to calculate how many hours a day characters must have had to spend scribbling – just as it is silly to ask how an omniscient author could possibly have discovered all he is supposed to know. All art depends on

1 Edward Fitzgerald to C. E. Norton, 4 April 1878, *Letters and Literary Remains* (London, 1902-3), III, 321.

convention, and all sensible criticism on recognising and allowing for it. Yet because Richardson was a 'historian' wedded to verisimilitude, he unwisely draws attention to the problem by fussing too much about it himself. He was an extremely early riser, and makes a point of insisting that his characters do likewise. Lovelace and Belford use short-hand. Sir Charles agrees that Harriet should pop in and out of company to keep her correspondents posted. Pamela and Clarissa hide paper and pens and ink so that we should not wonder where they got them. Yet the convention remains obstinately a convention, and it might have been better to tiptoe quietly past its clumsiness.

As characters multiply in *Grandison* there is a new problem of getting them all informed. At one point Harriet sends to Northampton Dr Bartlett's translation of (presumably) Grandison's copy of Mrs Beaumont's letter to the Marquesa della Poretta about Clementina (III, 85). This is made a little more plausible by the thematically public nature of the novel: Harriet and Sir Charles will not read each other's letters come upon by accident, but both deliberately open the bulk of their correspondence to an increasing circle as part of the theme of moral community. Yet this means not only a loss of intimacy and its self-revelation, but also that the convention can be heard to creak. There is an analogous problem about getting readers informed. Richardson, who knew his novels backwards, remarked how widely the relevant material on any given crux may be scattered[1]; and anyone who has tried to write on him will recognise the problem feelingly. It is extremely difficult to 'possess' such huge fictions and keep the experience fresh and complex in one's mind, and it is still more difficult, even when one remembers a point and roughly where in the story it comes, to put one's finger on it. Richardson supplies cross-references in footnotes, and indexes, but the problem remains.

The difficulty of 'harking back to make up', which is particularly important in 'History', is also increased by the letter convention. Necessary slabs of narrative look even more awkward

[1] Richardson to Lady Bradshaigh, 8 February 1754; Carroll, *Letters*, 281.

pretending to be letters. Richardson handles the problem quite well. He always tries to use the harking back to produce some other effect by its placing. In *Clarissa* there are effects of delayed understanding and sharp juxtaposition. In *Grandison*, where the two stories in parallel increase the problem, he carefully alternates slabs of narrative with sections of 'to the moment' and makes sure that the narratives are enlivened by our sense of the characters' response to them. The story of the wedding is made more spirited by splitting it between Charlotte and Lucy, writing in relay. Yet the letter convention creaks again whenever we see the telltale heading 'X – in continuation'.

Indeed many of the radical characteristics of the experience Richardson offers are effects of his convention. Dr Johnson speaks as ever for the common reader in his famous remark that if a man were to read Richardson for the story, he would hang himself.[1] His other famous comparison of Richardson and Fielding in terms of a watch,[2] may point to the far greater interior depth and subtlety of Richardson's insight into mind and heart; but the obverse is the far greater narrowness of range. With this again goes the intensity and introversion, which may amount to claustrophobia with some readers, and gave rise to Coleridge's comparison of reading Richardson with being in an overheated sick room,[3] while reading Fielding is like being out on a breezy lawn. Yet in comparing the two and trying to be just to either, we are bound to see how the defects are the obverse of the major qualities, and how inevitably both are the outcome of convention and form.

3

Both 'History' and 'Dramatic Narrative' are centrally concerned with the creation of highly complex characters (rather than archetypes or types), and this is a major distinction between the

[1] Boswell, *Life of Johnson*, ed. Hill-Powell, II, 175.
[2] Boswell, *Life of Johnson*, ed. Hill-Powell, II, 49.
[3] *Table Talk*, 5 July 1834.

different kinds of imaginative drive. In talking of the 'people' who inhabit all kinds of fictional world, the distinction of 'flat' and 'round' is a rough index of complexity. We all understand approximately what is meant; but the terms are imprecise because they take no account of the whole shaping vision in which those 'people' have their life, and which determines the kind of life they shall have. The more a fiction tends towards Fable, the more specialised and functional its people will be, since the chief reason for their existence is their role in fitting in with one another as parts of an analytic and authorial design. The subtlety, complexity, and penetration will be found in the design, rather than the individual components or attitudes, and they should never be considered in separation. We know all we need to know of Volpone, Tom Jones, and Mr Gradgrind, and if they became more complicated they could not work as they do. In Myth there is more 'lifelike' complexity, since the 'deep' structure of meaning is not already known, but is searched for within the lifelike; yet again there is considerable selectivity. It is the whole situation rather than the individual character which is important and revealing. Golding's image of the artist whittling away to get at a shape hidden in the wood is useful here[1]: the art discards as irrelevant a good deal about its people. Oedipus, Moll Flanders, and Ahab are potentially very complex, but the complexity is not the point. It is what they come to see and reveal archetypally about their worlds that is important, not the exploration of their individuality, their past, their development. All this is complicated, of course, by the co-existence in any work of more than one kind of imagination, but in so far as one kind dominates, the nature of the 'characterisation' is always a direct function of the form, and its 'success' depends altogether on what it is *for*. All 'flat' characters are potentially 'round', all 'round' characters are potentially 'flat'. The terms carry no evaluative charge unless and until they are related to the requirements of the form they serve, and then they are too crude.

In Richardson, character is all-important. His 'historian's' urge

[1] *The Inheritors* (London, 1955), final chapter.

is to capture the life of his main characters with the greatest possible complexity, and the fullest possible sense of development. The dramatic form depends on creating *through* the characters and allowing them to produce the changing situations. The letter convention is a device to get us 'inside' their minds. Hence every character in Richardson is basically complex; and how far the potentiality of a particular one is developed will be a function of the space available, rather than the nature of the imaginative process that is at work. If Mr Harlowe seems 'flatter' than the rest of his family it is because there is a special reason why we are not allowed to see enough of him. Servants like Joseph and Will are 'flat' because they function mainly to serve the action, but Joseph is 'rounder' than Will because he is given more space to reveal himself, and both could easily be developed much further. The subtlety of Richardson's form means that we are always aware of the complexity hidden behind the action. James Harlowe looks like a stage villain on the surface; but once we become aware of his hidden motivation, of the way he and Bella are 'acting', and how they are deliberately crushing some feelings and liberating others, he makes an effect wholly different from Blifil or Mosca. He can be given letters near the end that reveal a complex and suffering character. The drive of the art is towards actualising the potential complexity of every character, though this cannot possibly be achieved.

Yet, because we are involved in getting to know characters from within, part of the experience is of how they get to know others and themselves, and here 'flatness' has a real part to play. For all characters begin by knowing others 'flatly', and how this continues or changes is a function of character, and an important part of the total experience and the meaning. B is a 'flat' character to Pamela until the second pond scene, a 'round' character to himself, and potentially a still 'rounder' character to us if we can learn to see beyond the limitations of both; yet the 'flat' interpretations of each are part of the total experience, and too great a part if we do not read carefully. We experience a continual conflict between 'flatness' and 'roundness' both in the cognitive processes of the characters and in our own. Clarissa partly overcomes her tendency to categorise as she overcomes her ego; but never completely, because *moral* categories always seem more important to her than characteristic complexity. Belford grows into a 'historian', a medium for conveying understanding of both Lovelace and Clarissa, but as he does so he becomes less interesting as a character. The ability to enter the situations of others is both a discipline of the self and an extension of human sympathy – yet the loss of ego may be a loss of character-interest. The central experience of living in Lovelace's mind is of fascinating individuality, but of one that sustains itself by refusing to accept its own complexity or that of others, and that goes on trying to flatten character into type and attitude.

The tension comes from Richardson himself. There is an interplay in all his work of the Historian's imagination with that of Fable and Myth. There is a kind of moral insight which drives towards an understanding of complexity, but there is another kind of moral imagination which drives to Fable, 'flattening' characters into attitudes, types of virtue and of vice. The major drive is to explore the complex imperfection of Clarissa and Pamela, but there is also the tendency to intensify their 'perfection', make them 'exemplary' – or intensify the villainy of Lovelace. Insofar as characters are themselves moralists of the second kind as well as historians, it may be their morality as well as their ego that causes them to 'flatten' their vision of others. We see both a vividly characteristic fear, and a moralistic fabling, in Pamela's portrait of Colbrand, which plays against the Colbrand we see and hear for ourselves. The equally grotesque death scenes described by Belford, especially the death of Mrs Sinclair, show the temporary prevalence in him of the moral fabulist over the historian. This is as much 'heightening' as 'flattening', intensification goes along with selectivity as it was to do in Dickens. In *Grandison*, Fable and History do overt battle: Sir Charles is exhibited as a type in an art of analytic fable, Harriet as a character in an art of dramatic history. But whereas the idea of moral role allows Harriet to develop herself into the type she wishes to be, without losing her individuality and complexity because of the exploration of its cost, Richardson fails to develop Sir Charles into the character which lies latent in the type. On the other hand, insofar as Richardson's novels are religious, they also contain an element of Myth. (In the sense that Myth searches for a 'deep' structure of reality behind the apparent surface, it always represents a 'religious' view of the world – though this can be Marxist as easily as Christian.) We can most easily see in *Clarissa* the distillation characteristic of Myth, the X-ray vision which is finally revealed as the complexities of History are stripped away. The inquisition into the heroine finally takes her beyond herself into a mode in which her individuality is no longer important. As she sits in prison, she remains the individual we have got to know better than we know anyone in life, but she has become an archetype in an archetypal situation, where individual complexities no longer matter. We cannot any longer follow the last process of archetypalisation in terms appropriate to character.

Yet it is still the mode of History that dominates overall and proves the major mode of experience. We can see this particularly in the importance of development and growth in characterisation. Fable is an art of fixation, and changes are brought about by plot for analytic reasons. In Myth it is the vision rather than the character which changes. But the central experience of *Pamela* is to share the development of the naïve girl into the poised and confident young woman, and the same is true of our experience of growth in Clarissa, Belford, Harriet, Charlotte and Clementina. It is true also of our experience of Anna and Lovelace, though there is in them a resistance to change. (It is *not* true of Grandison.) The experience of living inside minds from moment to moment is essentially an experience of historical growth, though it may use Fable for analysis, and distil out into Myth at the end of *Clarissa*, or in the middle of *Pamela*.

We can see the dominance of History also in the central concern with integrity of character. In Fable the typical attitudes are 'given' and constant; the author manoeuvres them within his analytic patterns to make points. But in History the character has to be painstakingly established from within, and his integrity has to be tested to the point of disintegration if necessary, to prove its validity. In Myth the archetype learns to read his true situation, but what is discovered, whether it be Oedipus or Moll Flanders, is that it is situation which determines the human being. Indeed, as I argue in the next chapter, the lumping of Defoe and Richardson together as exponents of 'realism' has blurred the polar opposition between them. In *Moll Flanders* the central revelation is that what she is, what she can feel, and what she will do are all determined by her situation. Defoe's art implicitly denies integrity of character. Conversely, Richardson pits *Clarissa* against terrible onslaughts of circumstance, precisely to vindicate the integrity of her character against the worst her world can do. It is the characters in Richardson who create their situations, and discover the truth of their self-determination.

Complexity, growth and change, integrity and self-determination – these are then Richardson's primary concern in 'characterisation'. One must however insist again that the distinctions I have tried to draw between his dominant imaginative drive, and other kinds of imagination, do not themselves imply value judgement. There are as many kinds of 'reality' in fiction as there are ways of looking at life and forms of articulating vision in words. None is intrinsically better than another, for they ultimately translate into metaphysical stances, and we cannot allow some concealed 'reality principle' to determine our critical criteria. There are temperaments which will prefer one kind of imagination to another, ideologies which imply a ranking, social or cultural contexts in which one direction will seem more palatable or fruitful. But each kind of imagination must be judged in its own terms first, and what I am really concerned with is the establishment of the appropriate terms for Richardson. Moreover all fictions are conventional and artificial; and it is the more necessary to insist on this, the more closely art attempts to 'imitate' life. If one can speak of 'knowing' a character in Richardson in terms analogous to knowing somebody in life, there is still a crucial difference. For Richardsonian 'knowing' is a product of artfulness, a process which can be traced to a manipulation of words. How then do we get to know Richardson's characters?

The primary answers are the most difficult to demonstrate, since they depend precisely on the experience of living with characters over a prolonged period, from moment to moment, relatively free from authorial interference. Each dramatic scene adds its quota to our knowledge. We watch characters behave, catch their gestures and expressions, pick up the tones of their voices in direct speech, assess the things they say, and guess at their motives. In these respects watching Richardson's characters is like watching people in life. Next, we see each of them as he appears to and is analysed by the others, and so modify or extend our own more complex and inclusive analysis. This represents an artificial intensification of processes in real life. Finally, however, we listen to their own analysis of themselves and of others, their introspection, their consciousness on the wing. Richardson departs from life because it is words, and styles, that become preternaturally significant. Indeed all 'knowing' in his work is coloured by the point of view of the letter-writer, except for the most fully dramatised scenes. Richardson offers an orchestra of styles, and uses stylistic minutiae as he uses minutiae of behaviour. For 'styles differ too, as much as faces, and are indicative, generally beyond the power of disguise, of the mind of the writer'.[1] In his mature art, each of the correspondents has a perceptibly different style, and we not only sense the differences (as many admirers pointed out), but must also distinguish their implications. Furthermore the development and change in characters can be suggested by the modification of their style.

This would need a book in itself to analyse properly – and possibly a more valuable book than mine – but I can perhaps suggest a structure of investigation.

If Richardson's desired effect is to seem as though he had no style himself, only a number of distinctive styles, in practice it cannot really be like that. It is perhaps more realistic to think of

[1] Richardson to Miss Westcomb, ?1746; Carroll, *Letters*, 64.

him as commanding a stylistic range, which he proceeds to subdivide and discipline in different ways; so that what we need to inquire into is the nature of the subdivision and the discipline in each case. On the other hand there is also a degree of stylistic projection, in which he imagines and commands a language that is not his, and will increase the distinctive coloration.

Pamela provides a preliminary model. Richardson operates on a scale which stretches from his own analytic mode to a homeliness, colloquialism, and femininity which represent his fullest projection into a mind very different from his own – though it uses himself as all dramatists and actors do. The original Pamela was much more rustic than she is now, in both vocabulary and grammar. She used 'curchee' for curtsy, 'stockens' for stockings; the false concord 'you was', and many other rusticities of grammar; and had a more pronounced habit of running on with many 'ands' and 'buts', like conversation. She 'tricked herself up' before the clothes scene, and here the colloquialism has a feminine flavour too. Unfortunately, Richardson almost immediately began to revise the novel towards greater politeness, so that by the fifth edition (when he had learnt about concord himself, incidentally) she had become perceptibly less rustic. In his final recension, published posthumously in 1801, he pushed this still further with Pamela and much further with B, and took the opportunity also to safeguard the novel wherever possible against the misinterpretations and adverse criticisms it had suffered.[1] Yet if the book becomes less open to question and more dignified, it loses a great deal of its life and complexity. Eaves and Kimpel have shown that the original version of *Clarissa* was also much more colloquial and lively than the first edition.[2] There was clearly a continuous, and unfortunate, drive to politeness throughout Richardson's career, since each novel has a staple style more 'raised' but also stiffer than the last. I believe the first editions are preferable, though later ones do contain improvements in

[1] The revision is discussed in detail by Eaves and Kimpel, 'Richardson's Revisions of *Pamela*', *Studies in Bibliography*, 20 (1967), 61-88.

[2] Eaves and Kimpel, 'The Composition of *Clarissa*', 416-28.

some ways. In the final recension the greater politeness of Pamela tends to close the over-wide gap between the extremes of her style which allowed the 'High-Life' men to sneer that she talks 'like a *Philosopher* on one Page and like a *Changling* the next'.[1] Nevertheless, even as *Pamela* stands in the editions we read, Richardson preserves a good deal of homeliness, colloquialism and femininity, which create the first coloration of the little servant-girl's style. One would need to examine the conversational running-on, the parentheses and exclamations, the homely vocabulary, the vivid idiom ('madamed up', 'topsy-turvied', 'horrid cross', 'in a great pucker'). Other servants have this too – Richardson clearly felt that the idiom of the servant hall was much more lively than that of the drawing-room. Locations like the clothes scenes and the gossip-sessions with Mrs Jervis show feminine turns of phrase as well as subject matter – Richardson had a good ear for female idiom. These begin to give us 'the servant girl'; but there are also certain motifs that belong specifically to Pamela. One is the sort of signature tune that many dramatists use to mark characteristic speech, like Hamlet's habit of triple repetition. Pamela's 'Good Sirs' is one of these, and she has a characteristic vocabulary: sad, odious, vile, naughty, honest, innocent, virtue, sweet. Significantly, however, this begins to shade into stylistic features which are not only characteristic, but also have implications which become part of the novel's process of evaluation. Her 'sanctimonious' references to God (so easily and so often) grow into a far more serious exploration of providence. Her pronounced exaggerations, the vivid blacks and whites into which she translates the complexity of others, and the heightened idiom in which she thinks of them, both make her very 'real' to us, but are also criticised and ultimately transcended in the novel's exploration. Her literary allusions mark what would now be the 'scholarship girl', but their comedy is often part of her habits of self-dramatisation and self-pity which also come under the microscope. Her pertness and cheek, the quickness of her ingenuity and calculation, are

[1] Quoted by McKillop, *Richardson*, 67.

both a vital part of our sense of her liveliness, and are used to raise moral question-marks. On the other hand, we also have to note the stylistic register of her attempts to get outside herself in objective analysis. This can be done by the distancing techniques of 'thee' and 'thou', but also by approximating her style to Richardson's own analytic mode. Here colloquialism modulates to formality, antithesis, balance; subjective sentences become structured sententiae. Yet we must be on the look-out even here for stylistic suggestions of unconscious revelation.

To investigate these various layers would take much time and effort, but perhaps a brief quotation may suggest how many factors can be present in a confined verbal space. Mrs Jervis tells Pamela about B's remark, that if he could find a 'lady of birth' just like Pamela, he would marry her. 'I colour'd up to the Ears at this Word; but said, 'Yet if I was the Lady of Birth, and he would offer to be rude first, as he has twice done to poor me, I don't know whether I would have him. For *she* that can bear an Insult of that kind, I should think not worthy to be a Gentleman's Wife; any more than *he* wou'd to be a Gentleman, that could offer it.' The colloquial speech-rhythm is the base, with the colloquial idiom (coloured up to the ears) and grammar (Yet if I was). There is the Pamela-word 'rude', and the Pamela self-pity (to poor me). But the sentence modulates to a more formal structure of value in which 'he' and 'she' and 'gentleman' and 'worth' are set off against each other. Yet it contains not only the ambiguous blush, but the tell-tale verbal slip (used in *Clarissa*) which betrays female calculation and nascent feeling (I don't know whether I would have him). Often Richardson's command is uncertain, and there are over-wide gaps between the different layers, but here they co-exist quite naturally. And though there can be unconscious humour, much that seems comically pretentious and parodic is taken up meaningfully into the total verbal structure of exploration and evaluation. Her style is a 'bastard' mixed style, appropriate to her peculiar situation, and its mixture can be funny and silly, as well as lively, but it would be a mistake to take Richardson's naïvete for granted.

Lastly, of course, in this preliminary model, we should have to try to register the modification of the style that suggests Pamela's growth through the book. This would be difficult to demonstrate, yet we recognise that it is there. We should look for less homeliness and better grammar. Her sentence-structure becomes more formal and elaborate and colloquialism tends to disappear. The most morally questionable features are disciplined. Pertness is replaced by meekness; the exaggerations born of self-righteousness, suspicion, and fear, are replaced by an effusive gratitude. There are fewer dramatics, less calculation, though she never ceases to be the Pamela we have known. But, quite apart from our feelings about her more elevated character, many of which are complimentary, we make the awkward stylistic discovery that as Richardsonian characters grow better, their style may become less interesting. There is also a new kind of silliness in Richardson's attempt to make her talk like a lady: 'The charming Taste, you gave me, Sir, of your poetical Fancy, makes me sure you have more Favours of this Kind, to delight me with, if you please; and may I beg to be indulged on this agreeable Head?' (II, 358; *I*, *449*). Yet there can also be a straightforward plangency of Richardsonian high-seriousness two paragraphs later, in her final abjuring of pride.

In *Clarissa* it is the strategy of subdivision that gives the 'orchestra of style' its life and significance. The first division is the differing disciplines which produce Clarissa and Anna. Richardson gives Clarissa his own style, purged of its comic register, its linguistic playfulness, its inventiveness and whimsicality. She is 'Serious' and 'Gravity' (the nicknames of Richardson as a boy at school), her tonal range is from the serious to the melancholic. Hers is primarily an analytic mode in which words are taken seriously, weighed against one another, assayed by repeated examination. The structure of her sentences has a constant tendency to balance and antithesis, moving words into meaningful collocation or distinction. (Her first two sentences in the book weigh 'politeness' and 'sincerity', 'partiality' and 'judgement'.) There is a large conceptual vocabulary, aiming at precision. The movement has the steady progression of a mind thinking. More and more surely, she tries to discipline her ego, to apologise for talking about herself, to become objective – and though this may be morally admirable, it also explains why we should feel that her style is less interesting as she grows more truly virtuous. On the other hand, there are three kinds of modulation which make the style more lively. Along with the analytic power can go a verbal tartness, edged by petulance or anger. Betty remarks on her ability to 'say very cutting words in a cool manner, and yet not call names' (II, 121; *I, 321*), and it is the accuracy and point that makes the words cut. Then, in dramatic scene, and in introspection as the pressures on her mount, the whole movement quickens, the modulations become emotional, the voice is more spoken than thought or written. Finally her family all call attention to an organ note of feeling, which expresses itself not only in tears and gestures, kneeling, throwing up her hands, turning up her eyes, but also in another kind of style. Behind each of Richardson's main protagonists there lies a stage tradition[1]: Clarissa resists Lovelace in the pathetic language of contemporary 'she-tragedy'. This style is exclamatory, working by rhetorical repetition and amplification: 'Save me, save me, O my dearest Mamma, save your child from this heavy, from this unsupportable evil!' (I, 148; *I, 101*). It eventually rises to a serious theatricality: 'Be remorse thy portion! – For thine own sake, be remorse thy portion! – I never, never will forgive thee! – I never, never will be thine! – Let me retire! – Why kneelest thou to the wretch whom thou hast so vilely humbled?' (VI, 26; *III, 260*). The tendency of this 'high style' to lapse into the melodramatic and operatic is clear enough; yet our response is always governed by the seriousness of her situation, and modified by the tension between the different registers. For the operatic mode is always cooled by the modulation into the analytic

[1] On Richardson and the stage see McKillop, *Richardson*, 144-54; Leo Hughes, 'Theatrical Convention in Richardson' in *Restoration and Eighteenth-Century Literature, Essays in Honor of Alan Dugald McKillop*, ed. Carroll Camden (Chicago, 1963), 239-50; Konigsberg, *S. R. and the Dramatic Novel.*

one as soon as the crisis is over; while the analytic is saved from dryness by the pressure of feeling. There are effects of mutual compensation and control. Moreover the different registers are unified by the fact that the same moral currency governs both, and by the kind of integrity that makes Clarissa Clarissa. Whether she uses words with analytic precision or rhetorical amplification, she does not play with words or feelings, she does not 'act'. There can be excess and indulgence, failures to be wholly accurate or honest, but these exist within and are controlled by a linguistic medium that strives always for truth of word and emotion. Her moral imagination and strength of feeling can lead to grotesquerie, like her portrait of Solmes; or to image and allegory, like her papers, but these are felt to be registers of pressure by their difference from the norm, while their seriousness makes them 'Clarissa'. Stylistically as well as morally she strikes us, not as invariable, but as 'steady' and unified – somehow massive.[1]

For Anna, Richardson begins to liberate all that he had repressed in creating Clarissa. She opposes Miss Flippant to Miss Grave-airs: gay, playful, full of raillery. Her tonal scale overlaps with Clarissa's moral seriousness, but it moves in the opposite direction towards an irresponsible levity, breaching decorum; a teasing that can hurt as well as amuse. Where Clarissa weighs words, Anna asserts her sovereignty over them. She makes up language, distorting or combining words with hyphens, playing with them in new senses or forms. Her syntax represents the quick and volatile movements of her own moods, playful or scornful. It is much more dramatically *spoken* than Clarissa, with darts and jabs, turns and interjections, thrusts and ripostes. In dialogue, and imagined dialogue, she has a pronounced habit of breaking in on others, and twisting what they say. She has a special sex war vocabulary of scorn and contempt, and as 'man-wretches' turn into 'monkeys' and 'baboons' she opens a vein

[1] See also William J. Farrell, 'The Style and the Action in *Clarissa*', *Studie in English Literature, 1500-1900*, III (1963), 365-75; reprinted in Carroll (ed.), *Twentieth Century Views*, 92-101.

of animal imagery expressing her strong sense of superiority. Whereas Clarissa can be cutting when she is angry, Anna is more slashing (Bella uses a bludgeon). She is less inhibited by loyalty or fairness in turning a phrase or piling up a case; less verbally responsible in that the balance disappears from the syntax and the scrupulousness from the vocabulary. The effect is of a delightful freedom, zest, and vitality of language. If 'she-tragedy' lies behind Clarissa, Anna is the witty lady of Restoration Comedy. Yet the comedy depends on distance, on keeping experience and feeling at arm's length; the style which is so delightful, also shows the implications of such distance for mind and heart. She feels more quickly than Clarissa but less strongly; thinks more flexibly and sharply but less deeply. Her linguistic habits of interrupting and of playing with the words of others, her irony and sarcasm, make her a good acid test and probe; but they also reveal her egotism, and her failure to respond to and allow for others' feelings and integrity. To quote at length her teasings of Clarissa about 'conditional liking', 'punctilio' and 'delicacy', would be to demonstrate how, in mimicking and mocking, she shows up her friend's limitations; but also how her lightness contrasts with Clarissa's painful effort to be scrupulous. Though Anna plays with the language of feeling, 'throbs' and 'glows', she can do so more easily because she feels less herself, and is less concerned with the moral significance of feeling and behaviour. Eventually the limits of her compassion, and the touch of cruelty in her make-up, will be registered in the language of her hurtful letter after the rape (VI, 153 ff.; *III, 346 ff.*), which is inexcusable even in the light of her partial ignorance. She takes phrase after phrase from the pathetically incoherent letter Clarissa writes, after her escape from the brothel, and with cold anger draws mortifying inferences. She claims that Clarissa has broken her heart, but she shows the limits of that heart. The very habit of playing at a distance with what others say, that can be so amusing and testing, reveals its irresponsibility, and lack of imagination and understanding. When she does feel, the 'distance' produces staginess, as we see at Colonel Ambrose's Ball (VI,

447-9; *IV, 21-2*) and in her rhetoric over the coffin (VIII, 86 ff.; *IV, 402 ff.*). She can never really commit herself to feeling. Whereas the tensions in Clarissa's style exist within a uniformity of character, Anna's volatility begins to register in language a split personality: Miss Duessa against Miss Una. Richardson creates a style which is powerfully drawn towards Clarissa's world of feeling and morality; but which also reacts away to egotism, distance, levity, non-commitment. The contrast probes Clarissa; but Anna is also a constant relief and liberation from the remorseless pressure of absolutism and responsibility. She is more normative; and can act as a kind of lightning-conductor drawing off, in her parody, irony, and teasing, the reader's feelings of resistance to and withdrawal from her friend. Yet her style gradually reveals the implications of such withdrawal; of the divorce between language and experience.

The male correspondents then reverse the contrast in the order of their introduction. Lovelace is of course the great stylistic triumph of the book, and an endless source of linguistic fascination. He pushes each of Anna's characteristics to an extreme. If she is sovereign, he is Imperial. He has made his friends accept the stylistic convention of an Emperor addressing slow-witted vassals, and there is a continually feudal and condescending habit of both tone and vocabulary in his attitude to 'varlets' and 'rascals' – and female 'rebels' and 'rascalesses'. His Imperialism expresses itself in tone of address (Thee and Thou), in metaphors of power, warfare and conquest, and in his attitudes to language itself, which he invents and plays with more variously even than Anna. He opposes to Clarissa's conceptual framework and vocabulary, and to Anna's language of sex-war, the developed hypotheses and the special vocabulary of the rake's code. He continually takes up the girls' language, and builds it ironically or subversively into structures of his own, mimicking, parodying, distorting. The experience of his language is the polar opposite of that of Clarissa's, and is liberated also from Anna's degree of moral and decorous restraint. Whereas Clarissa uses the weight and substance of words objectively, to make herself confront and understand reality, Lovelace uses them to dissolve reality into the fantastic shapes which sustain his ego. He is far more imaginative than Anna, but his imagination is used to unrealise. Her vein of animal imagery, for example, is even more prominent in his style, but it is developed into sustained set-pieces: the bird in the cage, the marauding fox, the rooster and his hens. Imperial imagery develops into adolescent fantasies, like the harem picture of Anna and Clarissa. The move from image to fantasy is always amusing, but also is always used to distance and unrealise. He roars with laughter at his ability to translate the hysterical girl running from her father's door into 'the wind-outstripping Fair-one' (III, 30; *I*, *513*). The touch of grotesquerie, potential in Clarissa's moral imagination, is exploited for comically unrealising purposes in his zany image of Lord M, when he hears about the rape, 'shaking his loose-flesh'd wabbling chaps, which hung on his Shoulders like an old cow's dewlap' (VI, 223; *III*, *394*). Even the extraordinary portrait of Mrs Sinclair, as she terrorises Clarissa, imports a weird delight in surrealism into the 'real' situation, and takes our minds off Clarissa's terror by the distancing effect of caricature. He paints a mocking picture of himself and Belford as hermits in the old caves at Hornsey (VII, 18-19; *IV*, *42*) and parodies Clarissa's effect on his friend, and himself, in terms of the ridiculous statue in Westminster Abbey (VII, 331-2; *IV*, *252-3*). The touch of allegory present in Clarissa balloons into the unrealising allegories of Love and Conscience, which are designed to crush moral scruple (IV, 241-2; V, 242; *II*, *400*, *III*, *146-7*). Equally important stylistically is the creation of the quickness of Lovelace's mind. He is endlessly inventive, spinning plot and fantasy out of himself in zestful outpourings of language. His verbal reflexes are very fast. Where Clarissa debates seriously and carefully with herself, Lovelace blurs the issue in debating points, with speed and sleight of words. There is also the strongest contrast syntactically. Where the characteristic movement of Clarissa's mind is one of deliberation, Lovelace's style develops the volatility of Anna into a hectic, eddying verbal energy. This begins with his absolutely inveterate habit of dramatising himself and everything around him. Richardson perfects with Lovelace the use of the dash to mime the quick, darting, ever shifting kaleidoscope of a mind endlessly role-playing, and shifting roles in mid-stream or mid-sentence, to make a situation give up all its dramatic possibilities, as in his playacting before the fire scene. The zestful energy that makes him walk tall in his imagination and think of buffeting the moon with his hat, becomes more enjoyable to him the more hectic it can be made. 'Stamp, stamp, stamp up, each on her heels; Rave, rave, rave, every tongue - Bring up the creature before us all, this instant' (VI, 62; *III*, *285*). But most important of all is the development of Anna's volatility to the point where style can register a personality radically unstable. Every dramatist is potentially a chameleon, and with Lovelace Richardson gave full rein to this: if Anna is Duessa, Lovelace is Legion. The main tradition behind him is that of Restoration tragedy, and he himself is vividly aware of this, discriminating between the stormy rageful lover (which he prefers) and the softer kind, between Dryden and Otway. But he is also the rake in Restoration Comedy, giving his own title, 'The Quarrelsome Lovers', to the play he engages in. He writes the courtly love-epistle, he plays Othello and Milton's Satan, he is endlessly literary. He has a multiplicity of styles corresponding to the multiplicity of roles. But whereas some of them are self-pluming virtuosities (the old man, the gentleman-shopkeeper), the significant point is that many of the 'sympathetic' roles he plays with Clarissa really do represent sides of himself and what, with part of his mind, he would like to be. There is endless conflict between mask and face, and finally between different selves within himself. It is very difficult to detect which is the 'real' Lovelace, and the question can only be settled by watching him make his own final selection, and die in his chosen role. Lastly, however, we have to press the point made about Anna even more strongly: that it is because, for all his passionate talk, he cannot and will not commit himself to feeling; and because he sits so loose to all values but his own endlessly variegated egotism; that his style is so fascinating. He is Legion *because* he is Love-less, and because he represents an extreme series of dislocations between experience and language.

Belford is not introduced until the third volume, and his letters are infrequent until he takes up the narrative from the prison, when he becomes mainly a medium rather than a character. He is therefore always less 'there' to us than Clarissa, Anna, and Lovelace. What Richardson clearly does with him, however, is to start the Belford range from Lovelace at his most serious (when he is most affected by Clarissa), and bring it gradually towards Clarissa's world of morality and feeling. Belford is the sober rake who becomes the Man of Feeling in the new mode of Steele and Lillo. Even before he meets Clarissa, he is not as Lovelace would have us think, a heavy-footed imitation: indeed he is so little rakish in temperament that one can well believe his later insistence that it was only his admiration of Lovelace that made him his follower. His style, from his first letter, is nothing like Lovelace, but a medium whose seriousness and steadiness already remind us of Clarissa. He uses the imperial style, but the theeing and thouing, and words like 'eagleship' and 'elf', sit to the side of his sober arguments. Yet his style seldom has the pointed balance and antithesis of Clarissa's; its basis is rather a steady and painstaking accumulation, clause on clause, instance on instance, argument on argument. Conceptually he is hamstrung at first by his formal allegiance to the rake's code, so that he cannot offer arguments from morality or religion, but after he meets Clarissa he begins to renounce the limitation. He is not as intelligent as Clarissa; but when he fails to spot or guard against the openings he gives Lovelace to turn his arguments upside down, it is also because he lacks the levity of his friend, or Anna. His meeting with Clarissa, the death of his uncle, and the decline and death of Belton, all force him to think and to feel more deeply. His style becomes more plangent; the accumulated arguments stronger and more powerfully felt. Then Richardson liberates through him, as his other distinctive characteristic, a kind of imagination that is the moral counterpart of Lovelace's comic grotesque: the language of moral fable. He begins to use moral anecdote in his fourth letter, and develops the career of Belton into a full-scale Exemplum. He begins to develop a talent for grimly heightened detail, first 'realistically' in the death of Belton ('His eyes look like breath-stained glass' (VII, 208; *IV, 169*)), and then symbolically in the astonishing description of the death of Mrs Sinclair, which so shocked the Abbé Prévost that he refused to include the English barbarism in his translation. The description of the prostitutes in the morning confessedly derives from Swift, but the heightening of Mrs Sinclair goes well beyond the antiromanticism of the Lady's Dressing-Room or the magnified physical horrors of Brobdingnag (VIII, 55-7; *IV, 380-2*). She is made into an animated gargoyle, a horrifying personification of shapeless, uncontrolled Violence. (The 'tradition' for this goes back to the Middle Ages, through the monsters of Spenser and Bunyan, and also directly, through the pre-latitudinarian hellfire sermon.) Every repulsive feature, working with horrible verbal energy, adds its quota to the symbolism of 'the End of Violence and Disorder'; and the heightening is too unpleasant to be funny. The positive counterpart and contrast is of course his account of the death of Clarissa – but though the Man of Feeling veers towards sentimentality here, he still represents only part of Richardson, as the counterweight of Clarissa herself will show. When Belford takes over as the medium of narrative it is inevitable that we should tend to look through him rather than at him, and that he should cease to come across primarily as a character. Yet we are never safe in assuming that he is Richardson's mouthpiece. If he is ahead of Anna and Lovelace in feeling and understanding, he is always several stages behind Clarissa. His style continues to maintain a perceptible 'Belford' coloration; a hint of the ponderousness of Lovelace's 'awkward mortal' or 'sorrowful monkey'; a touch of the heightening that makes his dreams after he has seen the coffin, for example, so different from Clarissa's matter-of-factness. We are never allowed to forget that he is experiencing a new and unfamiliar atmosphere which disconcerts as much as it moves him. The hints of clumsiness and excess are not accidental, since Lovelace picks them up in mockery.

Clearly Richardson develops Belford less than the others, but there is enough to keep him part of the orchestration, the quadruple interplay of styles.

This produces in the texture an exact equivalent to the overall structure, where meaning is gradually defined by a process of repetition with variations, and continual cross-comparison. We can be confident that we are reading in the right way, when attention to the words themselves shows the same structural manipulation as the handling of the scenes. We should be concerned with the characteristic vocabulary of the correspondents, in which the meaning of words for each of them defines itself by rephrasing in a series of contexts; and with a continual cross-examination as characters submit one another's language to their own probing, irony, or subversion.[1] 'To be sure, he is far from being a polite man: Yet is not directly and characteristically, as I may say, *unpolite*. But *his* is such a sort of politeness...' (II, 173; *I, 357*). Clarissa defines politeness as she will define a whole range of value-words, but we shall also see the word as others see it in a wide variety of contexts, and measure the definitions against one another. Belford demands an assurance 'that thou meanest to do honourably by her, in *her own* sense of the word' (VI, 84; *III, 300*), drawing attention to the discrepancy. James Harlowe tauntingly redefines his sister's vocabulary in mid-sentence: 'your perverseness to him (*Averseness* I should have said, but let it go') (II, 25; *I, 256*), and the whole family try to translate her language into selfish peculiarity. Much of Anna's teasing is specifically linguistic: 'when you give new words for common things; when you come with your *curiosities*, with your *conditional likings*, and with your PRUDE-encies (Mind how I spell the word)' (I, 276; *I, 188*); 'my service to you my dear, and there is ceremony for your ceremony' (III, 293; *II, 177*); 'Were I in your place, and had *your* charming delicacies' (III, 261; *II, 155*). Each of these words will be taken up again and

[1] Some excellent work has been done on this by Irwin Gopnik, *A Theory of Style and Richardson's 'Clarissa'* (The Hague, 1970); to whose third chapter I am particularly indebted.

again, extended, examined, subjected to irony and parody, tested. 'Curiosity' develops a range of sexual suggestiveness, implied repulsion or attraction. The relations between prudence and prudery, moral approval and love, moral scruple and feminine pride, are examined not only by Anna and Clarissa but by Lovelace. He mimics Clarissa on punctilio for his own purposes, redefines her vocabulary in terms of female pride, translates it into his own 'plain English', brings out, in his account of a delicious verbal misunderstanding, the ironic relation between the physical and the moral meanings of 'delicacy'. Indeed *all* the characters are involved in this examination of words, seriously, or parodically, or both. As Betty Barnes genteelly takes her snuff, and Joseph pens his laborious epistles, we should be aware not only of ways in which they parody their betters, but of linguistic collocations of ingenuity and ingenuousness, pertness and impertinence, plainness and stupidity, that bear on our serious reading of their betters' language too.

Indeed, the orchestration of style is developed very cleverly outwards from the main four. To look back at the Harlowes is to see how, within their 'family' procedure of transforming Clarissa's language into a medium whose surface morality cloaks selfish greed and power, they are subtly differentiated by their stylistic relationships with the main correspondents. In Mrs Harlowe's style we see her daughter's, but with its linguistic and moral scruple evacuated and its feeling turned wholly inward on herself. Take Uncle John, remove the selfish inhibition of feeling, and increase the slightly ponderous seriousness to greater moral objectivity, and one has Belford. James and Arabella reorchestrate Lovelace and Anna in harsher, cruder terms. Lovelace's rhetorical storminess and Anna's teasing lose their 'play' and modulate into uglier passion and malevolence. Irony becomes heavy sarcasm, mimicry a taunting malice. The witty sovereignty over words is pedantry in James (whining vocatives, pervicacious) and abuse in Bella (pug's tricks, lovyer, hook-ins, creeper-on). The relationship of Anna with Bella, particularly, is brought to a head in parallel and contrast, in their slashing correspondence after the rape.

In another direction, minor characters are used to question the whole idiom of sententiousness. In this book, so radically concerned with moral analysis, the tendency of 'sentiments' to harden into cliché once language is divorced from the crucible of conflict, is splendidly parodied in the sententiousness of Uncle Anthony, Lord M, and the young clergyman Brand. The delight of Uncle Anthony is that he is a comic Mr Richardson, setting himself up as both the master of linguistic examination, and the master of the heart. 'Never, girl, say that is *severe*, that is *deserved.* You know the meaning of words. No-body better. Would to the Lord you had acted up to but one half of what you know' (VII, 113-4; *IV*, *105*). '*He that is first in his own cause*, saith the wise man, *seemeth just: But his neighbour cometh*, *and searcheth him*' (I, 233; *I*, *159*). His signature tune is the mandatory 'mind that', which is a pleasant parody of Richardson's own demands for close attention. But his claims to search language and the heart, and the sententiousness of his style, are allied with a coarseness of manner, a lowness of grammar and vocabulary, that call the whole quality of his mind in question. He is racily readable. Richardson gives him his most 'to the moment' style: the spoken intonation of the voice captured with the rapid movement of the dash, the frequency of interjection and turn, the colloquialism – and the result is that Uncle Anthony is remarkably 'there' to us. Yet the coarse worldly cynicism, the materialistic and commercial turn of mind, reveal the full result of puritanism taken over by the counting-house, the extreme of Harlowe-ness. 'Too ready forgiveness does but encourage offences', 'for the devil is love and love is the devil', 'self-do, self-have', 'what's sauce for the goose is sauce for the gander' (I, 238-41; *I*, *163-5*) – these 'sentences', allied with a vocabulary of racy tradesman's idiom, exhibit a 'common sense' in which we have to accentuate both words. For would-be moral sententiousness, divorced from the experiential testing of inner conflict and true relationship, and worn down to handled smoothness like money, goes dead and devalued. Uncle Anthony is a vulgar parody of Clarissa's scrupulous evaluation of language and feeling, and a beautiful linguistic creation of the Harlowe alliance of selfish greed and morality. If Clarissa's uncle marks a sententiousness gone low, Lovelace's uncle is the counterpart in high-life of moral sentiment become cliché. The garrulous, untidy, insensitive medium in which the collector's pieces of Lord M's 'wisdom of nations' are set, like coloured glass in a magpie's nest, again devalues their point. Again we are confronted with *sententiae* divorced from experience on the one hand, and discipline and scruple of intellect and feeling on the other. It is no surprise to find how easily Lord M can be manipulated by his nephew (as Uncle Anthony by his). He has a better heart than Anthony Harlowe, but the limits of his mind and of his moral sensibility are thrown into relief by his aspirations to wisdom. The letters of the insufferable and ambitious young clergyman complete the process of both parodying Clarissa and setting off her true quality. Here the satire is not merely directed at pretentiousness: the acquisition from classical Augustan education of a hoard of wise sayings, divorced from experience, and hence aridly pedantic. The point is revealed as a deeper one, when Brand's myopia is amplified in his imagined discourse with Clarissa. Behind the conceit and ambition, and the blindness they cause, is a radical worldliness. The classical sentences are meaningfully *pagan*; they can happily co-exist with self-pluming and social climbing; the education of a gentleman is allowed to become the denial of the Christian.

What is perhaps most interesting in all this is the degree to which parody becomes a central procedure of the novel. It was there in *Pamela* to a greater degree than has been realised, but in *Clarissa* it is omnipresent in scene, in style, in language, in characterisation. By surrounding his heroine with a whole series of distorting mirrors, Richardson can both allow for our criticism of her, and test her true quality. For an illustration of how far this goes, and in what surprising registers, we might conclude with a brief glance at Betty Barnes, Joseph Leman, and Dolly Hervey. Betty has been encouraged to ape her mistress Bella, and her substitution for Hannah in serving Clarissa is part of James and Bella's strategy of harassment. But the comment on

Clarissa of the cheeky maid is at least as important as her relation to her mistress. For she is not ill-natured; and as she gives Clarissa proverb for proverb, as she debates ingenious and ingenuous, and reveals her pride in an ability to say fine things, her impertinence has a moral as well as a social register. Clarissa is forced to confront not only a breach of social decorum, but an annoying parody of herself doing precisely what Bella says *she* does: show off morality and sententiousness for applause. The parody has its own small part to play in the complex investigation of Clarissa's pride. Similarly Joseph may strike us first in comic relationship with Lovelace. His mask of 'honesty' behind which he angles for Betty and the 'Blew Bore' inn, the parody of male sovereignty, the heavy-footed following of his paymaster's 'intricket' intrigue, the rustic spelling and coarse humour that play off against the aristocratic polish and wit, make it seem that the distorting mirror is primarily set to reflect a parodic image of Lovelace. Yet again the parody of Clarissa is ultimately more important, though more concealed. For Leman gets upset by the 'fessesshious' tag of 'honest' precisely because he really wants to be so. He does have a conscience that makes him uneasy about means and ends. It is partly because he wants to imitate Clarissa that Lovelace can deceive him into making her central mistake, 'to save mischieff' - 'for I am, althoff a very plane man, and all that, a very honnest one, I thank my God. And have good principels, and have kept my young Lady's pressepts always in mind: For she goes no-where, but saves a soul or two, more or less' (II, 370; *I*, *492*). We confront, stripped bare in a context of stupidity which must reflect back on his revered mistress, the central fault of taking on herself a wrong means for a good end, 'to prevent mischief', that she herself will see as the one false step that has led her into a wilderness of error. Finally Dolly Hervey, especially in the first edition, helps us to see that Richardson is not merely poking snobbish fun at simplicity and 'uneducated' style. He revised her letter (II, 327; *I*, *463*) to much greater politeness, but in its original state it was clearly designed to let a loving heart shine through simplicity of mind and many crudities of style. The touch of childishness is related to the childlike Clarissa that will appear in her deranged papers. All three of them provide simplifying mirrors of the heroine, which we use in defining her true likeness.

A stylistic examination of *Grandison* would reveal the same elaborate orchestration, in the 'dramatic' side of the novel. Rather than attempt to repeat the same kind of analysis, however, I prefer to draw attention to the third 'model' of the subdivision and discipline of Richardson's own style, which distinguishes *Grandison* from *Pamela* and *Clarissa.* The new departure is what one might call a binary division, splitting the whole book, and playing off against the whole dramatic orchestra of characteristic styles, a style from which drama and individual character have been exorcised. Sir Charles both writes and talks in the full sententiousness of moral argument and summary; dramatic introspection is banished; and dramatic scene regularly defused. This produces a stiffness, a formality, an unremitting solemnity which are major barriers for a modern reader. Not only, moreover, is Sir Charles never submitted to parody (apart from Harriet's crucial comparison with Adam); but he is also surrounded with continual paeans of praise which increase our alienation. If however one can control one's first impulse of annoyance, the stylistic analysis of the 'Sir Charles' side of the novel might proceed in two not uninteresting directions.

The first would be to attempt to pin down the kind of linguistic challenge that is presented by Sir Charles's elevations, absolutisms, and objectivities. For if the formality and stiffness are partly to be explained as the sad result of the humble printer's aspiration to high politeness, now reaching an unfortunate climax, there is also more to the problem than this. For they are not only deliberate, but designed to challenge precisely by their deliberation. The challenge, I think, takes two forms: the sustained insistence on a tone and vocabulary that we would never use; and the deliberate exclusion of kinds of syntax, tones of voice, registers of language, that play a vital part in our own living speech. We cannot explore the style of Sir Charles unless we see that the banishing of drama is *provocative.* The serious casuistry of the book shows itself not only in the challenge to argue about Sir Charles's actions, but also in the provocation to argue about his style. What does it do that we would not? As we noticed, Sir Charles first calls attention to his 'dialect' himself, when he insisted on referring to what is to be done with his father's body as 'interring' the 'venerable remains' (II, 110). When we have finished laughing, we may perhaps be ready to be struck by the weird precision of tone and vocabulary. Latin takes over from Anglo-Saxon with pompous results, but 'inter' insists on ceremonious respect as 'bury' would not, 'remains' insists on 'Sir Thomas' rather than 'corpse', and 'venerable' governs both, by insisting on incorporating into the language itself a formal recognition of the 'right' tone of veneration. It is not undertaker-jargon, for undertakers pretend what they do not feel, whereas Sir Charles is deliberately formulating a real demand on himself and his sisters. It turns out to be a pronounced verbal habit to lard his speech with adjectives which, equally deliberately, pin down and put on record his sense of the proper response: 'the condescending invitation' (in the complimentary sense), 'the amiable lady', the 'truly respectable persons', the 'worthiest of men'. Examples could be infinitely multiplied. He also has a habit of formally presenting people to one another, all the time, with a courtly summary of their best qualities. His language continually reminds everybody else, as well as himself, of what they should be feeling and how they should be acting. The nearest analogy, I believe, is with the language and style of diplomatic speech, which is equally elevated for the same reasons, and which equally insists, as it were, on objectifying the ideal function of everybody, rather than their fallible personalities. Here we reach the exclusiveness of Sir Charles's idiom, its banishing of most of the inflections and registers of language that make up our own. For the banishing of drama banishes all the less-than-ideal motives and impulses that give our speech its individual flavour, and all the registrations in tone, vocabulary and syntax that express our particular personalities and characters.

We reach the challenging paradox, that Richardson's ideal man has no subjective individuality at all – and that this is an important part of his function. His idiom is a deliberate objectivisation of himself, and of everybody else. Locked in those deliberate sentences, nothing but what he *ought* to say and feel can gain expression. The only conflict that is possible is when he cannot tell what he ought to express, or when he momentarily falls below his ideal of himself. In his very language there is embodied a curious invitation to a balletic dance of ideal behaviour, summoning the dancers to shed their ordinary selves, their less-than-ideal manners, and words, and tones, their defective individualities. In being struck with the artificiality, the 'unnatural' elevation, the admonishing and objectivisation, we must also take into account what they are *for*. They represent an extremism of style which is not a clumsy attempt to imitate high-life but a challenge to the fashionable and the middle-class alike. If we reject the challenge it cannot be on 'realistic' grounds, that people do not talk like that, for Richardson is not engaged in mimesis in the 'Sir Charles' side of the novel. It must be on the grounds that they *should* not talk like that, that the attitudes Sir Charles's language suggests are less ideal than he thinks, and this is the response of serious casuistry Richardson was most interested in provoking.

It is a great pity that there is not enough direct challenge to Sir Charles, stylistically, in the book itself. One direct confrontation on the subject would have done a world of good. On the other hand, the second direction in which stylistic analysis would be fruitful would be an investigation of the ways in which the two kinds of fiction, the dramatic and the anti-dramatic, proceed to influence each other. Unfortunately again, this is a rather one-sided story. In the Library, Sir Charles for the first time is in a situation where there is no 'ought' – or rather where 'ought' is highly perplexing. The result is that his speech suddenly begins to be genuinely dramatic. One great movement of the novel should have been the growth from that point to a complete interfusion, where the absolutist demands of the language of moral imperative were justified by the fully dramatised experience of introspection, the language of what *is* thought and felt, not only inescapably, but as part of moral fineness. This never happens; which is the book's great failure. All we have is a lesser kind of liveliness, when the influence of Charlotte and the idea of moral role liberate a serious teasing in Sir Charles. In the 'trial' scenes, and in the scenes with the Beaumonts and Lord W, there is dramatic syntax, a speaking voice, and a degree of playfulness, that make Sir Charles a bit more human and normative – but without sufficiently probing mind and heart as drama should do, since it has the effect of being 'put on' for strictly moral reasons. On the other hand, there is in Harriet a marked and interesting struggle to get outside herself, to live up to her chosen role, to become the Type she wishes to be, and this is registered in an interfusion of dramatic language and syntax with the 'Sir Charles' style. Here the two dimensions of the novel do come into intercourse: if it had happened the other way round as well, the novel would have been much more interesting linguistically, and in every other way.

What the whole stylistic examination of Richardson tends to bring out, moreover, is an intriguing set of paradoxes which *oppose* linguistic variety and liveliness to moral worth. It is the volatile characters, the witty ones, the ones who play with words as part of their egotism, who make the most lively and fascinating reading. It is the collected, steady, serious ones who register the moral fineness and discrimination, but who are by that very token, somehow inescapably heavier going. The more the characters improve morally in their growth within the book, the more the paradox is confirmed. We can register it again in another direction, with relation to objectivity. As objectivity grows, drama disappears; the less self-absorbed, the less interesting. Sometimes, as with Hickman, Richardson almost deliberately faces himself with an extreme assertion that the good and dull are preferable to the lively; and the Jane Austen of *Mansfield Park* showed her Richardsonian descent nowhere more clearly than in the subdivision of her own style that forced the same challenge on herself. In some depth of his mind, Richardson must have disapproved of the very qualities in himself that made him a notable dramatist, and created his most lively and fascinating styles. On the other hand, in style as in every other way, the greatest work comes when the two sides of himself most fully test each other.

4

As Richardson's art developed, so did his understanding of the implications of different kinds of drama. *Pamela* already shows a potential for tragedy, comedy, and melodrama; but in *Clarissa* he develops not only a greater technical grasp of what is involved in each of these directions, but a subtle ability to play them off in structural relationship, both overall, and within particular scenes.

The great invention of *Clarissa* can indeed be seen as the discovery of how to use comedy to probe tragedy. The comic mode, in Anna and Lovelace, is used to question, by distance and parody, the high seriousness and increasing involvement of the tragic mode that creates Clarissa. Whether Richardson actually learnt this from Shakespeare seems to me as unprofitable a question as whether *Clarissa* is strictly to be classified as tragedy; what is significant is that the probing of tragedy by comedy is as centrally 'Shakespearian' as the depth of characterisation and the mastery of human nature that were the distinguishing features of Shakespeare for the eighteenth century. To understand the fallibility of Pamela is to see that a comic counterpoint already existed in the early work; but in *Clarissa* the strategy is built into the central structure itself, and proceeds with a much subtler awareness of techniques of involvement or of distancing, and of techniques which combine both. Similarly, while intentional parody exists in *Pamela*, it becomes central in *Clarissa*.

The melodrama in *Pamela* comes mainly from the heightened imagination and fear of the heroine. Already, as in the 'Closet' scene, it can be used to produce a 'double-take' response, so that what is melodramatic from Pamela's point of view can be comic for us as we look at B – but without diminishing the heroine, since her feelings are made so real and so understandable to us. (Conversely there is a 'genuine' melodrama and a falsely rhetorical one, on the only occasion that B does 'attempt' to rape her.) Again, however, Richardson proceeds to develop with greater subtlety what had originally come about simply as the result of projection into different points of view. Clarissa herself is not melodramatic, but is continually involved in melodrama by others, especially Lovelace who thrives on it. Richardson however is well aware of this, and modulates it in several directions. He can subject his heroine to it, so that we hold in serious tension (in the fire scene) the weeping victim and the sardonic parody of courtship, with the residual strength of her underlying intransigence. Or he can explode it into farce, as in the scene where Clarissa bloodies her nose, or when she demolishes the whole melodramatic build-up around the 'crime' of Dorcas. Or – and this is where the call on his technique is most challenging – he can attempt to bring her *through* Lovelace's sensationalism to a grand melodrama of her own, as in the penknife scene, where the whole melodramatic idiom is transformed by the seriousness of her purpose, and the confrontation of Lovelace in his own currency of power. Whenever the 'grand' style falters in their altercations, the tension drops because of our sense of artificial heightening, but it can ring 'true' with a genuine strength and elevation paid for by the conviction that what is at stake is indeed the 'life or death' of the self, in which the grandeur of the situation demands the heightening. We distrust melodrama; Richardson's moral fervour embraced it. But though he can often fail by forcing a melodrama we feel has not been 'paid for', as in the death of Lady Grandison or the bleeding of Clementina; he is also aware at his best of the relationship between the sensational and farce.

In *Grandison* his awareness of the three modes is revealed in the deftness with which he arranges Charlotte, Clementina, and Olivia, as comic, tragic, and melodramatic mirrors to set off Harriet.

In *Clarissa*, too, the dramatist becomes aware of the moral implications of 'acting' and 'stage-managing'. Perhaps the greatest fascination of Lovelace is the study of the volatility and instability of the born actor, the 'perfect Proteus' – the difficulty for such a person of ever being truly 'sincere'. The endless variety of role-playing, the ceaseless interplay of mask and face, the contradictory stylishness of the multiple styles, are held in very serious fusion with Lovelace's difficulty in establishing who he is. Only when he is pushed to the point of disintegration can he select a final role; but unlike Clarissa, it can only be by suppressing an important part of himself. The impulse to stage-manage, to write comedy and tragedy of intrigue, and manipulate others into the roles one has selected for them, is also brought under the microscope, and developed to the sardonic misfiring of Lovelace's final scenario – but not until its full fascination has become as clear as its moral implications.

At the end of *Clarissa*, indeed, Richardson seems to realise that his deepest moral convictions run clean counter to the drama that gives his fiction its most vivid life. He makes drama die before his heroine does, by deliberately de-dramatising her as she reaches towards her apotheosis. Drama almost seems the mark of imperfection. (This had been, perhaps, implicit in the de-fusing of potential drama in the 'trial' of the elevated Pamela of the Continuation.) The process is built into the whole structure as *Grandison* gets under way, in the de-dramatising of the hero from the start, and the pitting of an anti-drama of perfection against a drama of imperfection.

As *Grandison* develops, however, a new solution is found. What had been seen as dangerous instability, deceit, and manipulating, is transformed into a process of moral self-creation. Whereas Charlotte (while she remains impenitent) and Olivia fix themselves reductively as Queens of Comedy and Operatic Melodrama, Harriet and Clementina gradually transform themselves into their chosen roles. The idea of 'raising' oneself above oneself, as an actress does to encompass a 'great' part, overrides a simpler view of sincerity. Sir Charles as stage-manager is similarly meant to show how a moral manipulation may offer people more satisfying versions of themselves than they perceive when imprisoned in their limited personalities.

In all these ways, the dramatist examines the activity of dramatising, and becomes increasingly aware of its implications for good and evil. The most significant implications of all, however, are those that we can only glimpse from the hindsight of two centuries.

In his *Study of Thomas Hardy*, D. H. Lawrence spoke of the supreme fiction as one which achieves, not a victory of the 'self' over the 'other', but an embrace and a marriage that is beyond both.[1] My study has sought to place at its centre the power of the dramatic imagination to strive towards this, because an imaginative projection into the 'other' is sought from the very beginning, in the process of creation itself. In projecting himself into his characters and allowing them to lead him, Richardson achieved real exploration, self-extension, self-transcendence. He threw differing facets of himself into dynamic conflict, by means of which he reached beyond his ordinary limits. What is most fascinating about this process, moreover, is that it can never be subject to full authorial control. The more one recognises his subtlety and his artistry, the more one realises that the model of 'the great artificer' is foreign to his kind of art. One responds to simple-minded assertions that he was an 'unconscious' artist with irritable demonstrations of how much more he knew about what he was doing than the critics who presume to patronise him. Yet his art so radically depended on being taken over by his imaginative projection, that it was indeed bound to proceed 'unconsciously' to a considerable extent. When one speaks of his 'awareness', one means the process by which he comes to grips with what he has already created, as a means of pushing it further, and further. In Blakean terms, the moral devourer is engaged in ceaseless dialectic with the imaginative prolific. He is a forerunner of romanticism in the sense that his imagination is that of Professor Abrams's lamp rather than the mirror. He is an extremist, working with a kind of excess that becomes fully thematic

[1] *Phoenix*, 515-16.

in Harriet Byron. He plunges into derangement, dream, the raised imagination, the heightened emotion, the fervent moral idealism, and his tactlessness is related to his strength and his courage. He often makes a fool of himself, but it is a folly one may learn to respect.

This means also that Richardson is the beginning of something that would have horrified him. To project oneself imaginatively into radically differing points of view is to embark on a road which leads to relativity. For the more convincingly these are 'done', the more it may come to seem that there is no such thing as '*the* story', only stories, only points of view, only ways of looking. In this direction Richardson points forward less to Henry James than to Conrad, Faulkner, Kafka, the *nouveau roman*. (I speak not of influence but of tendency.) Because of the nature of his basic creative process, Richardson is peculiarly open to differing interpretations. It is his great strength that Lovelace's vision is pursued as strongly and as honestly as Clarissa's.

Yet his final affinity is rather with the Jamesian concept of the artist, precisely because of his struggle to contain all the different ways of looking within an inclusive and definitive vision, allowing for all, but not reducible to any, or to relativity. He offers, as James does, the final illusion that 'the author' at his most imaginative, and 'the ideal reader' at his most perceptive, will meet at their fullest extension beyond the relativities, absolutely, and objectively. Yet Richardson does more than Henry James to banish his own voice from our primary experience. At his best it comes through (in the work itself) only in the convergence of the 'second voices' of the characters, none of which by itself can be 'his'. He gives both his characters and his readers even greater freedom than James. The later novelist is, arguably, the finer; better educated and with a far wider range; more keenly intelligent; more subtle and elaborate in his verbal artistry. Yet Richardson, I think, had a greater courage of imagination. No Jamesian character is pushed to the limit as Lovelace and Clarissa are; in no Jamesian novel does one feel the same degree of challenge to the author's own ideals. For this one can forgive even the tedium, the long-windedness, the lapses into didacticism and sentimentality.

It is true that Richardson feared his own imagination. His irritability when readers dared to question his exemplary protagonists, his impulse to deny his own complexities and cut down his fiction to the size of his ordinary quotidian self, are visible in the activities of what I have called 'Mr Richardson' within the novels, and of the Editor and commentator on them. Yet this is also evidence of how far 'the other' had been allowed its say. The Richardson one really cares about, the 'author' who only becomes visible by a full response to the creative dialectic of imagination and analysis in the texture and structure of the work itself, really does try to give his characters a freedom to pursue themselves, that in turn calls forth a correspondingly huge effort to include and resolve, and push the imagination even further. He did not perhaps write supreme fictions. Yet Richardson was I think the first novelist to merit comparison with Shakespeare in both the power to explore 'free' characters, and the struggle to comprehend and make the centre hold against the strongest challenge he could mount.

AN AFTER-WORD

What Richardson invented and explored was the novel as drama, and the epistolary convention is a means to that end. Yet it is obvious that we remain readers not spectators, and that what we respond to is the written word in the peculiar shape of a book of letters. If critics have been too concerned with the epistolary, and not enough with what it is for, there are nevertheless important ways in which the total response to Richardson is affected by the convention itself.

We are made unusually aware that our experience is literary. As Alan McKillop put it, 'the device of writing, editing, and even reading the novel within the novel is . . . essentially new'.[1] Richardson's are the first fictions where the actual composition of and the response to the novel, by characters and editor inside it, become part of our imaginative experience. Pamela produces a book, which B reads in instalments, and his sister as a whole. We watch Belford begin editing *Clarissa* before its heroine dies, and with her approval. Richardsonian characters sometimes think of themselves as being in a potential book, and always precede us as readers. The novels constantly call attention to themselves as books, carefully edited, indexed and cross-referenced, with typographical devices of emphasis: capitalisation, italics, pointing hands in the margin. So 'to the moment' experience of the letters themselves is accompanied and modified by an awareness of the retrospective activity, within the novel, of collecting them into a whole and grasping the coherence of the history they form.

The letter-convention is also part of the meaning in significant ways. Anthony Kearney has observed, in *Clarissa*[2], how the convention itself embodies and underlines the experience of isolation, vulnerability, and incomprehension. Clarissa's isolation begins to be created from the moment she is forced to write, when pastime becomes necessity, her only means of communication. Each letter within Harlowe Place, to Anna, and to her family at the end, increasingly mimes 'the painful reduction of human contact' by the fact that it is and can be only a letter, as well as by what it says. Also, as with Pamela, the vulnerability of letters becomes, first metaphorically, and then actually, an embodiment of the vulnerability of the girl herself in a power situation. When Lovelace steals letters, the rape has begun. When he forges them, his imperial vision of himself as demiurge, transforming persons and controlling situations to his will, is visibly enacted. Yet nothing brings home his total exclusion from the reality of Clarissa's world more powerfully than his abject dependence on

1 A. D. McKillop, 'Epistolary Technique in Richardson's Novels', *Rice Institute Pamphlet*, 38 (1951), 36-54; reprinted in Carroll (ed.), *Twentieth Century Views*, 139-151.

2 Anthony Kearney, '*Clarissa* and the Epistolary Form', *Essays in Criticism*, 16 (1966), 44-56.

the letters Belford so grudges writing, because they take him from Clarissa's side. Moreover the letter form itself enacts the Richardsonian vision of the complexity of human history: the 'distance' that separates each limited and partial viewpoint, the sheer time and effort that are necessary before there can be comprehension, before the fragments can be pieced into coherence.

In one of the most challenging treatments of *Clarissa*, John Preston pushes both these arguments a great deal further, to an existential view of the novel.[1] For him, 'Richardson . . . allows no insight beyond the written signs. They do not refer to a situation, they *are* the situation . . . The novel is in this sense *about* writing and reading . . . the characters . . . have become literature, even to themselves. The consequence of this is that those parts of their lives which cannot be shown to the reader seem not to exist at all . . . At the points where words fail, where syntax collapses, their existence collapses.' Kearney's isolation and vulnerability have become alienation. *Clarissa* 'is about literature as a process of estrangement'; writing to the moment is not only ' "the actual moment of experience" in "a continuous present", but the continuing experience of the present as a critical moment . . . The characters are all seen, all the time, in moments of crisis, moments in which they are severed from each other, from themselves, and from the future . . . moments when their connections with reality are imperilled, that is when they are involved in the process of writing and reading. Thus their crisis is the crisis of the novel itself, a crisis of form. And therefore it is a crisis for the reader as well.' Preston sees the reader as alienated, because although the letters need a reader, we are placed 'on the same footing as those characters who are emotionally involved, yet denied entry into the action . . . we grasp life as a literary experience . . . In fact there is no encounter with people at all, but rather with their written words.' There remain however two ways in which the novel 'places alienation . . . within reach of a concept of wholeness and freedom'. The activities of the editor, the apparatus of cross-reference, encourage the reader to achieve that 'heightened

[1] John Preston, *The Created Self* (London, 1970), chapters 3 and 4.

attention' to the whole which can produce an understanding denied to all the characters, and become a kind of 'love' never given to Clarissa in the book. (Though, in passing, Preston seems not to realise how many of the notes he cites were only added in the later editions.) And in Clarissa herself, he sees signs of a 'language that she believes in against all the weight of the book, the silent language of feeling and of reality' beyond words. In these ways the novel is tragic, 'not because it must exclude the possibility of relationship, but because it affirms the reality of what it must exclude'.

This is impressive, if rather abstract, but I think it is only a half-truth. The argument about alienation is unduly dependent on the tragic mode and end of *Clarissa*; the epistolary convention in *Pamela* and *Grandison* quickly re-emphasises that letters bear an opposite implication too. Any letter presupposes isolation, but it equally implies communication and aspires to community. *Pamela* ought to be an even grimmer study in alienation, since several of her letters are never delivered and the whole of her journal is written in a void; yet Pamela's pen is the agent of a community which is created by reading within the book,[1] and which images the creation of a community of readers outside. As we have seen, this was a major preoccupation of Richardson, and what *Pamela* had imagined, *Clarissa* actually brought about. Even in the tragic novel community begins to form before the end: the coming together of Belford, Charlotte, Anna, Morden and Hickman prefigures, however imperfectly, the community that a full cor-respondence – one recalls Lovelace's false etymology – between book and reader should create. If it is read to the moment, the reader acquires an intimacy with and an inner understanding of its fictive people greater in some ways than is possible in life. If it is also greater than that of the characters in the book, this is precisely because the reader possesses the whole correspondence as they do not. *Clarissa* may image aliena-

[1] John Dussinger points out that Pamela's 'moment of decision (like his) occurs in the process of reading B's letters'; 'What Pamela Knew: An Interpretation', *Journal of English and Germanic Philology*, 69 (1970), 387.

tion, but it drives towards community in the creation of its readers, and it actually produced the circle which encouraged Richardson to explore the idea of a Family of the Heart in *Grandison.*

Now this 'communication' cannot be merely a reaction to the image of its loss, but must spring from the form itself. Indeed, the real significance of Preston's argument, as it seems to me, is the illustration of the limits of even the most intelligent criticism when it is directed only to the convention, and insufficiently to the end it serves. To concentrate on the letters as letters, is to concentrate only on what is written; to concentrate on the letters as a means to drama is to see how much more there is than the words. It is surely not true that Richardson allows no insight beyond the written word? Indeed with every character and in every scene a reading to the moment engages us in a constant process of imagining through and behind words, in ways that the drama achieves *viva voce* with actors on a stage. The more dramatic the letters become, the less one is aware of them as written. The spoken voice begins to predominate, language and gesture become vividly present and spontaneous, the distance of the letter modulates into the involvement of the drama. Every detail of behaviour promotes inference, every unguarded word suggests more than is spoken, silences become pregnant with feeling, and style can reveal as much as a face. The basic process of creation is opposed to alienation, which is essentially an enclosure within the self. Richardson's dramatic method presupposes, both for the author in creation, and for the reader in response, a technique of projecting the imagination beyond the limits of any single vision, to an interplay of 'others' and a final comprehension.

Preston of course is not 'wrong'. His perceptions apply to the letters when we are most aware of them as letters. It is also true that any novel must remain written; that we can never achieve full inwardness with any fictive person; and that even writing to the moment cannot achieve what drama does with living actors on a stage.

Yet Richardson's basic form is an attempt to push his fictions as far toward the spoken, the inward, and the dramatic as he could. Hence the interplay between the epistolary and the dramatic seems to expose a paradox which must be contained in our response. The letters mime the fragmentation and anxiety of the moment – and Preston is illuminating on how the 'anxiety' of characters 'reveals itself as a form of punctuation', in the disjunction of to-the-moment syntax. But the dramatic interplay drives continually towards what Frank Kermode calls 'kairos' as opposed to 'chronos': time when the moment is 'filled with significance, charged with a meaning derived from its relation to the end', as against time as disjunct moments, in mere succession.[1] The letters enact the 'alienation' of the characters and their written words; the dramatisation of scene and consciousness tends to annihilate distance and promote intimacy and involvement. We are aware now of self-consciousness (Hazlitt's point) and now of spontaneity; of enclosure within each point of view, and of dramatic exploration towards a more inclusive vision. There is in Richardson both a desire to control character, reader, and meaning, and an impulse to liberate the imagination dramatically, and allow the characters and their readers to determine their own ways. But if either side of the paradox is to dominate, it must surely be the dramatic side. That is what Richardson claimed as 'new'. That is what makes his epistolary novels so different from others. That, above all, lay at the centre of his whole mode of creation, before the letters could be written.

[1] Frank Kermode, *The Sense of an Ending* (New York, 1967 reprinted 1970), 46-7, and on 'kairos' in Richardson, 51.

CHAPTER ELEVEN

Social Realism, Psychology – and Form

I

Misinterpretation of Richardson's novels is only one sign of inattention to their basic form. The modern tendency to reduce them to social realism or psychology is no less symptomatic and just as damaging; for the concealed implication is that we cannot take him seriously as an artist, and must find his true interest in non-fictive terms. We are tempted to substitute for the peculiar and complex ordering of the novels, and the patient effort to understand their imaginative formation, a reference of their contents to social 'reality', or to the individual psychology of the author, that must ultimately be superficial. For the contents of a novel are only intelligible with reference to the whole in which alone they find their orientation and meaning; and the author's attitudes cannot simply be lifted from the complex imaginative texture of his exploration. One agrees that literary criticism should not be insulated from sociology, psychology, history and philosophy; but what the experience of working closely with teachers of other disciplines has most clearly brought home to me is that the literary critic must do his own work properly in his own terms, before he can contribute to a useful dialogue. We have been encouraged to take Defoe and Richardson seriously by good critics, like Arnold Kettle and Ian Watt, whose main interest in the eighteenth-century novel has been in its relation to society. *The Rise of the Novel*, in particular, has become essential reading. The psychological dimension which contemporaries recognised in 'the master of the heart' was also bound to strike twentieth-century minds as throwing light upon the imaginer as well as the imagined. Yet the rescue operations which have sent readers to Richardson again have too often encouraged them to see him reductively, separating part from whole and content from form.

2

The idea that the novel, the new thing, is the product of a new society and is defined by its 'realistic' representation of the life of ordinary individuals in that society has been challenged on sociological grounds.[1] The representation of society by Defoe, Richardson and Fielding is clearly limited and partial; and 'realistic' novels have been produced by societies radically different in structure and intellectual climate. The idea is no less open to literary challenge. As a term in criticism, 'the novel' is almost meaningless. The most acceptable definition, E. M. Forster's 'a fiction in prose of a certain extent',[2] is mainly acceptable because it is so indefinite. The term did not come into general use before the end of the eighteenth century, and Richardson always used it as a term of abuse, for what his works were not. It is at best a collective noun for many different kinds of prose fiction, whose convenience lies in its looseness. We may say that the period 1678–1767 saw the invention of a number of new ways of writing fiction in prose; but their differences are quite as important as their similarities, and we might be well advised to include *The Pilgrim's Progress* and *Gulliver's Travels* among them if we hope to understand either the revolution in prose fiction or its relation to society adequately. Each is the product of a unique vision embodied in a peculiar use of language; what Coleridge called 'the shaping spirit of imagination' and

1 Diana Spearman, *The Novel and Society* (London, 1966).

2 *Aspects of the Novel* (London, 1927 reprinted 1961), 9; quoting Abel Chevalley.

Wallace Stevens, more accurately, 'the maker's rage to order words'.[1] The writer's reaction to society and its climate of ideas will be an important part of this, and he will be deeply affected by his lifetime's experience, but no writer does or can reflect social 'reality'. If we speak of 'reality' at all, we are bound to recognise that there are as many realities as there are angles of inspection and languages or media of articulation: physics, chemistry, sociology, poetry, painting. Within prose fiction, consequently, there are as many different relations to reality as there are ways of seeing with imaginative coherence and writing with verbal control. We cannot hope to understand how a writer sees society, until we understand how he sees. His 'realism' – or better, both for talking about the eighteenth century when there was no such word, and as more tentative, his 'verisimilitude': the way in which he pretends that his fiction is 'like' or 'true to' life – will be a direct function of his peculiar imaginative form.

Of course Defoe and Richardson were a new phenomenon. They came to fiction late in hardworking lives, Defoe at almost sixty, Richardson in his fifties. One had been failed merchant, journalist, pamphleteer and secret agent; the other a successful printer. Both were men of 'the City' not of 'the Town'; and in imaginative terms too their work was rooted on the other side of Temple Bar from the Augustan gentlemanly culture. So part of their value for us does indeed lie in the mapping of new territory in the new kinds of prose fiction they invented. There is a sense in which we can watch 'the City' becoming aware of itself and beginning to analyse its particular problems; in which we can turn to common men working in an upstart medium, not the poetry drama and witty satire of polite letters, for insight into the human implications of a new kind of society. Both men moreover were not only in the 'middle station' of life, but shared the relation to the puritan past of much of the middle 'class'.[2]

[1] 'The Idea of Order at Key West'.

[2] Diana Spearman warns, in *The Novel and Society*, of the distortion involved in thinking of eighteenth-century society in the 'class' terms of the nineteenth century and later.

Defoe was born in 1660, the year of undoing for the revolution of the 'saints' and the year in which John Bunyan went to prison. Richardson was born in 1689, the year after the bloodless revolution that ushered in the new era and saw Bunyan's death. In Bunyan's fictions we can watch the imaginative world of the defeated 'saint' turning into that of the bourgeois merchant in an allegorical landscape. For Christian, in the first part of *The Pilgrim's Progress*, 'the City' can only be the City of Destruction or Vanity Fair. Life, eternal life, begins with a headlong flight, fingers in ears, from his family and a godless society, and is won after incessant battling against the seductions and challenges of the world and the devil. In the second part of the *Progress* however, there is a tenderness and warmth of relationship in the pilgrimage of Christiana and her children, a renewed sense of the society which can extend – though still sundered from the City of Destruction – through the Christian family into a community of believers, even inside the walls of Vanity Fair. In *The Life and Death of Mr Badman*, the Christian conscience faces the challenge of conceiving the good life within the world of business and commerce itself. Defoe was a Dissenter like Bunyan; Richardson was not; but in their later situations and their different ways both share Bunyan's puritan concern with personal isolation and salvation, and the tensions between conscience and worldliness, community and individualism, 'economic' or religious. Behind their fictions lies not a literary tradition, but the puritan inheritance of domestic, devotional and instructive writing which sought to accommodate Christian the pilgrim with Mr Goodman the upright 'Cit'. So we may turn to 'that fellow who was pilloried', whose name Swift affected never to remember, for a new kind of awareness of the fiercely competitive and acquisitive world of 'the City'; of the poverty, dependence and crime that lay just beneath the prosperous surface; and of the challenge to integrity and human relationship from 'economic' individualism. We may also turn to the timid Fleet Street printer, whose fear of noblemen's servants so amused Dr Johnson, for a new kind of insight into the tensions of relationship indoors; the clash of love with duty, and of absolute morality with power, greed and pride; the assertion of integrity and community against the most difficult circumstances in a decadent society.

If it is the relation of prose fiction with society that concerns us, however, even this bald account throws up several problems. If 'the novel' is defined by 'realism' in such a way as to exclude Bunyan – and the disappearance of Bunyan from courses on 'the novel' would seem to be symptomatic – the continuity that links him with Richardson and Defoe is broken, for what seem inadequate reasons. Bunyan's fictions may not fulfil all the conditions of 'realism' set out in the first chapter of *The Rise of the Novel*[1] and applied to Defoe and Richardson, but his verisimilitude is no less striking in relation to previous fictions, though its focus is different. If the heart of the matter is a personal vision, embodying a lifetime's experience at a particular time and place – 'there', however universalised – expressed in a 'new' way in prose of a distinctively homely and characteristic style, and instantly recognised by contemporaries as 'like' their own experience, it is hard to see why Bunyan should be struck off the register.

Of course there is an essential difference. It lies in the basic form of Bunyan's imagination. From his mythic vision, with elements of fable (in my terms), using the convention of allegory, flow all the formal features of his treatment of people, situations, time and place. Yet once one makes the basic form of the imagination one's criterion, it is immediately obvious that the formal differences between the fictions of Fielding and those of Richardson and Defoe, are quite as striking. Also, Fielding was an Augustan gentleman as the other three were not. The son of a general, educated at Eton and Leyden, he followed a gentlemanly occupation barred to the others by religion and education, and

[1] Although, in the pages that follow, I question the approach of this influential book, my treatment would be grossly unfair if it were taken as an attempt to 'revalue' *The Rise of the Novel.* I am concerned only with what seem to me the limitations of certain assumptions. I pass by many excellences, and also Watt's own reservations: on Bunyan for example; or on the 'realism of assessment' in Fielding, which originally bulked larger than in the book as we now have it. Ian Watt reviews himself in *Novel*, 1 (1968), 205–18.

wrote a kind of literature suitable for gentlemen before he turned to the new low medium and tried to dignify it. He began indeed by mocking Richardson, as another gentleman of 'the Town' had begun *Gulliver's Travels* by mocking Defoe. His new way of writing, the 'comic epic in prose' – once one understands its sources in French epic theory, and particularly his favourite critic Le Bossu – succeeds in assimilating prose fiction to a classical tradition that could include Cervantes as well as Homer and Vergil. Form and style cohere in a kind of vision radically different from Richardson's. Dryden's distinction between epic and drama points to a basically different method of creation: Fielding is the epic writer, Richardson the dramatic. Richardson creates by projecting himself imaginatively into his characters, who create the developing situation. In Fielding it is our direct experience of the author's vision that is all-important, and he is always between the reader and the action. Moreover (like Dryden) Fielding looked at classical epic through the eyes of seventeenth-century theory. Le Bossu defined epic as 'a discourse, invented by art, to form the Manners, by such instructions as are disguis'd under the allegories of some One important Action'.[1] In other words, when Le Bossu looked at Homer and Vergil, what he saw was a great unified moral analysis, coming directly from the author, which the action and the people are there to articulate. In my terms, this is not history or myth but fable, which is always constructed 'artistically' – or 'artificially' in the complimentary eighteenth-century sense – for purposes of analysis. People and situations are 'allegorical' in that what most concerns us is their analytic point.

What 'comic epic in prose' means to Fielding, then, is a highly artful fable, with sufficient verisimilitude to engage the reader's sympathetic imagination and connect the fiction with contemporary life, but carefully constructed by the author to elaborate a single, unified moral analysis. It is done in comic terms, but this does not mean that the analysis is any less 'important' in

[1] Pope's translation; *A General View of the Epic Poem* prefaced to Pope's *Odyssey*, ed. Maynard Mack (London, 1967), Twickenham ed. IX, 4-5.

Le Bossu's sense; the author merely begins from the ridiculous, where the tragic epic begins from the sublime, as being more appropriate to the nature of his analysis of vanity and hypocrisy. It is properly prose rather than poetry, as the right decorum for comedy.

The formal difference between Richardson and Fielding is absolutely radical; a matter of their whole way of seeing, creating and ordering, long before there is any question of their moral or social attitudes. In Richardson 'the author' disappears; in Fielding he is omnipresent and all-important. We are always aware of his voice and using his eyes as he analyses for us and manoeuvres his personae into meaningful patterns, commenting directly on their significance. In Richardson the emphasis is on individual characters seen in depth and complexity, and the action is the inevitable outcome of character. In Fielding the emphasis is on the whole design, articulated by an elaborate authorial plot, and on the typicality of the personae or 'attitudes' – I borrow a suggestive term from Angus Wilson's novel – as functions of that design. Richardson wishes to persuade his reader of the verisimilitude of the experience; Fielding's novels are admitted artefacts, the significance and even the composition of which he continually discusses with the reader. As with Swift, who wrote still more obviously fabulous fable in *Gulliver's Travels*, it is the author's relationship with the reader that is central. Even when, in *Tom Jones*, 'the author' becomes less identifiable with Fielding himself and more unreliable; and the irony begins to turn like Swift's from the personae to the reader, to test his judgement; it is still the case that the central experience is of finding the true judgement which links the reader with the artificer behind 'the author', as they contemplate the made world together. It is a world unified by moral analysis rather than story. So the tales of Leonora and Wilson, or the Old Man on the Hill, are not to be regarded as regrettable excrescences breaking an important narrative unity. They are precisely moral fable at its clearest, and are there to alert us to the thematic and analytic centre of the whole pattern. It is even more foolish to deplore the 'author' chapters, which are quite as important as the story and sometimes more so. All this has important implications for 'character' – indeed there is a case for using a different word to mark the difference from Richardson. Fielding's people are mainly 'types', as always in fable, and we are not encouraged to 'get inside' them. 'I declare once for all, I describe not men but manners; not an individual but a species', he wrote in the Preface to Book 3 of *Joseph Andrews*, and though some of his people are more individualised than this suggests, we never get complex personalities. Rather his people are focussed from a sharply defined angle, and their effect depends on the way they fit in with one another as parts of the whole analytic pattern: the method of Jonson rather than of Shakespeare. Fielding prevents us from getting involved (where Richardson ensures that we are); he will use mock-heroic, or an elaborate and heightened rhetoric, to hold us at arm's length, keep us looking from the outside, and make us take the essential point of the scene within the whole pattern. Where Richardson varies style in order to reveal character, Fielding varies style in order to manipulate our attitude to what we watch. The deliberate artificiality of the plot is also distancing, with its coincidences and legerdemain; we never take its threatenings seriously. What one responds to is the brilliant performance of the great artificer himself, shaping and manipulating his analytic design, making his points with sharpness and wit, teasing us, but sharing with us his lucidity, his humour, his humane judgement.

We might have begun at the other end, as it were, by generalising about what is seen by each way of looking. Ignoring for the moment the last work of each, we might say that at the heart of Richardson's vision is faith; at the heart of Fielding's, charity. Richardson arguably sees sex too darkly in its violating and brutal aspects; Fielding arguably too brightly and naïvely. Richardson sees human consciousness as terribly complex; Fielding is confident in his ability to analyse behaviour in briskly ethical terms. Richardson has a vibrant awareness of sin and evil; Fielding seems a cheerful muscular Christian, whose vision is remarkably sunny at this stage, and who opposes to Richardson's absolutism a much more permissive morality of good nature. Yet for Richardson no human being is intrinsically evil; whereas Fielding flirts with a kind of Calvinism. Fielding's lens is wide-angled, social; Richardson's internal, much narrower, and individual. Richardson is exploratory, probing, challenging himself more and more agonisedly; Fielding genially demonstrates his culture and his values, confident in the approval of all good-hearted and right-minded readers. And so on. But even if such generalisations were not rather too bland, the significant thing would still be the relation of the vision to the fundamental way of seeing. In order to understand the opposition, we need to ask both why each vision should characteristically express itself in that particular kind of maker's rage to order words; and also why such a form should lead in such directions, in each case. Conversely, in the last work of both, where they have grown much closer together, there is a curious discrepancy between the attitudes, and the ability of the form to embody and explore them successfully. There was in any case a growing consensus between 'City' and 'Town' as the eighteenth century wore on. In several important ways the real 'positions' of Richardson and Fielding, in the hindsight of the history of ideas, were never as far apart as they (or later critics) thought, and they grew closer.[1] With Fielding's loss of faith in the sufficiency of the good heart alone, which had begun in *Tom Jones*, came the need for greater internalisation in *Amelia*; whereas in *Grandison* Richardson tried a wider social angle, and a more optimistic idealism, purging his imagined world of evil. Yet the problem in both cases is that they now appear to be writing against the grain of the way of seeing that produced their finest work, and both novels are seriously flawed. It is not enough to analyse the attitudes to society and morality, without inquiring into the tendency for the new wine to crack the old bottles.

The most interesting evidence of the radical difference in their whole way of seeing, however, is the inability to understand each

[1] See also William Park, 'Fielding *and* Richardson', *P.M.L.A.*, 81 (1966), 366-88.

other which goes deeper than any attitude. Richardson's misunderstanding of Fielding is well known; but Fielding's misunderstanding of Richardson is not only apparent in his mockery, but also in his praise. His letter to Richardson about the crucial fifth volume of *Clarissa*[1] breathes a generosity of spirit that puts Richardson's jealousy to shame. But it shows almost no understanding of what the volume is really about; and what he chooses to praise shows very clearly how he cannot but think in characteristically Fieldingesque terms. It is, of course, not at all surprising that the inventors of two such radically different new ways of writing, springing from such radically different ways of seeing, should proceed to misunderstand each other. What is perhaps surprising after two centuries of fiction is that one should still have to argue against the tendency to read either in terms of the other. It is probably inevitable that any reader will ultimately gravitate towards one kind of vision and consequently tend to be unfair to the other; yet we must surely seek to postpone that choice and discipline that tendency, at least until each has been grasped in his own terms. The surest way of being unfair is to assume from the start that both are doing the same kind of thing; and this is built into the definition of 'the novel' in terms of 'realism'. Seriously mistaken assumptions are clearly at work when a good critic can write that 'Fielding's stylistic virtues tend to interfere with his technique *as a novelist* (my italics), because a patent selectiveness of vision destroys our belief[2] in the reality

[1] First printed by E. L. McAdam, 'A New Letter from Fielding', *Yale Review*, 38 (1948), 300-10. See also Slattery (ed.), *The Richardson-Stinstra Correspondence*, 33 ff. Part of the letter is quoted by Eaves and Kimpel, *Richardson*, 294-5.

[2] The psychology of reading implied here is also rather naïve. Dr Johnson's robust common sense, in demolishing the 'illusionist' theory of the dramatic unities, is surely applicable *a fortiori* to prose fiction. The fact that part of the reading public they hoped to appeal to had a puritan suspicion of fiction as 'lies' may have caused Defoe and Richardson to pretend that their fictions were not fictive. Yet the pretence was increasingly transparent, and no modern reader 'believes' in the 'reality' of the 'report'. Rather, a reader's attention is caught and concentrated by the peculiar nature of the imagination that absorbs him; and what he comes to 'believe' in, if anything, is the quality of the vision. This may or may not include a concern for verisimilitude – but it certainly does not depend on that.

of report, or at least diverts our attention from the content of the report to the skill of the reporter'.[1] The inattention to form; the concentration on content; the definition of the novel as a 'report' of 'reality', quite irrespective of differing ways of seeing; the ignoring of the obvious truth that all fictions are patently selective, and that what is important is the nature and significance of the selectiveness involved in different kinds of maker's rage to order words; would all seem to demonstrate, not that the critic is foolish, but that his assumptions are effectively blocking his view. Fielding is accused of failure 'as a novelist' because of the central characteristics of his form of fiction.

If, then, we examine the idea that 'the novel' is defined by 'social realism', there are two kinds of literary distortion taking place, quite apart from the vulnerability to sociological criticism. If the stress falls on the relation of prose fiction to its society, the exclusion of Bunyan and Swift from 'the novel' involves a blurring of the cultural relation of Defoe and Richardson with Bunyan, and of Fielding with Swift, which is bound to affect the nature of the visions of all. If on the other hand the stress falls on criteria of form, the difference between Richardson and Fielding would seem quite as important as the difference between Richardson and Bunyan. We appear to be left with Richardson and Defoe as the only 'realists'. But what if the failure to attend to the basic form of each of these should be found to blur a radical opposition between them as well? I believe that this can be shown to be the case.[2]

Though both try to persuade us of the verisimilitude of their visions, each selects, and then intensifies, in ways that differ both from each other and from our experience of our lives. The main sense in which Richardson's characters become 'real' to us is through our inward experience of their consciousness; but in order to achieve this he becomes 'unrealistic' in several directions.

[1] Watt, *Rise of the Novel*, 30.

[2] I have argued the case that follows more fully in 'Defoe and Richardson – Novelists of the City' in the Sphere *History of Literature in the English Language*, IV, R. Lonsdale (ed.), *Dryden to Johnson* (London, 1971), 226-58.

His epistolary convention has its unrealistic side, as all conventions do. The letters we read are not like the letters we ourselves write; they are too long and too dramatic; and Richardson would have done better to let us accept them as convention, rather than try to explain the difficulties away realistically. He also has to keep his characters unnaturally passive and static in order to keep the correspondences going; or else contrive noticeably peculiar chains of transmission and narrative. Most of all, the very concentration on the inward life, and the intensity of his desire to probe the consciousness of his characters to the utmost, compels him to isolate them to an unnatural degree. There is always a kind of imprisonment, locking the characters into their conflicts hour after hour, day after day, over and over again. This is surely closing the door on common experience, and it produces a kind of claustrophobia which is nearer (as Coleridge hinted) to the tied-down continuity of nightmare than to ordinary life. So if it is the 'reality' of our own experience as conscious beings, living to the moment, that Richardson's fictions are most 'like', he both heightens to an unnaturally intense degree, giving us a degree of knowledge and awareness we never have in life, and concentrates on that kind of 'reality' to the exclusion of many other kinds. His idealism also drives him to imagine characters who may be 'too good to be true' – to the eyes of readers for whom 'realism' is all important.

Defoe's verisimilitude on the other hand is a matter of the thingishness of his world, the mass of circumstantial detail that creates very 'lifelike' situations. Yet we become even more aware than in Richardson of the extraordinary exclusiveness of the vision we inhabit. The experience is startlingly unlike the experience we have of our own living. The life of the senses is very largely missing: Crusoe's island never composes a landscape, and the richer the objects Moll Flanders devotes herself to acquiring, the more aware we become of their reduction to utility and price. The life of sensuality is also missing, except for an episode which marks the end of Moll's innocence. The life of human relationship is steadily attenuated: Crusoe sells Xury, has a strictly paternalistic master-slave relationship with Friday, and chooses wives for his colonists for their economic qualities. Moll's husbands are reduced to ordinal numbers, and most of her children are abandoned and forgotten. The life of consciousness is even more extraordinarily limited. *Robinson Crusoe* is psychologically most unrealistic: actual castaways were degraded by fear and loneliness and sank into apathy and animality in a far shorter time than Crusoe's twenty-eight years. (Crusoe also spends twenty-four years on his island before he longs for companionship, and never longs for women at all, in stark contradiction to the most common form of desert island day-dream.) In *Moll Flanders* reflections occur, not only in the commentary of the old woman looking back, but at the time. Yet they tend to be sited at moments when there is nothing to be done; or when they do occur in the heat of the struggle, they have no effect on how Moll acts. There is a constant dislocation between thought and behaviour. And if there is a kind of intelligence in Moll's ability to perceive, often at lightning speed, what a situation is and what moves it demands for her safety or profit, there is no life of the mind, no bringing of a situation to fully human consciousness.

The opposition between Richardson and Defoe begins, then, as an opposition between an 'internalised' and an 'externalised' vision: a verisimilitude of character and consciousness against a verisimilitude of material circumstance. Both, in their striking selectiveness and concentration, are 'unrealistic' in significant ways, and it is hard to see on what valid grounds they could be ranked on a scale of fidelity to the 'real'. Yet one is not offering adverse criticism – at least not yet. For it seems equally clear that these features of each 'shaping spirit of imagination' are inseparable from its nature, and essentially condition the quality of its insight. We are merely looking at surface symptoms; their cause and significance remain to be discovered, and will only be found by inquiring into the basic kind of imagination that is at work.

If Defoe's vision is extraordinarily selective, it is because his imagination is so taken up with what he sees as the essential human condition, archetypally. Though one can see what is meant by comparing his novels with law-court evidence, it is not that his vision and style can give us the truth, the whole truth, and nothing but the truth – any more than the courts can. It is rather that the account is stripped down to a basic 'factual' situation: what happened, and how, and why. But Defoe's stripping down is even more extreme. The law-court analogy helps us to add individual character and motivation to the long list of non-essential complications that can be excluded. Indeed, the basic imaginative drive in *Robinson Crusoe* is so selective, so intensely archetypal, that it is one of the best known European *myths.*[1] Crusoe is Everyman, isolated on his island in order to reveal Man as he essentially is in Defoe's imagination: alone, faced by a hostile environment, forced to shape it to his will or go under. He is driven by an energy which impels him forward from apparent security and makes him pit himself against the unknown, but which also enables him to cope with challenges and overcome. When the protections as well as the complexities of society are stripped away, it is Everyman's nature to know terrible fear; but the 'I' at the heart of him is resilient, resourceful, determined to survive, expand and profit.

The archetypal vision seems however to exist in two dimensions. *Robinson Crusoe* is both an economic and a religious myth. On the one hand we get an imaginative synopsis of the whole growth of economic man, concentrated into those twenty-eight years on the island. It is the way that the imagination strips away our normal consciousness that makes it so fascinating. We see every object that comes from the wreck with new eyes, and experience for the first time the true difficulty and grandeur of each of the steps and processes by which economic progress is made, because we appreciate their vital importance to the lonely human being in his archetypal struggle. Crusoe develops from

[1] See Ian Watt, '*Robinson Crusoe* as a Myth' in J. L. Clifford (ed.), *Eighteenth Century English Literature* (New York, 1959), 158-79; reprinted from *Essays in Criticism*, I (1951), 95-119.

the cave-man to the pastoral and agricultural stage; then gradually to the 'castle' is added the 'summer residence', the estate, and the colony, ruled first as governor, and finally as absentee landlord and capitalist. The novel is 'the City's' mythic celebration of economic man, but also, in its exclusiveness, a revelation of many of the implications of 'economic' individualism free from restraint. Yet the selectiveness and the freedom from normal social conditioning are also the source of the imaginative power and fascination. With another part of his mind, however, Defoe sees a no less archetypal vision of sinful man brought to regeneration by divine grace. The young Kreutznaer, fool of the cross, disobeys his earthly father in running away to sea, and the echoes of the prodigal son and Jonah suggest that this is a sin against the divine father too. He refuses to heed clear signs of warning, and cannot read the significance of his preservation, the 'accidental' sowing of the seed, and the insistent correspondence of the dates of his disasters and escapes. The realisation that the remotest corner of the universe is ruled by divine power and providence only comes to him in illness, when he is visited by the terrible apparition of God's angel; but through grace, and the neglected Bible in his sea-chest, he becomes converted. Moreover his musings on cannibalism and his instruction of Friday show that Defoe is concerned with the state of nature in religious and moral as well as economic ways. Only, how are we to relate the vision of 'homo economicus' to the vision of sinful Adam? The ungovernable impulse that sends Crusoe to sea is supposed to be his 'original sin', but it is the same impulse that makes him a hero and governs his success. And how is it that his conversion changes him so little? Yet we cannot dismiss the religious pattern as merely Defoe's conventional side; it is too insistent. This apparent contradiction of attitudes has given rise to fierce debate. Is it confusion or irony, and if ironic, is it conscious or unconscious?

We may however cut through the debate, and hit on a further decisive clue to the nature of Defoe's mythic vision, if we pay enough attention to the precise angle from which he sees, at a suitably notorious point. When Crusoe finds money in the wreck, the puritan's imagination seems suddenly to collide with the merchant's. Crusoe's plight makes money worthless, and he apostrophises the gold as Spenser, Milton or Bunyan might have done. But in almost the same breath, he proceeds to take it anyway, in the trader's knowledge that it might well come in useful later on. The contradiction certainly seems to produce an ironic effect – yet the homely garrulous style, which makes one feel close to the situation, seems oddly capable of holding apparent contradictions without discomfort. Still another part of Defoe's mind is already busy with the story-teller's interest in getting the hero off the wreck before a storm breaks. The opposite ways of looking are only part of a much longer and rambling syntactical unit, whose loose connections and bustling pace allow very different elements to rub along together quite easily. There is this, and that, and also this; the style is essentially episodic and works by addition, and what the passage is in miniature the book is as a whole. And yet . . . if we see through Defoe's eyes, is it not simply the case that money is both useless on the island and useful if Crusoe ever gets back to civilisation? *It all depends on the situation.* And since the situation includes the gathering storm, it might be sensible to take the coins where it would be foolish if the gold were in heavy bars, which would take time to load and might upset the raft. Defoe is not interested in character; he is interested in behaviour; but he always sees behaviour as governed by situation. (It is *our* assumption, that human beings ought to be consistent, that produces the 'irony'.) To understand this is to understand why Crusoe's conversion is not a change of character, any more than his sin was a character flaw. His conversion is, precisely, a vision, an opening of his eyes to a more accurate reading of the human situation, as his sin was to be blind. Once he has understood the true nature of the universe, how it is 'really' governed by God's will and not human impulse, the same energies which had led to disaster when God's messages were ignored, can lead to success when they are heard and understood, and divine vengeance gives way to grace and mercy. Conversion does not make Crusoe less worldly, it makes him more effective in the world. He is an erring economic man who becomes a God-fearing economic man and is blessed with success.

When the desert island myth is replaced in society, however, the implications of Defoe's peculiarly selective vision become more disturbing. In *Moll Flanders* the hostile environment, against which Everywoman fights her lone battle to survive, is the economic nature of society itself; and the key fact that its money economy is made for and directed by the male. Moll's only weapons are her sex, her wits, her courage and resourcefulness. Her main hope is marriage, but this is an economic institution in which most of the cards are in the hands of the male. Outside marriage, for a lone would-be gentlewoman without money, there is only the choice of poverty, or prostitution, or crime. This is the basic situation in which the various phases of Moll's career are played out. So we have another myth of the archetypal human situation, only in society this time, and another expression of Defoe's faith in the power of the isolated human being to survive, exploit, and profit. At the same time the setting in society makes us even more aware of the extreme selectivity of the vision, and the attenuation of what we think of as fully human life. Because Moll is placed in a world of human beings like herself, not a world of wild nature including some savages, the implications of her behaviour in her struggle to preserve and advance herself, and the cost in human terms, come home to us more sharply than in *Robinson Crusoe*. There seems consequently an even more radical discrepancy between the economic vision and the religious paradigm of sin, conversion and redemption. There is a constant dislocation between morality and behaviour in the younger Moll, but the 'moral' commentary of the old woman looking back over her career is also far from satisfactory. How seriously can we take her repentance and her self-evaluation? Her conversion in Newgate never suggests any thought of restitution, or inquiry after her only true husband and her abandoned children. Her new life is built solidly on the criminal foundations of the old, as are the lives of the 'reformed' governess and Jemmy. In the 'new world' she is still incapable of telling the whole truth about herself. Her repentance is purely the effect of fear and virtually ceases when the fear does.

Yet to have grasped how, for Defoe, everything depends on situation, may be to suggest how little one has said when one has pointed out these discrepancies. For not only do Moll's responses to other people ebb and flow according to the pressures of different situations, but she is also a perfect chameleon herself. It is significant that – unlike Robinson Crusoe – we never know her real name. She always takes on the shape that each situation demands; and in the key criminal phase when we see the implications of her world most nakedly, she has a different dress, accent, appearance and behaviour in every episode, to the point of passing as a man. Moll is determined by her situation. What she is, does, and feels will be what is necessary for self-preservation and advantage, and even when the iron hand of necessity is removed, she remains what her circumstances have made her. It is not that she is incapable of strong or genuine feeling; but we are always aware that the relation of what she feels to the contingencies of the situation is more direct and determined than it is in the world we ourselves inhabit. In one situation she can afford to do nothing but abandon a child, so that it is hardly mentioned. In another she can afford compunction but cannot afford to act on it. In yet another she can give herself the relief and satisfaction of expressing a mother's feelings to a high and even exaggerated degree – but accompanied by an alert response to the dampness of the ground. What is true of feeling is true also of moral consciousness and veracity. Moral reflection can occur at moments of stasis, disastrous or safe, but at the crunch it always comes second to self-preservation or advantage; and truth is always subject to strategy. Even religion, now, is seen as dependent on situation. Defoe has become a relativist of circumstance: the most basic 'reality' in *Moll Flanders* is that we are what circumstances allow us to be, and become what they mould. It is quite as important to see how perfectly Moll adapts herself to circumstance, and how indeed it is her openness to determinism that allows her to survive and prosper, as it is to remark the attenuation of life as we know it and the discrepancy between her behaviour and her morality or religion. If we object that Defoe is 'unrealistic', that our life is not like that, the reply is clear: it is our good fortune that our relationships and affluence hide reality from us. Strip away these protections, and the vision reveals Defoe's conviction both that man is essentially alone, and that he is essentially determined by circumstance – the subject of two of the most resonant passages from the *Serious Reflections*. 'What are the sorrows of other men to us, and what their joy? . . . Our meditations are all solitude in perfection; our passions are all exercised in retirement; we love, we hate, we covet, we enjoy, all in privacy and solitude.'[1] 'I am of the opinion that I could state a circumstance in which there is not one man in the world that would be honest. Necessity is above the power of human nature, and for Providence to suffer a man to fall into that necessity is to suffer him to sin, because nature is not furnished with power to defend itself, nor is grace itself able to fortify the mind against it.'[2]

Defoe's vision, then, has the characteristic features of myth: it deals with archetypes, not characters or types; and though verisimilitude is necessary to win imaginative consent to the ultimate 'truth', the vision is a kind of X-ray which renders shadowy much of the 'body' of ordinary experience in order to focus a more basic structure of 'reality' hidden beneath the surface. In this his affinity with Bunyan is clear, though it is masked by different conventions. The mythic visions also differ significantly however in the nature of the basic 'reality' each is concerned to expose. In the *Progress* there is a ruthless slicing through the secular to the spiritual action within the soul (though in the later work there is a progressive secularisation from the spiritual to the moral). In *Crusoe* the puritan supremacy of theology over ethics, faith rather than works, is maintained in the central

[1] Defoe, *Serious Reflections of Robinson Crusoe* (Boston, 1903), chapter 1, 4.
[2] *Serious Reflections*, chapter 2, 39.

reading of the universe, but already it is the secular situation which captures the imagination most fully. By *Moll Flanders* the mythic vision has become wholly secularised, and determinism by worldly circumstance has become the central 'reality'. The choice of convention is symptomatic of the tendency of the vision in both cases: allegory to fable in Bunyan; traveller's tale cum spiritual autobiography to rogue's tale in Defoe. More significantly still, we begin to understand how Defoe's episodic style and structure are also an important part of his meaning. He did not think of his novels as 'literature' requiring care and polish; he wrote at great speed and without revision, as many carelessnesses show. Yet this should not blind us to the fact that his vision *itself* involves a denial of integrity of character and coherence of consciousness. His art coheres, not by the relation of scene to scene, or of one aspect of character and consciousness to another, but by showing the same pattern of determinism by circumstance underlying all the episodic variety. There is this, and that, and this, and they may well seem contradictory; but look to the situation and they will all be seen to depend on that.

By now it should be obvious that Defoe and Richardson are poles apart, in almost every way. Richardson both 'sees' and creates from an opposite direction. He imagines by projecting himself into sharply individualised characters, each with a qualitatively different consciousness and language. It is the characters who create the developing situation, in ways that strike us as inevitable when Richardson is at his best. Neither style nor structure are episodic. The characters live from moment to moment, but in retrospect all the scenes cohere into consistent 'chains' of character development. 'Reality' is to be found in the activity and growth of consciousness above all, as the characters analyse and reveal themselves, one another, and their conflicts, with great subtlety and complexity. Where Defoe's myth is concerned to strip down to an archetypal pattern, Richardson's history is concerned to build up, necessarily at great length, an inclusive understanding of everything that goes to form personal identity. His best 'history of a young lady' tries to capture a full knowledge of Clarissa's inner life, her relationships, her conflicts, her growth, and her final choice of selfhood. To do this we must know Lovelace, and the Harlowes, and Anna, and Belford, and how they too choose what they will become. Where Defoe's archetypes are determined by circumstances, Richardson's characters determine themselves. As they do so, the relationship of morality and behaviour is exhaustively analysed, and the vision tends to deepen from the secular, through the moral, to the spiritual. Most significant of all, Richardson pits Clarissa against fierce onslaughts of circumstance, almost to the point of disintegration, in order to vindicate the integrity of her character against the worst her world can do to her. He is concerned precisely to affirm what Defoe denies and deny what Defoe affirms. Yet these are not mere 'views' about man-in-society. They involve the writer's whole way of seeing, ordering, and embodying his vision in words.

The assumption that 'the novel' is to be defined in terms of its social 'realism', then, both blurs the relation of prose fiction to society, and the cultural links and differences among the major writers; and also damages our understanding of the really significant qualities of vision, form and style, tempting us to divorce content from form and part from whole. We would do far better to clear it from our minds. We might then see that, though Bunyan, Defoe, Swift, Richardson and Fielding all have a kind of verisimilitude, the kinds differ considerably, according to the nature of the imagination that is at work, and the form and style which embody what the writer sees. Together they represent a major effort to come to terms imaginatively with a new society, but they could only do so by the discovery and development of distinctive ways of using and articulating the imagination, which remain permanently valuable. (In *Tristram Shandy*, all Sterne's major predecessors are present, and fiction turns in upon itself, examining the novelist's pretensions to explain life and communicate understanding: a short course on 'the novel' in itself.) Moreover no form of fiction is intrinsically 'better' than another, let alone more 'real'. Before we can evaluate we have to undertake the patient effort to grasp the peculiar nature of each imagination and how it governs convention, structure and style. I am well aware that my foreshortened treatment of Bunyan, Defoe and Fielding permits no such judgement here. Yet if, in another place, I would be prepared to argue that *Clarissa* is the most significant and valuable fiction before Jane Austen, this could not be because Richardson's form is more 'realistic' than others, nor because I prefer his attitudes to life. We cannot rest literary judgement on some 'reality principle' that turns out to be an ethical or metaphysical assumption. It could only be because of the way Richardson forced himself to probe the full implications of his chosen form, to face the difficulties inherent in his ideals, and challenge – to an extraordinary degree – the validity of his way of looking ... as the others, in my view, do not. But that is another story.

If it is the author's attitude to society that interests us, it also remains true that we shall inevitably simplify and distort his views if we do not base our account on a full understanding of his vision. If we wish to know what Mr Richardson in his everyday self thought about a particular social problem, it is a simple matter to quote from his correspondence. This will represent him fairly, and will show him as fairly representative, for there is little that is extraordinary about Mr Richardson. But if we wish to know what the 'Richardson' who really matters 'thought' about love, or sex, or marriage, or social distinctions, or duty, or anything else, there is simply no substitute for the work involved in reading him with a full understanding of the complexity of his imagination in its chosen form. I do not propose to summarise my own conclusions on such matters, which will be found embedded as they should be in the texture of my readings . . . for what they are worth. All I will venture to claim is that they may be worth more than the findings of those who think it enough to quote passages or ideas out of their formal context, or indulge in brash summaries of complex dramatic explorations. I have also tried to show how strikingly the dramatic imagination can alter the 'view' of the ordinary self. One sees why the historian or sociologist should often learn most, for their purposes, from second-rate work. It is easier to understand and to lift attitudes from, and is likely to be more representative. They may very well be more interested, for example, in a dozen ordinary poems of 1914–18 which 'contain' a given attitude, than in one or two extraordinary ones, like *Spring Offensive* or *Dead Men's Dump*, whose relation to the common experience of soldiers is far more complicated and oblique, and whose total vision is far less easily grasped. But the literary critic must insist that the insights of the major work are infinitely more valuable in themselves, because of the peculiar sensitivity and complexity embodied in their particular form and style.

3

Richardson is certainly the beginning of the 'psychological' novel, at least in English. He is primarily interested in consciousness, he probes deeper into the recesses of the mind than any other eighteenth-century writer, and this leads to the first really honest and revealing exposure of the 'unconscious' since Shakespeare. The nature of his creative process by dramatic projection, and the nature of his convention, the way that letters catch consciousness in process; produce an art that encourages reading between the lines. One is constantly discovering things about his characters that they do not know themselves. The concern with 'delicacy' and 'punctilio' demands that we become sensitive to every implication of speech and behaviour, so that the smallest points may become psychologically as well as morally significant. The more 'to the moment' techniques he invented, the more suggestive the experience became, as against the collected quality of retrospect. He developed the use of the dash to catch the quick movements of the mind, and was the first novelist to exploit the silence between words as the dramatist can. A very considerable part of his value is the light he can throw on the hidden promptings below the surface of the mind, and on the workings of the unconscious in dream and in derangement.

There is a subtle awareness, in his creation of Pamela, Clarissa,

Harriet and Clementina, of how love can grow beneath the threshold of consciousness, but give itself away in ambiguous turns of phrase and curious starts of feeling, when the mind is directed elsewhere. There is a sensitive exploration of how secret impulse can play against even the most determined efforts of self-analysis and moral role. The art focusses the hidden promptings of egotism, spiritual pride, and vanity, which not only undermine the moral behaviour of the good, but can be most dangerous when they disguise themselves as moral aspiration. Subtle, too, is the exposure of the rebellion of jealousy against moral role in Harriet and Emily; or of the unadmitted impulse to hurt Harriet that springs from Charlotte's feeling for her brother; or of the momentary psychic insurrection that produces Harriet's portrait of Sir Charles as a smugger Adam. Richardson explores the ways in which role-playing by the conscious mind can become a mask to hide or inhibit genuine impulses of a better nature in Olivia, in Charlotte, and especially in Lovelace. His villains are studies of egotism, not as a merely moral phenomenon, but as intimately bound up with a man's whole being and sense of identity. In the Harlowes and Lovelace the psychological probing lays bare the sadism behind conscious attitudes and motives, in a world of torturers and tortured, and there may be hints of masochism in the continued feeling of the victim for her tormentors, though there are certainly other things too. Lovelace, above all, is a marvellous study in obsession, a vivid creation of a mind forever beating against a cage of its own making, but desperately involved in the destruction of the only person he loves, because of his psychic revolt and withdrawal from her threat to his image of himself.

Even more startlingly modern is Richardson's imaginative grasp of how dreams can expose the unconscious, and reveal intuitions that the conscious mind cannot grasp; or will not admit. Clarissa's dream of the graveyard, Lovelace's dream of heaven and hell, Harriet's dream of the cavern and the baby, are not only intensely meaningful but a hundred and fifty years before their time. And the greatest triumph of all is the creation of Clarissa's derangement, though it has received virtually no critical attention. The revelation of the impact of the rape on Clarissa's psyche, and the disclosure of her inner struggle for identity, reaching gradually towards full consciousness, is the finest imaginative achievement of eighteenth-century fiction. Beside it, the derangement of Clementina is sentimental, yet if Richardson had managed an earlier grasp of the dangers of a heightened imagination as a source of schizophrenia, we might easily have had another coup by the 'master of the heart'.

Perhaps this is only to say in more detail what Diderot said: that Richardson 'carries the torch to the depths of the cave; it is he who teaches us how to discern the subtle, dishonest motives that are hidden and concealed under other motives which are honest and hasten to show themselves first'.[1] But Diderot then goes on with a fine flourish: 'He breathes on the sublime phantom which presents itself at the entrance of the cave; and the hideous Moor that it was masking, reveals himself' – and this is how 'psychological' criticism becomes reductive. The first sentence says there is more than appears on the surface; the second suggests it is the hideous Moor that is real, and the surface is only a phantom. Only what Iago sees is true. It has always seemed hideously easy for critics to slide from one position to the other. Pamela, from *Shamela* onwards, is a hypocrite with her eye on the main chance. Clarissa's prudery conceals an unhealthy masochism amounting finally to a morbid longing for death. Grandison is a prig who makes his 'morality' serve an urge to dominate that is no less powerful than Lovelace's. Validity is denied to the whole moral vision which spurred Richardson into writing *Pamela* in the first place, drove him to break Clarissa apart in order to reveal what she really is and vindicate her integrity; and led him in *Grandison* to pit an art of 'what ought

[1] 'Il porte le flambeau au fond de la caverne; c'est lui qui apprend à discerner les motifs subtils et déshonnêtes qui se cachent et se dérobent sous d'autres motifs qui sont honnêtes et qui se hâtent de se montrer les premiers. Il souffle sur le fantôme sublime qui se présente à l'entrée de la caverne; et le More hideux qu'il masquait s'aperçoit'. D. Diderot, 'Eloge de Richardson', *Oeuvres Complètes* (Paris, 1875), V, 215.

to be' against an art of 'what is' in order to resolve them. Once one has done that, it is easy enough to believe that Richardson was 'unconscious' of what his art was 'really' doing; that the critic knows better; and that criticism consists of showing the critic's superior understanding, with a patronising pat on the head for the lucky stroke which produced fictions that could so expose the plump printer, without his clothes, to the X-ray vision of wiser men. Richardson's painstaking History becomes a far simpler psychological myth (or fable), written by his critics.

Again the trouble lies in the failure to attend to the kind of imagination that is at work, and to the complexity and subtlety of the form which embodies the vision. By a cruel irony, Richardson's very achievement is made a stick to beat him with. It was his achievement to help us imagine characters so like people in real life that we seem able to analyse them in the same way. But 'people' in fiction are not like people in life. What we know of fictive characters is entirely dependent on the nature of the form and style that creates them, and we cannot understand what we know unless we understand how we come to know it, and the limits of that knowledge. The classic example of how technical difficulties can be responsible for 'psychological' impressions is the case of *Pamela* which I discuss at length in Chapter 4. Without playing false to the whole imaginative impression the book makes on us, we nevertheless must learn to distinguish which inferences are part of the imaginative texture itself, and which are produced by deficiencies of technique in a new way of writing, which Richardson would learn to remedy as his grasp of his medium improved. Even more vital, in a dramatic art which works by playing off one point of view against another, we must insure that we neither identify Richardson with his heroines, nor fall into the trap of adopting the point of view of a single character ourselves. As Diderot runs the danger of seeing only what Iago sees, we have to guard against the reductions of seeing only what Pamela sees as we look at B, or only what B sees when we look at Pamela, or only what Lovelace sees as we look at Clarissa, etc. If we fail to understand the demands of the form we cannot possibly achieve the inclusiveness of the vision. We have to learn to discipline our reading according to the maker's rage to order words, or we are bound to reduce the art to a caricature. On the other hand, once we do try to read in the way that Richardson wrote, one of the first things that we discover is that he is not only conscious of 'the hideous Moor', but engaged precisely in exploring how his characters either come to terms with what lies 'au fond de la caverne', like Pamela and Clarissa, or are destroyed by it, like Lovelace. The charge of hypocrisy is raised, and refuted, in the 24th letter of *Pamela*, but the fearfulness, faithlessness and egotism of the little servant-girl are subjected to prolonged examination by the dramatic and exploratory art. One of the few places in the continuation where Richardson's dramatic imagination is at full stretch again, shows him dissatisfied with his happy ending, and well aware that neither his hero nor his heroine have solved their psychological problems as much as that ending suggests. It is an even greater struggle for Clarissa to come to terms with her fear of sex, her readiness to cast herself as victim, her melancholy, and her morbid longing for death – or her spiritual pride, which is for Richardson at the heart of all. But however unaware of such things he may have been to begin with, he is driven by the nature of his art, and by sheer courage of imagination, to probe them all to the uttermost, to disintegrate Clarissa so that he can get at her very being, and discover whether her moral nature is a phantom or whether it is stronger than the hideous Moor. The readiness of the main 'psychological' critics to prefer the reductive simplicity of their own myths and fables to the painful efforts of Richardson's History is shown by their failure to examine the heart of the matter in Clarissa's derangement, her recovery, and her final attitude to sex, to human love, and to death. In *Grandison*, the degree to which we can probe the hero or the heroines psychologically is again determined by the two very different kinds of imagination that are at work. At the centre the form fails to fulfil its promise, and fails because the exploration of the hero is not psychological enough; but we cannot understand either the failure or how close Richardson came to success, until we understand the peculiar nature of what he was trying to do. It is only when we see how he tries to play one kind of vision against another that we see why Jane Austen and George Eliot admired the book, and chose to adopt its basic structuring (in different ways) as the model for *Mansfield Park* and *Daniel Deronda.*

At least, however, Diderot, and the kind of psychological criticism he typifies, concern themselves with Richardson's characters rather than the character of Richardson. What is a peculiarly twentieth-century phenomenon is the tendency to convert psychological criticism of the fiction into psycho-analysis of the author; though this follows naturally enough from the belief that he was an 'unconscious' writer who deluded himself about the real significance of his work. The ramifications grow wider and wider, however, as Richardson begins to be seen not only as an interesting case-study in himself, but as a representative case-study of the bourgeois mind of his own time and place, or of the bourgeois mind in general in England and America, or of the beginnings of the Romantic Agony in the Western world, or of 'a psychological division in the soul of man himself' – by which time we may well suffer from delirium of the depths. This sort of thing is a feature of twentieth-century criticism as a whole; but the treatment of Richardson often shows it at its most extravagant, one suspects, because he is so generally regarded as naïve that the critic feels uninhibited by the possibility of a shaping spirit of imagination. One is tempted simply to echo John Carroll's rebuke, in Richardson's words, to the gayest cavalier of all: 'Pray read, Madam, what you pretend to read'.[1] Yet this is too easy. By no means all exponents of this kind of criticism are quite so careless of the text or, for that matter, quite so honest in admitting that they are writing significant fictions rather than literary criticism in its more mundane – or disciplined – form. The approach can cast light, though of a necessarily limited kind if it is the novels themselves that interest one, rather

[1] 'Introduction' to *Twentieth Century Views*, 2, on Leslie Fiedler; see Richardson to Lady Bradshaigh, 4 January 1754, Carroll, *Letters*, 271.

than Mr Richardson or the bourgeois mind or the romantic agony. I do not propose to argue a full case in relation to any particular critic, hoping that the difference between my readings and the psycho-analytic ones will be clear enough. What might be useful, though, is to distinguish the four main lines along which critics of this kind work, and to suggest what is involved in each and in the process of generalising from them.

The first might be called the idea of authorial obsession. The critic fastens on what he takes to be an obsessive tendency of Richardson's subconscious, flourishing under the cover of his overt moral purpose. The obvious favourite is sex, often described as 'perverted'. The obsession may be revealed in the way that 'optical images' – 'like Clarissa in white clothes, kneeling in prayer, seen through a keyhole' – build up into significant symbolism. 'Let us consider the evolution ... of the "Clarissa symbol" itself ... pale, debilitated and distraught, with heaving bosom ... wilting like a broken lily on its stalk ... in torn clothes and with streaming eyes prostrated at the feet of her demon lover. The womanly quality which Richardson has made attractive in these images is that of an erotically tinged debility which offers, masochistically, a ripe temptation to violence.'[1] Or the obsession may be inherent in the method. *Clarissa* is 'a novel written about the world as one sees it through the keyhole. Prurient and obsessed by sex, the prim Richardson creeps on tip-toe nearer and nearer, inch by inch, to that vantage point; he beckons us on, pausing to make every kind of pious protestation, and then nearer and nearer he creeps again, delaying, arguing with us in whispers, working us up until we catch the obsession too. What are we going to see when we get there? ... Nothing short of the rape of Clarissa ... can satisfy Richardson's phenomenal day-dream with its infinite delays.'[2] The trouble is that neither 'image' nor 'method' are related to the dramatic form which creates to the

[1] Dorothy Van Ghent, *The English Novel – Form and Function* (New York, 1953 reprinted 1961), 48-9.

[2] V. S. Pritchett, *The Living Novel*, 10-11. (Compare Max Beerbohm's cartoon of Henry James)

moment and from moment to moment; nor to the full dramatic scene which governs interpretation; nor to the structured chain of scenes which build up into the complete meaning which must govern every part. Is it helpful to dwell on Clarissa's 'debility' to the exclusion of her moral and intellectual energy? Or on Lovelace's image of her as a lily, without any attention to her own very different use of the symbol on her coffin? Can we talk of keyholes without talking of the nature of what we see and how we see it? Richardson is a dramatic writer and not a symbolic poet; and even when what is seen is an image it must still be related to the sensibility of the narrator, who is only part of 'Richardson'. (It might also be valuable to see what becomes of the keyhole in Clarissa's derangement, and how the 'voyeurism' of the rape is related to the remarkable concern of Richardson, and Lovelace, that the inquisition should be public.) We cannot *see* Clarissa prostrate at Lovelace's feet without allowing for the lens: the sardonic parody of a proposal, and the insistence on her fundamental order, which in the scene as a whole curb melodrama and turn our response from prurience to moral discrimination. The most curious thing about Richardson's treatment of sexual 'attempts', even when they are what they seem and not shot through with comic misunderstanding or mock-heroic melodrama, is that they have so little to do with sexuality or prurience. If the form 'delays', has this nothing to do with the need to see over again from another point of view, or to explore by careful structured reorchestration, or to give the characters another chance, as part of their freedom to determine themselves? Ought one not finally to look to the end: and discuss Clarissa's own judgement of the spiritual pride behind her 'masochism', and her own view of the difference between a sexuality that is healthy and fertile, and one that perverts and destroys? It is not that there is no truth at all in what such critics see, but the accounts are reductive to the point of travesty.

The next 'line' might be called the idea of the significant category, or a version of the inkblot test. I think this is more interesting potentially, for the attempt to group Richardson's characters over his fiction as a whole – the bold and the mild young men, the bold and the grave girls, the old people, and so on – does throw up some characteristic habits of Richardson's imagination; and some correspondences not immediately obvious, like the ambition to 'dominate' that drives both Lovelace and Grandison. If this were done with enough care and scruple it could contribute valuably to a map of Richardson's imagination as a whole. But, again, the significance of every character in History can only be established in the full complexity of his or her development, and of the crosslights thrown by the existence and the analysis of all the other characters. Without this the characters will quickly turn into cut-out 'attitudes' or types – this line tends to turn History into fable rather than myth – and the relation both between the 'inkblots' and the author's mind, and between different versions of the same 'shape', will be seen far too simply. 'Even more than most novelists, Richardson is limited in his characters to a few staple types, which are stretched and chopped to fit various molds in his three novels'... 'The pervasiveness of fantasy in the creation of character is, I believe, Richardson's preeminent contribution to the novel; and the fantasies are mainly of dominance and subordination, as seem to have been those of the author himself.'[1] There is, again, some truth here. Barbara Hardy has argued an interesting case for seeing the novelist as a specialist in something we all do every day and night, tell ourselves stories, dream, and daydream.[2] There can be no objection to the idea that *all* novelists project their fantasies into their books. And Richardson did tend to repeat himself. Yet the reductive emphasis is very clear in the refusal to admit that what is really important is the peculiar way in which the 'fantasy' is worked out, and its relation to the conscious mind and ideals explored. It is not the 'stuff' out of which a work of art is 'moulded' that matters. Both a Grecian urn and a primitive cooking pot may be made out of mud. It is the artistic form and the workmanship which dictate the value.

[1] Morris Golden, *Richardson's Characters*, 1, 17.

[2] B. Hardy, 'Narrative', *Novel*, 2 (1968), 5.

No two works of art, even by the same man, can be 'moulded' alike; the very word betrays the misconception. Hence the relation of part to whole must differ significantly in each, and how significantly depends on an appreciation of the different wholes. The really interesting thing about the link between Lovelace and Grandison lies in the very different kinds of imagination that develop them, the very different kinds of crosslighting between them and the heroines, and the diametrically opposite emphasis on the moral implications of their role-playing. Lovelace's psychic urge to dominate, culminating in unmistakable sadism incomparable with anything in Richardson's own life and correspondence, expresses itself in obsessive fantasy and role-playing in order to disguise himself from himself, as well as from others. 'Acting' is seen as extremely dangerous, preventing integrity and sincerity. Lovelace destroys Clarissa rather than admit her superiority and so lose his imperial idea of himself. But Grandison turns a basically similar urge to totally different ends, in an art of moral idealism. He transforms his ambition to be the Grandest-son, and his pride, into a moral role. When he is accused of superiority he retorts that anyone can lessen this any time by behaving the same way, and proceeds to encourage everyone around him to do so. His 'fantasy' (or must we not say idealism?) expresses itself in works of active and practical benevolence. 'Acting' is seen as raising oneself to play a better part; right behaviour is seen as more important than sincerity; and deliberate role-playing can generate the proper feeling, in time. Whereas in B, Richardson has no interest in role-playing at all. B is the product of a cruder dramatic art, by an author who has not yet developed any understanding of the possible relations between 'acting' and morality. Merely to say that B, Lovelace, and Grandison, all express Richardson's own urge to dominate is, again, to flatten out both the significance and the life of his dramatic art.

The third 'line' is the Freudian idea of the censor, of totem and taboo, and of the interchange of opposites. '"Decency", as Bernard Shaw has reminded us, 'is indecency's conspiracy of silence, and the concern of the eighteenth-century moralists with feminine purity suggests imaginations only too ready to colour everything with impure sexual significances . . . The cause of this duality – in Richardson's time as in ours – is presumably that the tabooed object is always an indication of the deepest interest of the society that forbids'.[1] The intensity of an apparent aspiration in one direction is a tell-tale sign of a real interest in the opposite direction; the censor 'translates' the hideous Moor into the sublime phantom and we have to retranslate. (The activity of translating the surface fiction into the real analytic meaning is characteristic of fable.) Or again, there is the Freudian slip or association. 'Names are often a guide to unconscious attitudes, and those of Richardson's protagonists tend to confirm the view that he secretly identified himself with his hero – Robert Lovelace is a pleasant enough name – and even unconsciously collaborated with Lovelace's purpose of abasing the heroine: "Clarissa" is very close to "Calista", Rowe's impure heroine; while "Harlowe" is very close to "harlot".'[2] This is a very closed and self-confirming system: heads I win, tails you lose. If Richardson writes about rape he is prurient; but if he seems concerned about purity he is also prurient. Yet it never seems to work the other way round: one has not yet come across the Freudian essay that claims *Fanny Hill* as the product of an intense longing for purity. The critic seems surprisingly ready to dispose of the sublime phantom almost *a priori*. It is not only that 'Love-less' and 'Clarissima' cannot be taken seriously; but Belford's detailed discussion of *The Fair Penitent* (VII, 132 ff.; *IV, 117 ff.*), which draws a parallel between Lovelace and Lothario, but insists on the polar opposition of Clarissa and Calista, is presumably to be dismissed quite simply as the obfuscation of the Freudian censor. But the real objection is again to the failure to attend to the dramatic form and exploration. It is true that Freud has made us aware of the duplicity of consciousness, but Richardson was aware of this and explored it. He created by identifying himself with all his characters, quite as powerfully with Clarissa as with Lovelace,

[1] Watt, *Rise of the Novel*, 169, 171.

[2] Watt, *Rise of the Novel*, 236n.

and collaborated both with Lovelace's abasement of Clarissa and with Clarissa's abasement of Lovelace. We should certainly not take the surface texture at face value, but it is no less simple-minded to think that attitudes can easily be translated into their opposites. The only way of settling the interplay between the Moor, the phantom, and the censor, is the discipline of following the long dramatic conflict, with full attention to both conscious and unconscious attitudes, and seeing how it comes out. We shall certainly cook the book if we believe that Richardson is to be identified with Lovelace, and that Lovelace's 'Freudian' theory about the hypocrisy of the eighteenth-century sex-code (the product of custom and education, disguising the true sexual nature of women) is the right one. It is precisely to test that theory that the final phase of the tragedy produces its tremendous inquisition. We shall not understand Richardson's imaginative 'solution' without the most detailed and complex grasp of the dramatic conflict, of Clarissa's derangement and recovery, and of the nature of her final attitudes to love and to death.

The final 'line' is the idea of the Jungian myth. 'Though absurd, Clarissa has an archetypal greatness and a secret, underhanded, double-dealing association with the seeds of things, for she takes upon herself a social dream: the sterilisation of instinct, the supremacy of the "Father", the consolidation of society in abstraction, the cult of death . . . Her classic significance as love-goddess lies in the fact that she dies to promote not fertility but sterility.'[1] The passion of Clarissa and Lovelace identifies love and death, and 'symbolizes gratification, not of sensual life, but of a submerged portion of the emotional life whose tendency actually opposes gratification of the senses – the death wish, the desire for destruction.' 'Her mythical features still appear to us – for it would be a mistake to think that the Clarissa-myth does not still have deep social and psychological roots – in her two chief aspects: they appear on the covers of *Vogue* magazine, in the woman who is a wraith of clothes, debile and expensive,

[1] Dorothy Van Ghent, 'Clarissa and Emma as Phèdre', *Partisan Review*, 17, (1950), 826.

irrelevant to sense-life or affectional life, to be seen only; and they appear on the covers of *True Confessions* and *True Detective Stories*, in the many-breasted woman with torn deshabille and rolling eyeballs, a dagger pointing at her, a Venus as abstract as the *Vogue* Venus in her appeal to the eye and the idea alone, but differing in that she is to be vicariously ripped and murdered. Clarissa is a powerful symbol because she is both.'[1] I don't often see Venus Multimammia, but there is obvious truth here, of a kind. Yet the kind is sociological rather than critical. For the claim to critical depth, to dealing with 'the seeds of things', is significantly revealed as the reductiveness of the lowest common denominator. If we must concede (as I think we must) that there is a connection, which can be explained in psycho-analytic terms, between *Clarissa* and the *Vogue* cover, and between her Liebestod and the pulp magazine and paperback, do we not have to insist that this is a precise indication of how little we are saying in literary terms? For the world of difference lies in the power of Richardson's kind of imagination (History), and the power of his formal exploration (drama), and the power of his language (the subtle orchestration of characteristic styles), to take the lowest common denominator and transform it into complex and courageous self-examination. Between the simple indulgence of Jungian dream and the subtle probing of the 'master of the heart' there lies a chasm unbridgeable in terms of real significance. The sad thing is that the critic's own myth actually prevents the work of criticism: the investigation of what the novel eventually has to 'say' about instinct, 'the Father', the individual and society, love and death, through the appreciation of the form. 'It's clay', the critic exclaims, and goes home content.

When, on such bases, critics feel free to generalise about Richardson as 'representative' of his class and time, or of the bourgeois mind in Europe and America, or of a division in the human soul itself, the results are bound to be facile. For the soundness of any generalisation must depend directly on the truth of the particulars on which it is built. What is significant

[1] Van Ghent, *The English Novel*, 62, 50-1.

now is the way in which literary criticism moves via psychology, both Freudian and Jungian, into sociology. 'In reading Clarissa finally as a sexual myth, we are reading it as a construct of irrationals similar to a dream (although, in the case of myth, the myth-maker is "dreaming" not only his own dream, but society's dream as well).' So, 'the mythical representation of sexual relationships in *Clarissa* coincides with and deeply reinforces the mythical representation of social values and the values of family life. From each point of view, the book is a paean to death. Richardson is the great poet of the adolescence of our own acquisitive, aggressive culture.'[1] The focus moves from *Clarissa*, to Richardson, to his society, to a continuous culture. The heroine is not only the love goddess of Richardson's own perverted sexuality, she is the 'love goddess of the Puritan middle class of the English eighteenth century, of the bourgeois family, and of mercantile society';[2] and since Richardson's society is in continuity with our own, his dream still bears on ours. One fears, however, that this may be as unacceptable sociologically as it is reductive in literary terms. Fortunately one can choose a Freudian example which is more specific and subtle in both respects, but will show the change of gear and its results still more clearly. The critic is unhappy about 'assuming, as the Fielding interpretation suggests, that Pamela is only modest because she wants to entrap Mr B. It is surely better to regard her as a real person whose actions are the result of the complexities of her situation and of the effects, both conscious and unconscious, of the feminine code. Steele pointed out that prude and coquette are alike in that they have "the distinction of sex in all their thoughts, words and actions": the code that commanded the allegiance of Pamela and her author is itself open to either interpretation.'[3] Pamela is treated as a real person, and both her unconscious and Richardson's unconscious are interchangeably representative of the bourgeois sex code. Her hypocrisy is no

[1] Van Ghent, *The English Novel*, 61, 62-3.

[2] Van Ghent, *The English Novel*, 50.

[3] Watt, *Rise of the Novel*, 170.

longer a straightforward moral flaw, but hypocrisy it remains, in both her and her creator. Whereas – the charge is overfamiliar now – some attention to the dramatic exploration would have shown that Richardson was not unaware of the possibility of such hypocrisy, voiced the charge through B, and set out to explore and resolve it both in *Pamela*, and more powerfully and honestly in *Clarissa*. What is more interesting now is the amputation involved in what one might begin to call psycho-sociology. For though it is true that prude and coquette may be alike in that way – the Freudian opposites again – there is an important category missing. What about Steele, for instance? Unless we believe that sex has nothing to do with morals, it is not only the prude and coquette who are interested in it, in every detail of thought, word and action, but the analytic moralist too. But Richardson's dramatic imagination is a very different phenomenon from Mr Richardson's representative moral outlook. And the more we talk about the effect of liberating his unconscious through his dramatic imagination, the more significantly he both ceases to be representative, and explores his way to a unique judgement of the problems his mind and his society pose. Until we understand that judgement we cannot tell how far he is or is not representative. And only an appreciation of the formal workings of his imagination will reveal the nature of the judgement. We can only usefully think of him 'sociologically' when we have understood his art. One is very grateful for the formulation of the problem, which marked a long step beyond the Shamela-obsessed criticism that preceded it. Yet to treat Pamela as a real person and continue to identify her with Richardson is effectively to block one's view.

Though the impatience of twentieth-century readers with 'moralising' is a force to be reckoned with, the willingness to abandon Richardson's moral vocabulary that goes along with psychological criticism – let's do without the censor and the phantom – has its obvious dangers. If one is to come to terms with his subtle casuistry, it seems only sensible to try to live one's way into his language. One does not have to accept it, but one ought at least to know what one is rejecting. The attempts to substitute a fashionable psychological jargon will flatten the subtlety and empty out the imaginative life – unless the critic can show that he can be as subtle and complex as Richardson. One doubts whether the case is made by concluding that 'Richardson is the novelist of the conflict between the unrestrained urges of the ego, and the necessary restraints, imposed by the conditions of social living, to which that ego must adapt itself'.[1]

As psycho-sociology becomes more overt, the gap steadily widens between its concerns and those of the literary critic. Basing himself on Mario Praz[2] (though without his caution), and bringing to culmination nearly all the tendencies I have been discussing, the most dashing exponent openly proclaims his impatience with literary criticism and his awareness that he is writing a fiction he considers more culturally illuminating and alive. 'The novel proper could not be launched until some author imagined a prose narrative in which the Seducer and the Pure Maiden were brought face to face in a ritual combat destined to end in marriage or death.' Richardson achieved this and also made the sex war symbolise the class war. 'There is moreover an even deeper level at which the war of the sexes and classes is understood to represent a psychological division in the soul of man itself – and the conflict of ideologies which arises from this division. Lovelace and Clarissa are, as we have seen, the male principle and the female, Devil and Saviour, aristocracy and bourgeoisie; but they are also the head and the heart – what we would now call super-ego and (in somewhat expurgated form) id. Lovelace is above all things an intellectual . . . Clarissa the idealisation of all that lies beyond mere rationalism. Richardson as a champion of the heart over the head, a secret enemy of Reason, is the philistine's Rousseau, the Jean Jaques of the timid bourgeoisie . . . all Europe wept at Clary's end, felt itself

[1] Golden, *Richardson's Characters*, 192.

[2] Mario Praz, *The Romantic Agony*, tr. by Angus Davidson (London, 1933 reprinted 1960), 114-16.

redeemed by self knowledge as well as sympathy.'[1] From this point it becomes possible to follow Clarissa's daughters out of Europe into America, and in both serious literature and pop, to survey the whole gothick novel of Love and Death that is the fiction of America. The book is refreshing, stimulating, vertiginous, provocative and infuriating, just as its author wished. It is almost a pity to take it seriously, especially if one agrees that literature does not exist in a vacuum and that literary critics have been too 'genteel' in cutting themselves off from history, sociology, psychology, anthropology, linguistics, and pop-culture . . . as some have. Only, if there is to be dialogue about books, and if a whole edifice is to be erected on a reading of one book, only literary criticism will tell us whether the foundation is sound . . . and it is paper-thin, reductive in all the ways I have discussed. The more fascinating the width of the spectrum and the treatment of pop-works alongside good ones, the more infuriating the failure to establish the real nature of the good ones, and of the huge gulf that separates the generalisations one can draw from them, and from *Marjorie Morningstar*.

Of course the creator creates out of his subconscious as well as his conscious mind, and out of the collective subconscious of his class, society, nation, race. But how much are we saying when we have said as much? What gives a work significance is not its material but the nature of its workmanship, the quality of its form, the mastery of its medium, and the nature of the final understanding produced by these. The central feature of Richardson's art is that it is based on putting parts of his mind and ranges of his vocabulary in conflict with one another in order to explore and resolve that conflict. He probes, brings to light, orders . . . not always successfully. But when things go wrong, the first explanation is most often to be found in some

[1] Leslie Fiedler, *Love and Death in the American Novel* (London, 1967 reprinted 1970), 59, 68. The significance of Fiedler's splendid gaffes, like the belief that Pamela is a governess (later corrected), and that Lovelace is killed by Belford (uncorrected), is not merely the strong suspicion that he has not read the books; it is that for this kind of criticism the barest plot outline, or less, will suffice.

defect of the form, and only then and with great care is one likely to be able to explain why it happened, by reference to his psychology. It is not what was representative about Richardson that is interesting and significant, it is what was unique . . . his new way of writing, and what *that* enabled him to see.

4

. . . Only by the form, the pattern,
Can words or music reach
The stillness, as a Chinese jar still
Moves perpetually in its stillness.

The paradox is that it is a response to Richardson's strengths that causes the reductiveness. It is because, of all the eighteenth-century novelists, his History is the most concerned with verisimilitude, and his Drama the most concerned with consciousness, that his critics have tended to fasten on one element or another, inattentive to the nature of the shaping spirit of imagination that creates and orders the whole. To try to grasp those great still books – taking 'great' as a term of quantity! – is a long, difficult, and often tedious process as I fear I have abundantly shown. Perhaps the 'stillness' of which Eliot speaks is the response we make only to the really great work, when we are overcome with a sense of completion, harmony, wholeness, and communication so intense that another word would wreck it. Perhaps the frenzied conflict, the endless exploration, as well as the other Richardsonian faults, are a sign of his inability to reach the 'claritas' of the Chinese jar; as well as of his determination to try. I am certain this is true of my study. Yet just once – at the moment when one imagines one understands the meaning of the rape of Clarissa, and of the challenge Richardson's form has enabled him to pose, and meet in Clarissa's deranged papers – one may feel the stillness, and be moved. I think it is the courage of the imagination, the risks it is prepared to run; and also one's sense that, though the full History pressures of character, society, and the unconscious have been taken, yet Clarissa is miraculously free; that produce the single touch of awe one feels in reading eighteenth-century fiction. She is both grasped; and mysterious, self-existent, unpredictable. She is created both by the most remorseless analysis; and by letting the subconscious go in the dramatist's projection. She is both subject to the full conditioning of her and her creator's society; and yet her 'reality' is quite beyond the representative, as every sensitive contemporary felt, including Richardson's greatest rival and formal opposite. And the final treatment of Lovelace the inveterate actor, is uniquely right too. I do not find it surprising that the warmest tributes to Richardson have tended to come from other writers and from actors. It is also encouraging to find that among one's students, he has always found fit audience, though few. But only by the form . . .

Index

Addison, Joseph, 65; *Spectator*, 71, 86, 305
Allen, Walter, 393
Austen, Jane, 2, 295, 296, 480; *Mansfield Park*, 83, 320, 447, 486

Baker, Ernest, 8
Baker, Sheridan, 102
Barbauld, Anna Laetitia, 115
Battestin, Martin, 12
Beckett, Samuel, 400
Bible: Isaiah, 269; (parable of) Good Shepherd, 70; Job, 261, 270; (parable of) Prodigal Son, 70; Psalms, 231, 269, 270; St Matthew, 269; Song of Songs, 372, 379
Blake, William, 2, 237, 451
Brissenden, R. F., vii, 398
Bullen, John Samuel, 411
Bunyan, John, 438, 462, 463, 469, 474, 477, 478, 479; *Pilgrim's Progress*, 161, 460, 462; *Life and Death of Mr Badman*, 462
Burnett, Ivy Compton, 415
Burney, Fanny, 295, 296

Carroll, John, vii, 151, 411, 486
Chaucer, Geoffrey, 11, 315, 380
Cibber, Colley, 71, 219
Coleridge, Samuel, 94, 394, 410, 420, 460, 470
Conrad, Joseph, 452
Cowler, Rosemary, vii
Cowley, Abraham, 239
Crane, R. S., 12

Daiches, David, vii, 8, 69, 109
Defoe, Daniel, 19, 126, 170, 416, 418, 459, 460, 461-4; *Robinson Crusoe*, 416, 472-5, 477; *Moll Flanders*, 421, 425, 470-1, 475-8; *Serious Reflections*, 477; compared with Richardson, 469-81
Dickens, Charles, 313, 421, 423
Diderot, Denis, 483, 484, 486
Dobson, Austin, 7
Donne, John, 268
Downs, Brian, 8, 94
Dryden, John, 148, 239, 436, 464; *Absalom and Achitophel*, 240; *Of Dramatick Poesy*, 392-3
Dussinger, John, 456

Eaves, T. Duncan, vii, 71, 90, 101, 113, 137, 149, 361, 408, 413, 427
Edwards, Thomas, 393, 408
Eliot, George, 2; *Daniel Deronda*, 287, compared with *Grandison*, 292-4, 486

Farrell, William, J., 432
Faulkner, William, 415, 452
Fiedler, Leslie, 486, 496-7
Fielding, Henry, 11, 12, 57, 94, 125, 170, 219, 225, 282, 283, 306, 314, 315, 393, 398, 401, 416, 418, 420, 421, 460, 463-4, compared with Richardson, 465-9, 479; *Amelia*, 467; *Joseph Andrews*, 7, 23, 66, 71, 466; *Shamela*, 7, 8, 9, 13, 14, 15, 19, 71, 74, 77, 102, 398, 483; *Tom Jones*, 166, 283, 338, 416, 421, 465, 467
Ford, Ford Madox, vii
Forster, E. M., vii, 460

Garrick, David, 393
Garth, Samuel, 239
Golden, Morris, 8, 488-90, 496
Golding, William, 421
Gopnik, Irwin, 439
Green, F. C., 93

Habbakuk, H. J., 123, 127, 128, 129
Hardy, Barbara, 489
Haywood, Eliza, 71
Hazlitt, William, 94, 405, 458
Hill, Aaron, 74, 171, 393, 408
Hill, Christopher, 123, 267
Hilles, Frederick W., 410
Holberg, Ludvig, 7
Hughes, Leo, 431

James, Henry, vii, 242, 293, 367, 393, 408, 452; *The Awkward Age*, 415
Johnson, Dr Samuel, 101, 102, 167, 280, 287, 315, 420, 462, 468
Jonson, Ben, 393, 421, 422, 466
Joyce, James, 377

Kafka, Franz, 452
Kearney, Anthony, viii, 395-6, 454
Kermode, Frank, vii, 458
Kettle, Arnold, vii, 123, 459
Kimpel, Ben, vii, 71, 90, 101, 113, 137, 149, 361, 408, 413, 427
Konigsberg, Ira, 147, 431
Kreissman, Bernard, 8, 71
Krutch, J. W., 8, 69, 94

Laclos, Pierre, 393-4, 415
Lawrence, D. H., 106, 269, 451
Leavis, F. R., vii, 294
Lee, Nathaniel, 239
Lubbock, Percy, vii
Lyttleton, George, 219

McKillop, A. D., vii, 7, 71, 102, 282, 408, 428, 431, 453
Marlowe, Christopher, 273
Melville, Herman, 421
Middleton, Conyers, 71
Milton, John, 393, 474, *Areopagitica*, 94; *Comus*, 107; *Paradise Lost*, 223, 363-4, 436

Needham, Gwendolyn, 96

Otway, Thomas, 148, 239-40, 436
Owen, Wilfred, 481

Pamela Censured, 71
Pamela's Conduct in High Life (spurious continuation), 72, 428
Park, William, 467
Pinter, Harold, 400
Pope, Alexander, 71, 280, 401; *On the Characters of Women*, 179; *Rape of the Lock*, 60; *Essay on Man*, 335; *Eloisa to Abelard*, 367, 377
Povey, Charles, 71, 81
Praz, Mario, 496

Index

Preston, John, 455-7
Prévost, Abbé, 438
Pritchett, V. S., 107, 487-8
Proust, Marcel, vii, 367

Rattigan, Terence, 230
Rawson, Claude, 393
Richardson, Samuel, attitudes to duty and presumption, 37-42, 59-63; to prudence and faith, 42-57; whole duty of women; 58-64; problem of praise, 64-5; educative power of example, 66; concept of the family, 62-3; longing for secure relationships, 66-7; forgiveness, 67-70, 77-81; mixed fortunes of *Pamela*, 70-2; defence of *Pamela* in continuation, 72-8; his vanity and its effect on *Pamela*, 100-03; love of intrigue, 104-5; latent snobbery, 105-6; attitude to sex, 106-14, 237-8; virtue rewarded, 114-18; puritan introspection, 161, and moral community, 162; didactic revisions of *Clarissa*, 151, 182, 195, 203-4; view of evil, 173; demands for happy ending, 219-20; central issue of *Clarissa*, 241-2; attitudes to death, 268-72; his circle of admirers, 279-83, and their influence on *Grandison*, 283-5; interest in moral casuistry, 284-9; moral idealism, 290-1; problem of duelling, 306-9; moral importance of feeling, 313-16; morality of excess and its implications, 316-24; social realism, 123-9, 459-81; psychology, 481-98; psychoanalytic approaches to Richardson, 486-98.
Artistic awareness, 7-19; humour, 15-16, 18, 28, 90-2; use of parody, 28-9, 74, 216, 441-4; problem of access to B, 19, 23-4, 32-3, 56-7, 76, 96-100; B's point of view in continuation, 75-6; multiple viewpoint in continuation, 78-84; technical flaws of *Pamela*, 88-100; dramatic projection, 392-5; the 'second voice', 395-7; dramatic present, 397-401; 'play-book' technique, 401-3; dramatic soliloquy and self-colloquy, 403-7; self-revelation, 407-8; writing from moment to moment, 408; structuring, 409-11; fictive time, 411-14; length and relevance, 415-18; 'history' (compared with 'fable' and 'myth'), 416-18, 420-1; 423-5; disadvantages of letter form, 418-20; characterisation, 420-6; orchestra of styles, 426-48; tragedy, comedy, and melodrama, 448-9; moral implications of 'acting', 450-1; dramatic imagination and relativity, 451-3; epistolary novel and alienation, 453-8; his art compared with Fielding's, 465-9; with Defoe's 469-80.
Rosenberg, Isaac, 481
Rowe, Nicholas, 491

St John of the Cross, 260
Sale, William, vii
Shakespeare, William, 368, 393, 448, 453, 466, 481; *Hamlet*, 239-40; *King Lear*, 164; *Othello*, 154, 436; *The Tempest*, 152; *Twelfth Night*, 343, 370
Shaw, Bernard, 110, 490
Sophocles, *Oedipus*, 421, 425
Spearman, Diana, 460, 461
Spenser, Edmund, 438, 474

Steele, Richard, 65, 437, 494; *Spectator*, 71, 86, 305
Sterne, Lawrence, 412; *Tristram Shandy*, 414, 417, 479
Stevens, Wallace, 461
Swift, Jonathan, 11, 438, 462; 469, 479; *Gulliver's Travels*, 460, 464, 465

Tennyson, Alfred Lord, 418
Thomson, Clara, 7, 123
Thomson, James, 219
Tolstoy, Leo, 417

Van Ghent, Dorothy, 487-8, 492-4

Waldock, A. J. A., 364
Warburton, William, 398
Watt, Ian, vii, 8, 20, 95, 110, 123, 167, 459, 463, 468-9, 472, 490-2, 494-5
Wilde, Oscar, 313
Wilson, Angus, viii, 465